DATE DUE			

A HISTORY OF

MODERN CRITICISM

1750–1950

IN SEVEN VOLUMES

OTHER BOOKS BY RENÉ WELLEK

Immanuel Kant in England

The Rise of English Literary History

Theory of Literature (with Austin Warren)

Concepts of Criticism

Essays on Czech Literature

Confrontations: Studies in the Intellectual and Literary Relations
  between Germany, England, and the United States
  During the Nineteenth Century

Discriminations: Further Concepts of Criticism

Four Critics: Croce, Valéry, Lukács, Ingarden

The Attack on Literature & Other Essays

A HISTORY OF MODERN

Criticism: *1750–1950*

BY RENÉ WELLEK

VOLUME 5 *English Criticism, 1900–1950*

YALE UNIVERSITY PRESS
New Haven and London

Designed by James J. Johnson
and set in the Baskerville types.
Printed in the United States of America by
Vail-Ballou Press, Binghamton, N.Y.

Library of Congress Cataloging in Publication Data

(Revised for volume 5 and volume 6)

Wellek, René.
  A history of modern criticism.

  Includes bibliographies and indexes.
  Contents: v. 1. The later eighteenth century.—[etc.]
—v. 5. English criticism, 1900–1950.—v. 6. American
criticism, 1900–1950.
  1. Criticism—History. I. Title: Modern criticism.
PN86.W4   801.95'09   85–12005
ISBN 0–300–03378–8 (v. 5: alk. paper)
ISBN 0–300–03486–5 (v. 6: alk. paper)

The paper in this book meets the guidelines for permanence
and durability of the Committee on Production Guidelines for
Book Longevity of the Council on Library Resources.

10 9 8 7 6 5 4 3 2 1

CONTENTS

PREFACE TO VOLUMES 5 AND 6

THESE BOOKS have been long in the making. Several articles on individual critics were published over the years, scattered in periodicals, as the list of acknowledgments shows. They were all written with the overall scheme in view and with the intention of eventual inclusion in this project.

In planning this history of the first half of the twentieth century, I soon became aware that it could not be organized like the preceding four volumes, which moved easily from country to country: in the first volume, from France to England, and then to Italy and Germany; in the second, from Germany back to France, Italy, and England, and then again to Germany. In the third and fourth volumes, the chapters on the different countries were framed by chapters on French criticism from the first comparative literary historians to the symbolists.

It became obvious, however, that in the early part of the twentieth century the English and American world had emancipated itself from its earlier ties with the Continent—in practice, with France—and that the interchange was minimal. Certainly French, German, Italian, Russian, and Spanish criticism ignored the English and Americans almost completely. The situation was not quite so bleak on the other side of the Channel and Atlantic Ocean. Continental writers, philosophers, and aestheticians rather than critics began to influence English and American criticism. Marx loomed, though hardly with specific texts, behind much social criticism. In the United States, one can speak of a whole Marxist movement during the Depression of the thirties, and in England there was a brief flurry of Marxist criticism just before the outbreak of the Second World War. Two English critics, Christopher Caudwell and Ralph Fox, died fighting for the Republic in the Spanish Civil War. Freud, and in his wake the very different Carl Jung, began to affect literary criticism. Not only writers who professed allegiance to psychoanalysis as a method but also others who picked up only very general ideas about the role of sexuality, the unconscious, dreams, and such concepts as the Oedipus complex, repression, the collective unconscious, and archetypes began to appear on the critical scene. Bergson was for a time an important influence in England; and Nietzsche, mainly as a moralist or antimoralist, loomed in the background. But actual literary critics from the Continent remained virtually unknown.

An exception could be made for the French antiromantic polemicists such as Pierre Lasserre and the very different Julien Benda, who were known to T. E. Hulme, T. S. Eliot, Herbert Read, and others and who in America were read by Irving Babbitt. But they were really ideologues, propagandists rather than literary critics. Only T. S. Eliot and Ezra Pound had contacts with genuine French critics, Remy de Gourmont and Ramon Fernandez. Most important, though often hardly traceable in detail, was the influence of Benedetto Croce, whose early *Estetica* was translated in 1907. It seems to have been his only work which made any impact at that time. In America, Croce had his faithful expositor in Joel E. Spingarn, and an English philosopher, Robin Collingwood, shows his influence in his book on aesthetics, *The Principles of Art* (1934), and his writings on the theory of history. Contemporary Russian and German critics were totally unknown in the English-speaking world before the fifties. Thus treating the Continent apart from English and American criticism seems necessary and fully justified.

As the number of the studies outgrew the size of a comfortable volume it was decided to divide the work into two: English criticism in volume 5 and American criticism in volume 6. One can, admittedly, present a strong argument for the close relationship between the two traditions in this century. It is most strikingly proved by the fact that two Americans, Ezra Pound and T. S. Eliot, who came to England shortly before the outbreak of the First World War, not only deeply influenced subsequent criticism in both England and America but became the central figures in the shift of taste and change of theory in this century. An Englishman who deeply impressed criticism both in his native country and in America, I. A. Richards spent a good twenty years (1943–63) as professor at Harvard University, and G. Wilson Knight was a professor of English at the University of Toronto for nine years (1931–40) before he returned to his native England. Other English critics came to America at least as occasional lecturers and teachers in summer schools (William Empson, Herbert Read) or, like F. R. Leavis, went on organized lecture tours. Such an unacademic figure as D. H. Lawrence spent long periods in the Southwest of the United States but had written on American literature before he set foot on its soil.

The traffic went also the other way: besides those who decided to stay on in Europe—Eliot, Pound, and Santayana—we must not forget the effect that years of study in England must have had on American Rhodes scholars (J. C. Ransom, F. O. Matthiessen, Cleanth Brooks, R. P. Warren). Later in life others spent considerable time in England as visiting professors (Allen Tate, R. P. Blackmur, Lionel Trilling), and, of course, American students and professors were avid visitors in England and were frequenters and users of its libraries. The mobility of the twentieth century—with affluence and the increased speed of travel—made these contacts much more frequent than in preceding centuries, but even without personal relationships the exchange of books between the two countries was quick and often decisive in establishing and perpetuating reputations. English books appeared regularly, often after a year's delay, in American editions; and American books, less frequently, with English publishers. A study of these interchanges might show many discrepancies and inequities but would also show how the international booktrade has been a main vehicle for the spread of critical ideas.

While all this is true, one cannot, on the other hand, deny that English and American criticism in the first half of this century developed quite separately. The situation in the two countries was, for instance, in 1910 totally different. In England the Bloomsbury group began to dominate, and scholarship was in the hands of polite appreciators. In the United States journalistic criticism was in the hands of muckrakers and of the critics of the American business civilization who praised the naturalistic novel attacking the environment in which the writer was forced to live. In the universities a plodding factual scholarship ruled, though challenged here and there by the new humanists, who drew from Arnold inspiration for the preservation of the classical heritage. The two traditions differed profoundly, at least till the advent of the New Criticism, and even later the distinction remained very pronounced. The influence of the Leavises in England was feebly echoed in America, while figures such as Yvor Winters or Kenneth Burke remained local to the United States. Among American critics only Edmund Wilson was a success in England, and paradoxically he can, on many issues, be described as strongly Anglophobe. In writing a history of English and American criticism a separate order of exposition is inevitable even though the contact between the two traditions was intense.

The first volumes of this history carried an ample apparatus in the back, necessitated by the decision to print in the notes the original of all

translated excerpts quoted—from French, German, Italian, Russian, and
Danish. As all the quotations in these new volumes are in English the
need for such extensive apparatus is obviated. I still insist on full reference for every quotation, since one of the claims of this history is that
it is based on a verifiable examination of every book quoted, but now
instead of superscript numbers referring to notes assembled in the back,
I use abbreviated citations in the text whenever possible. When the reference is longer and would interrupt the flow of exposition, the documentation is still given in the greatly reduced notes.

The bibliographies list the books used, with the abbreviations, and a
small highly select number of comments about the authors or topics
discussed. There are today so many resources for bibliographical information, such as the annual MLA Bibliography, that it seemed unnecessary to list every item. The selection is focused on comment on the
literary criticism of the author discussed. Still, sometimes bibliographies
and general discussions are included when they seemed useful to a student of criticism.

Friends have made suggestions and criticisms over the years. Some
have read parts of the manuscript or commented on published articles.
I gratefully acknowledge in particular the help of my old friend and
collaborator Austin Warren, of Lowry Nelson, Jr., Barbara Rosecrance,
and an anonymous reader of my chapter on T. S. Eliot.

Over the years I have incurred obligations to institutions that have
supported my writing projects. I want to express my thanks to the Gug-
genheim Foundation, which awarded me a third fellowship in 1966–67.
I was a Fulbright lecturer in Germany, lecturing on American criticism,
in the spring of 1969. After my retirement from Yale University in 1972
I was a Senior Fellow of the National Endowment for the Humanities in
1972–73. I was invited by the Rockefeller Foundation three times for a
month's stay at the Conference and Study Center at Bellagio—in 1966,
1969, and 1977. I was a Fellow of the Cornell University Institute of
Humanities in 1977.

I also want to thank the libraries I have used. Without liberal access
to the Yale University Library this book could not have been written. I
also occasionally consulted the libraries of the University of California:
at San Diego, at Riverside, and at Santa Barbara, as well as the libraries
of the University of Washington at Seattle, the University of Iowa, Indiana University at Bloomington, Princeton University, and Cornell University; the British Library at London, the Bodleian at Oxford, the
Library of the University of Mainz, and the Alessandrina, the Library
of the University of Rome.

My editors at the Yale University Press, Ellen Graham and Jay Williams, deserve special thanks for their care, and so does Christopher Lemelin, who compiled the two Indices of Names.

R. W.

New Haven, Connecticut
April 1985

ACKNOWLEDGMENTS

I use the following articles of mine, sometimes expanded, cut, and changed.

Introduction: "Reflections on My *History of Modern Criticism*," in *PTL: A Journal for Descriptive Poetics and Theory of Literature* 3 (1977): 417–27. Reprinted in *The Attack on Literature and Other Essays* (1982), 134–45. Also in *Proceedings of the VIIIth Congress of the International Comparative Literature Association, 1976*, Budapest, Akadémia Kiadó (1981), 439–47.

"A. C. Bradley, Shakespeare and the Infinite," in *From Chaucer to Gibbon: Essays in Memory of Curt A. Zimansky* (1975), 85–103. Also in *Philological Quarterly* 54 (1975): 85–103.

"Virginia Woolf as Critic," *Southern Review* 13 (1977): 419–37.

"The Literary Criticism of D. H. Lawrence," *Sewanee Review* 16 (1983): 598–613.

"Ezra Pound's Literary Criticism," *Denver Quarterly* 3 (1976): 1–20.

"The Criticism of T. S. Eliot," *Sewanee Review* 64 (1956): 398–443.

"On Re-reading I. A. Richards," *Southern Review* 3 (1967): 533–54.

"The Literary Criticism of Frank Raymond Leavis," in *Literary Views: Critical and Historical Essays*, ed. Carroll Camden (1964), 175–99. Also "The Later Leavis," *Southern Review* 17 (1981): 490–500.

"The Literary Theories of F. W. Bateson," *Essays in Criticism* 29 (1979): 112–23.

INTRODUCTION TO VOLUMES 5 AND 6

METHOD AND SCOPE

I HAVE READ in the vast new literature on historiography, which, at least in the Anglo-American world, is dominated by the methods of analytical philosophy, but I have come away disappointed, for practically all these books and papers analyze problems that are of little or no relevance to the writing of a history of criticism. Most of these discussions are concerned with questions of moral responsibility or culpability, with normal or abnormal human behavior, with accidents such as sudden deaths and assassinations. We are to consider such problems as "Why did Brutus stab Caesar?" or "Why did Louis XIV die unpopular?" Hardly anywhere are the very different problems of a history of criticism even raised. We must go elsewhere for parallels, and possible models.

Obviously, the history of criticism differs profoundly from political, social, or economic history in one salient respect: the texts on which the history of criticism is based are immediately accessible, and they can be read, commented upon, interpreted, argued about, and criticized in turn, as if they had been written yesterday, even though they may have been written (like the *Poetics* of Aristotle) 2300 or so years ago. Thus the history of criticism is not history in the sense in which we write, say, the history of battles. The battle of Waterloo has to be reconstructed from recorded eye-witness accounts, from written commands or dispositions, or possibly from some physical remains, whereas texts such as Homer and Plato are present, just as the Parthenon is still present, or the frescoes of Giotto in the Arena Chapel. Still, the history of criticism differs from the history of art or music or poetry by not being faced with the task of having to translate from one medium (or, as it is now fashionable to say, from one language or code) into another. In writing the history of criticism we use and have to use the same language (even if we translate from ancient Greek), the language of concepts. In short the history of criticism presents the same problems as all histories of ideas: the history of philosophy, the history of aesthetics, of political, religious, and economic thought, of linguistics, and many other branches of learning.

We thus have some help and models. Not much unfortunately can be learned from other histories of criticism. The only general history that preceded my books, George Saintsbury's dating from 1901–04, is a deliberately antitheoretical, impressionistic history of literary taste. Saintsbury complains about the "error of wool-gathering after abstract questions of the nature and justification of poetry"[1] and hardly ever reflects on his method of writing, except to offer us an atlas and survey. More can be learned from R. S. Crane's review of J. W. Atkins's book on *English Literary Criticism: 17th and 18th Century* (1953). Crane rejects Atkins's summarizing of doctrines and wants a chronological analysis of specific texts, a "history without prior commitments as to what criticism is or ought to be," a history "without a thesis," an aim I consider impossible to attain and undesirable.[2]

More has been said about the writing of the history of philosophy. One can trace a history of the historiography of philosophy from Diogenes Laertius in the third century A.D. to the eighteenth-century compendia of Jakob Brucker (1742–67, five volumes) and Wilhelm Gottlieb Tennemann's twelve volumes (1798–1817) to Hegel's *Lectures on the History of Philosophy* (published in 1833–36 but based on manuscripts and transcripts by students sometimes dating back to 1815–16). All histories of philosophy preceding Hegel's can be called doxographies, that is, summaries and expositions of the doctrines of philosophers, arranged either according to schools (Platonic, skeptic, Epicurean, Stoic, etc.) or chronologically, with the ambition to do so neutrally, descriptively, though it is easy to detect the Leibnizian bias of Brucker or the Kantian of Tennemann. With Hegel the whole conception of a history of philosophy changed radically. In his introduction Hegel states resolutely that "the history of a subject depends closely on the concept one has of the subject." He admits that philosophy (and this would be even more true of criticism) has "the disadvantage compared to other sciences, that there are the most divergent views about what philosophy should and can do." But those who complain about the diversity of the manifestations of philosophy are, Hegel says with an unusual display of dry wit, like the man whom the doctor advised to eat fruit but who then refused cherries, plums, and grapes. "Diversity is thus not an impairment but an absolute necessity for the existence of philosophy. The study of the history of philosophy is thus the study of philosophy itself." The diversity of philosophy is conceived not as a random sequence but as "an organically progressive totality, as a rational continuity." Philosophy has a history which is "a necessary, consistent process." Every philosophy was necessary. None perished wholly. The newest philosophy, and he means his own, is the "result of all preceding philosophies." Hegel elaborates the paradox that in the "history of philosophy, though it is history, we still do not have to deal with anything that is past." "Truth," he says, "has no history, is not past."[3] For Hegel this implied the right and obligation of the historian to judge, to decide which ideas belong to the chain of development. The introductory reflections of Hegel's *History of Philosophy* are still pertinent today, also for a historian of criticism.

They raise the question I had to face. Is there such a subject as "criticism" which can be isolated from other activities of man, and does it show some kind of unity, focus, and continuity? I have answered "yes" to both of those questions, though, for instance, Benedetto Croce in his early pamphlet, *Critica letteraria* (1894), and Erich Auerbach in a review of the first two volumes of my *History of Modern Criticism* denied that criticism is a unified subject because of "the multitude of possible problems and crossings of problems, the extreme diversity of its presuppositions, aims and accents."[4] I am content to answer that criticism is any discourse on literature. It is thus clearly circumscribed by its theme, as many other sciences are, and the multitude of problems and approaches is precisely the topic of the books. One of its tasks is the sorting out of the different ways of defining and regarding the subject. A history of the concept of criticism, literature, and poetry is at the very center of the books.

While Croce and Auerbach see only the cherries, plums, and grapes and seem to deny the existence of fruit, other historians have tried to abolish the distinction between fruit and the whole of plant-life, or, to drop the metaphor, the distinction between literary and other criticism such as the criticism of art and music and have even denied that criticism can be discussed otherwise than as a branch of general history. There is an undeniable truth to the view that reality forms a seamless web, that any activity of man is involved with all his other activities. Literary criticism is related to the history of literature and the other arts, to intellectual history, to general history whether political or social, and even economic conditions play their part in shaping the history of criticism. Attempts have been made to make criticism simply a mirror of a specific time and situation. Thus Bernard Smith, in *Forces in American Criticism: A Study in the History of American Literary Thought* states emphatically that "literary criticism seemed to me more clearly related to social history than are poetry and fiction."[5] Criticism appears as "ideology"—not in the frequent sense of *Weltanschauung*—but as a false consciousness of reality, as a mere mouthpiece of specific literary or social trends. It becomes integrated into cultural history, becomes the expression of cultural change itself. We are confronted with the whole question of determinism, with the view that "everything must be treated not only as connected with everything else but as a symptom of something else."[6] I have discussed this whole question several times elsewhere[7] and can here only repeat my conclusion. Cause—in the sense defined by Morris R. Cohen— as "some reason or ground why, whenever the antecedent event occurs, the consequent must follow"[8]—is inapplicable in literary history or in the history of criticism. One work may be the necessary condition of another but one cannot say that it caused it. One must grant something to human freedom, to the decision of an individual. But we need not, in this context, move on this abstract plane.

As a historian of criticism I must make an attempt to describe the relationship of criticism to all the other activities of man without giving up the focus on the central subject. The relationship of criticism to the practice of writing must be constantly borne in mind. Sometimes there is the personal union of the poet-critic: most prominently in English literature, where poets such as Dryden, Wordsworth, Coleridge, Matthew Arnold, and T. S. Eliot are also landmarks in the history of criticism. Much criticism was written as a specific defense of a literary trend or school. I need only allude to the Schlegels as heralds of romanticism or to the Russian formalists as defenders of futurism. Criticism is closely related to aesthetics: it may be, as Croce argued, simply a branch of aesthetics, and I do discuss writers such as Kant, Schiller, Schelling, Ruskin, and Croce, though I try to steer clear of abstract speculations on beauty and the aesthetic response. Criticism is deeply influenced by philosophy: the empiricism of the British critics of the eighteenth century contrasts with the idealist and sometimes mystical assumptions of the German critics in the romantic period, as they differ from the positivists of the later nineteenth century in France. I could not ignore the impact of political history on criticism, when I discuss Madame de Staël expelled by Napoleon or the propagandist of liberal ideas, Georg Brandes, or the anti-Tsarist fervor of the radical critics in the Russia of the 1860s. I do on occasion think of the economic basis of criticism, the different class origins and allegiances of the critics. The German professors of the early nineteenth century (including Hegel) differ obviously in lifestyle from a Parisian bohemian such as Baudelaire or struggling journalists like the Russians, Belinsky, Dobrolyubov, and Pisarev.

All this is well and good, but we cannot get around the question raised in the quotations from Hegel. We must think of criticism as a relatively independent activity. No progress in any branch of learning has ever been made unless it was seen in comparative isolation, unless everything else was, to use the phenomenological terminology, "put into brackets." This isolation, which does not of course mean criticism for criticism's sake, is also a pragmatic imperative. A book, even a very long book, has to have some limits. If I had to discuss the relation of criticism to the practice of literature, I would have to examine, for instance, all the tragedies of Schiller or inquire whether Wordsworth actually wrote poetry in the common language of men. I would quickly abolish the unity of my subject matter, its continuity and development, and would make the history of criticism dissolve into the history of literature itself. Only by limiting the subject can we hope to master it.

But how can it be mastered? How can one reconcile the elementary fact that we have to do with texts that are present today and still think of them as part of the past, as history? One could argue that there is no history of criticism or even of literature. W. P. Ker has stated that the literary historian is like a guide in a museum who points and comments on the pictures, and Benedetto Croce, in many contexts, proclaimed that works of art are unique, individual, immediately present, and that there is no essential continuity between them. In criticism we can say that the problems discussed by Plato or Aristotle are still with us today. We have to do with what W. B. Gallie has strikingly called "essentially contested concepts."[9] We can take such concepts as "imitation," "tragedy," "form," "catharsis," to mention a few key-terms of the *Poetics*, and discuss them as if they were pronounced yesterday. We can ask: Are they true or not? Do they make sense? How do they apply to today's literature? I agree that there are persistent problems present even today, that Aristotle, Kant, Coleridge, Friedrich Schlegel, T. S. Eliot, and others ask questions that we are meant to answer, and they are often the same questions, though often differently phrased, with a new vocabulary. One of the functions of a history of criticism is to show the reader that what has been touted as a new discovery has been said many times over before. Modern criticism can be described as a constant process of rediscovery of old questions. But this whole idea of persistent questions has been challenged by the new historicism. It is said that Aristotle's concepts are not timeless but time bound, that "tragedy" means for him something very different from what it means for us, because he knew only the Greek plays. Every critic writes in his own time, encapsuled in his own time. I think we must recognize the danger of assuming timeless concepts too readily. We must be aware of the shifts of meaning and not be fooled by the occurrence of the same words or phrases. But this seems to me rather a challenge for the historian than an insurmountable obstacle. I cannot believe in the inscrutable past, in the closed cycles of time-spirits assumed in Hegelianism and such derivatives as Oswald Spengler or much of German *Geistesgeschichte* with its "medieval mind" or "baroque man."

I myself have written several papers on historical semantics, somewhat on the model of Leo Spitzer's studies on such words as *Stimmung* and *milieu,* papers on the concept of criticism, literature, period, evolution, and five period terms: baroque, classicism, romanticism, realism, and symbolism. But I have rejected the idea of organizing my *History* around the tracing of single concepts or "unit ideas" as recommended in Arthur O. Lovejoy's special method of the "history of ideas." It would break up the systems, admittedly often loosely put together and contradictory, of individual critics; it would make an understanding of their individuality and personality (which must not of course be thought of in biographical terms) impossible. Let us beware of the "trap of spurious persistence," as Peter Gay has called it, but still insist that we can understand the concepts and problems of even remote times and authors. False dilemmas have been pressed by modern hermeneutics. Man can understand someone with a perspective very different from his own. Wilhelm Dilthey has elaborated the view that men share a common potential to be other than they are.

We cannot, however, be content with the idea of the timelessness of criticism if we want to write history even though or because we recognize that concepts persist throughout history. If we dealt with concepts purely as present, we would write not a history of criticism but an introduction to critical problems on the occasion of Aristotle, Dryden, Lessing, Matthew Arnold, Hippolyte Taine, and others.

The history of criticism, as I conceive it, cannot be simply a discussion of timeless texts and must not be reduced to a branch of general or cultural history. We have to find a way of thinking of an internal history of criticism. Hegel assumes this for the history of philosophy, and so does Croce in the historical part of his *Aesthetics.* All philosophy and aesthetics are presumed to move toward the one divine event: the philosophy of Hegel or the aesthetics of Croce. These histories could be called "retrospective": they assume that philosophy and aesthetics have found their final resting point. I have been suspected of sharing this view and accused of "looking down at the history of criticism as a series of failures, as doomed attempts to scramble to the heights of our present-day glories," presumably represented by *Theory of Literature* (1949). But this is a misunderstanding of *Theory of Literature,* which is a tolerant and open-minded rehearsal of many theories, and this misunderstanding is refuted by the text of my *History.* I have a point of view. I have to make selections of texts and authors. The idea of a completely neutral, purely expository history seems to me a chimera. There cannot be any history without a sense of direction, some feeling for the future, some ideal, some standard, and hence some hindsight. But holding a point of view and even a specific creed cannot mean that other approaches or perspectives would remain invisible. The function of a book like mine is to expound the great diversity of views without, however, giving up one's own perspective. I should like to think of my *History,* to use the classification that John Passmore proposed for histories of philosophy,[10] as "elucidatory," as not "argumentative" or "polemical" in the sense of refuting a critic, but still not shirking from placing him; and not as cultural history, which would display doctrines only as representatives of a period or trend. Much in my books must be inevitably "doxographical," expository, for the books are supposed to be of use to others and to aim at the exposition of critical ideas from a firsthand study of the texts. Much is inevitably "retrospective": I cannot help selecting and judging from my own vantage point. Some is cultural history: I must suggest the way critics fit into their time. But I was always aware of the danger that critics would be treated as mere symptoms of their time and thus would remain without ties to the past of their arguments. The relationship between critics would cease to matter. I know the problem of novelty—the addition or emergence of new problems, the question of originality, the filiation of ideas. I do not think, for instance, that it is unimportant to point to the mainly German sources of Coleridge's theories. It locates him in intellectual history and prevents the kind of judgment pronounced, for instance, by I. A. Richards, when he makes him "the Galileo" of criticism, the forerunner of the presumed Newton.[11]

If we allow the possibility of different viewpoints, we are in danger of historicism and even complete relativism. But we need not grant such a conclusion. We can still adjudicate the merits of different ideas, see the relative justification of this or that formula or answer. We need not reconcile deep-seated contradictions and conflicts and claim a "synthesis" to overcome eclecticism. It seems to me that the conception of a greater or lesser understanding of the nature of literature or poetry is objectively determinable. Truth has no history, says Passmore echoing Hegel, but adds, "the discussion of problems has a history."[12]

How can such a continuity be conceived? In my early years I hoped that it would be possible to arrive at an evolutionary history of literature and criticism. On the model of the Russian formalists, one could think of literary history largely as a wearing out, of "automatization" of conventions, followed by an "actualization" of new conventions using radically new devices or concepts. One could think in terms of convention and revolt. Novelty would be the one criterion of change. But I have come to recognize that this scheme is far too simple, that it does not answer the basic question of the direction of change, and that the scheme implies a time-concept that is refuted by modern psychology. Today we recognize a potential simultaneity in a man's mental development. It constitutes a structure that is virtual at any moment. There is an inter-penetration of the causal order in experience and memory. A work of criticism is not simply a member of a series, a link in a chain. It may stand in relation to anything in the past. The critic may reach into the remotest history. An evolutionary history of criticism must fail. I have come to this resigned conclusion.

Nor can I accept the model proposed for the history of science in Thomas Kuhn's *Structure of Scientific Revolutions*. Kuhn argues that the canons of scientific theory and practice vary from period to period rad-ically, that there are what he calls "paradigms," or "disciplinary matrices" due to single scientific geniuses such as Copernicus, Newton, Lavoisier, and Einstein. They provide modes, belief systems, texts which Kuhn calls "exemplars." These paradigms are incommensurable, as there is no ac-cretion or accumulation of scientific knowledge except within a single paradigm. Even the words they use have different meanings. "How can they even hope to talk together, much less to be persuasive," says Kuhn.[13] It may be tempting to apply this scheme to the history of criticism. One could argue that there was a model provided by Aristotle and that this model was completely replaced by the romantic view, which presumably originated in Kant and Herder. In the twentieth century one could speak, at least in the English and American world, of a model provided by T. S. Eliot. It might be tempting to speak of completely irreconcilable points of view, to accept a pluralism of methods and thus to account for the present heightened difficulties of communication, for the Tower of Ba-bel, the confusion of tongues.

An attempt has been made to apply Kuhn's scheme to the history of linguistics in a collective volume *Studies in the History of Linguistics,* edited by the anthropologist Dell Hymes (1974). I was not convinced that lin-guistics has gone through such complete revolutions. There is a conti-nuity in the history of linguistics, as even some papers in the book prove convincingly. Linguistics is a cumulative science in spite of shifts of em-phasis and changing interests. I agree with Keith Percival's article in *Language* that accepting Kuhn's view would give rise to an "unhealthy situation": linguists would look upon "all theoretical disagreements as conflicts between rival paradigms, i.e., incommensurable viewpoints and use this as an excuse not to observe the ground rules of rational discussion."[14] The very same arguments hold true of criticism. There are no such complete revolutions in the history of criticism as Kuhn stipulates for the history of science. Nor are there periods completely dominated by one figure and one sacred text. While there are many different points of view, they can and must be discussed rationally. Criticism is an ongoing concern, with a future. I do not believe that things have been settled for good (as Hegel and Croce believed) nor can I believe that my views and those of my contemporaries will be replaced by completely different assumptions. There has been a continued clarification of problems throughout history, a growing core of agreement on many issues despite the ostensible conflicts. My own convictions, I hope, are never imposed or obtruded as a fixed, preconceived pattern.

The grouping by critics follows from my conviction that individual initiative rather than collective trends matters in criticism. Critics must never be considered merely as "cases." Both portraiture of critics, intellectual profiles, and a sense of trends and changing conditions make a history. But the order cannot be dialectical or strictly evolutionary. The more I study the situation of a specific time, the more I eschew easy labels and generalities. I trust that in mapping out the field I can indicate its scope and breadth like a surveyor by triangulation. I do not have to measure every foot of the ground. Some ultimate decision will have to remain with the historian. Whether I always made the right choices is a matter I cannot judge myself. As any author, I have to wait for the verdict of readers and critics.

In organizing these volumes I had the chronology of ascertainable facts in mind. There is a history of events which is quite distinct from the history of ideas. Critics are born and die in certain years; books and articles were published at definite dates. (A chronological list of books is provided in an appendix as in the earlier volumes.) But arranging them one soon discovers that the idea of a neat succession of critics and critical trends is far from clear: for instance, T. S. Eliot's highly influential and much quoted article "Tradition and the Individual Talent" was published in 1919 while the main writings of his supposed predecessor, John Middleton Murry, followed later. *The Problem of Style* dates from 1922. The lesson can be drawn that conflicting or contradictory doctrines existed side by side, that the dominance of a specific creed, to give an obvious example, the New Criticism, was always limited, confined to specific circles, supported by some reviews, opposed by others, ignored by many more. The chronological arrangement of these books is thus approximate, determined roughly by the sequence of the key books. But which are the key books or pronouncements is a selection made by hindsight. It allows me, for instance, to decide that the Chicago Aristotelians fall within my purview though their collective volume *Critics and Criticism* came out only in 1952 and thus follows my ostensible terminal date, as I judge that the crucial statements of R. S. Crane precede the year 1950. His essay "History versus Criticism in the Study of Literature" dates from 1935 and his teachings and polemics against the New Criticism span the 1940s while Northrop Frye's *Anatomy of Criticism* (1957), the basic book of myth-criticism, falls by its date outside my purview, though one could argue that his book on Blake, *Fearful Symmetry* (1949), anticipates the system expounded in *Anatomy* in many respects. The cutoff date 1950, announced years ago in the title of this whole series, means that I feel obliged to discuss every major critic established before 1950, though this leads to some ragged edges. For instance, R. P. Blackmur, who died in 1962, left a large manuscript on Henry Adams, which was printed only in 1980 but still forms an integral part of his achievement.

One more point should be emphasized. I focus sharply on the literary criticism of my figures and do not and cannot discuss their total work: their significance in a history of poetry or novel-writing or philosophy. The book would become unmanageable if I were to pay attention to the poetry of Yeats, Pound, and Eliot, to the novels of Virginia Woolf, E. M. Forster, D. H. Lawrence, and Wyndham Lewis, or even to the philosophy of George Santayana. A general knowledge of literary history of this time must be assumed. I am convinced that literary criticism is a distinct activity of man which is worth studying in its own right, just as I believe and would argue that there is a distinct group of writings called "literature" since antiquity. It deserves our regard for the aesthetic quality for what used to be called "beauty" and for its impact on men in solitude and on society in general. The world would be unimaginably poorer without literature and literature, in turn, needs the understanding, the sifting and judging provided by criticism.

1 : SYMBOLISM IN ENGLISH

THE FOURTH VOLUME of this *History* concluded with a chapter on the French symbolists, culminating in Mallarmé's theory of absolute poetry, as a contrast to Tolstoy and Zola, in whom art is identified with life. The discussion of criticism in English concluded similarly with the opposition between Oscar Wilde, the aesthete, and Bernard Shaw, the professed Marxist, which seems just as stark, though both came from the same place, Dublin, and were almost contemporaries.

Criticism in English shows no great changes until about 1910, when according to Virginia Woolf "human character changed" (*Mr. Bennett and Mrs. Brown* [1924], 4). We need not take seriously Virginia Woolf's exact pinpointing to acknowledge that about the second decade of the twentieth century the new art that is loosely called modernism began to emerge in most countries: the early Pound, T. E. Hulme, and somewhat later T. S. Eliot represent a break in the history of English poetry as they do in the history of criticism. Before their advent Victorian, vaguely romantic, or "aesthetic" views confronted a rising realism or naturalism, neither of which contributed anything new to critical thought, if we except the prefaces, hardly noticed at that time, which Henry James wrote for the New York edition of his *Novels and Tales* (1906–07).

W. B. YEATS (1865–1939)

One cannot speak in England of a symbolist movement, though a knowledge of the French began to penetrate in the 1890s. But William Butler Yeats developed a symbolist theory of his own which stands apart in some isolation and constitutes an impressive and coherent scheme of aesthetics, poetics, and even practical criticism. As Yeats is rightly considered a great poet, he deserves to be taken seriously as a theorist. He had arrived at his symbolism by his own road independently of the French movement, though he took, through his contacts with Arthur Symons, an interest in the French developments.

1

Yeats, at first glance, seems not to have the critical or even theoretical temper. In many ways he was the most credulous of men: he took occultism seriously, believed or professed to believe in the existence of fairies, demons, astral bodies, and ghosts, accepted telepathy and second sight, and as late as 1935 cast a horoscope for Lady Wellesley, though he was honest enough to express his surprise that "your profile gives a false impression" (*Letters on Poetry*, 37) compared to what he knew of her from personal contact. I shall not enter into the question, irrelevant for my purpose, of the extent to which Yeats actually believed in occult phenomena: he certainly on occasion treated his own obsession with some irony. Late in his life Yeats studied respectable philosophers— Berkeley, Schopenhauer, Nietzsche, Bergson, Russell, Whitehead, Croce, and Gentile—with persistence and some grasp of the problems involved in order to buttress an idealist philosophy, but one cannot say that he could distinguish clearly between an idealist epistemology and the age-old tradition of mysticism or even occultism. In the often comic discussion in letters with T. Sturge Moore, the brother of G. E. Moore, Yeats defends stubbornly the complete lack of distinction between a real black cat and the imagined black cat which the disturbed Ruskin supposedly threw out of the window. Sturge Moore clearly had the better of the argument (*W. B. Yeats and T. Sturge Moore*, passim [see index]).

Granting the absurdity of Yeats's assumptions about the nature of the world and dismissing the weird system developed in *A Vision* will not allow us to ignore their importance for the practice and interpretation of his poetry (a subject beyond my purpose here) but will make the paradox of Yeats's clarity and even sanity as a theorist of poetry so much the more striking.

Yeats, in his early years, was a prolific reviewer. He began, in 1886, at the age of twenty-one, with an essay on the "Poetry of Sir Samuel Ferguson" followed by a piece on Clarence Mangan (1803–49) and others in a campaign to sift through the Irish poetry of the nineteenth century: to disparage the merely rhetorical, patriotic, and sentimental tradition in favor of what he felt to be the genuinely popular and to advocate and praise the movement for the collecting and resurrecting of Irish folklore, in which he himself took a prominent part with *The Celtic Twilight* (1893). He plunged into the polemics about the Irish national revival, also in literature, defending a return to the national roots, to an "inherited subject-matter known to the whole people" (*A*, 116). In terms which would have been comprehensible to the Brothers Grimm, Yeats thought of art as "a traditional statement of certain heroic and religious truths, passed on from age to age, modified by individual genius but never abandoned" (298). Poetry and literature in general had, in Ireland, the function of defining and enhancing national self-consciousness and combatting the encroachment of the industrial civilization identified with the centralizing power of London. The view implied a rejection of the "muddy torrent of shallow realism" (*Letters to the New Island*, 176) and of the utilitarian and rationalist philosophy and science of the Victorian age (*A*, 77).

Yeats as a poet grew up with Shelley and Rossetti. Early he came under the spell of Blake, and in 1893 he collaborated with Edwin John Ellis in an edition of Blake's *Works, Poetic, Symbolic and Critical* in three large volumes. The edition, while severely criticized by modern scholars for its inaccuracies, had its importance in printing the Prophetic Books *in extenso* and providing a commentary with which Yeats hoped to "give to the world a great religious visionary who has been hidden" (*L*, 156). The exposition of Blake's "symbolic system" has been called a "disordered cataloging of symbolic colors, dualities, names, stories, images and body parts" (Bloom, *Yeats*, 79), but Yeats at least attempted, for the first time since Swinburne's embarrassed dismissal, to interpret the symbolism of the Prophetic Books, to make sense of the *Four Zoas*, and to describe Blake's cosmos, however inaccurate the details of his exposition may be. The first section of the "Symbolic System," called "The Necessity of Symbolism," expounds Swedenborg's and Blake's idea of two worlds, the one of the senses, the other of the intellect, which have their correspondences, and the view that the "chief difference between the metaphors of poetry and the symbols of mysticisms is that the latter are woven together into a complete system" (*WWB*, 1:238). Thus Yeats needed no French theories to embrace a symbolism which is a straight revelation theory. In the essays collected under the title *Ideas of Good and Evil* (1903) and in scattered articles, Yeats develops this ancient view. Art is not a "criticism of life" but a "revelation of a hidden life" (*UP*, 2:131). This hidden life to which art or poetry has access is sometimes conceived in terms that seem to anticipate the collective unconscious of Carl Gustav Jung but could be suggested also by Emerson's Oversoul or the Neoplatonist Anima Mundi. There is a "great mind and great memory" which can be evoked by symbols, for "our memories are part of one great memory, the memory of Nature herself" (*EI*, 28). In the very same essay, "Magic" (1901), the Great Memory, which is "a dwelling house of symbols" (79), is somewhat differently interpreted as "our minds giving a little, creating or revealing for a moment what I must call a supernatural artist" (36).

Somewhat earlier (1896) Yeats had spoken of the "little ritual" of verse as "resembling the great ritual of Nature." The poet "becomes, as well the great mystics believed, a vessel of the creative power of God; and whether he be a great poet or a small poet, we can praise the poems, which but seem to be his, with the extremity of praise that we give this great ritual which is but copied from the same eternal model" (*EI*, 202). A variation of the microcosm-macrocosm parallel is implied: the poet is a priest who celebrates a fixed ritual, whereas elsewhere, sometimes simultaneously, imagination is conceived as creatively collaborating with the Universal Mind, God or the supreme artist.

At times the expectations for the effects of art are put extravagantly. "The arts are founded on the life beyond the world, and they must cry in the ears of our penury until the world has been consumed and become a vision" (*EI*, 184), or, put differently, "we must cry out that imagination is always seeking to remake the world according to the impulses and the patterns in that Great Mind, and that Great Memory" (52). The apocalyptic gesture toward the "consummation of time" seems to demand an abolition of nature, a complete trust in vision, and shows little interest in the craft of poetry or its language. Mostly symbols are described in the vaguest terms. "A symbol is indeed the only possible expression of some invisible essence." Compared to the symbolic imagination which is revelation, fancy is mere amusement (116). Symbols are "blossoms, as it were, growing from immortal roots, hands, as it were, pointing the way into some divine labyrinth" (117). But Yeats does make attempts to distinguish between symbols, inherent or arbitrary (49), and emotional or intellectual, that is, "they either evoke ideas alone or ideas mingled with emotions" (160), with the assumption that present-day symbols are deplorably intellectual. For how, Yeats asks, "can the arts overcome the slow dying of men's hearts that we call the progress of the world, and lay their hands upon men's heart-strings again, without becoming the garment of religion as in old times?" (162–63).

This concept of symbolism seems rarefied and very general, but Yeats manages to use it as a critical tool successfully. In the good Coleridgean (and ultimately Goethean) sense, Yeats disparages allegory. It is "fastened to a big barnyard-door of common sense, of mere practical virtue" (*EI*, 367). Discussing Spenser, Yeats attempts to rescue him from what he considers a taint. "Allegory is not natural" to him (368); he is rather "a poet of the delighted senses" (370). "When Spenser lived the earth had still its sheltering sacredness"; his religion was a "paganism that is natural to proud and happy people," strengthened by the Platonism of the Renaissance (366).

When Yeats discusses Shelley's symbolism (under the misleading title "The Philosophy of Shelley's Poetry" [1903]), he attempts to ascertain·

his recurring images, towers and rivers, caves and fountains, and that one "star of his," concluding that Shelley's "world has grown solid under foot and consistent enough for the soul's habitation" (*EI*, 294). Later, however, when Yeats had emancipated himself from the overpowering influence of Shelley on his early poetry, he came to criticize Shelley for his Utopianism: "those theories about the coming changes of the world which he has built up with so much elaborate passion hurry him from life continually" (*E*, 149). In *A Vision* (1928) Yeats deplores that "Shelley lacked the vision of Evil, could not conceive of the world as a continual conflict." The justice of *Prometheus Unbound* now seems to him a vague propagandist emotion, and "the women that await its coming are but clouds" (*V*, 144). In a late introduction to *Prometheus Unbound* (1932) Yeats chides Shelley for "expecting miracle, the Kingdom of God in the twinkling of an eye" (*EI*, 419) and objects to what he considers his willful rationalism. "Shelley was not a mystic, his system of thought was constructed by his logical faculties to satisfy desire, not a symbolical revelation received after the suspension of all desire. He could neither say with Dante, 'His will is our peace,' nor with Finn in the Irish story, 'The best music is what happens' " (422).

Yeats has come to regard even Blake as something of a rationalist. "He was a symbolist who had to invent his symbols: and his counties of England, with their correspondence to the tribes of Israel, and his mountains and rivers, with their correspondence to parts of a man's body are arbitrary." Blake was "a man crying out for a mythology, and trying to make one because he could not find one to his hands" (*EI*, 119). Dante had Mary and the angels, Wagner his Nordic mythology, and, we may add, Yeats his Irish legends. Blake, he grants, had the symbolic imagination, "vision," "a representation of what actually exists really and unchangeably," not allegory. Yeats knows that Blake believed in the actual presence of the beings he saw with his mind's eye and considers this now a limitation. In a famous phrase he called Blake "a too literal realist of imagination" (119), and he speaks of "errors in the handiwork" (128). The assumptions shift from the symbol as somehow existing in the Great Mind to be discovered by the poet to the idea of the imagination inventing the symbols in an act that must not be deliberate, intellectual, arbitrary.

Sometimes, however, Yeats has a humbler conception of the symbol: closer to evocation, suggestion, or simply a cluster of metaphors. It may have been influenced by Mallarmé's or Verlaine's emphasis on suggestion. Yeats quotes, or rather misquotes, Burns:

The white [*recte wan*] moon is setting behind the white wave.
    And Time is setting with me, O!

and calls these lines "perfectly symbolical." "Take from them the whiteness of the moon and the wave, whose relation to the setting of Time is
too subtle for the intellect, and you take from them their beauty. But
when all are together, moon and wave and whiteness and setting Time
and the last melancholy cry, they evoke an emotion which cannot be
evoked by any other arrangement of colours and sounds and forms."
Calling this metaphorical writing, Yeats argues, does not suffice: "metaphors are not profound enough to be moving" (*EI,* 155–56). What is
needed is an interaction between words, "doing its work by suggestion,
not by direct statement" (*E,* 255).

Thus three kinds of symbolism are distinguished: suggestion, arbitrary
willful construction, and the only genuine symbolism: the discovery or
revelation of a supernatural world. But fortunately for criticism, Yeats
was able, within this frame, to restate many critical issues, trying always
to reconcile opposites. Thus the Imagination overcomes the dichotomy
of the universal versus the particular. It "expands away from the egoistic
mood; we become vehicles for the universal thought and merge in the
universal mood" (*WWB,* 1:242–43). "Ibsen and Maeterlinck have created
a new form, for they get multitude from the Wild Duck in the attic, or
from the crown at the bottom of the fountain [*Pelléas et Mélisande*], vague
symbols that set the mind wandering from idea to idea, emotion to emotion" (*EI,* 216).

Similarly symbol bridges the contrast between the sensuous and the
spiritual. In one sense Yeats grants that "all art is sensuous" (*EI,* 293):
we "only believe in those thoughts which have been conceived not in the
brain but in the whole body" (235), and "art bids us touch and taste and
hear and see the world, and shrinks from what Blake calls mathematical
form, from every abstract thing" (292). Art, he argues, "is a child of
experience always, of knowledge never" (317). He "cannot believe in the
reality of imaginations that are not inset with the minute life of long
familiar things and symbols and places" (296), but, on the other hand,
the "imaginative writer identifies himself with the soul of the world, and
frees himself from all that is impermanent in that soul" (286); "the end
of art is the ecstasy awakened by the presence before an ever-changing
mind of what is permanent in the world" (287).

This double view, sensuous and spiritual, yields Yeats a criterion for
judgment: mere realistic art, Stendhal's "mirror dawdling down the
lane," the art of Ibsen's *Doll's House,* Shaw, and Zola are disparaged. The
merely sensuous art (or what he considered to be so) of Keats with

"thoughts disappearing into the image" (*V,* 134) is inferior, too. Art, he says in an image made well-known as the title of Meyer H. Abrams's book on romantic criticism, turns from the mirror to the lamp (*Oxford,* xxxiii), because art cannot be a passive reception of either external reality or the evidence of the senses.

Art is necessarily an expression of personality, but, in Yeats's thinking, it is also necessarily impersonal, using the mask, the anti-self of personality. Speaking of his early years in London (1887–91), Yeats says: "I was soon to write many poems where an always personal emotion was woven into a general pattern of myth and symbol" (*A,* 101–02). Yeats makes a distinction between personality and character. Character is idiosyncratic. It is "continuously present in comedy alone" (*EI,* 240), whereas "tragedy is passion alone, and rejecting character it gets form from motives, from the wandering of passion; while comedy is the clash of character" (*A,* 318). Yeats's great effort to revive poetic drama in Ireland, and later in particular his attempts to imitate the Noh plays of Japan, fit into this scheme: plot, fable, intrigue, naturalistic scenery and acting are disparaged. Tragedy is centered on the great moments of lyricism, of unmixed passion: "tragedy must always be a drowning and breaking of the dykes that separate man from man" (*EI,* 241, and *UP,* 2:381). Yeats antagonized many critics and readers by excluding all war poets (even the admired Wilfred Owen) from his edition of the *Oxford Anthology of Modern Verse* (1931) on the grounds that "passive suffering is not the theme for poetry" (*Oxford,* xxxiv–v).

Personality in tragedy thus means an overcoming of egotism and hence, for Yeats, a joy even in suffering. We know from "Lapis Lazuli" that "Hamlet and Lear are gay / Gaiety transfiguring all that dread." "Tragedy is a joy to the man who dies; in Greece the tragic chorus danced" (*Oxford,* xxiv–v). In several eloquent passages Yeats speaks of the tragic joy, sometimes with overtones of Nietzschean exultation. "The arts are all the bridal chambers of joy. No tragedy is legitimate unless it leads some great character to his final joy. Polonius may go out wretchedly, but I can hear the dance music in 'Absent thee from felicity awhile,' or in Hamlet's speech over the dead Ophelia, and what of Cleopatra's last farewells, Lear's rage under the lightning, Oedipus sinking down at the story's end into an earth 'riven' by Love" (*E,* 448–49). Yeats speaks similarly of other examples: "Timon of Athens contemplates his own end, and orders his tomb by the beached verge of the salt flood, and Cleopatra sets the asp to her bosom, and their words move us because their sorrow is not their own at tomb or asp, but for all men's fate. That shaping joy has kept the sorrow pure, as it had kept it were the emotion love or hate, for the nobleness of the arts is in the mingling of contraries, the extremity of sorrow, the extremity of joy, perfection of personality, the perfection of its surrender, overflowing turbulent energy, and marmorean stillness" (*EI*, 255). The mingling or clash of contraries sounds Coleridgean or Blakean as an aesthetic principle, but it is also Yeats's own defiance and hatred of death: "We love aloud and mock, in the terror or the sweetness of our exaltation, at death and oblivion" (322). Creation, art, fame, and after-fame are somehow guarantees of survival beyond Christian immortality or Indian metempsychosis: *Non omnis moriar,* asserted proud Horace long ago.

Yeats, one could argue, always has it both ways, or rather he embraces both extremes and finds them reconcilable or, at least, compatible: the particular and the general; the personal and the collective; the sensuous corporeal and the supernatural; tradition and the individual genius; the suggestive and the solidly, fixedly symbolic, "market car and sky." A genuine dialectic, Hegelian in descent, permeates his theory of art. He ultimately yearns, as many before and after him, the very different T. S. Eliot included, for the unity of being and projects it into history as a reality of the past forfeited by modern civilization.

Yeats, in agreement with the medievalism of Ruskin and Morris, sees the Middle Ages as the age when man was still whole. Dante is quoted for the term "Unity of Being," comparing beauty to a perfectly proportioned human body in the *Convito* (*A,* 128). "Europe shared one mind and heart, until both mind and heart began to break into fragments a little before Shakespeare's birth" (129). It is not clear why the middle of the sixteenth century is here singled out as the turning point. After reading Whitehead's *Science and the Modern World* (1926) Yeats accepted the view that "mind split itself into mind and space in the seventeenth century" (*E,* 434), that "Descartes, Locke and Newton took away the world and gave us excrement instead" (325), a violently phrased restatement of Blake's distaste for Locke and Newton. Sometimes Yeats pinpoints the onset of disintegration at a specific date, "that morning when Descartes discovered that he could think better in his bed than out of it" (*A,* 130), presumably November 10, 1619, at Neuburg on the Danube, when he had three consecutive dreams that convinced him of his mission. At times Yeats seems to be of two minds: "I detest the Renaissance," he says, "because it made the human mind inorganic; I adore the Renaissance because it clarified form and created freedom" (*On the Boiler,* 27, suppressed in *E*). At other times he sees the process sensibly as a gradual deterioration, as a process of the specialization of man. "The enemy of this unity was abstraction, meaning by abstraction not the distinction but the isolation of occupation, or class or faculty," a statement that sounds almost Marxist but would be comprehensible to Morris, who read Marx, while Yeats disparaged Marx as "Macaulay with his heels in the air" (*E*, 424). Yeats himself refers to Ruskin, who knew that "machinery had not separated from handicraft wholly for the world's good" and that "the distinction of the classes had become their isolation" (*A*, 130). Yeats then quotes his own "Second Coming":

> Things fall apart; the centre cannot hold;
> Mere anarchy is loosed upon the world.

This is put sometimes in terms of the decay of religion. "I would found literature on the three things which Kant thought we must postulate to make life livable—Freedom, God, Immortality. The fading of these three before 'Bacon, Newton, Locke' has made literature decadent. Because Freedom is gone we have Stendhal's 'mirror dawdling down a lane'; because God has gone we can no longer write those tragedies which have always seemed to me alone legitimate—those that are a joy to the man who dies" (*E*, 332–33). The insistence on freedom implies a rejection of determinism, the mirroring of reality; the insistence on a belief in God condemns the same realism, the "accidental" meaning presumably the view that denies any plan in the universe, while the insistence on a belief in immortality justifies "tragic joy." Still, it requires here a Christian belief in a redemption or some judgment in afterlife rather than Nietzsche's tragic joy, which is a defiance of God. Yeats's belief in immortality affected his view of Valéry's *Cimetière marin*; he tells us that Valéry "just when I am deeply moved chills me." "In a passage of great eloquence he rejoices that human life must pass. I was about to put his poem among my sacred books, but I cannot now, for I do not believe him" (*V*, 219).

This rather simple scheme of the decay of poetry, a version of the "dissociation of sensibility," was greatly modified and elaborated in *A Vision*, particularly in the section "Dove or Swan" in a scheme with "historical cones," but little of these speculations, often illustrated with examples from art history, drawn from wide reading in Henry Adams, Flinders Petrie, Joseph Strzygowski, and later from Arnold Toynbee and Oswald Spengler, concerns literature. The scattered references merely confirm that Yeats thought that "the materialistic movement at the end of the seventeenth century, all that comes out of Bacon perhaps" (*V*, 296), is the beginning of a "breaking of the soul and the world in fragments." "The art discovered by Dante of marshalling into a vast antithetical structure antithetical material became through Milton Latinised and artificial." Eighteenth-century literature is seen as oscillating between the sentimental and the logical—"the poetry of Pope and Gray, the philosophy of Johnson and of Rousseau," with Johnson oddly considered logical. The modern novel with its "happy ending, the admired hero, the preoccupation with desirable things" has the undisguisedly antithetical disappear. One need not know anything about the gyres, tinctures, cycles, and the like to see the points of these remarks, nor is it necessary to grapple with the phases of the moon to appreciate the comments on writers and poets put into the different phases, often in the oddest combinations. It is hard to see how Calvin and George Herbert can belong to the same phase (172) or what Spinoza and Savonarola (125) or Rembrandt and Synge (163) could have in common. But Yeats can characterize Walt Whitman as "making catalogues of all that moved him" (114) or John Keats by his "exaggerated sensuousness, with little sexual passion, and intellectual curiosity at its weakest" (134). As a serious typology of psychological attributes the scheme has hardly anything to offer in its idiosyncratic combinations and identifications: for literary criticism nothing can be gained except some insight into Yeats's taste. This judgment cannot affect the interest of *A Vision* for the interpretation of Yeats's later poetry or any study of the workings of his mind.

Applied to poetics, the decay of the old world picture in Goethe, Wordsworth, and Browning is cited as proof that "poetry gave up the right to consider all things in the world as a dictionary of types and symbols and began to call itself a critic of life and an interpreter of all things as they are" (*EI*, 192). Yeats had read the following in an admired essay by Arthur Hallam: "Those different powers of poetic disposition, the energies of Sensitive, of Reflective, of Passionate Emotion, which in former times were intermingled, and derived from mutual support an extensive empire over the feelings of men, were now restrained within separate spheres of agency. The whole system no longer worked harmoniously, and by intrinsic harmony acquired external freedom: but there arose a violent and unusual action in the several component functions, each for itself, all striving to reproduce the regular power which the whole had once enjoyed."[1] Obviously the idea of the fragmentation of the human mind and the need for its reconstitution had become a commonplace.

Yeats does not see this process as either uniform or irreversible. "Imagination," he reasserts, "whether in literature, painting or sculpture, sank after the death of Shakespeare; supreme intensity had passed to another faculty," to the "harsh, almost unintelligible language" of philosophy, to the movement "from Spinoza to Hegel," "the greatest of all works of intellect" (*EI*, 396), "intellect" here having in Yeats's mind a meaning of ratiocination opposed to art. Yeats singled out Berkeley as the restorer of the world destroyed by Descartes, Locke, and Newton. "Berkeley has brought back to us the world that only exists because it shines and sounds" (*E*, 325). Berkeley is dear to Yeats as the reviver of European spirituality but also as an Irishman. Yeats, who earlier had detested the eighteenth century, came to appreciate and admire Georgian Ireland, especially Swift, whose *saeva indignatio* appealed to the "rage" of the old man, and Edmund Burke for the "restoration of European order" (337).

Among poets Blake and Shelley remained with him in spite of some criticism. Wordsworth is considered representative of the "soul's deepening solitude" that has "reduced mankind, when seen objectively, to a few slight figures outlined for a moment amid mountain and lake" (*V*, 134). He is "so often flat and heavy, partly because his moral sense being a discipline he had not created, a mere obedience, has no theatrical element" (*Mythologies*, 334). On the Continent there remains Balzac, "the only modern mind which has made a synthesis comparable to that of Dante" (*E*, 269). Yeats admired mainly *Louis Lambert* and *Seraphita*, the two books which have the most Swedenborgianism in them. But Yeats sees that *Louis Lambert* is "more or less materialistic" (*EI*, 438) and deplores that Balzac did not know either Berkeleian idealism or "our modern psychological research" (439, 441), referring to occultism. Putting an imaginary speech into Balzac's mouth, Yeats has him say: "My *Comédie humaine* will cure the world of all Utopias" (468). Balzac saved him from "Jacobin and Jacobite" (447), meaning apparently from both social radicalism and romantic conservatism. Yeats says in 1934 that he belongs "to a generation that returns to Balzac alone." He had read Tolstoy, Dostoevsky, and Flaubert twenty years earlier but had never opened them again (445).

One could collect Yeats's opinions on many nineteenth- and twentieth-century writers which often do not seem to keep the idea of decay in mind. Thus he thought that "England has had more good poets from 1900 to the present day than during any period of the same length since the early seventeenth century" (*Oxford*, xvi). But even the *Oxford Book of English Verse*, which in its selections shows an often idiosyncratic preference for friends, implies a definite standard of taste. Yeats obviously disliked the new 1930s group, also for political reasons: Auden, Spender, and Day Lewis. Joyce, Pound, and Eliot seem to him new naturalists who "leave man helpless before the contents of his own mind. One thinks of Joyce's *Anna Livia Plurabelle*, Pound's *Cantos*, works of an heroic sincerity, the man, his active faculties in suspense, one finger beating time to a bell sounding and echoing in the depths of his own mind" (*EI*, 405). Eliot's art "seems gray, cold, dry" (*Oxford*, xxi). "The worst language is Eliot's in all his early poems—a level flatness of rhythm" (*L*, 846). Yeats's opinion of Pound summarizes a long, ambiguous relationship. Yeats in earlier years had consulted Pound and taken his criticism and concrete suggestions meekly. Pound had been his secretary in the winter of 1914–15. They met many times over the years. Pound made him acquainted with the Noh plays of Japan. But Yeats's opinion of Pound's poetry remained remarkably stable: in 1913 he wrote that "Pound's own work is very uncertain, often very bad though very interesting sometimes. He spoils himself by too many experiments,"[2] and later in the *Oxford* anthology he comments that *The Cantos* have "more style than form," but that the style "is constantly interrupted, broken, twisted into nothing but its direct opposite, nervous obsession, nightmare, stammering confusion"; Pound is a "brilliant improvisator" (*Oxford*, xxv, xxvi). Yeats preferred Bridges, T. Sturge Moore, W. J. Turner, and Lady Wellesley. He is harshest toward his own "tragic generation," Dowson, Lionel Johnson, John Davidson, and two Irish compatriots most famous in their time. Shaw, though "a formidable man with an athletic wit," is in the enemy camp of abstraction, logical straightness. "Presently," Yeats tells us, "I had a nightmare that I was haunted by a sewing machine, that clicked and shone, but the incredible thing was that the machine smiled, smiled perpetually" (*A*, 188), or, with a different image: "He is quite content to exchange Narcissus and his Pool for the signal box at a railway junction, where foods and travellers pass perpetually upon their logical glittering road" (195). Yeats considered Wilde a mere wit. He was "essentially a man of action, that is he was a writer by perversity and accident" (189). He finds in Wilde "something pretty, feminine and insincere" and "much of that is violent, arbitrary and insolent" (*V*, 150), though before he had granted that Wilde "understood his weakness, true personality was impossible, for that is born in solitude" (*A*, 195). Wilde's poetry with its Victorian faults could not impress Yeats, but he came to except the *Ballad of Reading Gaol* as "a great, or almost great poem" (*Oxford*, vi, vii).

All these opinions—and examples could be multiplied from the correspondence in particular—show a developed taste anchored in a concept of poetry which has ancient roots and which bore fruit in the practice of a poet deeply involved with the Irish national revival and still in contact and affinity with a universal movement. I realize that in expounding it I have made it more rational, sensible, and coherent than when we study the individual essays with their divagations into the occult or into merely fanciful analogizing. Thus in the central essay on "The

Symbolism of Poetry," fine and subtle as it is, we are suddenly informed that Yeats once told a "seeress to ask one of the gods who, as she believed, were standing about her in their symbolic bodies, what would come of a charming but seeming trivial labour of a friend, and the form answering, 'the devastation of peoples and the overwhelming of cities' " (*EI*, 158). The story supposedly confirms the long-range effects of poetry, but nothing can persuade one that the predicted effect has or could come about. The whole argument (if it is one) collapses. Good arguments can be made against Auden's disparate view that poetry and the arts have made no difference to man's history, but Yeats's assertion that the world has changed "because of something that a boy piped in Thessaly" (158) remains an unsustained claim. Yeats's own impressive role as prophet, sage, philosopher, and statesman aborted in practice. Still, there is no point in complaining about Yeats's symbolism as Ezra Pound does:

> And Uncle William dawdling around Notre Dame
> In search of whatever
> > > paused to admire the symbol
> with Notre Dame standing inside it.
> > > > > > > > (*Cantos,* 1954 ed., 563)

Without the symbolism and the fantastic concept of the course of history there could be no poetry of Yeats. To speculate what poetry Yeats might have written without his beliefs seems the vainest of enterprises. What remains are the poems, or a few of them, and a defense of a symbolist view of poetry which he drew from old sources but supported by the impact of the contemporary symbolist movement in France.

ARTHUR SYMONS (1865–1945)

The main propagandist of the French symbolists in England was Arthur Symons, whose book on *The Symbolist Movement in Literature* (1900) was dedicated to Yeats. It served as a source of information and stimulus also to T. S. Eliot, as "an introduction to wholly new feelings, as a revelation" (*Sacred Wood* [1920], 4). In 1930 Eliot said, "I myself owe Mr. Symons a great debt: but for having read his book, I should not, in the year 1908, have heard of Laforgue or Rimbaud; I should probably not have begun to read Verlaine; and but for reading Verlaine, I should not have heard of Corbière. So the Symons book is one of those which have affected the course of my life" (*Criterion* 9 [1930]: 357). But the book should not be rated high as literary criticism. The introduction starts with Carlyle's view, claiming that "under one disguise or another [symbolism] can be seen in every great imaginative writer," but then saying that the symbolism of our day has "become conscious of itself." Contradictorily Symons claims that Nerval was at its origins though unconscious of it. He is finally content with calling symbolism a return to "the one pathway leading through beautiful things to the eternal beauty" (*SM*, 4). Symbolism is a "revolt against exteriority, against rhetoric, against a materialistic tradition"; it is an "endeavor to disengage the ultimate essence, the soul, of whatever exists." It is "a kind of religion." The essays themselves are elementary accounts, often biographical, with quotations of poems in French, of Nerval, Villiers de l'Isle-Adam, Rimbaud, Verlaine, Laforgue, Mallarmé (there two poems and a piece of prose appear in translation), and Maeterlinck. In the 1908 reissue Symons added a piece on the later Huysmans and in a revised edition of 1919 he added a few thin pages on Baudelaire, the most glaring omission from the original volume, with essays on Balzac, Mérimée, Gautier, Flaubert, the Goncourts, Léon Cladel, and Zola, who could not even pretend to be symbolists. Among the original essays the one on Verlaine is the most sympathetic: the one on Rimbaud is all secondhand biography plus a description of *Les Voyelles*; the one on Mallarmé gives some account of the Tuesday evenings at Mallarmé's flat and explains his view of language accurately: "Thus an artificiality, even, in the use of words, that seeming artificiality which comes from using words as if they had never been used before, that chimerical search after the virginity of language, is but the paradoxical outward sign of an extreme discontent with even the best of their service" (70–71). The short piece on Laforgue seems most successful in characterizing the poet: his self-pity, his laughter, his manner of not "distinguish[ing] between irony and pity" (60), but often, even in the good essay on Verlaine, Symons indulges in mere marginal fancies. Describing Verlaine's search for the right word he can say: "Verlaine knows that words are suspicious, not without their malice, and that they resist mere force with the impalpable resistance of fire or water. They are to be caught only with guile or with trust. Verlaine has both, and words become Ariel to him. They bring him not only that submission of the slave which they bring to others, but all the soul, and in a happy bondage" (48). This was then considered "creative criticism" but seems only an evasion of the job of criticism, which Symons declares impossible immediately afterwards: "It is not without reasons that we cannot analyze a perfect poem" (48). Symons has few critical tools: he has wide reading, some information, and sensibility. At his best, he can characterize by metaphor and even judge an author in relation to others.

He had come a long way to write *The Symbolist Movement*. He had edited Shakespeare, written an article on Mistral, and published a sober *Intro-*

duction to the Study of Browning (1886), which was praised by Walter Pater
in a review. In 1889 the young poet had been to Paris with Havelock
Ellis, written an article on Villiers de l'Isle-Adam, highly admiring the
Contes cruels, for Oscar Wilde's magazine, *Woman's World,* and made himself, after two more visits to Paris, a champion of K-J. Huysmans and of
Verlaine. The articles on Verlaine and his verse translations established
also personal contacts with the poet, who was then down-and-out, and
excited a desire to help him. Through Symons's efforts Verlaine could
lecture in London and Oxford and carry a substantial fee back to Paris.
In 1893 Symons wrote an article on the "Decadent Movement in Literature" in which symbolism and impressionism are considered alternative
labels. Symons then preferred decadence and defended it against the
usual accusations by arguing that decadence did not mean moral turpi-
tude or decay but "an intense self-consciousness," "an over-subtilizing
refinement upon refinement" (*Dramatis Personae,* 97). In the article on
Verlaine in 1891 Symons had referred to the "brainsick little school of
Symbolistes," and in the decadence article he speaks of Mallarmé's "jargon"
as "a massacre" (ibid., 109). It took time and the influence of his friend
from the Rhymers' Club, Yeats, to convert him to symbolism. Yeats, in
his turn, learned something about the French poets from Symons (see
his *Autobiography,* cited above, 213–14), and when in Paris in 1894 he saw
Axël in Symons's company and met Verlaine and Mallarmé. But Yeats
knew little French and needed no conversion to symbolism. Symons
needed it, but it was, after all, only halfhearted. One cannot doubt his
enthusiasm for the French poets but, as he himself says in the dedication
to Yeats, his turn toward mysticism "will probably be a surprise to many.
It will be no surprise to you, for you have seen me gradually finding my
way, uncertainly but inevitably, in that direction which has always been
to you your natural direction" (*SM,* xx). But Symons surely did not go
all the way, which may prove his good sense and his firm ties with his
original masters: Swinburne, Pater, and also W. E. Henley, whom he
celebrated rather oddly as the first pioneer of "Modernity in Verse" (*Studies in Two Literatures,* in *Collected Works,* 8:44f.).

The Symbolist Movement in Literature is the only book of Symons that is
still remembered. Some injustice is done here, for he has written prolif-
ically on almost every figure in English and French literature of the
nineteenth and early twentieth centuries, often within the limits of his
resources perceptively and critically. The essay on Donne (1899), for
instance, formulates well the quality of his passion. "It is a rapture in
which the mind is supreme, a reasonable rapture, and yet carried to a
pitch of actual violence" (*Figures of Several Centuries,* 97). George Mere-

dith is sharply characterized as a poet and the appreciation of Coventry Patmore's *To the Unknown Eros* is unusual if we contrast it with the critical attitude toward Francis Thompson. His work is "a splendour of rags and patches, a very masque of anarchy" (*Studies in Two Literatures*, 79), a feast of Trimalchio, "the heaped profusion, the vaunting prodigality, which brings a surfeit; and, unlike Trimalchio, it could not be said of him *Omnia domi nascuntur*" (ibid., 82). But there is a book which seems to me undeservedly neglected: *The Romantic Movement in English Poetry* (1909). It has, one should admit, an unfortunate scheme. Only writers who were born in the eighteenth century and died in the nineteenth century are included, and the essays on them are arranged in chronological order of birth, mingling brief, often witty sketches of a paragraph or two, treating poets from John Home (1722–1808) to Thomas Hood (1799–1845), with substantial essays on Blake, Wordsworth, Coleridge, Landor, Byron, Shelley, and Keats. The introduction fumbles with the question of the nature of poetry, the nature of romanticism, concluding that "poetry was realised as a personal confession, or as an evocation, or as 'an instant made eternity,' " which does not quite jibe with the view that "it was realised that the end of poetry was to be poetry" (*RM*, 20). But this insistence on poetry for poetry's sake allows Symons to ignore background, sources, historical development (he rejects Courthope and Brunetière expressly [10]), and to uphold a standard of the poetic moment, of magic, of intensity. It gives him the criterion to condemn the whole eighteenth century as an interruption of the great imaginative tradition of English poetry and to come down hard on Scott, Southey, and everyone else whom he considers writing versified rhetoric, didacticism, storytelling, or displaying mere descriptiveness or satirical cleverness. Still, Symons treats with great sympathy both John Clare (his discovery), and George Crabbe, though he complains, "How strange a delusion, that truth, without beauty, can have any place in art" (60).

The essays on the main poets abound in striking formulations which might be unjust or partial but often hit the mark. Blake, on whom Symons wrote a surprisingly sober expository book (1907) which makes him rather a Nietzschean than a mystic, is characterized as writing "a poetry of the mind, abstract in substance." "There are no men and women in the world of Blake's poetry, only primal instincts and energies of the imagination" (*RM*, 42). Wordsworth is seen as divided between his two voices, either prophesying in divine language or babbling like a village idiot (80). He is criticized for his inability to distinguish between "whim and intuition" (78). Coleridge's poetry is seen as culminating in *Kubla Khan*, which seems to Symons a poem like Mallarmé's in its "technique of dream" (140). Symons then attempts psychological portraiture, speaking of Coleridge's "passionless sensibility," "the dribbling overflow of choked-up feeling, a sort of moral leakage" (124), reflecting adversely on his "rhetoric of humility" (125) while praising the literary criticism to the sky. The essay on Byron is, considering Symons's professed standard of "magic," surprisingly favorable in its stress on Byron's sincerity, his raw and naked humanity, though Symons complains of "lack of atmosphere" and "lack of 'interior vision' " (248). Shelley is exalted as a lyrical poet. His message is slighted. He "teaches us nothing, leads us nowhere, but cries and flies around us like a sea-bird" (281), and Keats is depicted as a "natural animal to whom the sense of sin has never whispered itself" (304). He appears to Symons as a "forerunner of art for art's sake" (306). He lacks intellectual structure, is not troubled about his soul or the meaning of the universe (303, 311). Meditation brings him no inner vision (313). Symons makes much of his impersonality, passivity, and objectivity. "You have to get at Shelley's or Wordsworth's point of view; but Keats has only the point of view of sunlight" (314). This often sounds like the accepted interpretation before the modern revaluation: before Middleton Murry's *Keats* describing the struggle of his soul or Shelley being coopted by the socialists, not to speak of Foster Damon's or Northrop Frye's unriddling of Blake's Prophetic Books or the new feeling for Wordsworth's apocalyptic vision expounded by Geoffrey Hartman. But at the time of Symons there was merit in this summary. One could even say that the book is the last prominent display of metaphorical criticism dominated by a concept of poetry as the intense moment. Criticism by metaphor has a long tradition in England since Hazlitt and Lamb. It has a genuine function as long as the method achieves its aim of characterizing and evaluating. In Symons it does so most of the time, but sometimes it gets out of hand. Thus speaking of Landor's poetry he says that "a perfume clings about it, as if it had been stored for centuries in cedar chests and among spices." He then quotes

We are what suns and winds and waters make us

and tells us: "I have read the 'Hellenics' lying by the seashore, on warm, quiet days when I heard nothing but the monotonous repetition of the sea at my feet, and they have not seemed out of key" (179). On the very next page we are told that the *Hellenics* "are all in low relief; you can touch their surface, but not walk around them. . . . They resemble the work of Flaxman rather than the work of Greek sculpture," and so on. Soberly analyzed, Symons has told us that Landor's poetry draws on a long tradition, that the verse of the *Hellenics* is monotonous and that they have something of the rigidity, flatness, and lack of color characteristic of Flaxman. But Symons cannot say it straight out and has to spin his precious little fancies and display his fine writing.

T. S. Eliot in singling out Symons as the impressionistic critic whose charming verse "overflowed into his critical prose" fastened on a late, bad book, *Studies in Elizabethan Drama* (1919) (*Sacred Wood* [1920], 3). Eliot's trouncing of Symons's translation of Baudelaire ("Baudelaire in Our Time" in *For Lancelot Andrewes* [1928], 86–99) helped to consign him to oblivion. But both the *Studies in Elizabethan Drama* and the Baudelaire translations are works written after he had partially recovered from a mental breakdown in 1908. All his later work is not only scrappy and often incoherent but marred by obsessions which must be called pathological. Thus Baudelaire is described in crudely Satanic terms and even Conrad is seen "like a spider throwing out tentacles into the darkness. . . . At the center of his web sits an elemental sarcasm, discussing human affairs with a calm and cynical ferocity. . . . Behind that sarcasm crouches some ghastly influence, some powerful devil, invisible, poisonous, irresistible, spawning evil for his delight" (*Dramatis Personae*, 1–2). No wonder that mild Conrad protested: "I did not know that I had a 'heart of darkness' and an 'unlawful soul.' . . . I did not know that I delighted in cruelty and that shedding of blood was my obsession" (letter of August 1908, quoted in Lhombreaud, *Arthur Symons*, 232), but he forgave him and became his friend and neighbor in rural Kent, where Symons died in 1945, at the age of eighty, having long outlived his fame.

GEORGE MOORE (1852–1933)

Interest in the French symbolists was shown before Symons in the early writings of George Moore. Moore had gone to Paris from Ireland in 1873, and he lived there till 1880, at first attempting to become a painter and later joining in the swim of the French literary life, of which he gave a brash and enthusiastic account in *Confessions of a Young Man* (1888). There and in articles collected as *Impressions and Opinions* (1891) Moore gave sketchy and often poorly informed accounts of the new French poets. Moore was the first, in English, to tell the legend of Rimbaud's life and to describe Laforgue, "this Watteau of the *café-concert*."[1] He dismissed Mallarmé's poetry as "aberrations of a refined mind" though he admired the man. Gautier and Verlaine were his favorite French poets. He echoed the current distaste for Hugo and his treatment of God: "arm in arm he romps Him round the universe." The contrast between Verlaine's spiritual and musical poetry and his life appealed to Moore, for he had seen Verlaine in the squalor of his last days (*CYM.*, 340, 350; *Letters from George Moore to Edouard Dujardin* [1929]; "A Great Poet" in *IO*, 85–94). He had become a friend and correspondent of Edouard Dujardin and displayed some sympathy for symbolist theories though his early novels are rather naturalistic and even Zolaesque in theme and technique.

Moore returned to his native Ireland in 1901 and took part in the establishment of an Irish drama; but he was a late recruit to the cause of the Irish literary Renaissance and was never completely converted. He felt rather like Joyce that "an Irishman must fly from Ireland if he would be himself" (*Hail and Farewell*, Carra ed., 1:viii). The Irish episode was a failure: Moore quarreled with Yeats about a dramatic collaboration. His bragging, maliciously satirical, and even abusive account of his years in Ireland in *Hail and Farewell* (5 vols., 1911–14) confirms this view.

Only in Moore's later writings can one find anything that can be called criticism. *An Anthology of Pure Poetry* (1924) has a definite theory behind it which is expounded in the preface and in a dialogue of the *Conversations in Ebury Street* (1924). Pure poetry is poetry free from thought, ideas, morality, propaganda: it is free from personal emotion, a poetry of things and not of feelings. "The poet creates outside of his own personality." Moore complains that modern art "lacks innocency of vision." He admires Gautier's "La Tulipe" because it is not "blighted with the subjective taint" which he finds even in Keats's "Ode to Autumn" (*CES*, 223, 230; *APP*, 20; Moore, carelessly, speaks of Keats's "Sonnet to Autumn"!). Shakespeare's songs, some Elizabethan lyrics by Campion, Ben Jonson, Herrick, and others, a good deal of early Blake, "Kubla Khan," a few of Shelley's poems such as the "Hymn to Pan" and "The Cloud," Tennyson's "Mariana" and "The Lady of Shalott," much of Poe, and several pieces by Morris live up to this ideal and are included in the anthology. But nothing of Wordsworth except "The Green Linnet" qualifies. As to the sonnet on Westminster Bridge, Moore could not escape the "suspicion that it was not the beautiful image of a city overhanging a river at dawn that detained the poet, but the hope that he might once more discern a soul in nature." The poem "comes under the heading of proselytism in poetry" (*APP*, 30–31, 19–20). Moore's argument and the central criterion make sense, and his concept of "pure" poetry seems as good as that of Abbé Bremond, who identified it with prayer; or Valéry's austere intellectual ideal. But Moore could hardly have understood Marvell's "Nymph Complaining for the Death of Her Faun" when he included it in his collection. Moore wants not descriptions but images, pictorial clarity, the visual world he was seeking as a novelist and critic of novels.

In his early years Moore was deeply impressed by Zola. His first novel, *A Modern Lover* (1883), is a clumsy imitation of the master.[2] But Moore was soon aware of the limits of Zola and his methods (see "My Impressions of Zola," *IO*, 66–84, and *CYM*, 364, 380). He preferred the imaginative realism of Balzac and Turgenev. Moore finds "more wisdom and more divine imagination in Balzac than in any other writer" including Shakespeare and sees well Balzac's historical preoccupation, "his power of contrasting and opposing his own time with its immediate past."[3] Turgenev attracted him even more immediately, though Moore admitted the difference between "the fire and explosion of Balzac" and a "thinness, an irritating reserve" in Turgenev. Moore highly admired the short stories for "their abruptness and freedom of psychology" and tried to imitate them in his Irish stories, *The Untilled Field* (1903). He drew a facile contrast between the Western analytical novel and the Eastern straightforward tale, of which Turgenev seems to him representative. Moore knows of Turgenev's method of drawing on his experience and real-life models and remarks perceptively that Turgenev does not always understand his models: Bazarov remained opaque to his own author, and that is why Moore preferred *Virgin Soil* to *Fathers and Sons* (*IO*, 47, 60, 63–64, 58).

These early tastes in novelists are elaborated in the later books, *Avowals* and *Conversations in Ebury Street*. Moore had freed himself from the affectations of the nineties and recognized that *Impressions and Opinions* was a book of "odds and oddness," lacking in any unity of subject and language (*CES*, 36, 95). But in the new books, with their loose form of invented conversations, Moore began to indulge in worse vices than mere oddness. He displays violent prejudices, engages in elaborate games of pretending or parading ignorance, makes wholesale dismissals of almost the entire work of rival novelists, and unabashedly contradicts himself or changes his mind within a few pages. One can catch him in preposterous jugglings of opinions. Thus in the essay on Turgenev in the *Fortnightly Review* (n.s. 48 [1888]: 239) he said, "Tolstoy [*sic*] I have not read but he is only Gaboriau [an early crime novelist] with psychological sauce and that of an inferior kind," reproducing a witticism about Dostoevsky reported by Téodor de Wyzewa as Zola's (in *Revue indépendante*, January 1887). In 1894, however, Moore wrote an appreciative introduction to a translation of Dostoevsky's *Poor People* with a frontispiece by Aubrey Beardsley. There he confesses to having once written of *Crime and Punishment* that it was "Gaboriau with psychological sauce" and apologizes. "The desire to be witty led men into phrases which they afterwards" regretted. Still, the saying does not seem to him "wholly unwarranted."

Poor People is praised, but it cannot be as perfect as Turgenev because Turgenev is "the greatest artist since antiquity" (preface). Turgenev's and Balzac's competitors are systematically downgraded. *Madame Bovary*, we are told, is not as well written as *Eugénie Grandet*. Moore would like to expose "the stiff, paralyzed narrative, the short sentences trussed like a fowl, with the inevitable adjective in the middle of every one." He cannot understand the "strange belief in the inevitable word." But still Flaubert is better than Zola, Daudet, and the Goncourts (*A*, 235–37). Moore also disliked Tolstoy for his "ugly temperament," like "a wild beast, straining at the bars, trying to escape his animality." He is repelled by Tolstoy's "sizzling white light, crude and disagreeable" (*A*, 144, 132; *ES*, 13).

The comments on the English novel also tend to exaggerated violence of expression and easy dismissals. Since *Tom Jones* is an "entirely empty book without sensibility of any kind, mental or physical," it is not surprising that Moore rather admires Sterne. "*The Sentimental Journey* recalls antiquity perhaps more than any other book of the modern world," something like *Daphnis and Chloe* (*A*, 18, 21–23). He unfairly judges Scott by an inept page from *Waverley* that seems to him to come from a servant girl's magazine (33). The rejection of the "vile English tradition that humour is a literate quality" allows him to admit Dickens's natural spontaneous talent but to deplore its waste (79–81). It seems ungracious to speak of Thackeray's "meagre, sandy mind" (83) and in a deliberately frivolous exchange with John Freeman to make fun of George Eliot, though Moore admits *The Mill on the Floss* is "a well-modulated narrative." "George Eliot constructed well and solidly; her prose is rich and well balanced. But these qualities were not enough to save her from the whirling, bubbling flood of Time; her books have gone down like the mill," a judgment that must have been true in the twenties but has been belied by her revival, while Moore's own fiction does seem to have gone down like the mill (*CES*, 97–101).

Sometimes, however, Moore combines satirical analysis and harsh probing with a standard of probability, coherent and good writing, and manages to persuade or at least amuse the reader by apt quotation and skillful, tendentious retelling. Moore cannot miss in ridiculing *Jane Eyre* (*A*, 68ff.) and is brilliantly funny at the expense of Hardy and his "ill-constructed melodrama, feebly written in bad grammar." He retells a preposterous story from *A Group of Noble Dames* with devastating effect (*CES*, 135, 122f.). Moore also persecuted Henry James with his mordant wit. Though he admired him as "an extraordinarily able critic" he deplored his "lack of human instinct." "He mistook trivial comments about men and women for psychology." He is lost in trifles, in "weighing whether a woman should accept a cup of tea or reject it," in wandering through "a desert of qualifying clauses," in "bringing out a pack of fox hounds to hunt a rat." The kiss in *Portrait of a Lady* is "one of the worst in literature, proclaiming the fact that Henry James knows very little about kissing, and that it does not interest him" (*A*, 186–87). Still, Moore is not merely ungenerous to his rivals or insensitive to what smacks of romanticism. He praises Hawthorne and *The House of Seven Gables* fervently (95ff.). He preserved some of his early enthusiasms even when they did not agree with his novelistic aim: the admiration for Pater, "a greater writer than Flaubert," who "raised the English language from the dead," and for Landor, whom he places above Shakespeare, remains untarnished (198, 180; *CES*, 96). *Imaginary Conversations* are the model for the dialogues in *Avowals* and *Conversations in Ebury Street*, in which Edmund Gosse, Walter De La Mare, John Freeman, and others take a rather passive part. Moore's late books are much lighter, more volatile, far less studied than Landor's dialogues. There is a gulf between the imperious, doctrinaire Landor and the puckish Moore, who trusts only his sensibility, a "sense judgment" which he compares to the "caprices of the flesh" and "sexual affinities." Shortly after Anatole France had formulated the impressionists' creed, Moore was saying that criticism was "the story of the critic's soul" (*CYM*, 367–68; *IO*, 43, in article on Balzac [1889]; the preface to *La Vie littéraire* dates from 1888).

2 : *ACADEMIC CRITICS*

IN THE EARLY TWENTIETH CENTURY criticism found a home in the universities. Critics were professors, or rather professors became critics, and criticism became a subject of instruction. Whether this development has been good for the cause of criticism in abstracto is debatable, but in both Great Britain and the United States many critics *have* become "academic" and strongly feel that they are different from journalists. The man of letters who combined scholarship and journalism has almost disappeared. Middleton Murry and Edmund Wilson are exceptions which prove the rule.

The incorporation of criticism into the universities was a very slow process. One could argue that Hugh Blair, who in 1762 became the first professor of Rhetoric and Belles Lettres in the University of Edinburgh, was a critic, and that Thomas Warton, the author of the first *History of English Poetry* (1774–81), a Fellow of Trinity College, Oxford, was something of a critic. But none of the important critics of the early nineteenth century taught in the university: neither Coleridge nor Hazlitt, nor Macaulay, nor Carlyle, nor De Quincey, nor even the learned historian of European literature, Henry Hallam, a barrister. The situation changed slowly in the second half of the century. Matthew Arnold was elected Professor of Poetry at Oxford in 1857. He was the first to lecture in English in that venerable chair founded in 1704. Arnold served for ten years, giving a few lectures each year. Still, two books, *On Translating Homer* (1861) and *On the Study of Celtic Literature* (1867), grew out of his lectures, though Arnold's main literary criticism was written for magazines. Swinburne, John Addington Symonds, Walter Bagehot, and Leslie Stephen (who early had resigned academic ambitions) were not connected with a university. Only Walter Pater was a Fellow of Brasenose College, Oxford, a shy, retiring man whose impact came not from his teaching but from the spread of his writings.

The teaching of English literature became widespread in the nineteenth century but was not, of course, necessarily conducive to the cause of criticism. University College, London, had its Professor of English Language and Literature from 1828 on, but the Rev. Thomas Dale was rather a moralizing lay preacher. Henry Morley (1822–94), who taught at the same institution from 1865 to 1885, was a popular biographer who conceived of literature as "an embodiment of the religious life of England," as a collection of uplifting passages. Technical literary study was carried on outside the university. F. J. Furnivall (1825–1910), secretary of the Philological Society, founded the New Shakspere Society, the Early English Text Society, and many other such enterprises. Factual scholars began to come into the universities. A. W. Ward (1837–1924) began teaching at Manchester in 1866, and David Masson (1822–1907), the author of a monumental *Life of Milton,* held for thirty years (1865–95) the chair first occupied by Blair. Thus the teaching of English literature either meant antiquarian factual literary history (Ward propounded what he called *Realpolitik* and wrote a purely external *History of Dramatic Literature*) or was an unsystematic, often preachy or gushy commentary on men and books. The turning point was the appointment of George Saintsbury in 1895 to the Professorship of Rhetoric and Belles Lettres at Edinburgh. A strong defender of criticism, an outspoken critic, and later the first historian of criticism, he found a sounding board in the Academy. More modestly Edward Dowden (1842–1913) at Trinity College, Dublin, had developed critical interests even beyond his widely known book on *Shakspere* (1875); A. C. Bradley started in 1882 as Professor of Modern Literature and History at University College, Liverpool, and W. P. Ker, who in 1889 succeeded Morley at University College, London, was more than a learned medievalist.

Oxford and Cambridge held out longest. At Oxford a School of English was established in 1894 which required a "critical" paper for the final examination. But when the Merton Professorship of English Language and Literature was established in 1885, A. S. Napier, a philologist with no literary interests, was appointed, though Saintsbury, Bradley, Dowden, and J. Churton Collins had applied for it. Collins (1848–1908), who had done some editing of Cyril Tourneur, Lord Herbert of Cherbury, and Milton, did not take the rejection lying down and waged a relentless campaign for the teaching of English literature divorced from what he considered its shameful subservience to philology. He argued for a study of English literature in close relation to its background in the ancients, calling for the observance of standards of accuracy which he applied with some harshness in often captious reviews of Gosse, Saintsbury, and other luminaries of the time (see *Ephemera Critica,* 1901). Though his direct effect was only minimal (because he violated the accepted code of polite manners) he correctly recognized the enemies of the teaching of English literature. There were the upholders of a purely classical education who, not without reason, feared for the life of their subject and suspected the study of modern literature of dilettantism ("chatter about Shelley"), and there were the students of Germanic philology, interested only in Anglo-Saxon and the history of linguistic change. Thus the hope for English studies was in the imitation of the methods and standards of classical philology. Textual criticism, editing, commentary, antiquarian research in the Public Record Office were to establish English as a discipline of learning. An enormous activity of this kind has proliferated since then inside and outside the universities. It has, in spite of much pedantry, great achievements to its credit. Its history is outside the purview of this book.

WALTER RALEIGH (1861–1922) AND
ARTHUR QUILLER-COUCH (1863–1944)

English studies might have developed peacefully along these lines of antiquarianism, but surprisingly the Merton Professorship was divided in 1904 between English Language and English Literature, and Walter Raleigh was asked to fill the new post. When the newly established King Edward VII Professorship of English Literature in the University of Cambridge became vacant by the early death of its first holder, A. W. Verrall (1851–1912), a classical scholar who lectured on Dryden, Sir Arthur Quiller-Couch, a successful novelist known for his zeal in the cause of the Liberal party, was brought in from Cornwall. Both men, though very different in temper and outlook, shared a condescending attitude toward technical scholarship and a contempt for or at least suspicion of theory and criticism beyond "appreciation" and the "art of praise." They established what in Max Weber's terms one could almost call an "ideal type": the professor who is uneasy in his subject, decries literary criticism, and still spreads a hearty enjoyment of literature by reciting and commenting on the authors he loves. He is deeply afraid of an accusation of pedantry, hides his learning in understatement or whimsical pleasantries, and is nevertheless proud of being a gentleman, a select being, a knight both by title and in imagination. All his writings are about well established figures of the past; when he has to face the challenge of the new, he tries to ward it off by sneers and jokes. Walter Raleigh's *Letters* reveal a crudity of feeling and expression one would not have expected from the erstwhile aesthete who wrote a precious little book on *Style* (1897). The letters show his contempt for criticism: "The eunuch was the first modern critic" (1:220). "Critical admiration for what another man has written is an emotion for spinsters. Shakesp. didn't want it. Jerome K. Jerome is in some ways a decenter writer than Brunetière or Saintsbury or any of the professed critics. He goes and begets a brat himself, and doesn't pule over other people's amours. If I write an autobiography, it shall be called 'Confessions of a Pimp' " (1:268–69). "I never cared for literature as such . . . to me the learned critic is a beast" (2:239). With the contempt for criticism goes Raleigh's helplessness and sentimentality when he praises, for example, Christina Rossetti as the best poet alive. "The only thing that Christina makes me want to do is cry, not lecture" (1:164). The letters are filled with coarse or flippant judgments: Browning is "an educated, interesting, progressive pig" (1:164). Zola and Ibsen are "modern pigs" (1:215). Macaulay is "God's Ape—he stinks in my nostrils. Cheap, vain, poor, noisy, blind" (2:279). Raleigh gives vent to his prejudices: "There is nothing in Brandes: he is just a Continental Jew culture-monger" (2:281). Even Matthew Arnold must have been a Jew. "I know it, by his face, and his writing. My essay is on the cultured Jew" (2:383). Still, it is always unjust to judge anyone by his casual letters collected by the piety of a widow or pupil. A writer should be judged by his formal pronouncements, and there Raleigh comes off much better. In spite of his pretense of amateurishness he had considerable miscellaneous learning. The introduction to Sir Thomas Hoby's translation of Castiglione's *Cortegiano* (1900), whose ideal of the gentleman-scholar struck a sympathetic chord in his mind, is more than competent, and the *Six Essays on Johnson* (1910) were for their time a good foray to rescue Johnson from Boswell and Macaulay, to see him as the representative Englishman, as a moralist and critic and not merely as a bullying oracle.

The books on *The English Novel* (1894), *Milton* (1900), *Wordsworth* (1903), and *Shakespeare* (1907) are professedly introductions which contain, in a small compass, not only much information and description but some sane though hardly profound criticism. *The English Novel* sketches its history from the earliest times to the appearance of *Waverley*. The stress is on Fielding and Jane Austen while Richardson and Sterne are conventionally criticized: "Richardson's characters live in a sick-room but they would die in the open air" (160). Sterne is censured for "the inartistic intrusion of himself and his own feelings on a scene that might be pathetic enough if it were not marred by his self-consciousness" (198). *Milton* expounds the romantic view of Milton being of the devil's party. *Wordsworth*, organized around the obvious topics, the French Revolution, Coleridge, Poetic Diction, Nature, concludes that Wordsworth was a "true visionary" (213). *Shakespeare* is good at demolishing superstitions, concentrates deftly on essential topics, and is clearer than Bradley in distinguishing between fiction and reality. Raleigh sees, for instance, that there is no point in chiding Cordelia for her obstinacy. "If Cordelia had been perfectly tender and tactful, there would have been no play" (135). She is a character invented for the situation. Raleigh must allude to Bradley when he complains of critics who neglect the fact that some characters have "no full and independent existence; they are seen only in a limited aspect." The critics wrongly insist on "finishing his sketches for him" (135). Much in the book is trite: the emphasis on Shakespeare's irony and detachment seems overdone, but individual discussions such as the lengthy one of *Measure for Measure* are acute even if this one shirks the moral questions raised by the dénouement. Raleigh came from W. E. Henley's hearty imperialism. Men of action such as the Elizabethan voyagers, of whom he wrote with sympathy, are his ideal. During the First World War he undertook to write a history of the British Air Force. A first volume, *The War in the Air,* was published in 1922, but before he could complete the history Raleigh died of a fever contracted on a tour of duty to Baghdad.

Quiller-Couch was a much gentler soul. He wrote adventure novels in the wake of R. L. Stevenson but hardly a proper book of criticism. He collected his lectures in many volumes (e.g., *On the Art of Writing, Studies in Literature, On the Art of Reading, The Poet as Citizen*) and with the *Oxford Book of English Verse,* which he selected, influenced taste in poetry widely and profoundly. Quiller-Couch shares Raleigh's distaste for criticism. In his inaugural lecture (1912) he promises to eschew "all general definitions and theories" (*AW,* 18). In a lecture "On the terms 'classical' and 'romantic' " (*SL,* 1:76), Quiller-Couch ridicules these and similar terms. "Shakespeare, Milton, Shelley did not write 'classicism' or 'romanticism.' They wrote *Hamlet, Lycidas, The Cenci.*" "Gentlemen," he exhorts his audience, "I would I could persuade you to remember that you are English, and to go always for the thing, casting out of your vocabulary all such words as 'tendencies,' 'influences,' 'revivals,' 'revolts' " (*SL,* 1:79). German scholarship becomes his target during the First World War, and oddly enough he singled out Georg Brandes, a Danish Jew, as its representative. "A German bemuses himself with the theory that Wordsworth wrote naturalism or that naturalism wrote Wordsworth" (*SL,* 1:82), as if anybody had ever said or believed this. Quiller-Couch dismisses Croce and Spingarn (*PC,* 76–77) and can acquiesce in a simple relativism. "All critical discernment, or taste is relative" (*SL,* 3:208). "No book can mean the same to any two men" (*SL,* 3:211), but at times he can go off into vague idealistic declamations. "Platonic harmony is the principle of Poetry" (*PC,* 134). Man "by harmonising speech arrives at Poetry, and so a step nearer to the meaning of nature" (*PC*, 136). The combination of crude empiricism and lofty idealism, of miscellaneous learning and amateurish enjoyment, not only appealed to an eager student audience but also set the tone for much academic scholarship in the next decades. Quiller-Couch was, at least, a man of large tolerance: in 1917 he fostered the establishment of an English Tripos (the Cambridge term for an Honours examination) which stipulated questions on the history of literary criticism. In 1919 I. A. Richards began lecturing on the theory of criticism. On Quiller-Couch's urging a paper on the English moralists was added in 1925. The atmosphere was changing; the students became less numerous in Quiller-Couch's lectures, and he retired more and more to his home in Cornwall, to his yacht club and his house, The Haven, in Fowey. He died there in 1944.

A. C. BRADLEY (1851–1935)

The two men in the limelight at Oxford and Cambridge during the early twentieth century should not obscure a few scholars of that time who were critics. Of these, A. C. Bradley is clearly the most distinguished. His *Shakespearean Tragedy* (1904) preserves a high reputation and a wide reading public. Katherine Cook's *A. C. Bradley and His Influence in Twentieth-Century Shakespeare Criticism* has chronicled the ups and downs of Bradley's critical fortune: the violent reaction in the thirties and the later upswing. Oddly enough, among the dozens of opinions on her list, she missed John Middleton Murry's eulogy. *Shakespearean Tragedy* is, he says, "surely the greatest single work of criticism in the English language."[1] We may contrast it with the pride of F. R. Leavis in the "relegation of Bradley" achieved by him and the *Scrutiny* group. It brought home to the academic world "how inadequate and wrong the Bradley approach was."[2]

Both these extreme views lack historical perspective or any sense for Bradley's position in a history of thought and of thinking about tragedy and Shakespeare. Very few commentators realize some basic facts of Bradley's intellectual background. He was a disciple of Thomas Hill Green, of whom he said, fifty years later, that he "saved his soul."[3] Green is often described as the first Oxford Hegelian, though he should rather be labeled a Kantian who criticized Hume and empiricism. After Green's death (1882) Bradley edited his unfinished *Prolegomena to Ethics* (1883). Bradley's philosophical ambiance—the Oxford objective idealism—could not be clearer.

Also in aesthetic theory Bradley's antecedents are obvious. Hegel's philosophy of tragedy is the foremost model. Bradley called Hegel "the only philosopher who has treated tragedy in a manner both original and searching" (*OL*, 69). Bradley's exposition of "Hegel's Theory of Tragedy" (1901) is rightly considered the main clue to his own views. But Bradley was also a student of Kant, Schiller, and Eduard von Hartmann. In a note to the paper on "The Sublime," Bradley recognizes that his view is "perhaps nearer to Hartmann's than to any other" (37n). Bradley knew the main German critics of Shakespeare: he refers to Goethe, A. W. Schlegel, the Hegelian Heinrich Theodor Rötscher, Hermann Ulrici, Georg Gottfried Gervinus, Karl Werder, and Bernhard Ten Brink.[4] In discussing the structure of Shakespeare's plays, he acknowledges a debt to Gustav Freytag's *Technik des Dramas* (1873) (*ST*, 40, 63). Bradley was saturated in the whole German discussion of the tragic, a concept which was apparently almost unknown in England up to his time. According to the *NED*, the term "the tragic" occurs for the first time in John Morley's *Voltaire* (1872). "The tragic" was apparently felt to be a German invention, even in France. A letter of Marcel Proust's begins: "Vous allez voir tout le tragique comme dirait le critique allemand Curtius de ma situation."[5] The English, with their strong hold on the Aristotelian tradition, had discussed tragedy as a structure and its effect on the audience, the presumed catharsis. Friedrich Wilhelm Schelling, in 1795, was the first to break with this tradition and to look for the tragic in the dialectic of freedom and necessity.[6]

In discussing Bradley, one cannot avoid coming to grips with his philosophy, his aesthetics, and his concept of tragedy. Bradley thought he knew what tragedy is, and that he knew it because he had a concept of metaphysics.

A. C. Bradley is a convinced monist. Reality is one. There cannot be many reals. Pluralism, atomism, individualism are false. All finite existence is a "partial manifestation of the infinite." "Truth and reality prove in the end to be merely names for this idea or this infinite." "Evil is the attempt at complete isolation of the part from the whole." It is inevitable, for it is imperfection, and anything finite expresses the infinite only imperfectly. Religion arises because we recognize that we are imperfect, because we suffer evil and are evil. It is an attempted escape from the evil that men find they cannot escape otherwise (*IR*, 236, 241, 247; cf. 265f.). But at the end, Bradley believes, the moral order triumphs, harmony is reestablished.

Tragedy is an image of this world drama and, Bradley argues, Shakespeare grasped this drama correctly, exemplified and reaffirmed it. Tragedy is thus ultimately a *théodicée*, a defense of the world order. If, Bradley says expressly, the world were "the kingdom of evil, and therefore worthless," there would not be any tragedy, for nothing, neither suffering nor death, would matter greatly (*ST,* 327). Tragedy must be a collision of forces. The tragic hero in revolting against the order of the universe must perish but he must perish sublimely. "We feel that this spirit, even in the error and defeat, rises by its greatness into ideal union with the power that overwhelms it" (*OL,* 292).

It follows from this conception that mere passive suffering cannot be tragic. Job is not tragic (*ST,* 11). The hero must be responsible for his actions, must have freedom of choice, and thus cannot be a madman, cannot be governed by supernatural powers, and cannot be subject to pure chance (13–15), for otherwise he could not be judged on moral grounds. Ajax would presumably be excluded from the list of tragic heros, whatever the Greeks may have thought or Lily B. Campbell could argue.[7] A mad Hamlet is inconceivable: he puts on his "antic disposition." Lear, Bradley has to admit, goes mad, but his madness is a consequence of his free actions and is temporary. He recovers at the end. Nor can tragedy be determined by the interference of the supernatural: the witches in *Macbeth,* while not hallucinations, express Macbeth's desires, which were there before the appearance of the witches, and the Ghost confirms Hamlet's premonitions. Hamlet still acts or does not act as he chooses (343f., 139, 173f.). Pure chance would destroy tragedy. "We find practically no trace of fatalism" in Shakespeare's tragedies. Even in *Lear,* which is full of chance encounters, "the strict connection between act and consequence" is preserved (29, 284; cf. 15).

The hero need not be a moral man: he must, however, be a great man, a sublime man, who may be a criminal. Sublimity, Bradley says, "awakes through the check or shock which it gives to our finitude, the conscious-ness of an infinite or absolute" (*OL,* 53). There are no ethical distinctions among the sublimities. "That Socrates is not Satan, interests it [the Sub-lime] but little. What it cares for is the truth that, when they are sublime, they are all sublime, they are all the same; for each becomes infinite, and it feels in each its own infinity" (63). Thus Macbeth can be treated as a sublime hero on the same level with Hamlet, Othello, and Lear. Bradley knows that Macbeth committed a horrible crime, but he is a tragic hero of "frightful courage," "convulsed by conscience" (*ST,* 353).

Evil is like poison. "The world reacts against it violently, and, in the struggle to expel it, is driven to devastate itself. If we ask why the world should generate that which convulses and wastes it, the tragedy gives us no answer, and we are trying to go beyond tragedy in seeking one" (*ST,* 304). We would want to solve the mystery of evil, which to Bradley (and many others) seems insolvable, a mere datum of existence. The world rejects the evil, and moral order is restored. But this restitution of the whole is not simply a moral judgment. Bradley is very careful to avoid anything that would resemble the concept of "poetic justice," the distribution of prizes, though the catastrophe of a tragedy is, in his view, "an example of justice" (31). Still, it is a mysterious justice, for it often entails the perdition of the innocents: of Desdemona and Cordelia. Bradley defends the death of Cordelia rather oddly by exempting her from mortality. "What happens to such a being does not matter; all that matters is what she is. How this can be, when for anything the tragedy tells us, she has ceased to exist, we do not ask, but the tragedy itself makes us feel that somehow it is so." We are sent back to the "inscrutable ways of God," though Bradley always insists that the presence of Christian beliefs, a forecast of retribution in afterlife, would destroy the tragic effect. "Such [i.e., Shakespearean] tragedy assumes that the world, as it is presented, is the truth" (325). Bradley insists that the Elizabethan drama was "almost wholly secular." Shakespeare presents the world "substantially in one and the same way whether the period of the story is pre-Christian or Christian" (25). *Hamlet*, he concedes, while it "certainly cannot be called in the specific sense a 'religious drama,'" "uses popular religious ideas" freely and contains "a more decided, though always imaginative, intimation of a supreme power concerned in human evil and good, than can be found in any other of Shakespeare's tragedies" (174). But this is as far as he will go. In speaking of Cordelia, he endorses what we all must consider injustice. "The more unmotivated, unmerited, senseless, monstrous, Cordelia's fate, the more do we feel that it does not concern her . . . if only we could see things as they are (i.e., that goodness does not always prosper) we should see that the outward is nothing and the inward is all" (325f.). Here death and suffering are rather glibly dismissed as external on the grounds that man is only spirit.

While the world is spirit, it is made up of what F. H. Bradley calls "finite centers." There is nothing but souls, their community, and the infinite whole. In tragedy Bradley thus has to look at the characters first. The characters must be studied in their motives, must be treated as responsible beings whose motives determine their actions, involve them in a plot. Action issues from character, character issues in action. "The calamities and catastrophe follow inevitably from the deeds of men and the main source of these deeds is character." Bradley almost accepts— but not quite—the dictum that "character is destiny."[8] Character obviously cannot be merely an enslaving passion or a generalized humor type such as "melancholy adust," as some scholars argue.

Bradley's emphasis on character has elicited the sharpest criticism against his method and his specific interpretation. He does quite deliberately attempt to fill out the gaps in the depiction of a character, ponder what motivated him in the past or could motivate him in the future. He sees characters as figures on the stage who are to be understood and acted out as coherent human beings by an actor. Though Bradley may not have heard of Stanislavsky, his method resembles that of the Russian producer, who recommends that an actor envisage and even reconstruct a biography of the person whom he is to portray on the stage.[9] Bradley was perfectly aware of the difference between a character in a play and a person in real life, though one must admit that he lends himself to the charge of confusion between art and life on quite a few occasions. Some of these are pedantic or speculative projections which were effectively ridiculed in L. C. Knights's pamphlet *How Many Children Had Lady Macbeth?* (1933). Bradley, one should know, never asked this question, though in the notes there is a section "He has no children," in which we are told that "Lady Macbeth's child (I, iii, 54) may be alive or may be dead. . . . It may be that Macbeth had many children or that he had none. We cannot say, and it does not concern the play" (*ST*, 486, 489). Knights himself later ascribed the invention of the title to F. R. Leavis and apologized for its malicious effect.[10] Still, there are many cases that can be called confusions between life and stage. Some are sentimental projections, hypothetical questions, as when Bradley says of Desdemona that "if she had lived . . . her individuality and strength would have issued in a thousand actions, sweet and good, but surprising to her conventional or timid neighbours" (204), a statement that might be defended as an attempt at further defining her character, which combines kindness and timidity with a boldness and persistence shown in her marriage and her insistent pleading for Cassio. We might even defend speculating about Romeo's love for Rosaline, "which could have become a genuine passion if Rosaline had been kind" (*OL*, 326n), as a roundabout way of saying that Romeo was in love with love.

Other passages seem to take stage business literally, as if it were history. Bradley argues that Cassio was no younger than Iago, who is twenty-eight, for "a mere youth would not have been made Governor of Cyprus" (*ST*, 213), or that Cleopatra must have been a physically strong woman, for she raised Antony's heavy body from the ground to her tower (*OL*, 300), or that the court in *Hamlet*—after all, a mere stage-crowd—shows no sign of perceiving Claudius's leaving the play within the play as an accusation of murder (*ST*, 137n). As early as 1905, A. B. Walkley, then a well-known theater critic, singled out this passage as a "delightful naiveté."[11] Other passages could be called whimsical mental experiments, shifting a character into another play and speculating how he or she would have behaved in another situation. A whole page is devoted to the question of what Cordelia would have done in Desdemona's place and what Desdemona in Cordelia's (205f.; cf. 318). Similarly we are told: "Imagine Goneril uttering 'Had he not resembled / My father as he slept, I had done it' (*Macbeth*, II, ii, 14)" (370) and that "Posthumus would never have acted as Othello did" and "Othello would have met Iachimo's challenge with something more than words" (21). Bradley conjectures that "if the message of the Ghost had come within a week of his father's death . . . [Hamlet] would have acted on it as decisively as Othello himself" (116). All these passages might be accounted for as rhetorical devices to make us realize the different characters and situations more clearly. We might notice Lady Macbeth's awakening conscience, or we might see that Hamlet was not an abnormally speculative and sensitive nature, as Goethe and Coleridge thought, but was changed by the shock of his father's death and the incestuous marriage of his mother.

Still, there are passages in Bradley that do show a confusion of fiction and reality that seems almost incredible. Thus we are told: "when Desdemona spoke her last words, perhaps that line of the ballad which she sang an hour before her death was still busy in her brain, 'Let nobody blame him; his scorn I approve.' Nature plays such strange tricks, and Shakespeare alone among poets seems to create in somewhat the same manner as Nature" (206). Bradley apparently does not see that Desdemona is given the song to sing because it anticipates her last words. Charitably interpreted, however, the concluding clause might imply such recognition.

There are many of these indubitable confusions of fiction and reality, which, however, can be matched by as many that show that Bradley was very well aware that the plays were only plays. It is a totally unwarranted slur on Bradley to "suspect that he never went to the theater,"[12] for there is ample evidence in the printed works (and in reminiscences) that he was an assiduous playgoer. He refers to performances and actors such as Salvini as Othello and Sarah Bernhardt as Lady Macbeth (*ST*, 203, 379n). He disapproves of an unnamed actress playing mad Ophelia uttering an agonized cry of horror; he objects to actors who play Othello giving Desdemona a tap on the shoulder with a roll of paper instead of a slap in the face; he complains of having seen King Lear turn continually in anguish to the corpse of Cordelia in the very last scene; and he disapproves of all the actors playing Lear saying "Never" only three times when the Folio prescribes it repeated five times (165, 184, 292n, 293n).

Bradley states emphatically that "Shakespeare wrote primarily for the theatre and not for students" (*ST,* 158f., also 47). He knows that much in Shakespeare can be explained by the conditions of the stage and the technique of a play, where, as in a picture, a figure might be lightly sketched in the background. Thus Kent in *Lear,* he says, "is wanted mainly to fill a place in the scheme of the play" (295). Ophelia, he recognizes, "is merely one of the subordinate characters," for "it was essential to Shakespeare's purpose that too great an interest should not be aroused in the love story" (160). Bradley even generalizes that "a good deal is admitted for the sake of its immediate attraction and not because it is essential to the plot" (*OL,* 383), and recognizes "explanations offered to the audience" (*ST,* 222), a point of technique he finds merely "curious," while L. L. Schücking and E. E. Stoll have since made it the key for their interpretations of Shakespeare's characters. Bradley thinks that "nobody ever notices" (78) minute inconsistencies in a stage performance, though he examined more elaborately than anyone before the "Double Time" in *Othello,* a question first raised by John Wilson in 1849.[13] Bradley concludes sensibly that Shakespeare perhaps said to himself, "No one in the theatre will notice all this" (*ST,* 428). Still, Bradley does belong, after all, to the tribe of Lamb, who would rather read Shakespeare than hear him performed. He thinks that *Lear* is for the "inward eye," and that the witches in *Macbeth* belong, like the storm scenes in *Lear,* "properly to the world of imagination" (269, 340n). We can sympathize if we think of the rattle and lightning of Victorian performances in the style of Henry Irving.

The reaction against Bradley was not, however, focused only on his excessive concentration on character analysis. It is not true that he looked on Shakespeare's characters as "characters in a serious moralizing novel, something like *Middlemarch.*"[14] He expressly said that "to criticize Shakespeare's plays as a realistic novel would be merely stupid" and emphasized that the "psychological point of view is not equivalent to the tragic" (*ST,* 71, 127). Rather the reaction against Bradley came from several divergent angles: from those who, like Schücking, Stoll, G. B. Harrison, and Alfred Harbage, saw Shakespeare mainly as a purveyor of effective stage drama. It came from scholars such as Lily B. Campbell who rejected Bradley's concept of tragedy as unhistorical because they wanted to interpret it strictly in terms of Elizabethan humor psychology. It came also from those who wanted to have the plays looked at primarily as poems, as patterns of imagery and themes. L. C. Knights was the most effective polemicist, while G. Wilson Knight, the original expounder of the "spatial" approach to Shakespeare, recognized that Bradley felt the effect of atmosphere, imagery, and an implied metaphysics. Though

Knight objected to older Shakespeare criticism for its "essentially ethical outlook" and the whole "search for motives"[15] and specifically charged Bradley with having "on occasion pushed the 'character' analysis to an unnecessary extreme," he praised Bradley for having been the first who "subjected, what I have called the 'spatial' qualities of Shakespeare's plays to a considered, if rudimentary comment."[16] G. Wilson Knight later reasserted the claim that his investigations "can be considered to lie directly in the tradition of A. C. Bradley's *Shakespearean Tragedy,* which is too often wrongly supposed to be limited to the *minutiae* of 'characterization.' "[17] Atmosphere is one of Bradley's interests: that of *King Lear* in "its dim outlines like a winter mist," that of *Troilus and Cressida,* "intellectual, of an intense but hard clearness," that of *Macbeth,* "as if the poet saw the whole story through an ensanguined mist," while in *Othello* there is a "comparative confinement of the imaginative atmosphere" (*ST,* 247, 275, 336, 185), and *Coriolanus* has "scarcely more atmosphere, either supernatural or natural, than the average prose drama of to-day" (*M,* 77). Nor can it be said that Bradley entirely ignored imagery, which since Caroline Spurgeon's book has aroused so much interest. He pays attention to the animal imagery in *Lear,* which had been noticed before by J. Kirkman (*ST,* 266),[18] and he comments on Iago's incongruous preference for nautical phrases though he is described as a land-soldier (213). Nor can one say that Bradley ignores the poetry and the verbal surface of Shakespeare's plays. He knew that "poetry is words" that "it is an art of language," and he was aware of the "identity of content and form" (*OL,* 25; *M,* 27f.; *OL,* 15). "Poetry for Poetry's Sake" (1901), Bradley's inaugural lecture as professor of poetry at Oxford, states clearly and eloquently the view that poetry is "a world by itself, independent, complete, autonomous" (*OL,* 5), which is only an analogy to life. It is neither philosophy nor religion, though on occasion, Bradley does suggest that "wherever the imagination is satisfied we should discover no idle fancy but the image of truth" (394f.). Patiently Bradley explains the difference between "subject," which precedes a poem and is aesthetically indifferent, and "substance" (corresponding to the German *Gehalt*), which is within the poem. In poetry meaning and sound are one. "Form and content are one thing from different points of view" (15). Three years before the publication of *Shakespearean Tragedy* Bradley refutes the criticisms that will be launched against it. "When you are really reading *Hamlet,* the action and the characters are not something which you conceive apart from the words; you apprehend them from point to point *in* the words, and the words as expressions of them," and, on the next page, he asserts that the true critic speaking of characters and action, style and

versification apart, "does not really think of them apart" (15f.). The most
verbal of critics, William Empson, in his essays on "The Fool in Lear"
and "Honest in Othello," pays tribute to Bradley's "magnificent" analyses
of the plays, though he must reject Bradley's pious interpretation of
Lear's end as "turning the blasphemies against the gods into the orthodox view held by Mrs. Gamp that the world is a Wale." Still he agrees
with Bradley's concern for motivation. "I think it is clearly wrong to talk
as if coherence of character were not needed in poetic drama, only coherence of metaphor and so on."[19] Bradley would not have endorsed the
"poetic," "static," or "spatial" reading of patterns practiced by Wilson
Knight. He defines tragedy, like Aristotle, as a "story of exceptional ca-
lamity leading to the death of a man in high estate" (*ST,* 11, 12). He also
describes the construction of a Shakespearean tragedy very much in
terms of the Aristotelian concern for such distinctions as exposition, conflict, turning point, and resolution, though he uses the somewhat stream-
lined modernization of the *Poetics* he found in Freytag's *Technik des Dramas*
(40–78; on Freytag, 40n, 63). On the whole Bradley was wary of finding
symbolism and allegory in Shakespeare. Still, in discussing *Lear,* Bradley
sees that the opposing forces in their starkness raise the issue, as do Ariel
and Caliban. He sees "a tendency which produces symbols, allegories,
personifications of qualities and abstract ideas." Cautiously Bradley
concedes that "while it would be going too far to suggest that [Shake-
speare] was employing conscious symbolism or allegory in *King Lear,* it
does appear to disclose a mode of imagination not so very far removed
from the mode with which, we must remember, Shakespeare was perfectly familiar in Morality plays and the *Fairy Queen*" (264ff.).

   All these somewhat hesitant approaches to new themes and methods
of Shakespeare criticism are far outweighed by what seems to me, besides
the concept of tragedy and character analysis, Bradley's main method:
a description of the presumed emotional reaction of the audience, which,
when Bradley seems uncertain of its universality, is stated often bluntly
as his own personal reaction. Some of these reactions seem to be observed very subtly, though it might be impossible to prove their universality. Thus speaking of the Gravedigger scene Bradley comments: "Our
distress for Ophelia is not so absorbing that we refuse to be interested
in the man who digs her grave, or even continue throughout the long
conversation to remember always with pain that the grave is hers" (*ST,*
396). In a similar vein he suggests that "we are saddened by the very
fact that the catastrophe [of *Antony and Cleopatra*] saddens us so little"
(*OL,* 304). He meditates on the death of Coriolanus: "since his rival's
plan is concerted before our eyes, we wait with little suspense, almost

indeed with tranquillity, the certain end," and then carefully describes the last scene, in which Coriolanus is killed. "The instantaneous cessation of enormous energy (which is like nothing else in Shakespeare) strikes us with awe, but not with pity. . . . Life has suddenly shrunk and dwindled, and become a home for pygmies and not for him" (*M*, 94f.). In other contexts, statements about our feelings seem often merely fanciful, whimsical, or even downright sentimental. Especially his comment on Othello (which so arouses the indignation of F. R. Leavis that he denigrates Othello for his "obtuse and brutal egoism" and "ferocious stupidity")[20] seems extravagant in assuming in the audience "a passion of mingled love and pity" for Othello which "they feel for no other hero in Shakespeare." Even in the murder of Desdemona, "terribly painful as this scene is, there is almost nothing here to diminish the admiration and love which heighten pity" (*ST*, 191, 198). We might wonder whether the strangling is "almost nothing."

At times, the personal reaction is stated with almost ludicrous violence. Thus Bradley chides Octavius for being proof to Cleopatra's fascination. "We turn from him with disgust and think him a disgrace to his species" (*OL*, 302), or, commenting on Iago's suggestion that Othello should give Desdemona "a patent to offend, for it touches not you" (IV, i, 194), Bradley permits himself the outburst that "this is perhaps the moment when we most of all long to destroy Iago" (*ST*, 436). Most extravagantly, in the essay on *Coriolanus*, Bradley indignantly speaks of the "unspeakable baseness of [Aufidius'] sneer at the hero's tears." "I confess I feel nothing but disgust as Aufidius speaks the last words, except some indignation with the poet who allowed him to speak them, and an unregenerate desire to see the head and body of the speaker lying on opposite sides of the stage" (*M*, 98). What happened to the world of poetry, "independent, complete, autonomous," which is only an analogue to life?

These emotional reactions, carefully listened to, are also the basis of Bradley's rare adverse criticism of Shakespeare's art. Obviously and quite properly he assumes the greatness of Shakespeare's tragedies, which need no defense or praise. He lists, however, very much in the style of Dr. Johnson, Shakespeare's defects: loose construction, inflated language, and so on, explaining them, as usual, by the conditions of the stage and time.[21] But they are minor blemishes that do not concern Bradley's standards. Rather, coherence of character seems the criterion by which he condemns Iago's "alliance of evil and supreme intellect" as "an impossible fiction" (*ST*, 237). More subtly Bradley argues that it is "surely an error to regard *Antony and Cleopatra* as a rival of the famous four," not because, as he says elsewhere, it is "the most faultily constructed of all the tragedies" but because it does not live up to Bradley's idea of a tragedy. The tragic emotions, he argues, are "stirred only when such beauty or nobility of character is displayed as commands unreserved admiration or love; or when, in default of this, the forces which move the agents, and the conflicts which result from these forces, attain terrifying and overwhelming power. The four famous tragedies satisfy one or both of these conditions; *Antony and Cleopatra,* though a great tragedy, satisfies neither of them completely" (282, 260; *OL,* 305). But Shakespeare is considered most at fault in the depiction of the dismissal of Falstaff. Henry "had no right to talk all of a sudden like a clergyman: and surely it was both ungenerous and insincere to speak of [Sir John and his companions] as his 'misleaders.' " Shakespeare in these Falstaff scenes "overshot his mark." "He created so extraordinary a being, and fixed him so firmly on his intellectual throne that when he sought to dethrone him he could not" (*OL,* 259). There is truth in this, however much we may account for Henry's action if we conceive of Falstaff as a Lord of Misrule dismissed on Ash Wednesday.

King Lear makes the greatest trouble for Bradley's cosmic optimism. The catastrophe, he complains, "is not at all inevitable." "It is not even satisfactorily motived." The delay of Edmund in attempting to save Cordelia and Lear has no sufficiently clear reason. "The real cause," Bradley has to conclude, "lies outside the dramatic *nexus.* It is Shakespeare's wish to deliver a sudden and crushing blow to the hopes which he excited" (*ST,* 252–53). But still Bradley resists the impression that *Lear* is composed of "almost wholly painful feelings—utter depression, or indignant rebellion, or appalled despair. And that would surely be strange." It would be "a very serious flaw" which Bradley insists would be also an aesthetic flaw. He has to interpret the last scene as "The Redemption of King Lear" and find "its final and total result one in which pity and terror, carried perhaps to the extreme limits of art, are so blended with a sense of the law and beauty that we feel at last, not depression and much less despair, but a consciousness of greatness in pain, and a solemnity in the mystery we cannot fathom" (277, 278n, 285, 279). We are back at the beginning: at Bradley's overriding concern with a world that ultimately guarantees a meaning to human life and a moral order to the universe. A reading of *Lear* like that of Jan Kott's in terms of Beckett's *Endgame,* or Octavio Paz's as a "return to chaos"[22] would seem to Bradley not only false but incomprehensible. Though Bradley knows and even underlines the difference between religion and poetry, poetry finally appears to say the same thing. "Religion denies that real life . . . is the whole and final truth; and this is just what poetry, which asserts nothing, nevertheless suggests."²³ Tragedy is "a type of mystery of the whole world . . . it forces the mystery on us," or in other terms, "about the best poetry, and not only the best, there floats an atmosphere of infinite suggestion" (23; *OL*, 26). Infinite, and the infinite is the key word. It is the "object of worship," "no alien power but the goal of desire and aspiration. . . . Beauty, truth, goodness, if not identical with it, are its highest manifestations. It is the one and only power" (*IR*, 146). Thus it is highest praise for Bradley to say that "Antony touches infinity," that Hamlet, Falstaff, Macbeth, Cleopatra, "have a sense of the soul's infinity," while Henry V lacks it (*ST*, 83, 128; *OL*, 273).

We understand why Wordsworth, after Shakespeare, is for Bradley the most important English poet. Bradley was one of those students of Wordsworth who saw the "mystic," "visionary," and "sublime" aspect of Wordsworth's poetry. For Wordsworth, he says, "the 'visionary' power arises from, and testifies to, the mind's infinity," and "the feeling of this is, or involves, or is united with, a feeling or idea of the infinite or 'one mind' " (*OL*, 129, 139n). He defines this visionary feeling as "the intimation of something illimitable, over-arching or breaking into the customary 'reality.' . . . At its touch the soul, suddenly conscious of its own infinity, melts in rapture into the infinite being" (134). A late paper, "English Poetry and German Philosophy in the Age of Wordsworth" (1909), argues for "some particular affinities between Wordsworth and Hegel," deploring the lack of an adequate (i.e., idealist) philosophy in the England of Wordsworth's time. An elaborate comparison is drawn between Wordsworth and Hegel which must move on a high level of abstraction. They both, for instance, believe that "the inmost principle in man's mind is also the inmost principle in everything else," that "imagination is the way to truth," and that "there is a 'soul of goodness' in things which are, and that, in spite of evils, the 'inward frame of things' is wiser than its critics." Man must surrender himself to God, "in whom there is no negation that is not overcome." "Here the mind (there is but one) puts off its finitude; its implicit infinity is realized, its temporal life exchanged for eternity, and its mere humanity for divinity" (*M*, 107, 122, 125, 130, 136). Bradley, however, in assimilating Wordsworth to Hegel, recognizes that this parallel might also be drawn with Schelling or even Spinoza (125n) (as E. D. Hirsch has drawn it for Wordsworth and Schelling)²⁴ and that Wordsworth is not unique in his time. An eloquent exposition of "Shelley's View of Poetry" endorses Shelley's celebration of the imagination, though Bradley admits the limitations of Shelley's "beautiful idealisms of moral excellence" (*OL*, 169). The lecture on "The Letters of Keats" emphasizes Keats's view of "the regular stepping of Imagination towards truth" (235) while a late paper, "Keats and Philosophy" (1921), tries to show that Keats strove for a philosophical outlook (M, 189–206). Matthew Arnold is criticized for ignoring what is for Bradley central in Shelley: that behind life and the world "and entering into them" there is that "ultimate spiritual perfection which is also the ultimate *power.*" Both for Wordsworth and Shelley "there is a spirit in Nature, and Nature therefore is not a mere 'outward world.' And the spirit in Nature is one and the same with the spirit in man" (M, 158, 149). Thus the English romantic movement is for Bradley "the great ideal movement" (ST, 127), parallel to German idealist philosophy, to which he felt, in the version he knew from his Oxford days, a lifelong allegiance.

I have defined the historical position of Bradley's thought: its roots in German idealist philosophy and English romantic poetry. I have unraveled the different strands in Bradley's method: the theory of tragedy, the character analysis, the recording of personal reactions, but I have not answered the final question. Has Bradley succeeded in the task of a critic to deepen our knowledge and insight of his subject or to use Bradley's own stated ambition: have Shakespeare's tragedies assumed "in our imaginations a shape a little less unlike the shape they wore in the imagination of their creator"? (ST, 1). The answer, I think, must be in the affirmative. Whatever the debatable points and even mistakes of Bradley may be, he has grasped something true in Shakespeare, in the explanation of motives, in the evaluation of characters, situations, and whole plays, and in the definition of Shakespearean tragedy. Bradley, at least, should fortify us against false descriptions, misinterpretations, wrong evaluations, and inapplicable theories of tragedy. To give only a few examples from the enormous proliferation of Shakespeare criticism since Bradley's book: one can label as false the "inhuman—or superhuman" Hamlet of G. Wilson Knight, "whose consciousness—somewhat like Dostoevsky's Stavrogin—is centred on death" contrasted with Claudius, "a good and gentle king, in a state of healthy and robust spiritual life";[25] the Hamlet as Cesare Borgia of Salvador de Madariaga;[26] the Iago of Wyndham Lewis "who never lies";[27] the latent homosexual Iago of the Freudians;[28] the Coriolanus, "a character in a satyr play," whose invective if "fecal" and who is rightly named Coriol*anus* (invented by Kenneth Burke);[29] and many, many other grotesque distortions or fanciful whimsies concocted by critics who have lost all contact with the text. Bradley has again raised the most burning question of recent criticism: is there or is there not a correct interpretation? There are, indubitably, many incorrect ones.

Finally, one might reflect on the fact that the two Bradley brothers provided a philosophical background for two strands of twentieth-century English criticism. A. C. Bradley stands behind John Middleton Murry, whose book on *Keats and Shakespeare* (1925) is inconceivable without Bradley's conception of both Shakespeare and Keats.[30] F. H. Bradley, as has been increasingly realized since the publication of T. S. Eliot's Harvard thesis *Knowledge and Experience in the Philosophy of F. H. Bradley* (1964), has profoundly influenced the general outlook and critical vocabulary of the early T. S. Eliot.[31] Eliot wrote a laudatory introduction to G. Wilson Knight's *Wheel of Fire* (1930), though Wilson Knight came from Middleton Murry. Knight tells us that Murry's articles in the *Adelphi* acted on him "like an avatar."[32] He quotes Murry sounding like Bradley: "Great literature is the revelation of a harmony that cannot be interpreted. Art holds the place it does in our secret loyalties because it does reveal what cannot be uttered."[33] But Murry reviewed Knight's first books unfavorably and Knight found an unexpected ally in T. S. Eliot.

ELTON, KER, GRIERSON, AND GARROD

Bradley is still widely read and discussed. But other scholar-critics of distinction have almost disappeared from view. At least four of them— Oliver Elton (1861–1945), Walter Paton Ker (1855–1923), Herbert Grierson (1866–1960), and H. W. Garrod (1878–1960)—deserve attention.

Oliver Elton produced an extensive body of writing. After some translations from Icelandic and a monograph on Michael Drayton (1895), he contributed a volume on *The Augustan Ages* (1899) to Saintsbury's series "Periods of European Literature." Considering the small scale, it is a skillful survey of French and English literature with brief excursions into Italian, German, and Danish (Holberg). For the time the treatment of the French classics is very sympathetic, and some of the comment on individual works perceptive and even original. Thus Elton comments on *La Princesse de Clèves* "that it might be possible to resent a certain motherly and elderly tone that she [Madame de La Fayette] takes with her young people" (*AA*, 83) and that the solution of *Le Misanthrope* is tragic (123). Elton understands the assumptions of neoclassicism very well: that "nature" means "human nature" and "reason" the general sense of mankind rather than rationality (144–45). But the account of English literature seems vitiated by the view that "it does not express the essence but only an incident of the English mind" (3). Elton was to reverse this judgment.

His next book, *Modern Studies* (1907), contains much of critical interest. A paper on "Recent Shakespeare Criticism" is severe in its strictures of Brandes and cool in its criticism of Bradley's *Shakespearean Tragedy.* Bradley's manner is "a curious mixture of preaching at high pressure with a nervous, guarded Oxford accuracy of analysis" (*MS,* 93). Elton sees his "odd habit of treating" Shakespeare's characters "as if they were real" (104). Raleigh's *Shakespeare* seems to suffer from a narrow view of what is moral, and Elton detects "signs of a light, inexpensive, and not always covert scorn for the scholarship without which the author could not have written one page in security" (118). An essay on "The Meaning of Literary History" is a fine plea for world-literature in Goethe's sense. "Knowledge is international or nothing" (125). Elton comments on Hallam, Sainte-Beuve, "the greatest of literary historians" (132), Taine, the new French *littérature comparée,* and the recent organized study of literature in the United States. "These books" (he refers to Spingarn, Erskine, and Morris Croll) may lack tint, may forget "the truth that criticism is at last a fine art like friendship, and requires colour and personality" (137). Elton then discusses Courthope's *History of English Poetry,* worrying about the way Courthope reduces everything to a history of impersonal forces. Discussing his view of Marlowe's worship of *virtù* as the ruling mood of the Renaissance, Elton protests that "his real characteristic lies in the form, the voice, he gives to that impulse" (145). Finally Elton comments on Saintsbury's *Short History of English Literature,* praising it for its "timely betrayal of preferences" (155) but seeing its limitation in "almost excluding the intellectual stuff of literature" (152). Everywhere Elton shows a sure grasp of the issues.

Surprisingly Elton's article on the "Novels of Henry James" (reprinted in *Modern Studies*) seems to be unknown today. Considering its date (1904), it must have been the most thorough and the most perceptive conspectus of James's work. Elton comments, for instance, on the ending of *The American,* which "baffles men at the last moment by some malign turn of fortune," as characteristic of James. "He is fond of the cruel slip between the cup and the lip" (*MS,* 247). The interpretation of *The Wings of the Dove* seems to me superbly right, also for its emphasis on our sympathy with Kate Croy just because of her failure. The book, Elton says, "ends in a deep, resonant discord" (272), as there is a "profound, if muffled discord" (282) at the end of *The Golden Bowl. The Ambassadors* is seen as a "gently ironic comedy," as a respite between the two great novels treated at length.

After *Modern Studies* Elton embarked on his great project: a *Survey of English Literature* which eventually covered 150 years, from 1730 to 1880.

(*1780–1830* was published in 1912; *1830–1880*, in 1920; *1730–1780*, in 1932.) Elton's *Survey* has one indubitable virtue: he has examined every writer firsthand. He includes not only imaginative literature of high rank but even third-rate dramatists and novelists, and beyond the core of literature memoir-writers, historians, philosophers, theologians, literary scholars, and so on. Elton, in contrast to many of his rivals, is thoroughly familiar with the secondary literature; he pays scrupulous attention to American scholarship then frequently ignored or slighted. The books profess to be surveys and not histories, but they are not oblivious of movements and tendencies and the context of European literature. Contacts and influences and the impact of English literature abroad are often noted. The proportions seem almost always right, except that 1730 seems an artificial starting point which necessitates a retrospect to Pope and the age of Queen Anne.

These books are today neglected, mainly, it seems, because Elton is largely an expositor, judicious, level-headed, detached to an extent that negates his own requirement of color and personality. He defines his aim by using a saying of Hazlitt's on his title-page of the first series: "I have endeavoured to feel what is good, and to give a reason for the faith that was in me, when necessary and when in my power." He goes on to say that the book is "a series of judgments upon works of art," "really a review, a direct criticism" (*1780–1830,* 1:vii), an attempt "to receive, define, and re-impart the characteristic pleasure of each work of art" (ibid., 2:372). He somewhat anxiously professes that the "chronicler of letters has to hold fast to the artistic canon: not to pretend to be writing a history of thought or of knowledge" (*1830–1880,* 1:5), for applied literature can survive only by virtue of its form.

The promised direct criticism often lacks profile, some edge and sharpness. One cannot say, however, that Elton is reluctant to rank: he is not averse to occasional superlatives. Thus "Crabbe is the greatest novelist between Sterne and Scott" (*1780–1830,* 1:54). Scott is "the greatest of our lyric poets between Blake, or Burns, and Shelley: Coleridge not being excluded" (ibid., 1:310). Nor are we spared comparisons of greater or less. Burns is superior to Blake "not only because by his more constantly perfect form, but because he has more of plain humanity in him" (ibid., 1:114), a standard which might not impress us. Individual works of a poet are singled out with assurance: the "Ode to a Nightingale" is Keats's "greatest" (ibid., 2:247); Hazlitt's *Lectures on the Comic Writers* are "his most precious contribution to criticism" (ibid., 2:375). Elton often blames in strong terms. *The Castle of Otranto* is "unbearable" (ibid., 1:203). "The slow, lengthy, microscopic analysis" in *Emma* has "a certain hard repellent prolixity about much of it" (ibid., 1:197). There are unabashed comparisons between writers: between Balzac and Scott (ibid., 1:346), Thackeray and Tolstoy (*1830–1880*, 2:254–55), or Arnold and Sainte-Beuve. Sainte-Beuve has "no mission, and treats his readers as urbane and rational already. Matthew Arnold tries to scold and banter them into becoming so" (ibid., 1:270).

The individual chapters characterize the writers often perceptively: Byron, Hazlitt, Carlyle, and Ruskin are treated particularly well and by no means uncritically. At times Elton attempts an analysis of stylistic traits. He is especially interested in prose rhythm and comments on Burke and De Quincey in some detail. A passage from Browning's *Parleyings* is subjected to a grammatical analysis (*1830–1880*, 1:393) and neologisms of the Victorian age are marshaled (ibid., 1:90–91). Elton is not averse to tracing changes in poetic style. In discussing the eighteenth century he tells us that "describing the 'progress of poesy' in the eighteenth century as a simple conflict between the classical and romantic tendencies is to get into a morass" (*1730–1780*, 1:334), but he still quite rightly sees the beginning of a "transformation scene: a slow, hindered recovery of the artistic senses and of a rare style" (ibid., 1:333). His own taste, despite his sympathy of the literature of the eighteenth century, which, he now recognizes, "expresses, better perhaps than that of any other time, the permanent average temper of our race" (ibid., 1:vii), remains romantic or rather a tempered, subdued romantic, basically Victorian taste. The evenness, the constant weighing of pro and con can sometimes be disconcerting. Thus in the early series (*1780–1830*) Elton wrote an admiring page on Dr. Johnson as a "mystic, of his own kind," a heroic hypochondriac, while in the later *Survey, 1730–1780*, after a sympathetic account of his writings and a defense of his most commonly challenged critical opinions Elton can still point to his limitations. "To open a page of Lessing or Diderot is to be in another world of ideas" (*1730–1780*, 1:124). "We can hardly count Johnson among the great masters of wisdom; it would be unfair to contrast him with Montaigne or Goethe" (ibid., 1:131). One of the supporting arguments is that Johnson "was unable or unwilling to perceive [Sir Thomas] Browne's greatness of vision" (ibid., 1:139). In Elton there is a final moral vision. The peroration to the Victorian volumes praises the "intensely ethical, exalted, and didactic temper" of the age and three times speaks of the "quality of nobleness" of English literature between 1830 and 1880, which in Elton's view was followed by twenty years of decline, of "an ebb in English literature" (*1830–1880*, 2:366). Nonetheless, granting the Victorian taste and an excess of detachment, Elton's books seem to me still the best handbook of the kind, preferable to such rivals as Cazamian, Sampson, or Chew (in Baugh's composite volume).

The English Muse (1933) is something like an abridgment of the big books, "a companion to an imaginary, and most imperfect anthology" (preface). It contains accounts of periods in the history of English poetry not discussed before by Elton. We may be surprised by his praise for his newest poet, D. H. Lawrence, and the cool handling of *Paradise Lost*. "It fails to move the imagination" and "to make us feel either the presence or the power of evil" (238). The treatment of the metaphysicals shows imperfect sympathy. Donne's poetry is characterized as "highly irritant, disquieted and disquieting" and chided for "lacking simple and direct feeling for the beauty of the world" (210). The Victorian taste for both the simply felt and the sublime is reasserted.

Two later collections show Elton's broadening interests. In *A Sheaf of Papers* (1922) "English Prose Numbers" struggles with the problem of finding "a terminology which is neither pedantic and full of neologism, nor yet hampered by false associations" (163). Papers on the Russian poets Koltsov and Fet show his mastery of a new language. It led to a complete verse translation of Pushkin's *Evgeny Onegin,* to essays, collected in *Essays and Addresses* (1939), on Pushkin and Chekhov, and even to an interest in Karel Čapek, the Czech dramatist, whose stories and novels Elton read in the original. A late lecture, "The Nature of Literary Criticism" (1935), is something of a disappointment. Elton speaks of the critic as "identifying himself with the poet's mood and vision" and deplores the modern habit of never facing the question of "ranks and values at all" (*EA,* 216). But he himself does not face it properly. He takes refuge behind the duty of the "critic or teacher to make poetry easier, and not harsher, to his hearers; all his interpreting must be judged by his success in that adventure" (220). Elton accepts Croce's view of the autonomy of art and the independence of each single work of art. The only canon of value he recognizes is "inner harmony," which he, however, modifies by admitting "a harmony between discords" (231). But then he turns back to the more modest task: the attempt of criticism "to define once more the virtue of the *classics*" (237). If we take classics in a broad sense, Elton has defined his own work.

Walter Paton Ker is mainly remembered as an excellent medievalist whose first book, *Epic and Romance* (1896), clearly distinguished the Teutonic epic (with the *Chanson de Roland*) from the Romance romance both in form, the way of telling, and in the social background, feudal versus courtly society. His handbooks, *The Dark Ages* (1904), another volume in Saintsbury's "Periods of European Literature," and *English Literature:*

Medieval (1912), are succinct, wide-ranging, informative, and sane. They are the work of a true comparatiste who knew not only the Latin of the early Middle Ages but also all the different forms and stages of the Germanic and Romance languages from Iceland to Portugal. Ker was not only a fine scholar: he also thought systematically about the nature of art and poetry, poetics and literary history, and thus belongs in a history of criticism. He wrote a long essay "On the Philosophy of Art" for *Essays in Philosophical Criticism* (1883), a volume edited by Andrew Seth and R. B. Haldane (the later Lord Haldane) which has its importance in the history of British idealism. There Ker formulated the doctrine that art is "an end in itself" (*CE*, 2:241), that "its creations do not prove anything, they have no reference to things beyond themselves, they do not throw light upon the nature of things, they are themselves clear and definite objects." Works of art are "particular things" which "cannot be exhausted by any formula or expressed in words, as something whose relation to other things, to causes or effects or laws, is altogether a subordinate matter" (2:248). Hence "there is a point at which its history ceases, and only then does [the work of art] exist; before that it is not" (2:250). Works of art "remain intelligible in their own way, indifferent to science and history," "above the world of movement" (2:251), "raised above the flux of things" (2:259). Ker, however, seems to retract this abstract Platonism, saying that "art has its place in the development of human reason" (2:261) and that periods in art history "succeed one another according to the necessity of thought" (2:265), a Hegelian concept which seems implied also in his view that there is a "progress from art akin to religion to art akin to science" (2:168), where science presumably means knowledge, *Wissenschaft*. Ker preserved this double view of a timeless realm of art which is still somehow in relation to history. In an essay "On the Philosophy of History" (1909) he emphasizes the difference between political history and art history. "The historian of art is dealing with things present and alive," whereas "statesmen and generals are past and gone" (2:301).

Later this insight is specifically applied to literary history. In a lecture on Thomas Warton (1910) Ker defends the first historian of English poetry for his want of method. "Method, after all, is far less required in literary than in political history." "Literary history is more a guide-book than a geography" (*CE*, 1:100), or, phrased differently, "Literary history is like a museum, and a museum may be of use, even if ill arranged, the separate specimens may be studied by themselves" (in *On Modern Literature*, ed. T. Spencer and J. Sutherland [1955], an undatable fragment). He varies and develops these ideas, saying, "Art and literature are living things which assert themselves against the historian and cannot be made into a mere matter of narrative" (1:102), or, again, in an essay on Tennyson (1909): "The essence of a poem is that it should be remembered for what it is, not that it should be catalogued in an historical series in relation to what it is not" (1:261). This view has not, to my mind, been refuted.

Still, more and more Ker recognized the necessity of acknowledging historical change and the history of literature as a history of literary forms. In lectures at University College, London, given in 1912, he states expressly: "If the history of literature is to be properly a history, and not a series of biographies—lives of the poets and essays on their several works—then there must be a study of what is continuous and common, of the tendencies in which different authors share, the forms and fashions which they inherit, the origins of their art" (*Form and Style in Poetry,* ed. R. W. Chambers [1928], 50). He still insists that theoretically form is simply the poem itself. "The poem as an individual thing is all form; and what is not form in it is not poetry" (ibid., 98); a poem "does not live in its argument but in every single phrase and word and rhyme" (94). But then he modifies this Crocean emphasis on the unity, individuality, and uniqueness of a work of art by arguing that abstract ideas, patterns, genre concepts have an influence on the real work of poets: "The abstract form shows itself vital and inspiring" (101). Fashions in literature are fashions of the community at large. There are typical modes of development.

In practice, Ker wrote extensively on the history of prosody and particularly of stanzaic forms and constantly kept in mind the role of conventions, traditions, and poetical schools. The study of literature appears to him finally as a "compromise between taking poems as they stand on their own merits or as belonging to poetic schools, as stages in a process" (ibid., 165, dating from 1914–15), though Ker expressly disapproves of Brunetière's biological concept of genre evolution (*CE,* 1:328).

Ker quotes Flaubert's letter (1869, cf. this *History,* 4:11) which asks "when will the critic be an artist, but a real artist? Where do you know of a critic who cares about the work itself in an intense way?" and demands a study of its "unconscious poetics, its composition, its style, the point of view of the author," but Ker comments ruefully: "Yet that is in the future, if it is at all; we belong to the generation of historians" (*On Modern Literature,* a paper "On Criticism" [1889], 160). He remained a historian in spite of his ambition to become a critic, "to reckon every author as one individual, with his own particular story to tell, his own individual manner, his own value," and "not to judge abstractedly, but to see concretely, is the end and aim of it" (ibid., 162). Ultimately, with the exception of his analyses of metrical forms, Ker did not develop any analytical tools to satisfy his own ambition and the hopes of Flaubert. Most often he is content to substitute quotation for criticism and to point to the "ineffable" in poetry. He gave a lecture on Keats (1921) beginning with the helpless question "I ask you and myself what there is left to do or say" (*CE*, 1:224) and then went on quoting long passages with hardly any comment. Ker was a victim of the lecturing system.

He cared for Teutonic antiquity, for the Icelandic sagas, for Provençal lyrics, and for the "ocean of stories, the fortunate isles of romance" (*CE*, 1:147), but he also, somewhat incongruously, admired the eighteenth century as "one of the greatest ages of the world in artistic imagination" (*CE*, 1:76) and praised it for restraint, moderation, and "simple harmonies of spaces" (*CE*, 1:78). Burns was to him a "classical" author steeped in the conventions of Scottish poetry, though elsewhere he admits that there was no true classicism in English literature and nothing comparable to Racine (*On Modern Literature*, 220). Ker edited the *Essays* of Dryden with elaborate introduction and commentary but also lectured on Scott, Byron, Tennyson, and Browning and as Professor of Poetry in Oxford expounded Shelley, Milton, Pope, Molière, Matthew Arnold, Dante, and Boiardo (see *The Art of Poetry;* see *CE*, 1:305–35 for the Dante and Boiardo lectures delivered at Oxford), always praising, always commenting sensibly. But, like Oliver Elton, he could not emancipate himself from the basically eclectic, indiscriminately tolerant Victorian taste, its basic historicism.

Sir Herbert Grierson has earned the gratitude of all students of English literature by his edition, based on the manuscripts, of John Donne's poetry (1912), and his anthology, *Metaphysical Lyrics and Poems of the Seventeenth Century: Donne to Butler* (1921), which contains an introduction defining the "peculiar blend of passion and thought, feeling and ratiocination" (xvi) as the "greatest achievement" of the metaphysical poets. Eliot's essay "The Metaphysical Poets" was a review of Grierson's anthology, in the *TLS*.

Grierson's first book was a volume contributed to Saintsbury's "Periods of European Literature" on *The First Half of the Seventeenth Century* (1907). Like Elton's and Ker's volumes in the same series it was a skillful digest of information with a then unusual emphasis on Dutch literature, Hooft and Vondel in particular. The accounts of Italian and German developments are hardly more than compilations, and even the firsthand chapters on the English poets suffer from brevity and a lack of any overriding concept such as baroque. In discussing Donne, Grierson makes much of his "medieval scholasticism" clashing with his personal tone.

The book is limited to belles lettres: "exclusively literature conceived as an art" (360). Grierson's Inaugural as the successor of Saintsbury at Edinburgh, "The Background of English Literature" (1915), sketches rather the common assumptions of poet and audience in the knowledge of the Bible and the ancients throughout the history of English literature and deplores the decay of this "background." Kipling seems to him the first poet who made "no demand for a too literary and classical culture" (*The Background of English Literature*, 36). Grierson's Messenger lectures at Cornell University, *Cross Currents in English Literature of the Seventeenth Century* (1929), are then a study of the spiritual conflicts of the age, of humanism and puritanism from Spenser to Milton, whereas the late lectures *Milton and Wordsworth: Poets and Prophets. A Study of Their Reactions to Political Events* (1937) exult in the likeness of Grierson's two heroes to the Hebrew prophets, in the truth of their insights into the Puritan and French revolutions. At that time Grierson had turned to the task of editing a collection of the *Letters* of Sir Walter Scott (12 vols., 1932–37), and he wrote a life of *Sir Walter Scott, Bart* (1938) which supplemented and corrected Lockhart's.

Grierson's books and scattered papers collected in *Essays and Addresses* (1941) and *Criticism and Creation* (1949) have a tone of modest authority, a command of learning, also in the history of ideas, which includes an unusual awareness even of the work of Dilthey and Troeltsch in Germany, and a generous spirit which makes the disappointment with his *Critical History of English Poetry* (in collaboration with J. C. Smith, 1946) all the more acute. It is neither critical nor a history in the proper sense. It is not critical even within the limits of the "Victorian sensibility" with which the authors excuse their failure to do "justice to the poetry and criticism of the present day" (prefatory note). As it is impossible to isolate the exact shares of the two authors (J. C. Smith had edited Edmund Spenser and had written a little *Study of Wordsworth* [1944]), the book must be seen rather as a symptom of the state of literary history than as an expression of Grierson's personal views. One has to refer to Grierson's earlier writings to be convinced that his interest in the metaphysicals was something more than a misunderstanding. They are treated very briefly. Less than a page is devoted to Crashaw, merely to criticize him for "extravagance" and "ludicrous conceits" (*CH*, 165). Even George Herbert's "loving reasonable temper" is used only to excuse his "metrical flourishes" and "products of Fancy" (164). Pope is denied "enduring worth and influence" (220), and the view of his "penury of knowledge and vulgarity of sentiment" (127) is expressly endorsed. The romantics are treated in much greater detail. There are eighteen pages on Crabbe, compared to the twelve devoted to all the metaphysical poets together. Scott is exalted as a "great poet" who rises to "epic heights" (367). The attitude toward modern poetry is totally unsympathetic. The authors are puzzled even by Yeats, leaving "Sailing to Byzantium" to "younger readers, poets of tomorrow" (523). Instead we get fulsome praise of Laurence Binyon and hear even of the Rev. Andrew Young, Mrs. Rachel Annand Taylor, and Mrs. Fredegond Shove. The authors plead ingenuously that a "shift of sensibility" had occurred recently and that their "taste in poetry was formed in Victorian days." But this relativism would mean that there is no communication between generations, that the universe of critical discourse has to be broken up into splinters. Bad poetry is bad poetry as great poetry is great poetry, whatever its age and whatever our particular sensibility.

Even more disconcerting than the judgments is the helplessness of the authors in analyzing or even describing poetry. They merely ring changes on adjectives such as "superb, opulent, capital, lovely, delightful, charming." They think it worthwhile to quote Canon Beeching on a play by Samuel Daniel that it is "full from first to last of beautiful thoughts and beautiful writing" (92). They would tell us dogmatically that "blank verse is not the medium of satire" (72), that some poems of Sidney are songs and so "one remove farther from reality than the sonnets" (85), or that Milton's line "To save the Athenian walls from ruin bare" is "perhaps the most beautiful line in the language" (180), or that there is no such thing as free verse, which is a "contradiction in terms" (557). Reading Spenser, they tell us, is like "watching a color film move steadily across the screen to the sound of music" (83); *The Lady of Shallott* "is a landscape in water colour. And the picture is shown to the music of flutes" (442).

The book is not only poor criticism but also poor literary history. It shows an almost complete lack of awareness of the simplest methodological problems of writing literary history. The authors do not even attempt what one would think should be the preoccupation of a historian of English poetry: the continuity, the rise, the development, the changes and revolutions of the art of English poetry. They do not even clearly envisage the task of discussing a series of individual poets. Their method is a mere empirical hodgepodge of biography, bibliography, and anthology—mostly of small snippets, and indications of themes and verse-forms. They value biographical evidence very highly, to judge from the space devoted to it and to such complaints as the following: "We do not know enough of Thomson's [James Thomson, the Victorian poet] private life to connect his various moods in poetry with changes in his actual circumstances" (499). But nowhere is there a genuine attempt to use political, social, or even biographical contexts for an interpretation of the poetry. When any such gesture is made we get a simplistic view, such as the statement that the decline of Wordsworth's poetic powers was due to "overwork" (351).

This deplorable book merits attention as coming from a distinguished scholar. It is completely at sea as to the methods, aims, and even materials of literary history and reveals an ineptitude even at simple analysis which indicates that there was (or still is?) something radically wrong with the practice of literary history.

H. W. Garrod could easily be put down as a mere follower of Sir Walter Raleigh. I have quoted twice (in *Concepts of Criticism* [1963], 264, and in *Discriminations* [1970], 350) a passage that seems characteristic of this generation of scholars, in which Garrod praises criticism of poetry that "has been written *freest*, with the least worry of head, the least disposition to break the heart over ultimate questions" (*Poetry and the Criticism of Life*, 157). The critic, Garrod continues, "can afford to indulge his temperament. . . . He can be a creature of likes and dislikes." Many other indications—the praise of Hazlitt as "the greatest of English critics" (*PCL*, 150), the laudatory papers on Rupert Brooke, Humbert Wolfe, A. E. Housman, on the poetry of Robert Louis Stevenson, on Robert Bridges's *Testament of Beauty*, and on a topic such as "The Nightingale in Poetry"— set Garrod firmly in his time. There is no contradiction between such "impressionistic" criticism and concern for textual criticism. Garrod's edition of *The Poetical Works of John Keats* (1939), which lists variants in manuscripts and printed versions, is still considered a standard work.

But Garrod is not simply another case of the symbiosis of textual scholarship, external literary history, and impressionistic criticism so prevalent in England at that time. Actually he had a much more sophisticated view of poetry and criticism. Even a lecture on "how to know a good book from a bad" addressed to elementary school teachers shows that Garrod grasped the standard of authorial control and what he calls "to the point" writing, the whole concept of organic unity, and the ultimate appeal to the verdict of the ages, to tradition: "the only test that I know of a good book is the best books" (*The Profession of Poetry and Other Lectures*, 265). More ambitiously in another lecture, "The Methods of Criticism in Poetry," Garrod argues that there is "a solid body of agreed opinion" in the criticism of poetry (*PCL*, 155), and that all methods of criticism need to be used: the exegetical method, "appreciation" (which he disparages

as the "cooing and reciting school"), biographical studies, and criticism
in terms of political and social conditions. "I like all these methods" (160),
he says complacently, but then goes on to reject the subjectivism of Anatole France, arguing that there is a difference between recognizing that
truth is relative and partial and believing that truth is personal. Critics
cannot indulge in self-expression. Self-expression means nothing. Man
lives in a tradition: he is compelled to use words. He draws on other
minds. "I become aware how little, how nothing I have or am, which is
my own." "We are mere accomplices with the world." Even the great poet
expresses not himself, but "the prophetic soul of the great world." "It is
a commonplace that the success of a stage-play depends quite as much
upon the audience as upon the actors. . . . The public acts the play; and
in a sense it writes it" (165). Here some of the new extreme formulations
of the reader's share in creation are anticipated. There is truth in Garrod's rejection of the view that the poet is simply a mouthpiece of his
age. He may, he argues, live with his poetry in another age, even in the
age of Pericles (166). The objection to a unilinear concept of time is well
taken, but Garrod avoids a solution by escaping into the old idea of the
timelessness of poetry. "For poetry, nothing happens in time. If it did,
poetry would be history" (167). At the end he finds "no difficulty in
supposing that the world-consciousness which speaks in poetry is a consciousness before and after." "That makes it possible to speak of laws of
poetry," he says obscurely. Garrod knows of course the argument that
"there are no laws of poetry, because they are so often violated. By the
same token, there are no Ten Commandments" (153). If the poet proves
too much for the laws, they are changed as laws are changed in a state
without ceasing to be laws. But Garrod does not go any further: we need
not be conscious of these laws as we need not know the laws of our body.
He then continues with the anti-theoretical position that I quoted at the
beginning, out of context.

On some central issues (I would not call them laws but standards of
judgment) Garrod is of a divided mind. As a student of Aristotle he
accepts the universal and the type as standard and rejects consistent
realism: "to put in everything, and to let things speak for themselves.
But just this is the trouble of realism. If you let things speak for themselves, they will never be done talking. They perish of their own volu-
bility" (*PP,* 21), but then Garrod quotes an open letter addressed to him
by John Alexander Smith, an Aristotelian scholar, on *The Nature of Art*
(1924), which argues in terms explicitly derived from Croce, that poetry
consists "in a kind of hunger and thirst for that which is individual." Its
purpose is "to exhibit objects, not in their universal connexions, but in

their individuality . . . as wholes, as momentary perfections, as arrests of chance and the stream of appearance, each of them a something cogent in itself, a *that* and not a *what,* its own logic, its own living body—that is what all poetry is after" (*PP,* 25). But again Garrod evades a decision and takes refuge in his distrust of theory: "If a man comes to a conclusion, look to your spoons and forks; for there is no truth in him. I am left with the half of Aristotle and Wordsworth, of intellectualism and sensationalism, still on my hands" (28). There is ineptitude but also wisdom in Garrod's oscillations and gropings.

There are no vacillations in the small books on *Wordsworth: Lectures and Essays* (1923), *Keats* (1926), and *Collins* (1928). They are rather dogmatically stated, often opinionated and captious close readings of poems—not close readings in the sense of the New Criticism but examinations of the difficulties of understanding the words, phrases, and connections. The book on Wordsworth is the most dated today, partly because new manuscripts of the *Prelude* have turned up, and partly because Garrod's concern with ideology, with sensationalism, Godwin, and the model of Coleridge as philosophical poet seems excessive. The polemic against G. M. Harper's conception of Wordsworth is, however, justified: "The Byronic Wordsworth is on the whole more untrue, I believe, than 'Daddy Wordsworth' " (22), and the analysis of the preface to *Lyrical Ballads* is acute. Garrod professes "to adhere to interpretation, and to eschew literary criticism in the larger sense" (10). But this is hardly true of many pages, particularly the elaborate ranking of the poems in *Lyrical Ballads* (148–49).

The book on Keats sharply reasserts the old view of Keats as a poet of the senses. Garrod recognizes his political interests and his ambition to philosophize but thinks that in "this vacillation between the sense and mind, lies not his strength, but his weakness" (35). All the emphasis falls on the *Odes. Endymion* and the allegory of *Hyperion: A Vision* are disparaged. "I think him the great poet he is only when the senses capture him, when he finds truth in beauty, that is to say, when he does not trouble to find truth at all" (61). More recent criticism has gone all the other way.

The little book on Collins avoids all excess; it very properly dismisses Swinburne's gushing celebration of Collins's lucidity and instead examines the obscurities of his syntax, the difficulties of his diction, and comments often extensively on Collins's failure "to achieve true harmony between what he is saying and what he has already said" (76), even in the greatly admired "Ode to Evening."

"Jane Austen: A Depreciation" elaborates the objections Emerson made against the cult of Jane Austen: her world is narrow, a social back-water, she has no interest or grasp of public issues. "Her village has no room for either God or the poor. Nature is also rigidly excluded" (33). No one in a book of Jane Austen's has any work to do. Her plots are thin and monotonous, her ethical standards are low, tolerating "such worn and shabby institutions as simony, nepotism, and the marriage of convenience" (30). Garrod grants her only one merit: acuteness of observation, a skill in what he considers Theophrastian character-drawing. For all his donnishness Garrod seems to be a better critic than his peers in this group.

3: THE BLOOMSBURY GROUP

IN AN ESSAY on Bloomsbury Clive Bell doubts whether Bloomsbury ever existed and asks whether it is "a point of view, a period, a gang of conspirators, or an infectious disease" (*Old Friends,* 126). Still, he can tell us who belonged, in 1899, to a group of undergraduates in Cambridge, and who then met and continued meeting from 1904 on in a house rented by Vanessa and Virginia Stephen at 46 Gordon Square, Bloomsbury. The two sisters, daughters of the recently deceased biographer and critic Leslie Stephen, later married to Clive Bell and Leonard Woolf respectively, had friendly relations with the economist John Maynard Keynes, the biographer Lytton Strachey, the art critic Roger Fry, the theater critic Desmond MacCarthy, and the novelist Edward Morgan Forster. Bell shirks the question of whether there was anything in common to the aesthetic and critical outlook of these friends. Keynes, an early member of the group, considered the influence of G. E. Moore's *Principia Ethica* decisive. He quoted Moore's assertion that "by far the most valuable things, which we know or can imagine, are certain states of consciousness, which may be roughly described as the pleasure of human intercourse and the enjoyment of beautiful objects."[1] "Nothing mattered," said Keynes, "except states of mind, our own and other people's of course, but chiefly our own. These states of mind were not associated with action or achievement or with consequences. They consisted in timeless, passionate states of contemplation and communion, largely unattached to 'before' and 'after.'" An aesthetic approach to life is implied. "We repudiated customary morals, conventions and traditional wisdom. We were, that is to say, in the strict sense of the term, immoralists."[2] The recent biographies of Keynes, Strachey, Virginia Woolf, E. M. Forster, Vanessa Bell, and Vita Sackville-West, as well as the publication of an early novel by E. M. Forster, have immensely widened our knowledge of their sexual emancipation and emotional entanglements. But one cannot say that they remained apart from the world of action and achievement. Virginia Woolf, at least, became an ardent feminist, pacifist, and socialist.

Nor can one say that their aesthetics was simply that of "art for art's sake" or even a search for "timeless, passionate states of communion." With our broader perspective we can distinguish them clearly from contemporary critics. They never (or hardly ever) claim for the aesthetic state the status of mystical insight as Middleton Murry, D. H. Lawrence, or G. Wilson Knight would. They did not anticipate or share the classicism of T. S. Eliot, his view of the impersonality of poetry and the power of tradition, or his and T. E. Hulme's violent anti-romanticism. Nor could they accept I. A. Richards's psychological scientism and sympathize with F. R. Leavis's moralism. But this sense of distinction from the other main trends and figures of English criticism should not obscure the diversity of the actual critical views and practice of this group associated in friendship and in a cliquish self-conscious superiority. We have to discuss separately the criticism of each in order to bring out the individuality of the members of the group and to judge them not as cases but as critical personalities. We need briefly to consider the art critics Roger Fry and Clive Bell.

ROGER FRY (1866–1934) AND CLIVE BELL (1881–1964)

Roger Fry was, oddly enough, impressed by Tolstoy's *What is Art?*, not, of course, by his "preposterous valuation of works of art" but "by his luminous criticism of past aesthetic systems" and by his decision (derived from Eugène Véron) that art is not concerned with the beautiful but is "a means of communication between human beings" (*VD*, 292–93). This highly social and communal view of art is modified and sometimes contradicted by Fry's insistence on the purely personal reaction to a work of art. "The critic," he says, "must work with the only instrument he possesses—namely his own sensibility with all its personal equations" (285). Fry thus has to defend "the complete relativity of everything to human nature and the impossibility of talking at all about things in themselves. It's curious how difficult it is to root out the mediaeval habit of thinking of 'substances,' of things existing apart from all relations."[3] Fry still can say that "the greatest art has always been communal, the expression—in highly individualized ways, no doubt—of common aspirations and ideals," but he expresses fears about the freedom of the artist in a future socialist society, which he can envisage only as "aiming at human freedom," as "an organisation for leisure out of which art grows," a naively Utopian vision belied by recent history (*VD*, 62, 77–78). Ordinarily Fry argues that "the usual assumption of direct and decisive connection between life and art is by no means correct." Art "is open at times to influences from life but in the main self-contained—we find the rhythmic sequences of change determined much more of its own internal forces" than by external influences (9). He can even assert that "art has no connection with morals" and none with sex.[4]

In practice, Fry became the main advocate of post-impressionist art: he arranged the exhibition of November 1910 which showed Cézanne, Gauguin, Van Gogh, and Matisse for the first time in England, and he constantly argued for the rejection of both realistic and impressionistic art, accepting even the logical conclusion in abstract or nonrepresentational art. "Content," he argues, is "merely directive of form. . . . All the essential aesthetic quality has to do with pure form." Referring expressly to poetry, he asserts that "as poetry becomes more intense the content is entirely remade by the form and has no separate value at all."[5] Fry accepts the existence of a special art-emotion, but he admits that the ideal of pure art is only an ideal. In practice "the aesthetic emotion has greater value in highly complicated compounds than in the pure state." Art has a peculiar quality of "reality" which makes it a "matter of infinite importance." He concludes with a characteristic gesture of resignation. "Any attempt I might make to explain this would probably land me in the depths of mysticism. On the edge of that gulf I stop" (VD, 301–02).

Logically Fry later rejected the challenge of I. A. Richards to any kind of separate aesthetic experience. Richards's argument that in looking at a picture or reading a poem or listening to music we are not doing anything different from what we are doing on our way to the gallery or when we dress in the morning is unconvincing. Fry appeals to A. C. Bradley's lecture on "Poetry for Poetry's Sake" and discusses the conflict between pure form and representation which Richards disposed of by calling it "co-operative." Fry illustrates the spectrum from Breughel's representational art to Poussin's formal design and sees it as a tension and conflict (T, 2f., 8, 20). In his last years Fry was impressed by Charles Mauron, a Frenchman who later developed what he called "psychocritique." From him Fry drew the metaphor of "psychological volumes" in literature on the analogy of the plastic volumes in the fine arts (8).[6] Plastic, or tactile, is a term derived from Berenson which it seems impossible to transfer to literature with any precision. Fry's achievements were largely in educating the public in the new art of the century: in rejecting the illustrative realism of the Victorians and downgrading the contribution of the impressionists as a step in the right direction but lacking in the form and organization he found in Cézanne and the early Picasso. Fry has a skill in interpreting pictures, in finding a vocabulary for the description of art works (he owed something to Wölfflin on this

point) which was new in England, accustomed to the moralizing or
vaguely impressionistic vocabulary derived from Ruskin.

Actually, Clive Bell, with *Art* (1913), had a wider impact by the very
radicalism with which he stated his position and the invention of the
slogan of "significant form." It seems a good term to suggest that art is
form but form that means something beyond formal relations, points to
a reality, expresses or conveys an emotion. But in Bell the term *significant*
is used to reject any "representation" and "illusion." The "representative"
element, we are told, is "always irrelevant." "For, to appreciate a work of
art we need bring with us nothing from life, no knowledge of its ideas
and affairs, no familiarity with its emotions. Art transports us from the
world of man's activity to a world of aesthetic exaltation" (*A,* 27). In a
chapter entitled "The Metaphysical Hypothesis" Clive Bell suggests
rather hesitatingly that we prefer the aesthetic exaltation from a work of
art to that from a work of nature (a flower, the wing of a butterfly)
because we are moved by the emotion of the human creator, or even that
"significant form" is form behind which we catch a sense of ultimate
reality. Clive Bell refuses to return a positive answer to the question "Why
are we so profoundly moved by certain combinations of forms?" but
recognizes that "we become aware of essential reality, of the God in
everything, of the universal in the particular, of the all-pervading
rhythm" (43, 46, 48, 54). He even argues that "all artists are religious"
because "all uncompromising belief is religious." Art and religion are,
then, two roads by which men escape from "circumstance to ecstasy."
"The great ages of religion are commonly the great ages of art." But "to
criticize a work of art historically is to play the science-besotted fool. No
more disastrous theory ever issued from the brain of a charlatan than
that of evolution in art." Art does not progress (68, 71, 75). In similar
simple terms the question of art and ethics is decided. "To pronounce
anything a work of art," Bell asserts, is to make "a momentous moral
judgment." We assign it to a class of objects which bring about spiritual
exaltation (84–85). As to art and society, "the one good thing Society
can do for the artist is to leave him alone." Art, in turn, may "leaven
society; perhaps even redeem it," but it remains unclear how this could
come about except by some withdrawal which is also a purification. "He
who has once lost himself in an 'O Altitudo' will not be tempted to
overestimate the fussy excitements of action." What remains and "all that
matter are the aesthetic emotion and its immediate object" (167, 181,
190, 183).

Bell's book with all its gestures toward metaphysical and religious pretensions for art established for him a standard which allowed him also

to define his literary taste.[7] In literature he appealed to "an absolute standard based on the whole *corpus* of that art" which, as in painting, made him call "realists" such as H. G. Wells, George Moore, and Galsworthy "not artists at all" (*Potboilers*, 12, 11). He admired Hardy, Conrad, Virginia Woolf, Anatole France, and the new discovery, Proust. His little book on *Proust* (1928) rehearses well enough the standard complaints against his neglect of action, his long sentences, his snobbery, to defend him on every point. Bell explains Proust's method as "a series of carefully planned explosions by means of which the submerged past is brought into the present, the deep-sea monsters of memory to the surface." The form of the novel is defined as "a shape in time" and his outlook on love and life as nihilistic. But Proust had his illusions. "He believed that art and thought signify something" (*Proust*, 41, 45, 85). In the light of later Proust criticism the booklet will appear slight and modest. After Middleton Murry's essay in 1922 and the *English Tribute* to Proust (1923) to which Bell had contributed, Bell's enthusiasm marks a climax of the long love-affair of the English with Proust.

In an article on "The Creed of an Aesthete" (1922) Bell attacked Shaw's *Back to Methuselah* and its dismal prognosis by asserting that "people who really care for beauty do not care for it because it comes from God or leads to anything. They care for it in itself; what is more, that is how they care for all the fine things in life," and he argues that "the antecedents of Mozart's music and of my feelings have nothing to do with the value of either." Shaw in return called Bell "a fathead and a voluptuary" but more seriously argued that "we don't and won't, and can't live in the present." The clash between aestheticism and didacticism could not have been stated more succinctly.

Clearly these two art critics cannot be said to have formulated anything like a Bloomsbury creed. Their influence was far from pervasive and their writings too remote from concrete literary criticism to matter very much. We must take up the individual figures in the group to go beyond generalizations about aestheticism or impressionism and to see them at work as critics.

LYTTON STRACHEY (1880–1932)

Lytton Strachey's reputation rests on his biographies. His first great success was *Eminent Victorians* (1918), a collection of satirical sketches of Cardinal Manning, Florence Nightingale, Thomas Arnold, and General Gordon, which was followed by a much milder and even gentle biography of *Queen Victoria* (1921). But Strachey was also a literary critic who must

be seen somewhere in the wake of Sainte-Beuve and Pater, a deft propounder of a tolerant historicist creed, skeptical of theory and dogmatism, temperamentally in sympathy with the eighteenth century but
imaginative enough to admire Shakespeare, Milton, and the English romantics from Wordsworth to Beddoes.

Strachey's first paper, "Two Frenchmen" (Vauvenargues and La Bruyère), dates back to 1903, when he was 23. Its first sentence sounds a
main motif of his writing: "The greatest misfortune that can happen to
a witty man is to be born out of France." He was that witty man himself,
and the two moralists he discusses use what will become Strachey's main
forms of writing—aphorisms, meditations, and portraits. Even then
Strachey protests against a lack of historical sense. Against the odd view
of Vauvenargues's English translator that his work "betrays no sign of
the age in which it was written," Strachey argues that Vauvenargues was
rather "typically eighteenth century." In both writers Strachey recognizes
his own stylistic ideal: "absolute precision, complete finish, perfect proportion" (CC, 67, 69, 67), which he finds realized in the French tradition
and the French language in general.

His first book, Landmarks in French Literature (1912), is a short handbook written for the Home University Library which, often from sketchy
secondhand knowledge and with surprising omissions, manages to convey not only information but also genuine enthusiasm for the great classical writers of France, Racine and Voltaire in particular. The little book
displays Strachey's joy in evoking the age of Louis XIV.

> When the morning sun was up and the horn was sounding down
> the long avenues, who would not wish, if only in fancy, to join the
> glittering cavalcade when the young Louis led the hunt in the days
> of his opening glory? Later, we might linger on the endless terrace,
> to watch the great monarch, with his red heels and his golden snuff-
> box and his towering periwig, come out among his courtiers, or in
> some elaborate grotto applaud a ballet by Molière. (LFL, 64f.)

It displays his skill in characterizing—though Strachey indulges excessively in paradoxes, antitheses, and sometimes tiresome clichés. It displays his love of hyperbole: Voltaire's prose is "the final embodiment of
the most characteristic qualities of the French genius. If all that great
nation had ever done or thought were abolished from the world, except
a single sentence of Voltaire's, the essence of their achievement would
have survived" (180f.). More persuasively Strachey makes sometimes
genuine critical observations. La Fontaine's creatures

are animals with the minds which human beings would certainly have, if one could suppose them transformed into animals. When the young and foolish rat sees a cat for the first time and observes to his mother—

> "Je le crois fort sympathisant
> Avec messieurs les rats; car il a des oreilles
> En figure aux nôtres pareilles;"

this excellent reason is obviously not a rat's reason; nor is it a human being's reason; the fun lies in its being just the reason which, no doubt, a silly young creature of the human species would give in the circumstances if, somehow or other, he were metamorphosed into a rat. (113)

All the emphasis falls on the seventeenth and eighteenth centuries. The Middle Ages are surveyed hurriedly, and the Renaissance except for Rabelais is slighted. Surprisingly, Montaigne, we are told, "was neither a great artist nor a great philosopher; he was not *great* at all" (40). In the accounts of Pascal, La Rouchefoucauld, and La Bruyère there are quotations woven in and stressed which show a side of Strachey's mind not usually on display: his melancholy and low view of the human condition, an undercurrent he senses also behind Molière's laughter and admires in Voltaire and Rousseau at their gloomiest. But Strachey becomes positively lyrical when he exalts Racine against the neglect of the English, an argument he had expounded in an earlier essay,[1] or when he dilates on Voltaire, to whom he devoted several papers, concerning his stay in England, his dealings with Frederick the Great (to which he gives a different slant from that of Carlyle), and his tragedies, which he denigrates in favor of Racine's. Voltaire's plays are "mere *tours de force*," his characters are "marionettes" compared with Racine's "edifice of subtle psychology, of exquisite poetry, of overwhelming passion" in spite of the "whole intolerable paraphernalia of the Classical stage" (*BC*, 129, 132, 130).

In two cases Strachey directly challenges comparison with Sainte-Beuve. The essays on Mademoiselle de Lespinasse and on Madame du Duffand have the same topic as Sainte-Beuve's *Lundis* on these two ladies. Strachey even tells the same anecdotes, for example, that of Père Massillon suggesting the present of a "threepenny Catechism" to the young girl who became Madame du Duffand.[2] Though Strachey uses the same quotations, he still comes out well in the comparison. Strachey's essays are better organized, freer of redundancies, finer in psychological penetration, more moved and moving, as when he quotes Dante at the end of the essay on Mademoiselle de Lespinasse or concludes with the farewell letter Madame du Duffand wrote on her deathbed to Horace Walpole.

Sainte-Beuve at the same juncture ends with the sentimental business about the dog Tonton.[3]

Still, it is not right to limit Strachey's literary criticism to his praise of the French classical age. The English eighteenth century is as much his domain. The essays on the English letter writers which belong to Strachey's earliest work (1905; *CC*, 3–64) center properly on Lady Mary Montagu, Lord Chesterfield, Horace Walpole, Gray, and Cowper, while Walpole and Lady Mary are the subjects of other essays. The late lecture on Alexander Pope (1925) excited the resentment of the growing community of Pope's new admirers by a passage in which the verses of the *Satires* and the *Epistles* are said to resemble "nothing so much as spoonfuls of boiling oil ladled out by a fiendish monkey at an upstairs window upon such passers-by whom the wretch had a grudge against" (261–77). But the lecture should be corrected by an earlier review which recognizes Pope's tenderness, his power of affection, his sincere and generous friendship with the Blounts, his profound admiration for Swift, and his devotion to his mother, sufficient amends to make Pope's moral character a "battle-ground of discordant emotions."[4] The emphasis of both the lecture and the early review is, however, on Pope as "an artist of supreme genius" who "succeeded in expressing passion, not by means of his medium, but in spite of it." The defense of Pope's poetry against Matthew Arnold, of the couplet as a stimulus precisely with its purely arbitrary conventions,[5] of the poems' sensuous beauty, occasional harsh realism, and poetic criticism of life, fits in with Strachey's general admiration for almost all major English authors of the eighteenth century, "that most balmy time" of "sweet reasonableness" (*PM*, 156f.). Strachey defends Restoration comedy against the extremes of Macaulay's moral indignation and Lamb's belief in its fairy-tale irrelevancy. Pure comedy "depends for its existence on the construction of a conventional world in which, while human nature and human actions are revealed, their consequences are suspended. The characters in Comedy are real, but they exist *in vacuo*" (47). The praise of Vanbrugh dwells on the contrast between his architecture, "the embodiment of massive grandeur," and his drama, "all light and air" (*CC*, 160). An essay on James Thomson comments, in a rare stylistic observation, on the "use of the definite article" in the *Seasons* to produce "the most indefinite effects." Strachey vastly prefers *The Castle of Indolence*, which he sees as anticipating the early work of Keats (*SE*, 155, 158). But Strachey cared more for letter writers, historians, and biographers than for poets. Gibbon's *Decline and Fall of the Roman Empire* is "a masterpiece of enormous erudition and perfect form" (*PM*, 156) and Boswell triumphed as a letter writer and biographer because he had "no pride, no shame, and no dignity." "Boswell was *ex hypothesi* absurd; it was his absurdity that was the essential condition of his consummate art" (91).

Strachey's sympathy with the century fails in one respect. He cannot accept its criticism. Dr. Johnson, he thinks, "was not, in essence, a critic of literature; he was a critic of life." Johnson had breadth and sanity of outlook but his aesthetic judgments, while "almost invariably subtle, or solid, or bold," were never right. He "judged authors as if they were criminals in the dock." He did not understand tragedy. He "never inquired what poets were trying to do," whereas Strachey considers "the first duty of [the critic] not to criticise, but to understand the objects of his criticism." He praises "the quality of sympathy without which all criticism is a vain and empty thing" (*SE*, 6of.; *BC*, 60, 61, 64, 61; *SE*, 110f.). Sympathy, however, means not surrender but rather tolerance, detachment. Hume appeals to him with his "consummate success in the divine art of impartiality. And certainly to have no axe to grind is something very noble and very rare. It may be said to be the antithesis of the bestial" (*PM*, 141). With such detachment Strachey looks at the literary stockmarket. "Donne still rising, Stevenson rapidly collapsing, Shakespeare safe, Wordsworth a good sound investment, but he yields only 2½ percent," a metaphor since exploited by T. S. Eliot and Northrop Frye (*CC*, 155). Strachey simply recognizes several standards. "It is strange to reflect that, until quite lately, the notion that there might be more than one species of literary excellence was almost unknown to criticism," he says, and he acts on this insight (*Spectator* 101:266; quoted by Sanders, 77). He can admire both Racine and Shakespeare, Pope and Hardy, Donne and Dostoevsky. *Elizabeth and Essex* (1928), his last biography, should not have come as a surprise. Much of his criticism had been devoted to Shakespeare. One essay, "Shakespeare's Final Period" (*BC*, 41ff.), protests the view propounded by Dowden and Brandes that Shakespeare's last plays reflect serenity and harmony. Strachey quotes passages of bitter despair, virulent denunciation, and gross laughter to ask whether "in this world of dreams, we are justified in ignoring nightmares." He concludes, extravagantly, that Shakespeare was "bored with people, bored with real life, bored with drama, bored, in fact, with everything except poetry and poetical dreams." The last period is not "serene, nor benign, nor pastoral, nor 'On the Heights' " (Dowden's label) (51, 52, 56). But Strachey's answer seems as sentimental as the serenity of its propounders. Oddly enough, at the beginning of this essay Strachey questions the "tacit assumption, that the character of any given drama is, in fact, a true index to the state of mind of the dramatist composing it" (41), only to dismiss it as outside the purpose of the essay, though one would think an answer might undermine the whole thesis. More soberly, in a later essay, the introduction to George Ryland's *Words and Poetry* (1928), one of the first books to pay close attention to Shakespeare's verbal art, Strachey again disparages Shakespeare's later works. "Character has grown unindividual and unreal; drama has become conventional or operatic; the words remain more tremendously, more exquisitely, more thrillingly alive than ever" (*CC*, 287). In the great Shakespearean tragedies Strachey always recognizes "the immense complexity and passionate force" (*Spectator* 102:185; quoted by Sanders, 89). His last unfinished essay on *Othello* (1931) is an effort to push Coleridge's unconvincing argument for Iago's "motiveless malignity" even further. Shakespeare, deliberately changing Cinthio's story, "determined that Iago should have no motive at all" (*CC*, 289ff., 295).

Of all Shakespeare's contemporaries Strachey admired Donne most, as a "religious, sensual, erudite, passionate and argumentative" poet, singling out "The Anniversaries" as his most characteristic work as early as 1913 in a review of Grierson's great edition (*SE*, 91f.). Strachey also shares in the revival of Sir Thomas Browne, whose style he sees reborn in Dr. Johnson, Burke, and Gibbon. "*The Decline and Fall* could not have been precisely what it is, had Sir Thomas Browne never written *Christian Morals*" (*BC,* 30).

Strachey had a weakness for the romantic poet Thomas Lovell Beddoes, whom he extolled as "The Last Elizabethan." Beddoes belongs with Spenser, Keats, and Milton. "Who cares about what Milton had to say? It is his way of saying it that matters; it is his expression" (*BC*, 211). The divorce between art and life, matter and style, sound and sense is here reasserted with a gross simplification. Usually Strachey struggles with the issue more discreetly. He admires Wordsworth for his grandiloquence, his mixture of Latinized diction and Anglo-Saxon which he illustrates by the effect of the word "diurnal" in the verse "rolled round in earth's diurnal course, with rocks, and stones, and trees" (*SE*, 164). In contrast, Strachey praises Hardy's new volume of verse as "full of poetry; and yet it is full of ugly and cumbrous expressions, clumsy metres, and flat, prosaic turns of speech" (*CC*, 182). He sympathizes with Hardy's pessimism, with the little cruel scenes of human failures and hatreds, regardless of the quality of the verse, and he can find good words even for Carlyle's "grim satiric humour" though his "ears are deafened by the roar and rattle of that inexhaustible artillery" of his style (*PM*, 183).

Strachey's wide sympathies fail before mysticism and prophecy. Blake, "an intellectual drunkard," becomes the occasion for condemning mysticism for its "lack of humanity" (BC, 188, 187). The "prophetic" Victorian is his special aversion. Yet in the atmosphere of Bloomsbury's enthusiasm for Dostoevsky he was carried away. An essay on the *Brothers Karamazov* is surprisingly laudatory, though Strachey is upset by its loose composition and the feverish atmosphere (*SE*, 174). He likens Dostoevsky to Jacobean dramatists but has the good sense, rare at that time and place, to see Dostoevsky also as "A Russian Humorist." He comments on Madame Epanchin in *The Idiot* and on Stefan Trofimovich in *The Possessed*. Stefan is a nineteenth-century Don Quixote whose death recalls that of Cervantes's hero (*CC*, 168ff., 173).

Strachey, the son of General Sir Richard Strachey, who had a long career in India, reacted violently against the Victorian age, "its incoherence, its pretentiousness, its incurable lack of detachment, its incapability of criticism," its "eccentricity and provincialism" (*CC*, 174, 175; *PM*, 182), to quote from articles and not from *Eminent Victorians*, which with their mocking tone gained him the reputation of a callous "debunker." But Strachey's literary criticism, with all the limits of his sympathies, errs rather by indiscriminate sympathy. The point of view is historic. Strachey is thinking in terms of a history of sentiment. He envisages a "historian of manners [who] might draw up an instructive series of moral fashion-plates, which would display, for each preceding generation, the good and evil most in vogue" (*CC*, 115). Roman magnanimity, medieval holiness, Renaissance virtue, eighteenth-century "humanity" are recalled. Strachey evokes and sometimes imitates the exuberance of the Elizabethans, the baroque splendor of Sir Thomas Browne, the "glowing, living, soaring and enchanting" art of Racine (*BC*, 130), the peace of the Augustans, and what he considered the coarseness and narrowness of the Victorians. His criticism can be thought of as exemplification of such a historical scheme.

VIRGINIA WOOLF (1882–1941)

Almost everyone who has discussed the criticism of Virginia Woolf has labeled her an "impressionist" and has quoted a passage from her essay on "Modern Fiction" (1919): life is "a luminous halo, a semi-transparent envelope surrounding us from the beginning of consciousness to the end." The new novelists are exhorted: "Let us record the atoms as they fall upon the mind in the order in which they fall, let us trace the pattern, however disconnected and incoherent in appearance, which each sight or incident scores upon the consciousness" (*CR*, 149). Here she speaks, however, about life and the new novelists including herself, defining her ambition, and not about criticism. Her own criticism, though often metaphorical and even whimsically personal, is wrongly described in terms of "atoms falling on the mind" and even of "patterns scored upon the consciousness." Philosophically, Virginia Woolf was no idealist, no Bergsonian, not even a British empiricist, but a fervent adherent of G. E. Moore, whom she studied with real effort in 1908 and quoted even in her novels.[1] Moore advocated a modern "realism," that is, he distinguishes between acts of consciousness and objects related to but distinct from those acts. Particulars exist outside of the mind. While Virginia Woolf's views must not be pressed into a philosophical scheme, she clearly aims, at least in her criticism, at grasping an object, and she did not and could not approve either of the solipsism implied in Anatole France's "adventures of the soul among masterpieces" or Pater's view of man's imprisonment in his own mind and body or of the imposition of one's ego on works of art demanded by "creative criticism."

Virginia Woolf did not, of course, ignore the share of art in the composition of her essays, deft, well-ordered, well-phrased, nor could she neglect the importance of the practitioner's experience for the critic. She goes very far in denying the value of criticism not nourished by the "excitement, the adventure, the turmoil of creation." The critics "who get to the heart of the matter" are Keats, Coleridge, Lamb, Flaubert, rather than academic professors such as Walter Raleigh—who, she recognizes, actually had a hankering for a life of action and despised criticism—or such a cautious, decorous journalist as Edmund Gosse, who "like all critics who persist in judging without creating forgets the risk and agony of childbirth" (CDB, 90; M, 91). Still, Virginia Woolf is entirely aware of the distinction between creation and criticism and often assigns a limited and even humble function to criticism. The critic is to tell us how to read, is himself a "common reader" in a sense in which she deliberately misread Dr. Johnson's "rejoicing to concur with the common reader" in the Life of Gray. Virginia Woolf's reader reads for his own pleasure. "He is guided by an instinct to create for himself, out of whatever odds and ends he can come by, some kind of whole—a portrait of a man, a sketch of an age, a theory of the art of writing," all demands quite remote from Johnson's common reader, who is simply a reader "uncorrupted by literary prejudice," free from the "refinements of subtilty [sic] and the dogmatism of learning" (CR, 11).

Virginia Woolf does concern herself with the "portrait of a man"—many of her essays are biographical, and she herself practiced the art on a larger scale in her book on Roger Fry (1940) and even in Orlando

(1928), a fictionalized account of the Sackville family over the centuries. She is also concerned with a "sketch of an age," often evoking the social setting and the atmosphere of a bygone period; or she does, on occasion, say something about a "theory of the art of writing," reflecting on the share of consciousness, on what she calls the "undermind," or asserting the importance of "conviction," "a rare gift" she found in Chaucer, "shared in our day by Joseph Conrad in his earlier novels" (*CR*, 23).

Still, she is aware that none of these concerns of the common reader are central to the business of criticism. She can even ridicule the preoccupation with biography. Commenting on Defoe, she complains that the date of his birth, his ancestors, his occupation as a hosier, his wife and six children, his sharp chin can take up much more time than reading *Robinson Crusoe* through from cover to cover (*SCR*, 42). It seems to her a "wise precaution to limit one's study of a writer to the study of his works" (*GR*, 167). Still, she always returns to the view that "somewhere, everywhere, now hidden, now apparent in whatever is written down is the form of a human being" (*CDB*, 175). But she envies the Greeks who "remain in a fastness of their own. Fate has been kind there too. She has preserved them from vulgarity. Euripides was eaten by dogs; Aeschylus killed by a stone; Sappho leapt from a cliff. We know no more of them than that. We have their poetry and that is all" (*CR*, 32). "The only question of any interest is whether that poetry is good or bad" (*SCR*, 218). Virginia Woolf drowned herself. Her biographer and nephew, Quentin Bell, has not, alas "preserved" her "from vulgarity."

Similarly, she loves to sketch the minutiae of an age, to evoke its peculiar atmosphere, to tell "the lives of the obscure," to speak of the Pastons and their letters as an introduction to Chaucer or of Hakluyt's *Voyages* as the "Elizabethan lumber-room." She often sees writers of the great masterpieces in terms that would have been comprehensible to Hippolyte Taine or her father as "the outcome of many years of thinking in common, of thinking by the body of the people, so that the experience of the mass is behind the single voice" (*ROO*, 97–98). But she reflects that Shakespeare's plays "are of no use whatever as 'applied sociology.' If we had to depend upon them for a knowledge of the social and economic conditions of Elizabethan life, we should be hopelessly at sea" (*GR*, 19). Great art transcends the ages but is rooted in its age. Virginia Woolf did not believe in art existing out of time and place or in *l'art pour l'art*, as she has often been accused of doing. She has a lively historical sense, a feeling for the color of England in different ages, and a feeling, rare at that time, for the changes in the audience of literature and the interplay between author and reader, text and response. Thus she speaks of the early readers of Sidney's *Arcadia*: "Each has read differently, with the insight and the blindness of his own generation. Our reading will be equally partial. In 1930 we shall miss a great deal that was obvious to 1655; we shall see some things that the eighteenth century ignored" (*SCR*, 32). A book, she knows, "is always written for somebody to read," for "writing is a method of communication" and "to know whom to write for is to know how to write." The fate of literature "depends upon a happy alliance" between writers and readers (*CR*, 205, 206, 207, 209).

Several times Virginia Woolf sketches a history of the economic support of English literature, contrasting the single patron, Sidney's Lady Pembroke, with the "vast miscellaneous crowd" of later times, quoting Goldsmith's well-known account of the decline of patronage in the eighteenth century (*CDB*, 3–4). She worries continually about the role of reviewing in her own time. In an extravagant article she proposes its abolition on the grounds that favorable and unfavorable reviews cancel each other out nowadays. She makes the unpractical proposal to replace reviewing with interviews of the author with a critic who would proffer advice for a fee (127–42). The importance of reviewing for the reading public rather than for the writer is hardly considered. She is rather concerned with the writer's declared or implied attitude to his readers. Samuel Butler, George Meredith, and Henry James were still conscious of their "public, yet superior to it." "Each despised the public; each desired a public; each failed to attain a public; and each wreaked his failure upon the public by a succession, gradually increasing in intensity, of angularities, obscurities, and affections which no writer whose patron was his equal and friend would have thought it necessary to inflict" (*CR*, 206). This is merely one example to support the truth that "undoubtedly all writers are immensely influenced by the people who read them." Comparing the readers of Cervantes to those of Thomas Hardy, she thinks that "the reader of today, accustomed to find himself in direct communication with the writer, is constantly out of touch with Cervantes." She doubts that Cervantes felt the tragedy and the satire of *Don Quijote* as we feel them and suspects him, gratuitously it seems to me, of being as callous as was Shakespeare (or, I would correct, Henry V) in dismissing Falstaff. "As for knowing himself what he was about—perhaps great writers never do. Perhaps that is why later ages find what they seek" (*CDB*, 177–78). It is the theme taken up later by the Polish phenomenologist Roman Ingarden, who speaks of "indeterminacy" or even of "empty spots" in a work of literature, which generations of readers are free to fill in their own way.

There is, I would argue, a "structure of determination" which prevents

arbitrariness, and Virginia Woolf knows this when she attempts to describe, characterize, and evaluate the world of the novelists she studies.
She seems, deliberately, to create a counterpart to the essays of her father,
Leslie Stephen, which are also concerned with the world of the English
novelists but judged always with the standards of a social morality: Stephen praises them for recognizing the "surpassing value of manliness,
honesty, and pure domestic affection" or condemns them for morbidity,
cynicism, or cloudy idealism.[2] Virginia Woolf goes about it differently.
She wants to master the "perspective," understand "how the novelist orders his world" (SCR, 43), "the one gift" of the novelist "more essential
than another," "the power of combination—the simple vision" (PM, 166).

From her essays we could abstract a history of the English novel from
Sidney's Arcadia to Conrad and Joyce, not in terms of "origin, rise,
growth, decline and fall" (SCR, 43), of the evolutionism of her father
and his time which she expressly rejects, but in individual portraits or
vignettes which characterize or evoke the particular world of the writer.
Sidney's Arcadia has a "pictorial stillness," with "verse performing something of the function of dialogue in the modern novel." The characters
are like ambling phantoms. Sidney's grasp upon them is so weak that
"he has forgotten what his relation to them is—is it 'I' the author who is
speaking or is it 'I' the character?" Such a genuinely critical observation
makes acceptable the conclusion that "all the seeds of English fiction—
romance and realism, poetry and psychology" lie latent in Arcadia. We
might even admire her saying that "by degrees the book floats away into
the thin air of limbo. It becomes one of those half-forgotten and deserted
places where the grasses grow over fallen statues and the rain drips and
the marble steps are green with moss and vast weeds flourish in the
flower-beds. And yet it is a beautiful garden to wander in now and then;
one stumbles over lovely broken faces, and here and there a flower
blooms and the nightingale sings in the lilac-tree" (34, 38, 40, 41). It is
a method now completely out of fashion and generally deprecated, but
it has its function and its respectable ancestry in Lamb, Hazlitt, and Pater.

Less fancifully she can characterize Robinson Crusoe, a "masterpiece"
with narrow limits. "There are no sunsets and no sunrises; there is no
solitude and no soul. There is, on the contrary, staring us full in the face
nothing but a large earthenware pot. . . . We must hastily alter our proportions throughout. . . . Man must be reduced to a struggling, life-pre-
serving animal; and God shriveled into a magistrate whose seat,
substantial and somewhat hard, is only a little way above the horizon"
(SCR, 45).

Her favorite eighteenth-century novelist is Laurence Sterne. His world

is not, however, "altogether the world of fiction. It is above." Virginia
Woolf argues that Sterne is "not an analyst of other people's sensations.
Those remain simple, eccentric, erratic. It is his own mind that fascinates
him, its oddities and its whims, its fancies and its sensibilities; and it is
his own mind that colours the book [*Tristram Shandy*] and gives it walls
and shape." Laurence Sterne is the most important character in the book.
The other characters "are a race apart among the people in fiction.
There is nothing like them elsewhere, for in no other book are the characters so closely dependent on the author. In no other book are the writer
and the reader so involved together." In *Tristram Shandy* Sterne seems to
her "witty, indecent, disagreeable, yet highly sympathetic." He succeeds
in making us "feel close to life" but at the same time, paradoxically, shows
us "a life which has nothing in common with what, in the shorthand of
speech, one calls 'real life.' " "Shandy Hall, the home of cranks and eccentricities, nevertheless contrives to make the whole of the outer world
appear heavy, and dull and brutal, and teased by innumerable imps"
(*GR*, 135, 134, 172, 171). Though Virginia Woolf wrote an appreciative
introduction to *The Sentimental Journey*, she voices her embarrassment at
the display of virtue. "We are never allowed to forget that Sterne is above
all things sensitive, sympathetic, humane." She misses "the variety, the
vigour, the ribaldry of *Tristram Shandy*," but even in the *Journey* she finds
"a backbone of conviction to support him." Sterne was "a stoic in his way
and a moralist, and a teacher," and finally "a very great writer" (*SCR*,
73, 75). Still, her essays, perceptive of the man and his world, are dis-
appointing: she has nothing to say about Sterne's main claim to originality, his writing a novel about the novel, his parody of the conventional
novel, his handling of time—all those qualities which have since made
Sterne a pivotal figure in the history of fiction.

As we move into the nineteenth century, Virginia Woolf's essays combine more and more judgment with evocation and description. The essay
on Jane Austen is almost entirely favorable. Discussing her early story,
The Watsons, Virginia Woolf finds in it all the elements of Jane Austen's
greatness. "Think away the surface animation, the likeness to life, and
there remains, to provide a deeper pleasure, an exquisite discrimination
of human values." "It is against the disc of an unerring heart, an un-
failing good taste, and almost stern morality, that she shows up these
deviations from kindness, truth and sincerity which are among the most
delightful things in English literature." Virginia Woolf sees Jane Austen's
limitations clearly: "She could not throw herself wholeheartedly into a
romantic moment. She had all sorts of devices for evading scenes of
passion. Nature and its beauties she approached in a sidelong way of her

own" (*CR*, 138, 140, 141–42). Her figures, Virginia Woolf comments elsewhere, "are bound, and restricted to a few definite movements" (35). But that reticence is admirable: "How definitely, by not saying something, she says it; how surprising, therefore, her expressive phrases when they come" (*GR*, 54). Virginia Woolf thinks of Emma saying to Mr. Knightley at the Westons' ball, "I will dance with you," "which though not eloquent in itself, or violent or made striking by beauty of language, has the whole weight of the book behind it" (*CR*, 35). Little is said which could be called aesthetic criticism, though Virginia Woolf alludes to the "more abstract art which, in the ball-room scene [of *The Watsons*], so varies the emotions and proportions the parts that it is possible to enjoy it, as one enjoys poetry, for itself, and not as a link which carries the story this way and that" (*CR*, 138). With her last finished novel, *Persuasion*, Virginia Woolf argues, Jane Austen began to overcome her limitations. The sensitivity to nature is new. An emotion of love (which Virginia Woolf assumes is drawn from her own experience) is expressed for the first time. A new Jane Austen seems to emerge. Virginia Woolf speculates what would have become of her if she had not died at the age of forty-two. "She would have been the forerunner of Henry James and Proust" (144). After A. C. Bradley's essay on Jane Austen (1911) had begun to reestablish her fame, Virginia Woolf's enthusiasm for the writer whom she called "the most perfect artist among women"[3] was, with E. M. Forster's admiration and R. W. Chapman's editions, the main stimulus of the new cult.

In contrast, Virginia Woolf is decidedly cool to Walter Scott. There is an ironical sketch about the grand setup of Scott's household called "Gas at Abbotsford." In a discussion of *The Antiquary* she complains of his "execrable style." Scott used "the wrong pen, the genteel pen to describe the intricacies and passions of the human heart." Surprisingly, we are told that "the Waverley Novels are as unmoral as Shakespeare's plays" and that "you may read them over and over again, and never know for certain what Scott himself was or what Scott himself thought," an idea easily refuted by any close student. Still, Virginia Woolf thinks that Scott excels in depicting "the emotions not of human beings pitted against other human beings, but of man against Nature, of man in relation to fate" (*M*, 63, 64, 66, 68).

Jane Eyre and *Wuthering Heights* provide an easy contrast. Charlotte Brontë's tremendous force goes into the assertions "I love," "I hate," "I suffer," while there is no "I" in *Wuthering Heights*. Rather Emily Brontë speaks of "the whole human race" and "you eternal powers . . . The sentence remains unfinished. It is not strange that it should be so." Virginia Woolf thinks that Emily "looked upon a world cleft into gigantic disorder and felt within her the power to unite it in a book," an assertion that takes the mysticism too seriously and is unsupported by any evidence (*CR*, 156, 158–59, 158).

George Eliot is seen in the perspective of her biography, "raising herself with groans and struggles from the intolerable boredom of petty provincial society," finally entering into the union with George Henry Lewes which isolated her from society. Virginia Woolf admires *Middlemarch* most as a "magnificent book which with all its imperfections is one of the few novels written for grown-up people." She is, however, troubled by George Eliot's heroines. "They bring out the worst of her, lead her into difficult places, make her self-conscious, didactic and occasionally vulgar." "They cannot live without religion" and have "the deep feminine passion for goodness." George Eliot is equally unable to portray a man, fumbling when she has to conceive a fit mate for her heroine. The emotional scenes like the end of *Mill on the Floss*, with Maggie Tulliver drowned, clasping her brother in her arms, "drag her from her natural surroundings." One wonders what remains of her work except the agricultural world of her remotest past. "The searching power and reflective richness of the later novels," though acknowledged, remains unaccounted for (*CR*, 163, 167, 170, 169).

Virginia Woolf is even more critical of Meredith. Reading *Richard Feverel*, "we at once exclaim how unreal, how artificial, how impossible" its characters are. The scene may be splendid, the landscape a part of the emotion, but Meredith is not among the great psychologists and his teaching "seems now too strident, too optimistic, too shallow." The later books are even "meretricious and false" (*SCR*, 206, 211, 212), "charred bones and masses of contorted wire." Virginia Woolf would have liked a touch of realism—"or is it a touch of something more akin to sympathy?"—"It would have kept the Meredith hero from being the honourable but tedious gentleman that . . . we have always found him." In *The Egoist*, Meredith "flouts probability, disdains coherency, and lives from one high moment to the next." Still, Meredith, she grants, has imagination, has "the power of summoning nature into sympathy with man and merging him in her vastness" (*GR*, 49, 51, 52). Meredith is a "rhapsodist," lyrical in sensibility but "extremely conventional as a mind." He belongs to the great eccentrics like Donne, Peacock, and Gerard Manley Hopkins, not a bad company, we might think (*SCR*, 207, 208, 213).

Hardy is obviously a much greater writer in Virginia Woolf's eyes. She glosses over "an extreme and even melodramatic use of coincidence" in his early novel, *Desperate Remedies*, and merely alludes to the conflict within "a faithful son of field and down, yet tormented by the doubts and despondencies bred by book-learning." When she comes to speaking of *Far from the Madding Crowd,* which "holds its place among the great English novels," she can only lyrically evoke its atmosphere in a long metaphorical passage. "The dark downland, marked by the barrows of the dead and the huts of shepherds, rises against the sky, smooth as a wave of the sea, but solid and eternal," etcetera, etcetera, but then she generalizes sensibly about the types and situations in the novels. "The woman is the weaker and the fleshlier, and she clings to the stronger and obscures his vision." Love is the great fact of human life. "But it is a catastrophe; it happens suddenly and overwhelmingly, and there is little to be said about it." We do not really know Hardy's characters. "His light does not fall directly upon the human heart." Each man is battling with the storm, alone. "We do not know his men and women in their relations to each other, we know them in their relations to time, death, and fate." Virginia Woolf disapproves of "convicting" Hardy of a creed, of "tethering him to a consistent point of view." The reader should know "when to put aside the writer's conscious intention in favour of some deeper intention of which perhaps he may be unconscious." Only *Jude the Obscure* justifies the charge of pessimism. Its "misery is overwhelming, not tragic." Virginia Woolf defends even the violence and melodrama of the books as due to "a curious peasantlike love of the monstrous for its own sake," as part of "the wild spirit of poetry which saw the strangeness of life itself, with no symbol of caprice and unreason too extreme to represent the astonishing circumstances of our existence." She forgives all the shortcomings and failures of Hardy, "the greatest tragic writer among English novelists" (*SCR,* 223–33 passim).

Virginia Woolf has a similar sympathy for Conrad. She admires his vision and his "implacable integrity, how it is better to be good than bad, how loyalty is good, and honesty and courage." She vastly prefers the early books: *Typhoon, The Nigger of Narcissus,* and *Youth* (*CR,* 223, 225). *Lord Jim* falls apart. The second half does not develop satisfactorily from the first. Conrad "sees his people in flashes; it explains what we may call the static quality of Mr. Conrad's characters." An atmosphere of profound and monotonous calm pervades the book. The idea is simple, but the texture is extremely fine (*TLS,* July 27, 1917). The later fiction, however, fails to come up to her expectations. She reviewed *The Rescue* unfavorably. She misses a "central idea which, gathering the multiplicity of incidents together, produces a final effect of unity." It is just "stiff melodrama" (*TLS,* July 1, 1920; *WD,* 26). *Nostromo* suffers from "a crowding and suffocating superabundance" (*TLS,* March 14, 1918). The later Conrad was "not able to bring his figures into perfect relation with their background." "He was not sure of the world of values and convictions." She sees a conflict between the seacaptain and the talkative Marlow. There is something "somnolent, stiff, ornate" (*CR,* 223, 228), even "pomposity and monotony" in Conrad, and once she even denies him the honor of being an English writer. "He is too formal, too courteous, too scrupulous," a foreign aristocrat, without intimacy and humor (*CDB,* 80, 77).

The standard of judgment implied in these essays is the preference for the universally human, for the power of generalizing, of creating situations and characters which (like Hardy's characters) persuade us that there is "something symbolical about them which is common to us all" (*SCR,* 228). "Imagination is at its freest when it is most generalized." In contrast, two novelists whom she discussed remained subjective, particular. George Gissing uses personal suffering as his only theme. She approves of Gissing's purpose of making us think of the "hideous injustice in the system of society" but considers him "self-centered," limited by "narrowness of outlook and meagerness of sensibility" (*SCR,* 200, 201). A very different writer, George Moore, writes also only about himself. He lacks all dramatic power. Not one of his novels is a masterpiece. "They are silken tents which have no poles," she says strikingly. *Esther Waters,* though it has "a shapeliness which is at once admirable and disconcerting," is a failure. The "scenes and characters are curiously flat. The dialogue is always toneless and monotonous" (*CW,* 146, 148). Still, she thinks George Moore "has brought a new mind into the world, he has given us a new way of feeling and seeing." He "liquidates the capricious and volatile essence of himself and decants it in [his] memoirs" (*DM,* 156, 160). But she does not even try to define the nature of this new mind.

Henry James, one would think, must have been very important for her practice as a novelist. She reviewed *The Golden Bowl* carefully and descriptively as early as 1905.[4] But the critical pronouncements show a divided mind. She does not much care for the ghost stories. "The horror of *The Turn of the Screw* is tame and conventional." "Quint and Miss Jessel are not ghosts, but odious creatures much closer to us than ghosts have ever been." "The Great Good Place" is a failure because of James's lack of "visionary imagination" (*GR,* 60, 63, 65, 66–67). She complains that in *What Maisie Knew* the "characters seem held in a vacuum at a great [re]move from the substantial lumbering world of Dickens and George Eliot or from the precise crisscross of convention which metes out the world of Jane Austen" (121). In *The Wings of the Dove* James becomes "merely excessively ingenious. . . . After all this juggling and arranging of silk pocket handkerchiefs, one ceases to have any feeling for the figure behind. Milly thus manipulated disappears. He overreaches himself" (*WD*, 39). Virginia Woolf likes *The American Scene* ("very quiet and luminous"), and the "wonderful" *Notes of a Son and Brother* even more (*Letters* 1:304; *DM*, 134). We owe to Henry James and to Hawthorne, she says, "the best relish of the past in our literature—not the past of romance and chivalry, but the immediate past of vanished dignity and faded fashions." She alludes to James's "late and mighty flowering" and calls him "English in his humour, Johnsonian in his sanity" (*DM*, 134, 152, 154). "The courtly, worldly, sentimental old gentleman" whom she met in 1907 seemed to her, however, something of a figure of fun, to judge from the letter in which she described his convoluted questions (*GR*, 72; *Letters* 1:306), and in a review of Joseph Warren Beach's *Method of Henry James* (1918) some deep hostility comes to the surface. James is called "vulgar, a snob, an American." His characters are "tainted by the determination not to be vulgar; they are, as exiles tend to be, slightly parasitic; they have an enormous appetite for afternoon tea; their attitude not only to furniture but to life is more that of an appreciative collector than an undoubting possessor." She reflects that "one had rather read what he meant to do than what he actually did do." Still, she admits the interest of his later books, "not a plot, or a collection of characters, or a view of life, but something more abstract, more difficult to grasp, the weaving together of many themes into one of them, the making out of a design" (*TLS*, December 26, 1918). She seems to be describing her own procedures. But she did not, publicly, discuss the relation to James beyond these remarks.

   She defined her own position most clearly in regard to her immediate predecessors, Arnold Bennett, H. G. Wells, and John Galsworthy. These are her best-known essays, particularly "Mr. Bennett and Mrs. Brown" (1924), which is one of a series of articles rehearsing the theme that the novels of the three authors are encumbered by loads of detail, by "bushels of fact."[5] "You cannot," she says elsewhere, "cross the narrow bridge of art carrying all its tools in your hands" (*GR*, 22). But the attacks on Bennett and company surely overshoot the mark. To say that their books leave one with a "feeling of incompleteness and dissatisfaction," that "in order to complete them it seems necessary to do something—to join a society, or, more desperately, to write a cheque," is hardly true of *The Old Wives' Tale*, *The Man of Property*, or *Tono Bungay* (*CDB*, 109). The charge that Bennett's ideal is "an eternity of bliss spent in the very best hotel in Brighton" does not apply even to *Imperial Palace*, and Wells can hardly be called "a materialist from sheer goodness of heart," though we may agree with her complaint about "the crudity and coarseness of his human beings" (CR, 147). Virginia Woolf resented Arnold Bennett's criticism of her novel *Jacob's Room*, which asserted that the work contained "no characters that vitally survive in the mind."[6] She turned the tables on him when she considered him not interested in human nature but in "rents, freeholds, copyholds, and fines." She effectively quotes the beginning of Bennett's *Hilda Lessways*, minutely describing a row of houses (CDB, 109), to support the general charge against a fashionable novelist as providing plot and "an air of probability embalming the whole so impeccably that if all his figures were to come to life they would find themselves dressed down to the last button of their coats in the fashion of the hour." Her own novel, on the contrary, "would have no plot, no comedy, no tragedy, no love interest or catastrophe in the accepted style, and perhaps not a single button sewn on as the Bond Street tailors would have it" (CR, 148–49). She pleads that we should tolerate "the spasmodic, the obscure, the fragmentary," even "the failure" of a new novel, for she believed that "we are trembling on the verge of one of the great ages of English Literature" (CDB, 119). Virginia Woolf proclaims the end of realism and prophesies the age of a novel of sensibility.

She was, however, disappointed with the new experimental novelists. One would expect her to welcome Dorothy Richardson. She praises her for discarding "the old deliberate business" and sympathetically describes her method, which she does not call "stream of consciousness." "The method," she continues, "if triumphant, should make us feel ourselves seated at the centre of another mind, and, according to the artistic gift of the writer, we should perceive in the helter-skelter of flying fragments some unity, significance, or design." She grants that Dorothy Richardson "achieved a far greater sense of reality than that produced by the ordinary means," but she finds herself, after all, "distressingly near the surface . . . never, or only for a tantalizing second, in the reality which underlies these appearances" (CW, 120, 121, 122). No doubt Virginia Woolf felt that with similar methods she herself had reached this deeper reality.

D. H. Lawrence upset her profoundly in private, though her only review, of *The Lost Girl* (1920), complains rather that the book is conventional. "We read Mr. Lawrence as one reads Mr. Bennett—for the facts and for the story." Virginia Woolf never alludes to the crucial episode of the book, the story of the heroine Alvina with Cicio in the mountains of the Abruzzi. To say that "little by little Alvina disappears beneath the heap of facts recorded about her," and that "the only sense in which we feel her to be lost is that we cannot longer believe in her existence" (CW,

159, 160), sounds as if Virginia Woolf had not read this admittedly incongruous but very Lawrentian part of the otherwise traditional Bennett-like book. Her later "Notes on D. H. Lawrence" (1932) profess that up to 1931 "he was known to [her] almost solely by reputation and scarcely at all by experience." His reputation was that of "the exponent of some mystical theory of sex." She disliked "The Prussian Officer," which left no clear impression except "starting muscles and forced obscenity." The two collections of poems, *Nettles* and *Pansies,* seemed to her "like the sayings that small boys scribble upon stiles to make housemaids jump and titter." But now she read belatedly *Sons and Lovers* and found it "clear cut, decisive, masterly, hard as rock, shaped." She admires the "rapture of physical being" evoked, for instance, in the scene in which Paul and Miriam swing in the barn. But she keeps her distance: she sees the dissatisfaction of a man of the common people who wants to get into the middle classes, and, contrasting him with Proust, she thinks that he "continues no tradition, is unaware of the past, of the present save as it affects the future. As a writer, this lack of tradition, affects him immensely" (*M*, 93, 94, 96, 97). When she read the *Letters* collected by Aldous Huxley (1930), she reacted with abrupt jottings in her *Diary*: "Lawrence is airless, confined. . . . I don't want 'a philosophy' in the least. . . . I don't like strumming with two fingers—and the arrogance." She protests against Huxley's saying that Lawrence is an "artist." "Art is being rid of all preaching. . . . Lawrence would only say what proved something" (*WD*, 182–83). Similar pronouncements can be found scattered through the *Diary* and the *Letters,* but her shrinking from what seemed to her his aggressive masculinity is clear enough.

Her attitude toward Joyce is somewhat similar. T. S. Eliot praised *Ulysses* in conversation, and Harriet Weaver wanted her to publish the book with the Hogarth Press (*CR*, 234). Nothing could be done about it, for at that time nobody could have found a printer for *Ulysses* in England. But her own view of the book is far from wholehearted admiration. Publicly she called it "a memorable catastrophe—immense in daring, terrific in disaster."[7] In the *Diary* she is more explicit: "Genius it [*Ulysses*] has, I think; but of the inferior water. The book is diffuse. . . . It is pretentious. It is underbred, not only in the obvious sense, but in the literary sense. A first rate writer, I mean, respects writing too much to be tricky; startling; doing stunts" (*WD*, 48). Elsewhere she complains of "the damned egotistical self which ruins Joyce and [Dorothy] Richardson" and of a "cheap, smart, smoking-room coarseness."[8]

She saw through Aldous Huxley, whom she liked personally, very early. Her review of *Limbo* (1920) recognizes that he is clever, amusing, and

far too intellectual and bookish. "It is well to leave a mind under a coun-
terpane of moderate ignorance," she advises him, but she obviously did
not take her own advice, at least in her criticism (*CW*, 149; *TLS*,
February 5, 1920). She was immensely well-read and reviewed even me-
diocre novels with patience and sympathy. Her reviews of such forgotten
novelists as Elinor Mordaunt, L. P. Jacks, W. E. Norris, Leonard Merrick,
and the still remembered Frank Swinnerton and Joseph Hergesheimer
are extremely indulgent though never without some reservations (see
CW, passim). She got "tired of being caged with Aldous, Joyce and Lawrence,"[9] thought that the new novel had failed to keep its promise, and
felt herself to be more and more alone and unappreciated, reacting ir-
ritably to satirical attacks against her and Bloomsbury, such as those of
Wyndham Lewis, or to disparaging comments in *Scrutiny*.[10]

The two collections of her essays she herself edited, *The Common Reader*
(1925) and *The Second Common Reader* (1932), were arranged in the chronological order of the authors discussed. In an article entitled "Phases
of Fiction" (1929), she classified the English and foreign novelists as if
they were present simultaneously in her bookshelves. The apparently
detached typology leads, however, to the kind of novel she herself preferred and practiced. She begins with "truth-tellers," Defoe, Mau-
passant, and Trollope; discusses "the Romantics," Scott, Stevenson,
and Mrs. Radcliffe; comments briefly on "Character-mongers and
Comedians," Dickens, Jane Austen, George Eliot; on "Psychologists" such
as Henry James, Proust, and Dostoevsky; "Satirists and Fantasists," Peacock and Sterne; and finally the "Poets," Tolstoy, Meredith, Emily
Brontë, Melville, and again Proust. She concludes, however, with an admission of the inevitability of mimesis. "The novel is the only form of
art [she forgets the film] which seeks to make us believe that it is giving
a full and truthful record of the life of a real person." It is "inevitable
that the reader . . . should go on feeling as he feels in life." But the
novelist should control the human sympathy. "Indeed the first sign we
are reading a writer of merit is that we feel this control at work on us.
The barrier between us and the book is raised higher." "The balance
between the power of bringing us into close touch with life" and "style,
arrangement, construction" is considered the main achievement of the
great novelist who gives us "an epitome" as well as an "inventory" of life
(*GR*, 141–45 passim). In commenting on Percy Lubbock's *Craft of Fiction*
(1921), the book that had expounded the Jamesian concept of the novel
most authoritatively, Virginia Woolf admits that novels "bristle with
temptations. We identify ourselves with this person or that" and "the
book itself, the form escapes," as Lubbock had complained. But she does

not care for the term *form*, which she wrongly considers as coming from the visual arts (as if Plato and Aristotle had never lived). It suggests to her the visual and the static. She thinks of the novel as being constituted in "the very process of reading itself," a very modern concept. "It is not form which you see, but emotion which you feel." But she grants that beyond emotion there is "something which though it is inspired by emotion, tranquilises it, orders it, composes it," which "places certain emotions in the right relations to each other," a result which she would not want to call "form" but rather "art" (*M*, 157, 158–59).

Many of her judgments of the novelists are based on an answer to the question whether this right balance between life and art is achieved or whether there is a preponderance of one or the other which upsets it. Considering her friendship with E. M. Forster, her review of *Aspects of the Novel* is surprisingly disapproving. She complains that Forster is silent about the novelist's language. He censures patterns she cares for. Beauty is suspect to him. "Fiction is treated as a parasite which draws sustenance from life and must in gratitude resemble life or perish." She concludes, not limiting herself to Forster, that "if the English critic were less domestic, less assiduous to protect the rights of what it pleases him to call life, the novelist might be bolder too. He must cut adrift from the eternal tea-table. . . . The story might wobble; the plot might crumble; ruin might seize upon the characters. The novel, in short, might become a work of art" (*M*, 110, 111, 112). That is what she wanted to achieve herself, even at a price. Forster, in *Howards End*, "having recorded too much and too literally," wavers between realism and symbolism. "The hesitation is fatal. For we doubt both things—the real and the symbolical" (*DM*, 169), an ambiguity that she considers a failing, even a disaster: she always insists on consistency, coherence, the observance of the writer's perspective, and finds that only "lesser writers introduce two different kinds of reality into the same book" (*CR*, 236). One wonders whether she is not warning herself against the dangers incurred by her own novels.

The balance of life and art is one criterion. Another is the contrast of national types and traditions. Virginia Woolf was acutely aware of the class character of English fiction of the nineteenth century. All the novelists were "fairly well-to-do middle class people." She welcomes the coming disappearance of classes and does not regret that this, very likely, "will be the end of the novel as we know it." It may become extinct like poetic drama (*M*, 132, 151). Virginia Woolf waxes satirical about the "nieces of Earls and cousins of Generals" in English fiction. "Our ignorance of the aristocracy is nothing compared with our ignorance of the working classes." There are "no gentlemen in Dickens; no working men in Thackeray. One hesitates to call Jane Eyre a lady." Virginia Woolf can only conclude with a question mark about the "art of a truly democratic age" (*SCR*, 193, 196, 197).

Yet she does recommend one remedy against the limits of English fiction: the Russian novel. She belongs to the early English enthusiasts of the Russian novel and was carried away not only by Turgenev, Tolstoy, Dostoevsky, and Chekhov but also by rash generalizations about the Russian soul, the "entirely new conception of the novel," "larger, saner and more profound than ours." "Could any English novel survive," she asks, "in the furnace of that overpowering sincerity," "their undeviating reverence for truth?" (*GR*, 49, 50). In her well-known essay "The Russian Point of View," the enthusiasm reaches fever pitch and the generalizations become often dubious. "The simplicity, the absence of effort, the assumption that in a world bursting with misery the chief call upon us is to understand fellow-sufferers 'and not with the mind—for it is easy with the mind—but with the heart'—this is the cloud which broods above the whole of Russian literature." It is a cliché to speak of the soul as "the chief character in Russian fiction" and an error to say that in Russian novels "there is none of that precise division between good and bad to which we are used" (*CR*, 173, 177, 178). The contrast she draws between Annabella in Ford's *'Tis a Pity She's a Whore* and Anna Karenina compares the incomparable. "The English girl is flat and crude as a face painted on a playing card; she is without depth, without range, without intricacy," whereas "the Russian woman is flesh and blood, nerves and temperament, has heart, brain, body, and mind" (61). English and Russian fiction seem to her "immeasurably far apart," though, on occasion, she grants the English "a natural delight in humour and comedy, in the beauty of the earth, in the activities of the intellect, and in the splendours of the body," supposedly absent from the Russians (153).

Fortunately these sweeping generalizations are modified in the many essays on individual authors. She sees the difference between Dostoevsky and Tolstoy and formulates it in the terms derived from Merezhkovsky's antithesis. "Life dominates Tolstoi as the soul dominates Dostoevsky." Virginia Woolf obviously prefers Turgenev, Tolstoy, and Chekhov to Dostoevsky. She admired Tolstoy as "the greatest of all novelists" (*CR*, 181, 179), as "genius in the raw. Thus more disturbing, more 'shocking,' more of a thunderclap, even on art, even on literature, than any other writer" (*WD*, 319). She reviewed a translation of *The Cossacks*, admiring Tolstoy's insight: "Nothing seems to escape him" (*TLS*, February 1, 1917). Dostoevsky rather stunned and bewildered her. Finally she confessed that one cannot read Dostoevsky again after reading Turgenev, "who wrote and rewrote to clear the truth of the unessential. But Dostoevsky would say that everything matters" (*WD*, 203). She sides with Turgenev, his "rare gift of symmetry, of balance"—Turgenev, whose books are not "a succession of events" but "a succession of emotions radiating from some character at the center" (*CDB*, 54), presumably like Mrs. Ramsey in *To the Lighthouse* or Mrs. Dalloway. Virginia Woolf reviewed two volumes of Constance Garnett's translation of the minor Dostoevsky. She praises fairly routinely *The Eternal Husband* for its insight into "the dim and populous underworld of the mind's consciousness where desires and impulses are moving blindly beneath the sod." "Intuition is the term which we should apply to Dostoevsky's genius at its best." But she does not know what to do with *The Double*: "The whole of its amazing machinery seems to spin fruitlessly in the air." It seems to her "an elaborate failure, with all its brilliancy and astonishing ingenuity" (*TLS*, June 7, 1917). She does not care for *The Gambler* either, which seems to her a "second-rate work of a great writer" "worth reading if only because it is apt to offer us the very best criticism of his masterpieces." She knows that *The Gambler* was written "at an almost inarticulate speed" and thinks "his passion rushes into violence, his scenes verge upon melodrama, and his characters are seized with the inevitable madness or epilepsy." "To control this tendency there is not in Dostoevsky, as there is always in Tolstoy, a central purpose which brings the whole field into focus" (*TLS*, October 11, 1917). In her reviews of Chekhov's stories she discriminates sensitively among them, defending their inconclusive endings, "though they leave us feeling melancholy and perhaps uncertain, yet somehow or other they provide a resting point for the mind—a solid object casting the shade of reflection and speculation" (*TLS*, August 14, 1919).

The English-Russian contrast preoccupied her almost as much as the male-female. There is here no need to speak of her feminism, of *A Room of One's Own*, of her pleas for "leisure, money and room to themselves" so that women could write, not only to vent their grievances in novels which are "dumping grounds for the personal emotions" but also to become writers who could define their own sense of values, even in politics and social criticism, and who finally would achieve a greater impersonality which would "encourage the poetic spirit" and would make them speak out about "our destiny and the meaning of life." Virginia Woolf was acutely aware of the handicaps and restrictions imposed by law and custom on women writers in the past, but she deplored the effects of resentment and self-assertiveness on women writers. "The vision loses its perfect integrity, and with that, its most essential quality as a work of art." But Virginia Woolf was of two minds about femininity in literature. Sometimes she wants a feminine literature, though she has doubts about any common characteristics of feminine writings in the past. "Jane Austen can have had nothing in common with George Eliot; George Eliot was the direct opposite of Emily Brontë." But she also complains (not too seriously, one hopes) about the "sentence made by men; it is too loose, too heavy, too pompous for a woman's use" (*GR*, 84, 83, 80, 78, 81). "Charlotte Brontë, with her splendid gift for prose, stumbled and fell with that clumsy weapon in her hands. George Eliot committed atrocities with it that beggar description" (*ROO*, 80). Virginia Woolf praises Dorothy Richardson: "She has invented, or, if she has not invented, developed and applied to her own use a sentence which we might call the psychological sentence of the feminine gender" (*Nation and Athenaeum*, May 19, 1923). Fortunately Jane Austen and Emily Brontë were not trying to write like men (*ROO*, 112). Virginia Woolf dislikes overtly, self-consciously virile writers: D. H. Lawrence, Norman Douglas, and James Joyce. In a sharp review of Hemingway's *The Sun Also Rises* she objects not only to his crude and flat characters and conventional technique but also to his machismo (*GR*, 90–92). But ultimately she can contradict herself and say "a writer has no sex." "The greatest writers lay no stress upon sex one way or the other" (*CR*, 208; *GR*, 90). "Any emphasis, either of pride or of shame, laid consciously upon the sex of a writer is not only irritating but superfluous" (*CW*, 26). She quotes with approval Coleridge's saying that "a great mind must be androgynous" (*TLS*, February 7, 1918). At least theoretically and imaginatively in her books she overcame the division of the sexes.

Virginia Woolf was mainly interested in the novel and in biography. Her interest in poetry, at least in her printed criticism, is limited and somewhat perfunctory. She thinks that "very little of value has been said about poetry since the world began" (*SCR*, 218), and she did not add to this slender store. She was puzzled by the mere presence of rhyme, which seems to her "not only childish but dishonest," and considered the poet's rhythm, "which keeps up its perpetual beat on the floor of the mind," the essential distinction. Modern poetry shirks contact with life and is absorbed by the self. She argues that older poets wrote about other people (e.g., Byron in *Don Juan*, or George Crabbe) and asks the new poet to get out of himself—though "after a long preparation and commerce with himself"—just as Shakespeare did when "Hamlet, Falstaff and Cleopatra rushed him into the knowledge" of the English language (*DM*, 210, 212, 214, 202, 223). Virginia Woolf is shocked by coarse and vulgar expressions in recent poetry, annoyed by its ugliness—"the nightingale of Eliot sings 'jug, jug to dirty ears' " (GR, 16) and puzzled by its obscurity. She is particularly harsh toward the "destructiveness" and "emptiness" of the Oxford group, among whom she singles out Louis MacNeice for particular disapproval (M, 145, 142). But this lack of sympathy with modern poetry, including Yeats and T. S. Eliot, should not obscure her appreciation of narrative poets such as Chaucer or Elizabeth Barrett Browning, whose *Aurora Leigh* she tried to rescue from oblivion, or her admiration for Donne, who "still excites interest and disgust, contempt and adoration" (SCR, 182–92, 30). She defends allegory in Spenser's *Faerie Queene*: "Passions are turned into people," are given amplitude and depersonalized. "Who shall say that this is the less natural, the less realistic?" But she dislikes the stanzaic form of the poem. "The verse becomes for a time a rocking horse." We are confined in "one continuous consciousness which is Spenser's" (M, 28, 29). Again and again she voices her preference for the novel and the drama because they require the writer to enter into other people's minds.

This is also her ideal of criticism. "Do not dictate to your author; try to become him. Be his fellow-worker and accomplice." "Everywhere else we may be bound by laws and conventions—there [in art] we have none" (SCR, 235, 234). Virginia Woolf seems to appeal to the tradition descending from Lamb and Hazlitt via Sainte-Beuve and Pater to her friends. But Virginia Woolf's essay on Hazlitt is extremely critical of his person and mind. He seems to her a divided and discordant mind with "so much energy and yet so little love for his task." His essays are "dry, garish in their bright imagery, monotonous in the undeviating energy of their rhythm." She disapproves of his closed mind—"his own and it is made up" (SCR, 160, 162, 163)—and gently but insistently rejects the moral and political preoccupations of Macaulay, Matthew Arnold, and her father's "intemperate candour." Her own principle is "simply that the essay should give pleasure." "Not a fact juts out, not a dogma tears the surface of the texture." "It must be pure from dullness, deadness, and deposits of extraneous matter." But surely this passage exalting an ideal of pleasing the reader by a smooth surface of the noncommittal is quite inadequate to her actual practice. In the same review she disapproves of the genteel essayists of her time in vehement terms unusual in her writings. "We are nauseated by the sight of trivial personalities decomposing in the eternity of print." She asks for "backbone," "some fierce attachment to an idea," even for an "obstinate conviction" (CR, 219, 211, 212, 216, 220). In praising Coleridge's criticism as "the most spiritual in the language" and his notes on Shakespeare as "the only criticisms that bear reading with the sound of the play still in one's ears," she formulates his power "of seeming to bring to light what was already there beforehand, instead of imposing anything from the outside" (*TLS*, February 7, 1918). Reviewing Spingarn's *Creative Criticism* she can endorse the conception of criticism established "thanks to Sainte-Beuve and others." "We try to enter into the mind of the writer, to see each work of art by itself, and to judge how far each artist has succeeded in his aim," a repetition of Goethe's well-known formulas. She concludes that criticism is not creation but "an interpretation" of art (*TLS*, June 7, 1917).

Though she may not have importantly contributed to a theory of literature or even of the novel, Virginia Woolf has accomplished the task of the critic: she characterized many of the main novelists and judged them acutely, blending characterization and judgment, for she knew that judgment arises out of the description and interpretation. Occasionally she may be arbitrary or whimsical, but in her best essays she achieves what she granted that Hazlitt succeeded in doing. "He singles out the peculiar quality of his author and stamps it vigorously" (*SCR*, 165).

E. M. FORSTER (1879–1970)

E. M. Forster seems to uphold the aesthetic point of view even more extremely than the other members of the Bloomsbury group. A late address (1949) opens with the declaration: "I believe in art for art's sake" and develops the theme by endorsing the view that "a work of art—whatever else it may be—is a self-contained entity, with a life of its own imposed on it by its creator. It has internal order. It may have external form" (*TC*, 96). The lecture repeats a much earlier statement: "A poem points to nothing but itself." With it (*The Ancient Mariner* is the example used) "we have entered a universe that only answers to its own laws, supports itself, internally coheres, and has a new standard of truth" (89). The order of art, its internal harmony, is expressly contrasted with the disorder of society. "Ancient Athens made a mess—but the *Antigone* stands up. Renaissance Rome made a mess—but the ceiling of the Sistine got painted. James I made a mess—but there was *Macbeth*. Louis XIV—but there was *Phèdre*" (99–100). Criticism thus considers "the object in itself, as an entity, and tells us what it can about its life. The second aim is subsidiary: the relation of the objects to the rest of the world," social conditions, the biography of the author, and so on, which make criticism stray either into psychology or into history. Such criticism may have its contact with the object but it is "no longer with a work of art" (*TC*, 123). A curious distinction is here made (reminiscent of phenomenology, which

Forster could hardly have known) between the art-object and the work of art, the aesthetic object, somehow contained in it.

The emphasis on the self-enclosed work of art leads Forster to a by no means unavoidable rejection of the historicity of art. In a famous image at the beginning of his lectures, *Aspects of the Novel* (1927), he asks us to visualize the English novelists "as seated together in a room, a circular room, a sort of British Museum reading-room—all writing their novels simultaneously" (*AN,* 12), and this image is developed to mean that "all through history writers while writing felt more or less the same," for human nature does not change. There is partial truth in the motto "History develops, Art stands still" (23; cf. 157–58). Forster thus, at least for the purposes of these lectures, dismisses "classification by chronology," any attempts to "relate a book to the history of its time, to events in the life of its author, to the events it describes, and above all to some tendency." "Four hundred years is nothing in the life of our race, and does not allow room for any measurable change" (15, 17, 24) is his extravagant assertion of stability. Forster appeals to T. S. Eliot's demand that the critic see literature "*not* as consecrated by time, but to see it beyond time"[1] and he disparages the life in time as "so obviously base and inferior" to the "life of values" that he can minimize the role of story in the novel and see the point of Gertrude Stein's endeavor to abolish time, even though he considers her experiments a failure (41–42). The enmity toward time leads in Forster to a preference for space in a novel— not the spatial form discerned later by Joseph Frank in Flaubert or Joyce, but space in a simple geographic sense. "Space," Forster tells us, "is the lord of *War and Peace,* not time." The reason why the end of Tolstoy's novel, in spite of Nikolay's and Natasha's "partial decay," is not depressing is that the novel "has extended over space as well as over time, and the sense of space until it terrifies us, is exhilarating, and leaves behind it an effect like music" (39). But this is sheer fancy: Nikolay and Natasha do not conclude the novel. It ends with Nikolenka thinking of Pierre and his own father Andrey, "looking forward to doing something with which even he would be satisfied." Forster is arguing here against Percy Lubbock's discussion in his *Craft of Fiction* (1921) where Lubbock speaks of "Youth and Age, the flow and ebb of the recurrent tide" as the theme of Tolstoy's novel (31). But the appeal to the "immense area of Russia" seems as irrelevant critically as the concomitant disparagement of Arnold Bennett's *Old Wives' Tale* for showing the effect of time on the two sisters (40, 39).

Viewing it thus unhistorically, Forster can analyze the novel in its main aspects. Story, people, plot, fantasy, prophecy, pattern, and rhythm are his topics, and he loosely mixes an analysis of the strata of a novel with an attempt at a typology of the novel. Forster is content with the trivial definition of a novel as "any fictitious prose work over 50,000 words"—thus shirking the question of the short story or novella—and with dismissing foreign influence on the English novel (*AN*, 9, 10). As he minimizes the story and considers plot merely a story with the "emphasis falling on causality" (82), he must care most for the "people," the characters in the novel. The best pages of the book argue that people in a novel can be "completely understood by the reader, if the novelist wishes. Even if they are imperfect or unreal they do not contain any secrets." This is why "novels, even if they are about wicked people, can solace us; they suggest a more comprehensible and thus a more manageable human race, they give us the illusion of perspicacity and of power" (46, 62). Forster complains that among the main facts of human life—birth, food, sleep, love, and death—man cannot directly experience and hence cannot depict the first and the last and does not make much of food and sleep in the novel. Thus love bulks enormously—disproportionately so. Forster, however, drops this topic and then makes the distinction between "flat" and "round" characters: "flat" means predictable "humour" types such as Mrs. Micawber and Caleb Balderstone (in *The Bride of Lammermoor*); "round" characters such as Becky Sharp have the capacity of "surprising in a convincing way" (75). Similar distinctions have been made before. Aldous Huxley comes nearest when in an essay on Chaucer (1923) he speaks of Anatole France portraying his characters, "as it were, in the flat and not in three dimensions," while Chaucer's "slightest character sketches are always solid and three-dimensional."[2] But Forster's metaphor of "flat" versus "round" has deservedly become established as a fortunate formulation.

Forster considers point of view of secondary importance, deliberately rejecting Lubbock's insistence on the Jamesian doctrine. Forster argues that *Bleak House*, while "all to pieces logically," is successful, whereas Gide's *Les Faux-Monnayeurs* shows too much self-consciousness to be more than "interesting." The novelist has the "power to expand and contract perception (of which the shifting viewpoint is a symptom)"; he has the "right to intermittent knowledge" (*AN*, 77, 78). There is no law to hold him to a consistent point of view. But Forster endorses the Jamesian "exit author" dogma, though halfheartedly. The writer should not "take the reader into his confidence about his characters." Fielding and Thackeray harm their novels by "bar-parlour chattiness," but comments (such as those of Hardy and Conrad) "about the conditions under which he thinks life is carried on" are allowed (78, 79). A criterion of illusion may justify this distinction. It remains unclear why a writer can speak about life in general but must not comment about his characters.

Forster cannot keep the discussion to the aspect of the novel as structure. He is oddly silent even on what one might consider basic, the language of fiction, its words. Rather he makes some attempt at a typology of the novel. Under the heading of "Fantasy" such incongruous books as *Tristam Shandy* and Beerbohm's *Zuleika Dobson* are listed, and under "Prophecy" something is said about Dostoevsky, D. H. Lawrence, "the only prophetic novelist writing today" (*AN*, 132), *Moby Dick,* and *Wuthering Heights.* One wonders about the justice of saying that "no great book is more cut off than *Wuthering Heights* from the universals of Heaven and Hell" (135).

At the end Forster enlarges on an aspect of composition he calls pattern and rhythm, commenting on the way Strether and Chad, in *The Ambassadors,* change places, and on the rhythm that pervades Proust's huge series, apparently so chaotic and disjunctive.

Ultimately the book disappoints, though individual comments—harsh on Meredith, dismissive of Joyce (*Ulysses* is a "dogged attempt to cover the universe with mud")—are interesting as throwing light on Forster's taste and his own position in the history of the English novel (*AN*, 113). We can supplement these *obiter dicta* from other essays: the praise of Jane Austen, his "favourite author," the dismissal of Walter Scott, whose "continued reputation" he finds "difficult to understand," the unbounded admiration for Tolstoy ("no English novelist is as great as Tolstoy"), and the praise of Proust, whose *A la recherche du temps perdu* seems to him probably the second greatest novel after *War and Peace* (*AH*, 162; *AN*, 31, 11; *TC*, 226).

Forster's personal concern for Virginia Woolf, expressed in an essay on her early novels (1925) and in a memorial lecture (1941), shows his appreciation for her innovations. He believes that she is the only writer (with the exception of Joyce) who tried to change the form of English fiction, so remarkably stable from Fielding to Arnold Bennett (*AH*, 128). Still, Forster is not unaware of her shortcomings. He shares the common view that Virginia Woolf failed in depicting living people. "I feel that they do live, but not continuously" (144, 149) is his concession, or, differently phrased, she could give "life on the page," but not "life eternal," such as that of a character "remembered afterwards on its own account, as Emma is remembered, for instance, or Dorothea Casaubon, or Sophia and Constance in *The Old Wives' Tale* (127). Still, he sympathizes with her rejection of the naturalist tradition. He can jeer at Sinclair Lewis. The heroine of *Main Street* is quoted as saying, "I brought some snapshots

down to show you," and photography is oddly dismissed as "a pursuit
for the young" (*TC*, 257).

Ultimately we must conclude that Forster, in spite of the apparent
advocacy of "art for art's sake," applies standards of realism to literature
and to his own novels. He cannot get away from them as a novelist.
Somewhat ruefully he concludes that "the novel is not capable of as much
artistic development as the drama: its humanity or the grossness of its
material (use whichever phrase you like) hinder it" (*AN*, 150). He defends
Virginia Woolf either by saying that "she is a poet, who wants to write
something as near to a novel as possible" or by saying that "she liked
writing, liked receiving sensations—sights, sounds, tastes—passing them
through her mind," liked combining and arranging them. But then he
concedes that she did not avoid the pitfall, the "Palace of Art," that
"bottomless chasm of dullness . . . really a dreadful hole into which the
unwary aesthete may tumble, to be seen no more." Yet somehow, after
all, she "escaped the hole" because she liked writing for fun, because
"literature was her merry-go-round as well as her study," a feeble apology
which points to a central deficiency of Forster's criticism, his refusal to
think clearly about the creative process, the status of the work of art and
its function (*TC*, 258, 250, 251, 252).

As a good empiricist he disparages theory and criticism. Aesthetic
theories are "beds of Procrustes." As examples Forster invokes only the
obsolete issues raised by Tasso's and Corneille's struggles with authority
and the entirely different political troubles of Shostakovich. Criticism for
Forster has one practical function, "the sensitive dissection of particular
works of art," but this cannot be meant literally, for "the apparatus is
nothing, the specimen all." Without the specimen, the indistinct work of
art, the "education through precision" will not get far. Forster finds value
even in an outrageously gushy fancy of Walt Whitman on Beethoven
(*TC*, 116, 117). The ambition of criticism to "become co-creator" is dismissed as "presumptuous." "The claim of criticism to take us to the heart
of the Arts must be disallowed" (124, 127). Criticism is of little use to
the writer except in trivial matters. "The gulf between the creative and
critical states" (129) is unbridgeable, for Forster, conscious artist as he
was, considers creation ultimately unconscious. He uses several times the
image of the artist "letting down a bucket into the unconscious" (121,
91), arguing that any creator is surprised by his own creation. "Kubla
Khan" is invoked, and Claudel's saying: "Et l'ayant dite, je sais ce que j'ai
dit," which confirms him in the view that the critical state is "grossly
remote" from the creative (122, 123). It is a failure of his own criticism
when Forster is satisfied with gestures toward love and affection as stan-

dards of criticism or tells us, in a crude image, that "the novelist must bounce us" as Dickens "bounces us" (*AN*, 26, 76, 77). Forster remains, at least in his criticism, enclosed in the tradition of a critical realism—in contrast to Virginia Woolf's or Lytton Strachey's greater breadth and finer perceptions.

DESMOND MacCARTHY (1878–1952)

Desmond MacCarthy can be described as the most conservative critic of the group. His concept of criticism is practically Arnoldian: it "must be largely a 'criticism of life' . . . a discourse upon human nature and upon good and evil" (*C*, 152), as the writer (presumably the novelist or playwright) will "create or suggest a rational coherent ideal" of life. MacCarthy remarks, justly I think, that we will be surprised how much of the criticism of Goethe, Coleridge, Sainte-Beuve, Baudelaire, Arnold, is concerned with this question (19, cf. 286; 152). It is the standard of criticism of George Santayana, whom MacCarthy admires as "the greatest of living critics" (18). When in the preface to his most ambitious collection, *Criticism* (1932), MacCarthy formulates his ideal, he rather rehearses Sainte-Beuve's view of the critic as a "creature without a spiritual home" whose "point of honour is never to seek one," whose "first obligation is to permit himself to be absorbed in the vision of a writer." What matters most is sympathy and the power of the "critic, when he is expounding the literatures of the past, to put the reader at the point of view from which its contemporaries saw that literature, at the same time, of course, judging it from its own; and, confronted by contemporary literature, to show its relations to the world to-day." MacCarthy, in accord with Hennequin, anticipating a strong modern concern, thinks that "the psychology of the reader of a book is almost as much a part of the [critic's] subject as the book itself," though in practice he says little about it (vii, ix). Sometimes, the function of the critic is defined modestly as "not limited to comparison, analysis, and judgment; he may simply make us feel what he has felt." At such moments, MacCarthy admires Leigh Hunt and Swinburne, "the most magnificent sounding board for rapturous admiration," as critics (*H*, 175). He seems to advocate "appreciation" and "impressionism" when he criticizes Leslie Stephen as the "least aesthetic" of critics and complains that he is "deficient in the power of transmitting emotions he had derived himself from literature; he seldom, if ever, attempted to record a thrill" (*Leslie Stephen* [1937]). But in most of his writings MacCarthy is himself a moralist who judges from an ideal of a sane but somewhat gloomy and disillusioned view of life.

MacCarthy belonged to the early admirers of Proust in England. Proust's appeal, he argues, is due to the hope he raises that "aesthetic experience may, after all, fill the place of religious experience—probably a vain hope," he admits. While praising the books he concludes by suspecting the man. "How I should have missed in him, as a man, contact with the common massive satisfactions of life, and the steadiness of fundamental good-nature" (C, 198, 209). This commonsense standard makes MacCarthy reject "obscurity as a literary defect," mysticism as "nearly always pretentious and insincere," Catholicism as "capitulation" (141). MacCarthy is out of sympathy with most modernist experimentation and irrationalist philosophies. He admires D. H. Lawrence as "a religious prophet who was mistaken for a pornographer" but his mysticism is "nonsense to those" (and MacCarthy must consider himself one of them) "to whom belief in civilization seems a first condition of sanity" (253, 257). MacCarthy acknowledges that Lawrence's criticism of modern civilization has some truth in it, and he was deeply impressed by the imagination and vitality of his collection of poems, *Pansies.* MacCarthy has, however, no use for Freudian psychoanalysis: it "has had a bad effect on fiction because it offers easy short-cuts to psychological profundity." A novel by May Sinclair, *The Life and Death of Harriett Frean,* is used as a horrifying example (172, 176–80). The whole turn to subjectivity and to the technique of stream of consciousness does not appeal to him. Even Virginia Woolf, whom he admired personally, is criticized. "She gave us, as it were, not the train itself, but the draught a train makes as it flies by" (173). Joyce, though MacCarthy recognizes his "prodigious talents" and linguistic inventiveness, seems to him "a frightened enslaved mind. Much of *Ulysses* is cold, nasty, small and over-serious." The book is "far too much of a self-administered purge" (304, 303, 300). The stream of consciousness is a new artificial convention as artificial as any other. Gertrude Stein is a target of his ridicule. MacCarthy produces a page from *Pitman's Commercial Type-writing Manual* ("she likes a side-saddle; he is laid aside; he has skill," etc.) to dismiss her writing as "piffle" (261, 265). MacCarthy has no use for the "idea that the stuff of literature is a mass of words which can be arranged like coloured pebbles to make a pattern." It "undercuts almost the whole conception of what makes literature valuable to man" (269).

Not surprisingly MacCarthy has little to say about lyrical poetry and its techniques. He apologizes for the "uncertainty of judgements on poetry" as due to "our shifting moods" (C, 81). When in 1921 he reviewed T. S. Eliot he defined his general attitude as "subtle, tender, disillusioned, complicated and cool" and spoke of his "self-productive pride, reserve and sensibility of the dandy-like Laforgue." Eliot is labeled an "ironic sentimentalist" (92, 95, 96). Nowhere does MacCarthy look at the technique of poetry, even when he writes about Donne, Browning, and the highly admired Patmore (36, 68, 74).

MacCarthy achieves many of his effects by a technique of comparison. Eliot's modern curio shop with a few choice objects in it contrasts with Browning's curiosity shop, "a huge, rambling place, cobwebby, crammed, Rembrandtesque"; Joyce's "superstitious horror of the body and sex" contrasts with the "gay stoicism" of Rabelais; the "sceptical, aesthetic, amoral" Proust with the "emotionally lachrymose, and sentimentally moral" Richardson (C, 91, 300, 299, 213).

MacCarthy's preoccupation was with theater criticism, much of which is necessarily ephemeral. But he also wrote on his favorite dramatists. His heart went out to Ibsen and Chekhov. Ibsen's theater was for him a "theatre of the soul." Ibsen's role of social reformer is less important. "Society changes quickly; the soul hardly at all; it is that which makes his work permanent." It is that which "enables him to mingle with a realism which has even a perverse kind of commonness, fantastic symbols—rat wives, wild ducks, houses with lofty towers." Ibsen remains "the dramatist of the future," "our poet," as MacCarthy hopes for a "violent revulsion towards a philosophy which respects the individual and his happiness" (H, 62, 60, 65). Chekhov further defined a philosophy "never formulated," a "feeling rather than a thought," that though "precarious and empty, just because that is all, there is a kind of sacredness about it" (81).

Reviewing Eliot's *The Use of Poetry and Criticism*, MacCarthy can endorse his view that art and poetry cannot be a substitute for religion. "But poetry can help us to do one thing which religion helps us to do, to love life spiritually, that is to say, intelligently and disinterestedly" (H, 132). Intelligent and disinterested are good adjectives to qualify MacCarthy's criticism. They do not suffice to make him, as Lord David Cecil would want us to believe, "one of the best literary critics that England ever produced" (vi). He remains a minor, appealing figure.

4: THE NEW ROMANTICS

EZRA POUND AND T. S. ELIOT have so much dominated our conception of the new criticism in the twentieth century that other writers of the time have receded into a limbo. But it is impossible to ignore the group of critics—J. M. Murry, D. H. Lawrence, and G. Wilson Knight—whose conceptions of criticism and literature restate romantic or at least irrational attitudes which are still with us today. One cannot trace in that time a neat succession of trends, groups, and creeds. Rather, the most diverse points of view were voiced simultaneously, and in spite of deep differences even such antipodes as J. M. Murry and T. S. Eliot were in frequent personal contact. To establish their exact relationship, the priorities and chronology in which they adopted, developed, or invented key ideas, is a task that would require more space than this book could allow.

JOHN MIDDLETON MURRY (1889–1957)

The central figure of the group was John Middleton Murry, who played a great role both as editor of the *Athenaeum* and the *Adelphi* and as the author of a long row of books on criticism and almost every question under the sun. Few of his books can be obtained today. He appears usually as the husband of Katherine Mansfield, as the friend and foe of D. H. Lawrence, and possibly as the author of a book on *Keats and Shakespeare* (1925), which is often dismissed for its tone of adoration and the strained comparison implied in the title. When we look more closely, however, at his actual writings on literature, particularly *The Problem of Style* and the collections of early essays, we arrive at a different judgment. While Murry's political and religious ideas underwent quixotic gyrations, his outlook on literature was remarkably coherent, comprehensive, and, in its time and place, innovative or at least restorative. Murry revives the romantic concept of poetry as implying "some sort of Pantheism" (see "Thoughts on Pantheism" in *Things to Come*, 221), a belief in the unity of the world he often calls "organic." An acceptance of order, of death, and of evil follows. Every man is conceived as struggling for such an apprehension of the nature of the universe, as going through a process of maturing that he designates with Keats's term "soul-making." All great poetry is there to lead us to this insight, which is finally beyond reason, or at least beyond words. Murry ascribed great significance to a moment after the death of Katherine Mansfield when he felt at first utterly alone and then came suddenly to the recognition that "I *belonged,* and because I belonged, I was no longer I" (*TUG,* 43). He thought of this experience in 1923 as a mystical illumination, but nothing so portentous is needed to understand a view of the universe and of poetry perfectly comprehensible to Goethe, Coleridge, Carlyle, Emerson, or Blake.

Poetry (like all art and imaginative literature) is conceived as conveying a truth that is inexpressible in rational terms. "It does reveal what cannot be uttered" (*TUG,* 265). It is "the result of an effort to bring unthinkable thoughts and unsayable sayings within the range of human minds and ears" (*D,* 159). Poetry thus is emphatically not thought. "Poets do not have 'ideas,' they have perceptions. They do not have an 'idea'; they have comprehension" (*AL,* 199; cf. 56). Thus there is no philosophical poetry. "The universals of poetry are not concepts, nor have they conceptual equivalents" (*CM2,* 55). We recognize poetry by the impossibility of translating it into conceptual terms. A test of its authenticity is an affirmative answer to the question whether its meaning "could be conveyed to us by no other means" (*TUG,* 265). Like Eliot, Murry might have said that "in truth neither Shakespeare nor Dante did any real thinking."[1]

Murry, like Eliot, expounds a psychology of creation. Poetry is "rooted in emotion, and it grows by the mastery of emotion, and its significance finally depends upon the quality and comprehensiveness of the emotion" (*AL,* 147). Murry speaks rather vaguely of an original "perturbation of the poet's being" (*PS,* 24) but is wary of the old standard of "sincerity" and of tracing a poem back to some determined experience in the poet's life. "The essential quality of great artists," he recognizes, "is incommensurable with biography. They seem to be unconsciously engaged in a perpetual evasion of the event. All that piety can do for them is beside the mark" (*AL,* 113). Murry states that "the greater the man is, the more completely is an event merged in his inward reaction to the event. Not what happens to, but what happens *in* him, is the subject of our care; not what he suffers, but what he becomes" (*D,* 232–33). The syntax and the cadence remind one of Eliot's saying: "The more perfect the artist, the more completely separate in him will be the man who suffers and the mind which creates,"[2] but the argument can rather be paralleled in the subtle reflections made by Wilhelm Dilthey on the concept of *Erlebnis.*

Murry describes the process of transformation of the originating emotion into a work of art, or rather the conditions under which emotions can become effective in a work. In terms reminiscent of Eliot's "objective correlative" (though Murry never uses the term) Murry declares the necessity that emotions must be "symbolized in the objects which aroused them" (*PS*, 26). "The object is at once the cause and the symbol of the emotion" (97). He sees this process in the analogy of crystallization, drawn from Stendhal's simile for falling in love in *De l'amour,* in which the "writer's accumulation of emotional experience" forms itself about his characters "like crystals about a string dipped into a saturated solution" (31). Crystallization "of a large and structural kind" (105), "a created world" (41), emotions "systematized into a self-consistent whole" (75–76), "a complete projection of this personal emotion into the created thing" (35) are so many circumlocutions for the process of symbolization which, when successful, Murry calls "style." It is possibly from Goethe that Murry derives this exalted view of style, distinguishing it from "personal idiosyncrasy" (Goethe's *Manier*) and from the mere "techniques of exposition" (8).

Style or simply good poetry achieves its end by concreteness, solidity, palpability, by metaphor, by what John Crowe Ransom would call "texture." But Murry insists that the image need not be visual. "The precise visual image," he argues, "plays a very small part" in metaphor. "True metaphor, so far from being an ornament, has very little to do even with an act of comparison." It "becomes almost a mode of apprehension" (*PS,* 12–13). "Try to be precise, and you are bound to be metaphorical: you simply cannot help establishing affinities between all the provinces of the animate and inanimate world" (83). In the Oxford lectures on *The Problem of Style* (1922) and in an essay on "Metaphor" (in *CM2*), Murry develops an argument for the necessity of metaphor in "exploring the universe of quality and charting the non-measurable world" (*CM2*, 9). The greatest mastery is shown in a "succession of subtly related images" that produce "a harmonious total impression" (10). Murry shows how Shakespeare transformed a passage from North's translation of Plutarch describing Cleopatra's barge from an "inconsequential panorama" into an "organic unity" (12). But the acute observations do not satisfy Murry: he has to quote Coleridge saying that images are "modified by a predominant passion" and appeal to the imperious need of the poet to "impart life to the apparently lifeless" (13); thus he must conclude that "however much we struggle, we cannot avoid transcendentalism, for we are seeking to approximate to a universe of quality with analogy for its most essential language through a universe of quantity with a language of identities" (15). Murry is content with a gesture toward mystery, considering poetic images to be "miracles forever inviolable by intellectual analysis" (14). Still, the interpretation of metaphor as the main instrument of poetry was a fine restatement of an ancient insight.

What Murry aims at is something he calls a "metaphysic of poetry." Over and over again he repeats that particularity, concreteness, is the main device of poetry (an insight possibly learned from Bergson), but at the same time he still tries to identify this particularity with universality, just as he sees no contradiction between personality and impersonality. He argues that the particular, the image, the symbol, the specific plot, in harmony with the poet's emotion, or even myth, whose "structural possibilities depend upon its intelligibility" (*AL,* 40), imply always a universal which is, however, accessible only through the particular. It cannot be formulated in conceptual terms: this would require a belief that "there is a faculty of mind superior to the poetic." There is in great poetry a system of values which is "not a system at all. It satisfies, yet it cannot be analysed. The order is there, but it is the inscrutable order of organic life" (*CM*2, 59). Thus Shakespeare or any great poet is a "revealer of the real." "By the impact of that seemingly imperfect reality upon him, something is created in himself which declares that it is perfect" (60). It is this visible salvation that great poetry does offer. "It faces the real, it extenuates nothing: shrinks from nothing: it gives us life as it is" (62). "The poet's revelation of the perfection kindles in our souls the desire to be able, with unaided vision, to see the perfection for ourselves" (62). It is an "immediate apprehension of the unity of the world" (*TUG,* 179). Murry must conclude: "There is no escape. Religion and literature are branches of the same everlasting root" (164).

Still, Murry does not agree with the Abbé Bremond in identifying poetry, or at least pure poetry, with prayer. The poet's act of apprehension is not, according to Murry, Bremond's "incomplete mystical experience" (*CM*2, 20; see also *Things to Come,* 210–19). It is rather a single and entire mental act. In poetry "intellect and emotion, mind and heart, regain their lost unity within us." Poetry stimulates "the organic entirety of an experience" in us. We gain "integration," at least "a momentary union of thought and feeling. That will always be, relatively to our normal and necessary dissociations, joyful and beneficent" (*CM*2, 27). It brings us "into that 'fellowship with essence' than which, while we enjoy it, we can ask no more" (28). Murry quotes Macbeth's speech "Tomorrow and tomorrow . . ." and finds "undreamed-of riches, even in ultimate despair; a glory is shed over the road to dusty death. This despair is not despairing, because it is complete" (29). Something like Eliot's unified sensibility is here made an instrument of apologetics, of a theodicy which inspires Murry's often turgid celebrations of the blessings of poetry, for himself and for mankind.

If poetry is exalted, criticism must be, too, for it reveals the true nature and mission of poetry. "True criticism is itself an organic part of the whole activity of art" (*AL*, 11). It settles the "system of values" by which a work is to be judged (179). "To justify literature—this is the object and aim of modern criticism" (*CM2*, 33), and this justification will necessarily consist of an exposition of the ideal of life implied in literature. Inevitably criticism requires a scheme that allows it to establish a "hierarchy of values" (*AL,* 180), to arrive at a judgment that "in the last resort is an ethical judgement" (*CM*, 246). Murry appeals to Aristotle, who had "a conception of art as a means to a good life" (*AL*, 4). "The imitation of life in literature was for Aristotle, the creative revelation of the ideal actively at work in human life" (5). But in his usual way of thinking— which always has it both ways—Murry can say that "an ideal of the good life *must inevitably be aesthetic*" (8). "Art is autonomous, and to be pursued for its own sake, precisely because it comprehends the whole of human life" (12). Murry endorses what he assumes to have been the Greek view: the Greeks' "approach to life and their approach to art are the same; to them, and to them alone, life and art are one. The interpenetration is complete; the standards by which life and art are judged the same" (9). Obviously this is not only Murry's ideal but a description of his practice. A journal entry tells us of his early recognition that "criticism depended on values—a delineation of what is good for man. And I had to find out,"[3] a justification of his relentless search for a social Utopia.

But this emphasis on the good life is often contradicted, at least on the surface, by the description he gives of the method of criticism. It is sometimes formulated deceptively, when he says, "I subscribe whole-heartedly to the famous dictum of Anatole France that criticism is the adventures of a man's soul among books. More and more criticism appears to me an intensely personal affair" (*D,* 9). But actually Murry rejects impressionism when he quotes (as Eliot did before him) Remy de Gourmont saying that "the whole effort of a sincere man was to erect his personal impressions into laws" and condemns as no critic the "man who is content to record his own impressions, without making an effort to stabilize them in the form of laws" (*CM*, 239–40). The critic, he argues, needs "a system of principles, refined out of his more constant reactions, to control momentary enthusiasms and passing disgusts" (242). It would be "a foolish and impercipient reaction, to revive the impressionistic criticism which has sapped the English brain for a generation past" (*AL*,

200) out of dissatisfaction with "logic" and "ideas." Ultimately the method recommended by Murry is the age-old ideal of identification, of a complete submission which leads to "a sudden communication, a sudden communion rather" (D, 14). The true critic should say that "the more he can lose himself in the object, the more himself he is" (9). In exalted language he speaks of "touching a mystery. . . . There is a moment when, as though unconsciously and out of control, the deeper rhythm of a poet's work, the rise and fall of the great moods which determined what he was and what he wrote, enter into me also. I feel his presence; I am obedient to it, and it seems to me as though the breathing of my spirit is at one with his" (13–14). When Murry wrote his book on Dostoevsky he claimed: "All that happened—I speak, of course, of my sensation' only—was that the objective 'pattern' of Dostoevsky had declared itself, through me as an instrument" (Between Two Worlds, 368–69). Such a claim for inspiration, for some superpersonal imposition, is rarely put so confidently. Mostly Murry asks the critic "to have an apprehension of the unique and essential quality of his author" (PS, 34). He needs to have "patiently worked his way into the creative centre" (35); he must "convey the effect, the whole intellectual and emotional impression made by the work he is criticizing" (8). The critic must "define the unique quality of the sensibility which necessitated this expression" (CM, 245). Murry sees no contradiction in saying that the "function of criticism is primarily the function of literature itself, to provide a means of self-expression for the critic" (240) and that "a good criticism is as much a work of art as a good poem" (245). He aims at a synthesis of objective and subjective criticism, of self-assertion and submission, of the personal and the impersonal.

Murry's position is illuminated by his controversy with T. S. Eliot on the issue of classicism versus romanticism. Annoyed at the attempt to exalt David Garnett's Lady into Fox as a "great victory of classicism," when the novel seemed to Murry "about as classical as carved cocoanut" (TUG, 78), he declared: "I think it is very true that I myself am a Romantic" (80). Murry took the offensive by asserting that "in England there never has been any classicism worth talking about: we have had classics, but no classicism. And all our classics are romantic" (81). "The English writer, the English divine, the English statesman, inherit no rules from their forbears: they inherit only this: a sense that in the last resort they must depend upon the inner voice" (82). Romanticism is for Murry "individualism," "the discovery and discrimination of inward reality" (82, 84). Eliot had an easy game of ridiculing Murry's appeal to the inner voice as "remarkably like an old principle formulated in the new familiar phrase of 'doing as one likes' " and developing this satirically and snobbishly: "The possessors of the inner voice ride ten in a compartment to a football match at Swansea, listening to the inner voice, which breathes the eternal message of vanity, fear, and lust." Closer to Murry, Eliot suspects him of "a form of pantheism which I maintain is not European."[4] In his rebuttal Murry distinguishes between two kinds of romanticism: the romantic who "retires defiantly into the fortress of the ego" (*TUG*, 139) and the romantic (the kind he feels he is) who sees reality as "an organic and living whole," leading to an insight into "an underlying harmony in the external universe" achieved by a contact between "the finite soul and the infinite soul of which it is a manifestation" (49–50). This was in 1923. The controversy petered out but was renewed in 1926. Eliot invited Murry to restate his position and Murry, in a piece entitled "Towards a Synthesis," tried to refute the accusation of "anti-intellectualism" and reliance upon a capricious "inner voice" by a plea for a synthesis between "intuition" and "intelligence," for which Murry used the term "reason," "generated by the friction between intuition and intelligence" (*New Criterion* 5 [1927]: 312). Reason is here given the exalted sense in which it was used by Wordsworth and Coleridge. It is another version of attempts by Murry and many others, including Eliot, to define a new wholeness, a new undivided being, a new totality. Eliot's comment, however, rejects what he considers a false reliance on intuition, on making "poetry a substitute for philosophy and religion," each of which Eliot tries to keep in its proper place. Eliot now accuses Murry of relativism and Bergsonism. "What is true for one age is not true for another and there is no external standard" (*Monthly Criterion* 6 [1927]: 344–46). But this seems to do injustice to Murry. Murry, for instance, expressly disapproved of the "truly Hegelian spectacle of forms evolving out of forms in everlasting self-generation" (*PS*, 69) and always asserted "a system of values" which is not merely personal or time-bound. The other criticisms of Murry's position by Father M. C. D'Arcy, T. Sturge Moore, Charles Mauron, and Ramon Fernandez, the last two translated by Eliot, all rebuff Murry's rather pathetic attempt to reach a reconciliation.[5]

Actually Murry was often surprisingly sympathetic to classical points of view. An article on Lessing is almost panegyric about the "very great critic," "the most truly Aristotelian, of all the great critics since Aristotle" (*CM2*, 142). A review of Irving Babbitt's *Rousseau and Romanticism* is also highly laudatory. Murry appreciates his commitment to judgment and agrees that "the vital centre of our ethics is also the vital centre of our art" (*AL*, 170). Murry also likes his indictment of the gospel of progress and shares his fear that science might control human values, but he shrinks from an encounter with his views on the romantic poets. Later, Murry defended Babbitt's humanism against Eliot's view of its dependence on orthodoxy. Humanism and orthodoxy are irreconcilable. Eliot "to regain tradition has condemned himself to incessant mental suicide" (*New Adelphi* 2 [1929]: 198).

Still, Murry's attitude toward Eliot's criticism was far from unfavorable. In 1920 he wrote to Katherine Mansfield: "He is the only critic of literature that I think anything of" (Lea, *Life,* 72). Murry rejected, understandably, Eliot's view that the true critic is the poet. Eliot "has to smuggle the anomalous Aristotle in on the hardly convincing ground that 'he wrote well about everything,' and has, moreover, to elevate Dryden to a purple which he is quite unfitted to wear" (*AL,* 11). But the review of *The Sacred Wood* (in *New Republic* [April 13, 1921]: 194–95) praises Eliot's "critical intelligence of a high order and sensibility of an unusual kind" and gives a good exposition of Eliot's critical ideal: "to disengage and distinguish the precise emotion evoked by the object as a whole." Murry understands Eliot's standard of impersonality, sets it off well from the Parnassian ideal, and focuses on his discussion of comedy, the continuity between Marlowe and Ben Jonson in particular. Murry objects only to Eliot's manner as "often unfortunate, portentous and disdainful" and considers it a tactical error in "not doing his utmost to eliminate the traces of a superior attitude." But Murry's review has conspicuous omissions: he says nothing of Eliot's concept of tradition or the objective correlative. Later more disagreements come into the open: Murry protests against Eliot ranking Dickens below George Eliot and Stendhal (*P,* 178), and he violently disagrees with Eliot's view that "Seneca stands in the same relation to Shakespeare as Aquinas does to Dante." That "Shakespeare expressed an inferior philosophy in the greatest poetry" seems to him "surely nonsense" (*PCM,* 1, 13). But the main criticism is the then-current one of the cleft Eliot. Eliot is not "a true-blue classicist however much he might like to be" (*TUG,* 144). Murry finds "an inward contradiction between the profession of classical principles such as his and the content of *The Waste Land*" ("The 'Classical' Revival," in *Adelphi* 3 [1926]: 592). "The poem expresses a self-torturing and utter nihilism." There is an "internecine conflict between his understanding and his being" (594). Murry was baffled by the assertion of a "classical revival" in England and tried to distinguish between the "cynical" writers, Lytton Strachey, David Garnett, and Aldous Huxley, and the two "serious" writers, Virginia Woolf and T. S. Eliot, who were purported to be in league with them but to Murry appeared to be sailing under false colors. They were no classicists. They were "unusually fine critics" but exercised a "prodigious intellectual subtlety to produce the effect of a final futility." Both *Jacob's Room* and *The Waste Land* seemed to him failures, "experimental, alembicated, obscure" (*Adelphi* 3 [1926]: 590–91).

It is an error to see sharply drawn battle lines in criticism at that time. Eliot reviewed Murry's early play, *Cinnamon and Angelica*, with great interest in the issue of the poetic drama, later to become his own preoccupation (*Athenaeum* [May 14, 1920]: 635); he wrote favorable accounts of Murry's "brilliant" book on D. H. Lawrence (*Criterion* 10 [1931]: 768) and the "very good book" on Shakespeare (*Criterion* 15 [1936]: 708–10) and after Murry's death contributed a generous foreword to a posthumous collection of Murry's essays (*Katherine Mansfield and Other Literary Studies*, vii–xii), lauding him as a "literary critic first and foremost" who "in exploring the mind and soul of some creative writer, explored his own mind and soul also." Eliot recalls personal meetings and singles out essays by Murry which struck him in the past. Murry resumed reviewing Eliot in the last years of his life. A long, leisurely essay on the plays describes and analyzes them, praising *The Cocktail Party* as "an admirable play" (*UE*, 172) but consistently complaining of Eliot's alternatives for his characters between "ascetic vocation on the one hand and unloving marriage on the other" (183). Murry must proclaim the possibility of happy marriage against what he considers Eliot's nausea at sex. Incidentally Murry expresses his puzzlement with Eliot's later poetry as beautiful but "too hard for [his] understanding" (189).

Murry, in the book published in the year of his death, *Love, Freedom and Society* (1957), compared Lawrence and Eliot, thinking of himself as "representing something in between" the two (letter, 1955, quoted in Lea, *Life*, 346). In the conclusion, however, he declares: "I am, profoundly, with Lawrence rather than Eliot." Nevertheless, he defends Eliot's spirituality as belonging to a venerable tradition which he feels "will not serve to carry us through what is to come" (*Selected Criticism, 1916–1957*, ed. R. Rees, 302). Eliot and Murry disagreed on the issues of religion, society, and sex, but they were not so far apart in criticism as the disagreements may indicate.

One would expect that Murry would approve of G. Wilson Knight and that Eliot would not. Actually the opposite is true. Knight later acknowledged his profound debt to Murry and wrote favorably about his criticism (even of his book on Swift: see *Poets in Action* [1967], 176–78), though setting himself off, saying, "[Murry] wrote from his own spiritual experience, I from the imagination" (*Neglected Powers* [1971], 359). But Murry reviewed *Myth and Miracle* skeptically. He doubted the evidence for Shakespeare's "transcendental apprehension" and Knight's assumption that "poetic power and visionary power are indistinguishable. Poetry is one thing, religion is another. . . . The religious and the poetic judgement must be kept distinct," an injunction that Murry did not always observe himself. Murry questions Knight's ascription of portentous significance to the use of music in the later plays. "Resuscitations, miracles and enchantments lend themselves to pretty stage effects" enhanced by music, "provided it is sweet and low" (*TLS*, August 8, 1929). The objections to *The Wheel of Fire* are even stronger. "I can scarcely recognise some of the plays after they have passed through the process of 'interpretation' to which [Knight] submits them." Murry argues against the whitewash of good King Claudius and Knight's view "that the something that *is* rotten in the state of Denmark is Hamlet himself." Knight imposes "a dangerous, because empty schematism" (see *Adelphi*, n.s. 1 [January 1931]: 342–43). He stands the play on its head. Murry obviously was not impressed by Eliot's laudatory preface.

The two great critics of Shakespeare were for him Coleridge and A. C. Bradley. Coleridge is "the greatest critic of Shakespeare" (*AL*, 195), *Biographia Literaria* is "the best book of criticism in the English language" (184), but Murry dislikes Coleridge's philosophizing. His "submersion in the tepid transcendentalism wrought havoc upon Coleridge's mind" (184). He sees him as a rationalist who tried to seduce Wordsworth to write a philosophical poem and who defended a false distinction between the language of poetry and the language of prose. Murry admires Coleridge's practical criticism most: the pages on *Venus and Adonis* show him "at the summit of his powers as critic" (186). Bradley's book on *Shakespearean Tragedy* Murry considered "the greatest single work of criticism in the English language." Bradley is "the most genuinely imaginative critic our country has produced. . . . He, rather than Coleridge or Hazlitt, was the critical consciousness of that [romantic] age" (*Katherine Mansfield and Other Literary Portraits*, 114, 119).

The admirer of Bradley had no use for I. A. Richards's view of tragedy as indicating that "all is right with the nervous system." Murry questions whether "we should read *King Lear* only to find out that." Richards's view is "purely emotional and subjective. We feel it, and that is all," but Murry argues that "except we know the nature of the object, nothing can be deduced as to the nature of the subject." Richards leaves the "tragedy out of the reckoning." "It is tedious, no doubt, to be compelled thus painfully to indicate that an egg is an egg and not a taste." Murry necessarily rejects Richards's demolition of the "revelation" theory. He defends the knowledge conveyed by poetry as the "real in its particularity."

Murry acknowledges that we experience "joy and serenity" through tragedy, but there would not be joy and acceptance in the tragic experience
if it did not have "its roots in outward life" (in *Things to Come,* 178, 180,
182, 186).

The same assertion of the objectivity of a poem, the same distrust of
psychologizing, motivates Murry's criticism of Empson's *Seven Types of
Ambiguity.* "A poem," Murry believes, "is an incantation, a word of immediate power, compelling the wandering mind to response in a certain
order." It is "an organic whole," whereas Empson sees only the parts.
The book "is incontinent, and obscures rather than explains" (*PCM,* 81).

Comment on F. R. Leavis is rather sparse and late. Murry reviewed
his book on Lawrence, complaining, predictably, of the overrating of *The
Rainbow* and *Women in Love* and questioning the "extreme eulogy" of
St. Mawr. Murry concludes, justly I think, that Leavis "has made a brave
and stimulating effort to separate Lawrence's art from his doctrine but
in order to do it has been compelled to a tacit expurgation. The doctrine
is always there" (*PCM,* 87, 90). Murry seems not to be aware that the
same criticism could be made of his own book on Lawrence. In *Unprofessional Essays* (1956) Murry came to the defense of Fielding against Leavis's
dismissal of Fielding from the Great Tradition. He tries to explain Leavis's boredom with Fielding as arising from his preconceptions and protests incidentally against Leavis's singling out of Dickens's *Hard Times* for
praise (*UE,* 21). Though the emphasis of the essay is on an exposition
of Fielding's morality, Leavis appears as an honest but obtuse dogmatist,
hidebound by his theories.

Murry's last review discussed R. P. Blackmur's *The Lion and the Honey-
comb* and Allen Tate's *The Man of Letters in the Modern World.* He sees that
T. S. Eliot is the "primary scripture of the new canon of which
Mr. Blackmur and Mr. Tate stand high among the theologians," but he
finds them "impressively and dishearteningly arcane," complains of the
"complexity, intensity, scholasticism and concentration on a narrow range
of subject-matter," of "something portentous" about the New Criticism.
Mainly he voices misgivings about a "dysgenic union: between academic
criticism and the private worlds" (*London Magazine* 4 [1957]: 67, 69).
Murry resolutely remained a freelance writer, a journalist, a man of
letters.

The preceding pages have described Murry's theory of literature and
criticism and defined his position in a history of criticism. Still, Murry's
reputation rightly depends on his monographs and the essays devoted
to individual writers. *Fyodor Dostoevsky* (1916) was Murry's first biography,
an attempt to describe the evolution of the writer toward salvation (mean-

ing reconciliation, acceptance), a salvation proposed to humanity and implicitly to Murry himself. Murry ignores Dostoevsky as an artist almost completely, declaring that "Dostoevsky is not a novelist, and he cannot be judged as a novelist" (48). He could not represent life, "as he was obsessed by the *vision* of eternity" (37). His characters are "disembodied spirits. They have the likeness of men, we are told, but we know that we shall never look upon them" (47). "Their bodies are but symbols." Stavrogin, for instance, "is not a man but a presence" (161). Murry reflects: "It may be there really was no Smerdyakov as there really was no Devil, and they both had their abode in Ivan's soul. But then who did the murder? Then of course it may have been Ivan himself, or, on the other hand, there may have been no murder at all" (228), and, we may add, no book. The sense of phantasmagoria, of allegory with total disregard for what may be called Dostoevsky's realism, is conveyed so strongly that the novels are not only allegorized—often in obvious ways ("Rogozhin is Body, Myshkin is Soul" [152]; Nastasya is "not a woman but the embodiment of Pain" [152]—but also vaporized to become merely stages of Dostoevsky's spiritual pilgrimage from despair and pain to suffering and to a final acceptance and reconciliation with life (43). The stages are conceived of as not only marking Dostoevsky's progress but also charting the epochs of human consciousness, eventually leading to a faith in humanity which Dostoevsky claimed to be peculiarly Russian. "No one who looks steadily upon the nineteenth century can deny that the Russian spirit alone in modern times has taken mankind a great stride nearer to its inevitable goal. In Russian literature alone can be heard the trumpet-note of a new word." In Tolstoy and Dostoevsky "humanity stood on the brink of the revelation of a great secret" (263), but we are not told what this secret may be, except an "open secret": love, humanity, reconciliation, acceptance of evil, and death.

The book has been called by D. S. Mirsky "Pecksniffian sobstuff."[6] We may wonder how Murry can confidently assert that Dostoevsky "knew that belief in God as a person, the faith of religion as we understand religion, was denied him for ever" (44). We may puzzle why he declared "Svidrigailov" to be "the real hero of *Crime and Punishment*" (113), and we can correct his hasty reading when he says about Nastasya that "at the door of the church where [she and Myshkin] have been married, she leaves him for Rogozhin" (148). One may deplore the fervent tone, the whole strident claim for Dostoevsky's belief in the regeneration of mankind, but one can hardly deny that Murry correctly perceived that Dostoevsky expected a miracle, a Utopia around the corner.

Murry's book is the high point in England of Dostoevsky's impact as a "revelation." He becomes the incarnation of the spirit of Russian literature. "Russian literature," Murry tells us, "has done more than any other single influence to diminish the prestige of the French conception of literature" (*D,* 47), "French" meaning here *l'art pour l'art,* the well-made novel in the wake of *Madame Bovary.* Russian literature is exalted for its concern with conduct, with the harmony of human faculties, for its tolerance for the failings of men, which Murry finds compatible with the concern for the right life and the hunger for the absolute. Russian literature, he concludes, is "more Christian than any literature has ever been" (63). It is "historically, the fulfillment of our own" (69), answering the striving of Wordsworth, Shelley, and Keats for "an apprehension of harmony which includes, and by including, justifies all evil and pain" (72). Russian literature appears thus as a continuation of the English romantic movement.

Murry is thinking mainly of Dostoevsky and Tolstoy, whom he manages to see in some kind of harmony with his great antipode. But Chekhov became Murry's second and greatest love. He is to him "the last great writer" (*D,* 78), not only in Russia. He disagrees with the usual view of Chekhov as gray, depressing, and painful. Chekhov "goes there, without hope, without belief; it is the last of all forlorn quests: and he brings back the Grail in his hands" (78). In similar exalted terms: "There is no harmony, he cries, and the very sound of his voice echoes the music of the spheres" (76). Chekhov was "the perfectly free man; a man who has freed himself from all fears and has found that within himself which enables him to stand completely alone" (100). Murry remained an individualist even when he embraced socialism and some version of communism. But he deluded himself about Russia many times: in November 1916 he could praise Shestov in an introduction to a translation of the *Essays,* saying, "In Russia things of the spirit are held in honour above all others" (*EI,* 26). Russia was a dreamland: it was wartime and the Russians were Britain's allies.

But Murry's real masters, the two poets he admired beyond any other, were Shakespeare and Keats. *Keats and Shakespeare* (1925) put the two names on the title page though the book is about Keats and only exploits Keats's enthusiasm for Shakespeare to draw a strained parallel. Murry makes much of Keats's dramatic ambitions and sees him moving to greater objectivity, speculating about the vain hopes of writing a great drama. But *Otho the Great* contradicts this prediction. Keats never could have been a dramatist. Murry writes, as in his *Dostoevsky,* a spiritual biography with Keats as "a hero of humanity" (5), a poet who saw poetry "as a distinct and separate mode of attaining that final truth . . . the truth

of the soul, which comprehends and reconciles the partial truth of the
heart and of the mind" (26). Murry sees negative capability as "the only
road to a true personal identity as it is the truth itself" (49). Keats confirms his view of impersonality as the "true way to personality" as "self-
annihilation is a means to self-achievement" (53). This theme allows
Murry to write his "most intimate history in terms of his rejection first
of Wordsworth, then of Milton, in favor of a deeper and unchanging
loyalty to Shakespeare" (41). In ever new variations Keats is depicted as
resolving the discord of beauty and pain, the chaos and contradictions
of the world. Keats "is discovering the harmony which unites man to the
animal universe; he is revealing to himself and to us that things must be
as they are" (120). *Hyperion* is the pinnacle of Keats's actual achievement,
but Murry wishes to show that Keats "was greater, far greater than his
actual achievement." He wishes to present him as "the perfect type of
the great poet" (70), a man who possessed his own soul and became a
complete man. The soul, as Murry interprets Keats's famous letter, is
slowly created by "submission of consciousness to unconsciousness"
(138). Poetry is thus "one of the few roads that remains open to the
eternal reality that is less directly and less fully expressed in religion"
(144). Pure poetry contains a revelation, "a knowledge of the unity and
harmony of the universe which can be reached only through the individual's knowledge of unity and harmony in himself" (147). While *Hyperion* is Keats's greatest poetic achievement, the culmination of his
spiritual progress is *The Fall of Hyperion,* the vision of Moneta, "the poetic
vision of God—of a godhead immanent in the changing and enduring
reality of the world" (183), the poet's acceptance of death.

This overall scheme should not conceal the fact that Murry in the first
book and in many supplements and revisions (*Studies in Keats* [1930],
Studies in Keats: New and Old [1939], *The Mystery of Keats* [1949], and *Keats*
[1955]) sensitively commented on the letters, on Keats's personal relationships to Fanny Brawne (about whom he changed his mind), to Fanny
Keats, and others, and, in elaborate comparisons with Wordsworth, Milton, and Blake, on almost every one of Keats's poems, *Endymion,* "On
First Looking into Chapman's Homer," "On Visiting the Tomb of
Burns," and others. Murry slights *Isabella* because it does not yield much
for his conception of Keats, and he is apt to give grossly biographical
readings to poems that lend themselves to this procedure. "La Belle
Dame sans Merci," for example, *is* Fanny Brawne (124). But it should be
granted that Murry conveys both the spiritual and the erotic struggle of
the man, the tone and sense of his letters and poetry, even though Murry
overdoes the transcendental and even "mystical" element. Murry for-

mulated the main problems of later Keats criticism, though he seems
now out of favor with Keats scholars. Morris Dickstein, author of *Keats
and His Poetry* (1971), is an exception. Much in Murry is superseded or
needs correction or toning down, but he succeeded in rescuing Keats
from the "aesthetic" misreading still dominant in H. W. Garrod. He took
seriously Keats's struggle for self-awareness and maturity, movingly depicted in the letters, without succumbing to the temptation to systematize
the "Mind of Yeats" as Clarence D. Thorpe did in his influential book.

Murry's book on *Shakespeare* (1936), though long contemplated and
anticipated in early articles, parallels the Keats book, exploiting the concept of negative capability as the key. "In the moral world the finest type
of character may be achieved through having none; in the world of art,
perfection of style begins where manner ends; in the world of spirit,
absolute identity supervenes on self-annihilation" (30). The theme of all-
embracing sympathy, of the identity of objectivity with empathy, is, as in
Keats, often abandoned in favor of identifying Shakespeare with a particular character in the plays. There is the Shakespeare Man: Hamlet.
"We can imagine Shakespeare acting like Hamlet, whereas we cannot
imagine him acting like Lear, or Othello, or Macbeth" (324). There is,
on the other hand, the Shakespeare Woman: "She is Desdemona, and
Imogen, Perdita and Miranda" (231). The sonnets allow Murry to speculate wildly while admitting that it is all conjecture. He says three times
on one page (106) "I believe" and appeals to his "obstinate feeling that
the sonnets as a whole are the work of three years" (113). Then there are
Shakespeare's ideal Englishmen: the Bastard in *King John,* "one of the
most splendid of Shakespeare's creations" (162). Murry then notices that
the monolingual English gentleman-suitor of Portia in *The Merchant of
Venice* is, like the Bastard, called Falconbridge; Murry "regrets that he
did not marry Portia; he would have made a nobler husband than Bas-
sanio." "The Bastard's Portia is a French princess; her name (as it would
be in Shakespeare) is Kate" (169). We are asked to assume an identity
between the Bastard and Henry V. But mostly Murry does not engage
in such sentimental speculations. He is aware of the writings of L. L.
Schücking, E. E. Stoll, and W. W. Lawrence and agrees that "the situations [in Shakespeare's plays] are generally prior to the characters" (209).
He sees that it was "precisely by reason of the compulsion the audience
exacted upon his genius that he became the greatest *dramatist* of the
world" (134), though for Murry "the poetic and dramatic act are indis-
solubly entwined together" (286). Oddly enough, Murry ranks *King Lear*
as "definitely inferior to the other three 'great' tragedies of Shakespeare"
(337), lacking in "imaginative control" and "poetic spontaneity" (342,

348). Murry prefers *Coriolanus,* on which he had written two earlier, not uncritical essays (*D,* 265–85, and *CM,* 34–35), and *Antony and Cleopatra,* where Murry's obsessive theme of the love-death pursued in the Keats book finds its fullest expression: "The total self-sacrifice of one human being for another in death, is the only true symbol we have and can recognize for Love" (378). Murry, however, rejects the allegorical interpretations of the last plays, feeling "certain that allegory was alien to Shakespeare's mind" (392), but still he sees the last period as revealing a "man longing for spring, in nature and in the hearts of men: cherishing the reality of the rebirth of nature, and the dream of reborn Man" (408).

The book, in spite of all its lacunae and shortcomings, does give, I think, the "sensation" of Shakespeare (vii). It should be supplemented by Murry's essays on Shakespeare and Shakespeare's critics. He constantly resists the attempt to make Shakespeare the propounder of some abstract creeds or propositions as "the 'idea' bacillus" (*AL,* 198), when King John is described as illustrating the idea of treachery, and he resists realistic standards, well understanding stage conventions and imaginative flights. He can go into raptures about "The Phoenix and the Turtle," calling it "the most perfect short poem in any language" (*D,* 25). It is used to illustrate Murry's constant groping toward a description of the nature of genuine poetry. "The Phoenix and the Turtle" is "high above the plane of intellectual apprehension: what we understand is only a poor simulacrum of what we feel" (*D,* 23). It is both "crystal-clear" and "mysterious" and twenty pages later "obscure, mystical, and strictly unintelligible" (23, 43). Ultimately Murry can only point to what he considers poetry.

His idea of poetry is clarified by a glance at his many essays and pronouncements on English poets from Chaucer to T. S. Eliot. Chaucer is obviously outside his ken. He can say that "Chaucer is not what we understand by a great poet; he has none of the imaginative comprehension and little of the music that belong to one" (*AL,* 153). In a lengthy discussion in *Heaven—and Earth* (1938; the American edition is called *Heroes of Thought*) Chaucer is used as evidence for the parasitism of the medieval Church and the plight of the village community. Spenser is the "poet's poet"—the tradition of English poetry is rooted in Spenser, but today he "belongs to the archeology of literature" (*CM2,* 65). He was obsessed by the "passion of formal beauty," while "the morality is a mere convenience, or a useful theme, and the imagery quite often mere decorative fancy" (*CM2,* 74). *The Faerie Queene* is seen quite unhistorically. "Spenser's aim was to write a great poem in the English language; it could be *about* anything that great poems were about" (*CM2,* 69). Murry singles out the Sixth Book and the *Epithalamion* for praise, recognizing that this is a common view. Murry shares Keats's and Eliot's view that Milton represents a deviation from the continuity of English poetry. "He all but killed the English tongue" (*PS*, 109). "He petrified the poetry which he reformed" (*PCM*, 5). Murry "would give all *Paradise Lost* for the *Areopagitica*," which had moved him to tears (*Heaven*, 165). *Samson Agonistes* is "a superb museum piece" (*PCM*, 2) which "bears in it the marks of a long brooding over injuries, in the spirit of self-righteousness. It may be perfect but it does not live. It has no charity" (*Heaven*, 177). We can anticipate Murry's low opinion of eighteenth-century poetry, except for the five: Collins, Smart, Chatterton, Cowper, and Gray. "One killed himself, and three died melancholy-mad" (*D*, 163). Actually Murry made a further exception, in one of his deftest essays, for the poetry of the Countess of Winchelsea (1661–1720), her "genius for the intangible" (*CM2*, 175), knowing, of course, that she was a very minor poet. The essay on Collins recognizes "a sensibility overweighted from the beginning by a precious literary instinct" (*CM*, 89), a sensibility "deadened by the aesthetic preoccupation interposed between it and direct experience" (*CM*, 90), but praises "The Ode to Evening" and "How Sleep the Brave" lavishly and incidentally comments on Pope as a "Master of Wit in the best Metaphysical sense" (*CM*, 93), a perception developed later by F. R. Leavis.

Murry's concept of poetry was mainly determined by the English romantics, primarily by Keats. The comments on Wordsworth, however, are surprisingly meager and unsympathetic. Once he suggests that "Wordsworth's disintegration was due to the influence of his own theories upon himself." Upset by Coleridge's criticism of natural language in *Biographia Literaria*, "Wordsworth from that time forth indulged in it pretty freely; he achieved *simplesse* rather than simplicity" (*PS*, 201). Chronology is ignored, the relation is stood on its head. The comment on Wordsworth in *Heaven—and Earth* deplores his turn to conservatism in the tone of "The Lost Leader." Only a late essay, "Coleridge and Wordsworth" (in *Katherine Mansfield and Other Literary Portraits*), makes amends, recognizing the early Wordsworth, "a man for whom the vastness and the unity of the world were a *real experience of the world*" (74), a man who had "a real mystical experience" quite apart from Christianity (80). But Wordsworth is only the foil to describe Coleridge's disintegration, his self-deception in "believing there was an identity between Wordsworth's experience and his own" (87), illustrated by "Dejection: An Ode." The essay is psychological and biographical and moralizes haughtily about Coleridge's behavior to his family and friends. An inward decay is supposed to have begun with the trip to Germany in 1798. "He began to be eaten away by his sense of sin" (90), apparently at the loss of his second child during his absence. It is an unproved speculation which denies the achievement of the later Coleridge. In the same context in *Heaven—and Earth* in which Murry speaks of Wordsworth's turn to conservatism, Shelley draws favorable comments for his radicalism. In a late essay comparing Keats and Shelley, Murry explains his preference for Keats and speaks of Shelley's poetry as "abstract, intellectual, metaphysical," faults he admits to be his own (*Katherine Mansfield and Other Literary Portraits*, 240).

Murry's discovery (though Arthur Symons and Edmund Blunden had preceded him) was John Clare, whom he lauded as a "finer artist than Wordsworth," who "had a truer ear and more exquisite instinct for words," though Murry recognized that Clare lacked Wordsworth's scope and "principle of inward growth" (*CM*, 110). Murry admired Clare as the "love poet of nature," for his "impulsive tenderness" and his "unwearied eye watching the infinite process of Nature" (126, 121, 115). A late essay entitled "Clare Revisited" (in *Unprofessional Essays*, 1956)— which is as perceptive as anything he had written in his youth—pays more attention to Clare's mental derangement, his dreams of a lost paradise, and his resentment against the land enclosures. "Enclosure—imprisonment: both of himself and wild nature and the old order was 'freedom' for them. His mind clung to it with passionate and undying regret" (*UE*, 106).

The great Victorians seem not to have interested Murry much. G. M. Hopkins, on whom he wrote before his rise to fame (*Aspects of Literature*, 1920), left him cold. "The failure of his whole achievement was due to the starvation of experience which his vocation imposed upon him" (*AL*, 60). Murry's admiration goes out to Hardy as a poet. He must have been one of the first to prefer the poet to the novelist and to see that Hardy's poetry was not "a late and freakish flowering" (122) or a "curious simulacrum of his prose" (124) but a work of magnitude and depth in its own right. Murry brings to bear his criterion of visionary power: a poem is a "veritable epiphany," "an act of plenary apprehension" (132). Commenting on another poem, Murry develops a theory of the poetic process which he calls "two-fold." The poet discovers a symbol, establishes an equivalence between feeling and some external object, and then sees its significance, recognizes "the all in the one" which is "the specifically poetic act" (135). It seems hard to uphold such a distinction or to see such a sequence. Murry himself did not use these two stages later. But Hardy passed the test: he is a major poet.

Murry was cool toward most contemporary English poets. Early he had attacked the anthology *Georgian Poetry* (*AL*, 139–49). He appreciated Edward Thomas, John Masefield (150–56), and Walter De la Mare very mildly; *The Wild Swans of Coole* by Yeats seemed to him a failure. Yeats "has the apparatus of enchantment, but no potency in his soul" (45). Murry quotes: "I am worn out with dreams . . ." and takes it as a pitiful confession of defeat (42). Eliot's poetry, we saw, he considered a failure.

But Murry's interests were not confined to English poetry. From stays in Paris he also knew a good deal about France and French literature. His favorite poet was Baudelaire, whom he saw in the company of "intellectual romantics, in rebellion against life" (*CM*, 160), a group in which he included Stendhal, Nietzsche, and Dostoevsky. Murry rejects the label "decadent poet" and Arthur Symons's view of Baudelaire as a "singer of strange sins" (180). Baudelaire as a poet was "strong, masculine, deliberate, classical," even "heroic" (158). "The texture of his verse is very hard"—Murry's expression for what in ancient rhetoric would be called "austere harmony." In Baudelaire's poetry, he observes, "all living things" are reduced "to a condition of immobile solidity" (165). Murry describes his dandyism, combined with a sympathy for the oppressed and loathing for the bourgeois. His sentiment of suffering and his dream of escape by belief in God elicit Murry's entire sympathy.

Murry rarely paid attention to German literature. But the two chapters on Goethe in *Heaven—and Earth* show a surprisingly wide knowledge of Goethe's writings. They are an exposition of Goethe's Spinozism, concern with nature, and wisdom, with well-phrased claims of his enduring importance: "He was the first man who was really aware of man's true place in the realm of nature. . . . His historical consciousness is a new event in human history." Murry seems, at first, to share the view that Goethe was "a jack of all trades and master of none," disparaging his dramas, novels, and prose style. But he sees the mistake: Goethe was neither the last of the great dilettanti nor an all-round master. He sees his greatness, his daemon, the mastery of life, and has only the reservation: "He lacks the accent of suffering, the knowledge of the price of experience" (*Heaven*, 244). An article on Hölderlin, while introductory— as a review of Ronald Peacock's book had to be—shows a sureness of touch, a wide range of reference, and closes with a good observation: "Diotima is much rather a Beatrice guiding him to a *vita nuova* than a priestess of Plato's 'Symposium.' " Hölderlin referring to her "Madonna head" gives the case away. There was an unresolved conflict between Greece and Galilee in his mind (*PCM*, 26).

Murry's interest in fiction was much more limited, if we consider his concern for Dostoevsky or Lawrence motivated by their doctrines. But it was by no means nonexistent. The Russian novelists were used by Murry as contrast and refutation of what he considered the aberrant development toward the art novel. The criticism of Flaubert starts from this point. "The invention of 'Art' has done no good to art" (*CM*, 225). The cult of Flaubert as "the greatest writer who ever lived," particularly flourishing in England and America, seems to him preposterous. He is unimpressed by Flaubert's agonies. "It is not easy to see why the value of a writer's work should depend upon the completeness of his incineration on the altar of Art" (206). Murry disparages his imagination, his use of metaphor, recognizing only his "visual pageantry." Flaubert "had a bourgeois horror of the bourgeois" and suffered from a "strange absence of inward growth" (208, 210). Murry finds *Salammbô, La Tentation de St. Antoine*, and *Bouvard et Pécuchet* "inwardly hollow." Only *Madame Bovary* is praised, while *L'Éducation sentimentale* is dismissed as "a work of history rather than literature" (211, 218). Murry preferred Stendhal. He admired his tragic attitude toward life, his belief in man's duty to be a tragic hero (237). He calls him "a miniature, desiccated Shakespeare" (230), ambiguous praise which rejects the label "hedonist" and assimilates Stendhal to Shakespeare's attitude to life. But Stendhal "had not a shred of a sense of humour" (236). Murry had the singular merit to have written first in English, in July 1922, on Proust's *A la recherche du temps perdu*, "the subtlest of all modern psychological fictions" (*D*, 118) during Proust's lifetime. He had met Proust in Paris briefly. Murry accurately forecast the then unpublished conclusion and saw that the book was "in essentials the story of its own creation" (118). He described the duality between "the psychological history of modern mentality and an anatomy of modern society" (115), but he never entered into any discussion of technique, though he predicted that Henry James's *Critical Prefaces* "may some day occupy a place analogous to Flaubert's correspondence" (*PS*, 21).

   In the English novel Murry's taste remained traditional. He seems not to have written extensively on any of the standard novelists except for a late paper defending Fielding (*UE*). The interest in George Gissing (interpreted in terms of his erotic life) and a friend, Henry Williamson, belongs also to his last years (in *Katherine Mansfield and Other Literary Studies*). The new developments in fiction he felt as the "break-up of the novel," as the end of storywriting. He deplores James's "undue preoccupation with technique" and the "hypertrophy of his style" (*PS*, 21–22). He called *Ulysses* "a work of genius" but also "a gigantic aberration, the last extravagance of romanticism" (*D*, 146–47). He then reviewed *Ulysses* much in the same tone (*The Nation and Atheneum* 31 [April 22, 1922]: 124–25), totally unshocked at a time when the book had to be smuggled from Paris. Murry admires most the Circe chapter, a "transcendental buffoonery" (he calls it *Walpurgisnacht*), as "revealing a genius of the very highest order, strictly comparable to Goethe's or Dostoevsky's" but complains about obscurity and the "curse of nimiety, of too-muchness that hangs over the whole" (125). There is sense in saying that "the strongest part of [Joyce's] talent is magnificently comic" (*D*, 151).

Of all the novelists D. H. Lawrence absorbed Murry most. It was not, of course, the novelist alone but rather the prophet and the friend and foe. There is no need to retell the ups and downs of the relationship, which dates back to 1913, nor to discuss the accuracy of Murry's *Reminiscences of D. H. Lawrence* (1933) nor the way Lawrence used Murry as a model in his fiction, caricaturing him in such a story as "Smile." But Murry did write reviews of Lawrence's books during his lifetime, and *Son of Woman* (1931) is not merely a biography of Lawrence which as Graham Hough complains "proceeds throughout to blame the works for not telling the story [of Lawrence's life] right"[7]: it also contains literary criticism, judgments on books and ideas. Murry's reviews written in the twenties following the break with Lawrence harshly condemn the novels after *Sons and Lovers*. *The Lost Girl* shows "a very obvious loss of imaginative power," though it is a competent novel, more closely knit than *The Rainbow*. But the "corrupt mysticism" is condemned. Lawrence "would have us back to the slime from which we rose" (reprinted in *R*, 217). *Women in Love* is "five hundred pages of passionate vehemence, wave after wave of turgid, exasperated writing" (220). Murry asks, "Is Mr. Lawrence a fanatic or a prophet? That he is an artist no longer is certain, as certain as it is that he has no desire to be one" (222). Rather oddly, *Aaron's Rod* pleased Murry as "gay, careless, persuasive." "To read *Aaron's Rod* is to drink of a fountain of life." Lawrence has achieved serenity. *Aaron's Rod* "is the most important thing that has happened to English literature since the war. To my mind it is much more important than *Ulysses*. . . . *Ulysses* is sterile; *Aaron's Rod* is full of the sap of life" (231). *Fantasia of the Unconscious* is praised as a criticism of our civilization independent of either Freud or Jung (241; cf. an even more laudatory review in *The Nation and Athenaeum,* overlooked in *R*). Murry prophesies that "Lawrence must inevitably become a figure of European significance" and calls him "incomparably the most important writer of his generation" (242). A review of *Birds, Beasts and Flowers* praises Lawrence's knowledge of nonhuman life (250), but short notices of *St. Mawr* and *The Plumed Serpent* register disappointment, and a longer review of *The Collected Poems* voices refusal to abandon "intellectual consciousness": "a suicide that we neither will nor *can* commit" (262). Still, Lawrence is "very like a great prophet in the continuity of Jesus, with a message essentially the same and with comparable power of dynamic utterance," though Lawrence, Murry knows, refuses "to face the fact of Jesus" (266–67). A review of *Lady Chatterley's Lover* calls it, "for all its incompleteness and its still smouldering rage, a positive, living and creative book," a "cleansing book, the bringer of a new 'katharsis' " (275, 271). In spite of the rift in their friendship Murry continued to treat Lawrence as a very great writer but refused to share his anti-intellectualism and judged his books by a standard of approximation to serenity and good sense.

This is basically the view expounded in *Son of Woman* (1931), though the book caused offense for its strident condemnation of Lawrence as a "prophet of a false religion: which denies and will not understand the reality of Spirit" (352) and its suggestion that Lawrence was "almost a sexual weakling" (52). Murry appeared as a traitor, a Judas who after Lawrence's death took revenge for Lawrence's rejection of his friendship. We do not have to enter into this acrimonious dispute to see that Murry handles two critical questions which he keeps pretty clearly apart from biography: Lawrence's ideology, his so-called love ethic, and his success as a novelist. Murry seems to me substantially correct in describing and interpreting the ideology, the hatred of modern civilization which Murry seems to share or, at least, to understand, and Lawrence's view of the relationship between the sexes, "the intensity of loathing for woman in the sexual relation" (44), his demand that woman submit to man completely, abjectly, renouncing any claim to her own satisfaction and consenting even to physical abuse. Murry, in his revulsion from this creed, tries to divorce it from the art of the novelist and comes up with a ranking of the books that falsifies the evidence of their respective power. He is, I think, quite right in praising *Sons and Lovers* as Lawrence's "greatest book." "If Lawrence is to be judged as the 'pure artist,' then it is true that he never surpassed, and barely equalled, this rich and moving record of a life" (23). *The Rainbow* and *Women in Love* appear chaotic and obscure in comparison. Though Murry praises the opening of the chapter "Anna Victrix" in *The Rainbow*, saying that there is "nothing more beautiful or more powerful in all Lawrence's writing" (75), the implied view of marriage and the "ultra-phallic otherness" (134) of the Birkin-Ursula relationship is condemned as "a lie or as many lies." *Fantasia of the Unconscious* is called then Lawrence's "greatest book" (171) and *Aaron's Rod* "the greatest of his novels" (141); *Sons and Lovers* is apparently forgotten in each case. *The Lost Girl* is praised for the "magnificent chapters"

(149) on life in the Alban mountains. The novel appears as the "decisive moment" of Lawrence's recovery, of his revulsion against the former nostalgia. "A man must not put off his humanity; the allurement of the pre-mental world is a temptation, a lure to death" (151). *Aaron's Rod* accomplished the recovery. There is "more of the essential Lawrence in this than any other of his novels" (220). Murry sees the "sheer detestation of woman" which underlies *Aaron's Rod*. Sex is the supreme disaster. "All the insistence on sex and the blood-consciousness, which is the constant obsession of all his books . . . was in his own secret judgment, a self-violation, a sin against the light" (287). Murry thinks of *The Plumed Serpent* as an "imaginative achievement," as Lawrence's "greatest work of 'art' " (318), where "art" means a willed contrivance. But *St. Mawr* seems to him feeble, "febrile and sentimental in temper, unstable and incoherent in substance; it is a monument of Lawrence's disintegration" (338). *Lady Chatterley's Lover* has become a "wearisome and oppressive book" (369), while *The Man Who Died* is "a wonderful story; one of the most wonderful stories in the world—the masterpiece of a great and dying genius" (372), though a few pages later it is called "a childish dream" (381). In the attempt to exalt Lawrence to a Christlike figure whom "Jesus would have loved as his own brother" (377), Murry tries to rescue the rational core of his doctrine, the criticism of machine civilization, the need to confront our sensual nature, while brushing aside, with some embarrassment, the sinister implications of the worship of the dark gods. This attempt falsifies Murry's view of the books. It does not affect *Sons and Lovers* but leads to the paradox of demoting *The Rainbow* and *Women in Love,* clearly Lawrence's most individual and powerful books, and exalting *Aaron's Rod,* which is full of padding, local satire, travel descriptions, and remains morally indecisive and obscure. *Son of Woman* emphasizes Murry's shortcomings as a critic: his excessive involvement with the man and the doctrine behind the books which distorts his usually sound literary judgment.

The two later full-sized books on *William Blake* (1933) and *Jonathan Swift* (1954) are much more impersonal attempts at interpretation, suggesting self-imposed tasks. The Blake book gives a straightforward exposition of the doctrine which an unsuspect expert, Northrop Frye, predicted would "remain one of the best and closest studies of Blake's poetry and thought."[8] Without trying to adjudicate the rightness and wrongness of Murry's readings, the discussions of "There Is No Natural Religion" and of *Milton* strike me as particularly perceptive. *Milton* is considered Blake's "prophetic masterpiece," a "unique, imperishable, and inexhaustible work" (*Blake*, 218). The book, more sober than the books on Keats, Shakespeare, or Lawrence, is marred again by easy generalizations, parallelisms between Blake and Lawrence, Blake and Marx, and by the refusal to see Blake in the situation of his time. To say, "Albion [in *America*] has nothing to do with the England of George III and Pitt" (95–96), seems patently false, and one wonders why a poet can be considered "great among the greatest" for his "teaching of the final unity between Eternity and Forgiveness" (254). It suited Murry then to declare Blake "a great Communist," the reference to Marx obscuring his usual view that "the classless society is . . . inconceivable except as a Christian society" (*In Defence of Democracy* [1939], 190).

The book on Swift was, Murry admitted, "a sort of challenge to myself—to write a book on someone with whom I could not *possibly* identify myself" (letter, 1953, in Lea, *Life*, 240). He aimed at the "*ne plus ultra* of objectivity" (ibid.). It has been admired as Murry's "finest book" (341), but as a biography it has been superseded, and the attempt at psychoanalysis which picks up Aldous Huxley's suggestions in an essay on Swift in *What You Will* (1929) and christens Swift's preoccupation wih scatology "the excremental vision" seems to me a wrong step toward Norman O. Brown's fancies. Nor can one be convinced by the speculation based on a single letter (April 17, 1696) that the rejection of Swift's suit for Jane Waring was such a long-lasting traumatic experience and that, on the whole, a mind like Swift's should or could be interpreted by his obscure relations to women. The book is uncharacteristic of the best of Murry.

Murry needs rehabilitation today. This survey must have shown his enormous range, the coherence of his taste and opinions, the deftness of his formulations, and the theory of literature behind his varied pronouncements. This theory is now out of fashion, at a time when literature can be reduced to language games cut off from any reference to reality and criticism be made a science or pseudo-science which deliberately shirks any value judgment. Murry provides an antidote with his belief in the cognitive value of literature and in criticism as value judgment. At his best, he avoids a revelation theory, an identification of literature and religion as well as of literature and philosophy, seeing literature as a symbolization of emotion. He has discussed the metaphorical method of knowledge perceptively and has described the poet's struggle for self-identity and clarity. There is something to be said even for his variety of hero-worship. His great poets live a life of allegory, present an exemplary struggle with themselves, the world, and their work. He knows that a critic has to deal with an object that challenges him, that he must ap-

proach in humility in order to grasp it sympathetically. He knows that
correct interpretation, a sense for specific quality, leads to right judgment.

I am aware of his shortcomings and have, I know, minimized them:
he can be nebulous, turgid, pretentious, even bombastic. He makes gestures toward mystery that encourage the new obscurantism. But we may
have to admit that there is a final barrier, that genius or merely the
quality of great poetry cannot be completely accounted for, that Murry
had a feeling for the transcendent that cannot be dismissed if we want
to understand the great poets (and not only the romantic poets) of the
past.

D. H. LAWRENCE (1885–1930)

If John Middleton Murry is the romantic critic *redivivus,* D. H. Lawrence
will appear as the most extreme irrationalist. He wants to "release us
from the horrid grip of the evil-smelling old Logos" (*Apocalypse* [1932],
171); he detests abstract philosophy including the "beastly Kant" (*P,* 520);
he constantly appeals to "blood-consciousness," or "phallic consciousness," to the "solar plexus," the "dark gods," so many metaphors for the
subconscious, the instinctive, the utterly spontaneous and intuitive. Literary criticism seems to have no chance whatever, though Lawrence was
obviously a radical critic of industrial civilization, sexual morality, and
human relationships in general.

Still, F. R. Leavis could call him "the finest literary critic of our time—
a great literary critic if ever there was one" (*Scrutiny* 6 [1937]: 352), and
the one book of literary criticism Lawrence published during his lifetime,
Studies in Classic American Literature (1923), has been praised by Edmund
Wilson as "one of the few first-rate books that have ever been written on
the subject" (*The Shock of Recognition,* 2:906). Clearly it will not do to
underrate Lawrence's intelligence, shrewdness, and power of pungent
formulation. Actually his concept of literary criticism was a good restatement of an age-old creed. "Literary criticism," he tells us, introducing
a harsh attack on John Galsworthy, "can be no more than a reasoned
account of the feeling produced upon the critic by the book he is criticizing. Criticism can never be a science: it is, in the first place, much too
personal and in the second, it is concerned with values that science ignores. The touchstone is emotion, not reason. We judge a work of art
by its effect on our sincere and vital emotion, and nothing else." "A critic
must be able to *feel* the impact of a work of art in all its complexity and
force. . . . A critic must be emotionally alive in every fibre, intellectually

capable and skilful in essential logic, and then morally very honest" (*P,* 539). Sainte-Beuve remains to him a great critic "who has the courage to admit what he feels, as well as the flexibility to *know* what he feels." Here Lawrence explicitly recognizes the role of the intellect and even of logic while still reserving first place for an instinctive taste or insight. In many contexts, in letters and in reviews, Lawrence voiced his opinions vividly, sometimes truculently but often perceptively: the short reviews of Hemingway's *In Our Time* and of Dos Passos's *Manhattan Transfer* (363–65), the introductions to translations of Verga (223–31, 240–50), and to Edward Dahlberg's *Bottom Dogs* (267–73), and even the demolition jobs on H. G. Wells's *World of William Clissold* (346–50) and on John Galsworthy are good traditional criticism. *The World of William Clissold* "is all chewed-up newspaper, and chewed-up scientific reports, like a mouse's nest" (350). Lawrence retells with comic indignation, for instance, a story, "The Apple Tree," to show up Galsworthy's class-bound snobbery and vulgar sentimentalism.

Lawrence has good things to say about the novel. He has a grand view of the novelist's mission. "The novel is a great discovery: far greater than Galileo's telescope or somebody else's wireless" (*P2,* 416). "Being a novelist I consider myself superior to the saint, the scientist, the philosopher, and the poet who are all great masters of different bits of man alone, but never of the whole hog." "Whole hog" means here total man—soul, mind, and body—from which the novelist creates or should create so that he can cause "a tremulation on the ether which can make the whole man alive tremble" (*P,* 535). The novel can help us "to live as nothing else can" (532): it reveals (as does all art, presumably) "the relation between man and the circumambient universe, at the living moment" (527). "The novel is the highest example of subtle inter-relatedness that man has discovered" (528). For obvious reasons Lawrence pondered the relation of the novel to morality and specifically to pornography. He disapproved of overt moralizing. Morality is "that delicate, for ever trembling and changing balance between me and my circumambient universe," while moralizing, tendentiousness, is as if "the novelist put his thumb in the scale, to pull down the balance to his own predilection" (528)—and that is for Lawrence immorality. He admits that "the novel is not, as a rule, immoral because the novelist has any dominant *idea,* or *purpose.* The immorality lies in the novelist's helpless, unconscious predilection" (529), in sentimental, "sweet" novels, in blood-and-thunder novels, in smart cynical novels, in any art that falsifies reality and real relationships. He agrees that "every work of art adheres to some system of morality. But if it be really a work of art, it must contain the essential criticism on the morality to which it adheres" (476). Understandably, Lawrence was much concerned with freeing the novel from prudish restraints in sexual matters. We all know of his posthumous victory in England. The trial, in 1960, of *Lady Chatterley's Lover* broke the taboo on four-letter words with a vengeance, but Lawrence himself in his treatise on "Pornography and Obscenity" and his spirited defense "A propos *Lady Chatterley's Lover*" was anxious to make a distinction between frank depiction of sex and pornography. "Even I would censor pornography rigorously. Pornography is the attempt to insult sex, to do dirt on it" (175), whereas he argues that his own fiction does away with both sentimentality and obscenity.

Lawrence professes no interest in the "critical twiddle-twaddle about style and form" (*P,* 539), and he ridiculed Clive Bell's term *significant form* (566–67). He disapproved of the "craving for form" in the novel after Flaubert and singled out Thomas Mann as "the last sick sufferer from the complaint of Flaubert" (312). Oddly enough, Lawrence identifies Aschenbach, aged fifty-three in Mann's *Death in Venice*, with Thomas Mann and sees Mann as "old" and superannuated, though he was thirty-eight years old in 1913. "Even *Madame Bovary* seems to me dead in respect to the living rhythm of the whole work" (313). The maxim "nothing outside of the definite line of the book" seems to him stultifying: the human mind cannot "fix absolutely any definite line of action for a living being" (308). He thus defends a loose organic form: "We need an apparent formlessness, definite form is mechanical" (248). He sounds almost Crocean, saying that every work of art has its own form, which "has no relationships with any other form" and which "admits the existence of no other form" (454). He defended the form of *Sons and Lovers* by saying, "All rules of construction hold good only for novels which are copies of other novels; a book which is not a copy of other books has its own construction" (*L,* 299), and argued—parrying objections to the first version of *The Rainbow* (then called *The Wedding Ring*)—that "you mustn't look in my novel for the old stable *ego*—of the character. There is another *ego*, according to whose action the individual is unrecognisable, and passes through, as it were, allotropic states which it needs a deeper sense than any we've been used to exercise, to discover are states of the same single radically unchanged element" (*CL,* 282).

The rejection of the well-made novel, the concept of unique, fluid form and indeterminable character sound like defenses of the innovations of what could loosely be called modernism. Besides, Lawrence was a strong advocate of free verse. But this is deceptive. Lawrence detested psychologizing, the "self-important mentalities" (*Lady Chatterley's Lover,* ch. 13) of Proust. In a jeering attack that lumps Dorothy Richardson, Proust, and Joyce together, they are accused of preoccupation with petty trivialities. " 'Did I feel a twinge in my little toe, or didn't I?' asks every character of Mr. Joyce or of Miss Richardson or of M. Proust" (*P*, 517); Joyce and Richardson "strip their smallest emotions to the finest threads. . . . It is really childish, after a certain age, to be absorbedly self-conscious" (518). In a letter Lawrence complains more violently of an installment of *Finnegans Wake* in *transition*: "My God, what a clumsy *olla putrida* James Joyce is! Nothing but old fags and cabbage-stumps of quotations from the Bible and the rest, stewed in the juice of deliberate, journalistic dirty-mindedness—what old and hardworked staleness, masquerading as the all-new!" (*CL*, 1075), and, on the same occasion, "James Joyce bores me stiff—too terribly would-be and done-on-purpose, utterly without spontaneity or real life" (1087). Lawrence wanted fictional characters and books to be "alive," to be "quick." Quick, he tried to explain, "means the man in the novel must have a quick relatedness to all the other things in the novel: snow, bed-bugs, sunshine, the phallus, trains, silk-hats, cats, sorrow, people, food, diphtheria, fuchsias, stars, ideas, God, toothpaste, lightning, and toilet paper" (*P2*, 420). But this does not get us much further than E. M. Forster's round and flat characters. In practice, in Lawrence, the live character is always the instinctual man or woman. All writers are "phallic worshippers. From Balzac to Hardy, it is so. Nay, from Apuleius to E. M. Forster. Yet all of them when it comes to their philosophy, or what they think-they-are, they are all crucified Jesuses" (417). They all suffer from this duplicity of overt and latent meaning.

This sense of the double bottom, of the subtext, the latent meaning, pervades all of Lawrence's criticism. He is one of the unmaskers, convinced that the conscious intentions of the artist may run counter to his deep-felt allegiances. This contrast is an old idea in criticism: well known to the Schlegels, prominent in such diverse unrelated critics as Dobrolyubov in Russia and De Sanctis in Italy, and used by Engels in his famous letter on Balzac. It is memorably formulated by Lawrence: "Never trust the artist. Trust the tale. The proper function of the critic is to save the tale from the artist who created it" (*S*, 13). The earlier version amplifies this, saying, "The artist, who writes as a somnambulist in the spell of pure truth as in a dream, is contravened and contradicted by the wakeful man and moralist who sits at the desk" (*SM*, 18).

Lawrence looks for symbols in literature, which he distinguishes, in the fashion inherited from Goethe via Coleridge, from allegory. "Allegory is narrative description using, as a rule, images to express certain definite qualities. Each image means something, and is a term in the argument and nearly always for a moral or didactic purpose" (*P,* 295–96). They don't 'mean something.' They stand for units of human *feeling,* human experience. A complex of emotional experience is a symbol. And the power of the symbol is to arouse the deep emotional self, and the dynamic self, beyond comprehension. Many ages of accumulated experience still throb within a symbol. . . . No man can invent symbols. He can invent an emblem, made up of images: or metaphors: or images: but not symbols" (296). Myth for Lawrence implies a view of history that is often another version of the "dissociation of sensibility," the growing alienation of man, the artist's conflict with society. Sometimes this historical scheme is derived from Lawrence's wide reading in prehistory, anthropology, and philosophies of history, in Frobenius, Jane Harrison, Houston Stewart Chamberlain, and many others, ascribing to a mythical Atlantis, a fanciful Mexico, Africa, or Etruria, the status of the primeval wholeness now decayed. Sometimes the same society is assigned to the Middle Ages, "the grandiose, violent past of the Middle Ages" (*P2,* 318), or simply to the old peasant civilization, in Sicily or Sardinia, or the old English countryside before industrialization. Sometimes it is thought of simply as a decay of wholesome sexuality. Lawrence sketches a history of English poetry in these terms. Chaucer was "lovely and fearless," but Shakespeare is already morbid with the fear of sexuality. " 'Drink to me only with thine eyes' sings the cavalier" (as if Ben Jonson had been a cavalier). "The physical consciousness gives a last song in Burns." "Wordsworth, Keats, Shelley, the Brontës are all post-mortem poets." Swinburne and Wilde tried "to start a revival from the mental field" (*P,* 551–52), meaning that they, like the French symbolists, were intellectuals self-consciously reviving sexuality. But Lawrence admired Swinburne as "the greatest English poet" after Shelley, "the last fiery spirit among us" (*CL,* 474).

Lawrence conceives of himself as destined to reconstitute this original unity of man, to reconcile the mind and body, to establish the proper harmony between male and female—not necessarily the biological sexes, but in a theory clearly derived from Otto Weininger, to whom he alludes (*P,* 393), as poles between which every individual takes or rather has to take an intermediate position. This scheme of sexual psychology, combined with the scheme of history, which is not just primitivism but a Utopia of rebirth, becomes the main standard by which he judges books and characters in books. Characters are frequently discussed without any regard to their function in a book, simply as human beings living today whom he examines for their morals and asks for right behavior in a situation abstracted from the book. Literary criticism breaks down. Law-rence simply allegorizes books, destroys the content of a book or the pattern of a writer's mind and uses them to expound his own ideology.

This comes out clearly in his discussions of Tolstoy and Dostoevsky. Tolstoy's *Anna Karenina* is grossly misinterpreted when Lawrence sees it merely as displaying Anna and Vronsky unable "to live in the pride of their sincere passion and spit in Mother Grundy's eyes" (*P2*, 417), a judgment several times repeated and made worse when Lawrence mis-interprets Tolstoy's motto, "Vengeance is mine: I shall repay," as if Tol-stoy identified the "vulgar social condemnation" of Anna and Vronsky with "divine punishment" (*P*, 247). Lawrence condemned the later ascetic Tolstoy, exaggerating the discontinuity between the early and the late stages, opposing the "marvelous sensuous understanding" of the younger man to the "philosopher with a very nauseating Christian-brotherhood idea of himself" (*P*, 479; *P2*, 421). But Lawrence disliked even *War and Peace*, calling it "downright dishonourable, with that fat, diluted Pierre for a hero" (*P2*, 423), and with more justification speaks of Prince Nekh-lyudov in *Resurrection* as a "muff," as "dead as lumber" (420, 416).

Dostoevsky is treated with embittered hostility. Some of the violence of Lawrence's pronouncements must be ascribed to his distaste for Mur-ry's exaltation of Dostoevsky, to the whole English cult of Dostoevsky and the Russians during the First World War years, but essentially it is mo-tivated by Lawrence's contempt for Dostoevsky's religion, which he sus-pects of hypocrisy. The early letters vary in stridency: *Crime and Punishment* "is a tract, a treatise, a pamphlet" (*CL*, 54). He did not care for *The Possessed*: "Nobody was possessed enough really to interest me. They bore me, these squirming sorts of people: they teem like insects" (430). But the same letter attempts a reasonable classification of Dos-toevsky's characters according to their will and a criticism of what might be called his angelism. "The whole point of Dostoevsky lies in the fact of his fixed will that the individual ego, the achieved I, the conscious entity, shall be infinite, God-like, and absolved from all relation, i.e. free" (431). Even earlier this is phrased as a condemnation. Dostoevsky was "a pure introvert, a purely disintegrating will—there was not a grain of the passion of love within him—all the passion of hate, of evil. It has come, I think, now, a supreme wickedness to set up a Christ worship as Dos-toevsky did: it is the outcome of an evil will, disguising itself in terms of love" (332). "Dostoevsky, mixing God and Sadism, he is foul" (420). Most extravagantly, Dostoevsky's books and Murry's study of him are called, "offal, putrid stuff." "Dostoevsky is a rotten little stinker" (492), and even more drastically: "Dostoevsky, like the rest, can nicely stick his head between the feet of Christ, and waggle his behind in the air" (470). A poem sums it up:

> Dostoevsky, the Judas,
> with his sham christianity
> epileptically ruined
> the last bit of sanity
> left in the hefty bodies
> of the Russian nobility.
>
>   ("Now it's happened" [*CP*, 536–37], from *Pansies*, 1929)

But when Lawrence was induced to write a preface to *The Grand Inquisitor* (1930) he assumed a calm tone, retelling the legend, but misread its point completely. Dostoevsky supposedly says there, "Jesus, you are inadequate. Men must correct you. And Jesus at the end gives the kiss of acquiescence to the Inquisitor" (*P*, 283). "Jesus kisses the Inquisitor: Thank you, thank you, you are right, old man" (290). But surely Jesus Christ does not accept the arguments of the Grand Inquisitor. He answers them in the only way religion can answer atheism—by silence and forgiveness. The Inquisitor is refuted by the kiss. Alyosha immediately afterward kisses Ivan, forgiving him his atheism, answering his "revolt" with Christian love. Ivan knows this when he says, "That's plagiarism. You stole it from my poem." The rest of the novel—Father Zossima, Brother Markel, the conclusion with Alyosha promising the boys immortality—testifies, as well as Dostoevsky's other writings, fictional and journalistic, to the correctness of this interpretation and the wrongheadedness of Lawrence's, which, surprisingly, has been echoed widely.

What can one say when Lawrence writes that Chekhov "is a second-rate writer and a willy wet-leg" (*CL*, 1109)?

This revulsion against the greatest Russian writers was a denial, after all, of the "enormous amount" they had meant to Lawrence earlier. "Turgenev, Tolstoy, Dostoevsky—mattered almost more than anything, and I thought them the greatest writers of all time." But now (in 1916) he realized "a certain crudity and thick uncivilised stupidity about them" (*L*, 387–88). He deplored their self-consciousness, their probings into the soul. "That is almost the whole of Russian literature: the phenomenal coruscations of the soul of quite commonplace people. That's why the Russians are so popular. Every character in Dostoevsky or Chekhov thinks himself *inwardly* a nonesuch, absolutely unique" (*P*, 227–28). Lawrence prefers the terse, straightforward art of Verga writing about Sicilians who have not got "our sort of subjective consciousness," who have no soul in our sense of the word (228). "Anything more un-Russian than Verga it would be hard to imagine: save Homer." He made one exception among the Russians: he had discovered Vasily Rozanov. Reviewing *Solitaria* he praised him for having "more or less recovered the genuine pagan vision, the phallic vision" (369), though he suspects him to be "a pup out of the Dostoievsky kennel" (367). The other book then translated, *Fallen Leaves*, interested him less as "just fragments of thought jotted down anywhere and anyhow" (388).

Lawrence was happier with his predecessors at home. He realized "with something of a shock how much finer and purer and more ultimate our own stuff is" compared with the Russians (*L*, 388). A long study of Thomas Hardy, written in 1914 but not published until 1936, wanders all over the place but does contain, when it finally settles down to a consideration of the novels, some witty retelling of the absurd plots of the early novels and good comment on the role of the setting, Egdon Heath, in *The Return of the Native* (*P*, 415). Lawrence rejects Hardy's metaphysics and with the usual contrast between overt and latent meaning thinks that "turning to the earth, to landscape, then he is true to himself" (480). Lawrence denies, however, that the position of Hardy's heroines—Eustacia, Tess, and Sue—is tragic. "Necessarily painful it was, but they were not at war with God, only with Society. . . . And the judgment of men killed them, not the judgment of their own souls or the judgment of Eternal God" (420). "There is," he feels, "a lack of sternness, there is hesitating between life and public opinion, which diminishes the Wessex novels from the rank of pure tragedy" (440). But other contexts show that Lawrence actually did not rank tragedy in general highly. This little poem must be taken literally:

> Tragedy looks to me like man
> In love with his own defeat.
> Which is only a sloppy way of being in love with yourself.
> I can't very much care about woes and tragedies
> of Lear and Macbeth and Hamlet and Timon.
> They cared so excessively themselves.
>
> (*CP*, 508)

In a vivid account of theatricals on Lake Garda Lawrence condemns *Hamlet* as "repulsive in its conception, based on self-dislike and a spirit of disintegration" (*Twilight in Italy* [1916], 122). He sees Hamlet in contrast to his prototype Orestes as "a mental creature, anti-physical, anti-sensual" (124). Lawrence approves of the reconciliation at the end of the *Oresteia* but finds the final duel in *Hamlet* merely foolish. Later he repeats that "the real 'mortal coil' in Hamlet is all sexual; the young man's horror of his mother's incest, sex carrying with it a wild and nameless terror which, it seems to me, it had never carried before" (*P*, 551). In spite of all of Lawrence's revulsion against his time, he remained a Utopian, full of messianic hope, and disapproved of tragedy.

The discussion of Hardy's main novels unfortunately quickly degenerates into a criticism of the main characters in terms of Lawrence's schematic sexual typology. For instance, Arabella in *Jude the Obscure* is defended, while Sue is denigrated. Arabella is not so coarse as Hardy made her out to be (*P,* 489). Sue is not a woman: she had no love for Jude. But how could Lawrence or anybody else know that Arabella— who throws a pig's pizzle at Jude, sticks the pig to bleed it slowly to death, and deserts Jude in total incomprehension of his ambition for learning— was less coarse than Hardy depicted her as being? Lawrence's criticism here and in many instances suffers from a common critical vice: the confusion of fiction and reality, the use of fiction to illustrate a theory or preconception.

Similarly a thesis or rather several theses on national psychology, history, and sexual typology are imposed on American writing in *Studies in Classic American Literature* (1923). The chapters exist in earlier versions published in *The English Review* in 1919 and 1920. These are more sober and straightforward: less strident in tone, less Carlylese, less exclamatory in style, but also less pungent and impressive. The national psychology which is at the basis seems to me, however, preposterous in its wild generalizations. "The essential American soul is hard, isolate, stoic, and a killer" (*S,* 73). "In America, nobody does anything from the blood. Always from the nerves, if not from the mind." "Ghastly Americans, with their blood no longer blood. A yellow spiritual fluid" (96). "The American has got to destroy. It is his destiny. It is his destiny to destroy the whole corpus of the white psyche, the white consciousness" (93). "America hurts because it has a powerful disintegrative influence upon the white psyche" (60). The Americans (all Americans?) are depicted as thinned out, intellectualized, hating "the old European spontaneity" (16), but at the same time as demonic, destructive. Lawrence detests what could be called the idealist tradition in America. "You *must* look through the surface of American art, and see the inner diabolism of the symbolic meaning. Otherwise it is all mere childishness" (93). Or, "You have got to pull the democratic and idealistic clothes off American utterance, and see what you can of the dusky body of *IT* underneath" (18). Lawrence does this, first, by denying that the pilgrim fathers came for freedom of worship. Rather, as the earlier version develops it, they had "a gloomy passion to destroy or mutilate life at its very quick, lusting in their dark power to annihilate all living impulses, both of their own and those of their neighbour" (*SM,* 25). Then Benjamin Franklin is satirized for his utilitarian Philistinism. "He tries to take away my wholeness and my dark forest, my freedom" (*S*, 28). Oddly enough, Franklin is considered some kind of dark plotter who "has done more to ruin the old Europe than any Russian nihilist" (30–31); how remains obscure, unless we take him as the symbol of the shallow Enlightenment and technology.

James Fenimore Cooper is ridiculed for social snobbery and lip service to egalitarian democracy. He was "a gentleman in the worst sense of the word" (*S*, 56). The "white novels" are condemned but the *Leatherstocking Tales* are praised, particularly for the "stark stripped, human relationship of two men," Chingachgook and Natty Bumpo, "deeper than the depths of sex" (63). The tales create a myth of a new relationship. "The two childless womanless men, of opposite races,"are "the clue, the inception of the new Humanity" (69). The Deerslayer is "a man who turns his back on white society," "an isolate, almost selfless, stoic, enduring man, who lives by death, by killing, but who is pure white. This is the very intrinsic-most American" (73), and suddenly this lonely man, and earlier the two men, are seen as containing the germ of the future.

Poe, in contrast, belongs entirely to the past. "Ligeia" is interpreted as "a ghastly story of the assertion of the human will, the will-to-live and the will-to-consciousness, asserted against death itself. The pride of human conceit in *Knowledge*" (*S*, 85). Poe is for Lawrence the representative of excessive self-consciousness, of extreme intellectualism, and of the "ghastly disease, love" (92), love meaning here romantic spiritual love contrasted with healthy sex. He ridiculed it also in Dante and Petrarch, who had their "spiritual concubines," Beatrice and Laura, but babies with other women (*P*2, 422).

There is no overt discussion of transcendentalism in the *Studies*, but in a review of Stuart Sherman's *Americans* (1923) Lawrence expressed his opinion of Emerson sufficiently. He is an "idealist." Quoting "I am surrounded by messengers of God who send me credentials day by day," Lawrence jeers that Emerson forgot that there are many messengers. "He knew only a sort of smooth-shaven Gabriel. There was a whole bunch of others. But Emerson had a stone-deaf ear for all except a nicely au-reoled Gabriel qui n'avait pas de quoi" (*P*, 317).

But the prime example of Lawrence's method of unmasking is Haw-thorne's *Scarlet Letter*, "a masterpiece in duplicity and false excitement" (*P*, 319). The book is allegorized into a "colossal satire" (*S*, 98) on the destructive love of woman. Hester Prynne is a demon, a witch, a devil, as Pearl is a devilish girl-child, a little demon who married an Italian count (a detail invented by Lawrence). Dimmesdale was seduced by Hes-ter but took his revenge in the public confession at the end. The Scarlet

Woman became a Sister of Mercy (*S*, 122). Hester is characterized as a
Great Mother, is called "oriental," which in Lawrence's weird spiritual
geography means also that "the aboriginal American principle is working
in her, the Aztec principle" (134). Chillingworth is a malevolent soul,
somebody like Francis Bacon, while Dimmesdale is "the whole clue of
Dostoevsky" (140). This is developed in the earlier version—"Dostoevsky's whole essence is in the last days of Arthur Dimmesdale" (*SM*, 153)—
and further allegorized fancifully: "The world is like Dimmesdale [and
thus like Dostoevsky?]; it has its Chillingworth in the dark races. It has
its Hester in Germany" (*SM*, 153). Lawrence considers the surface meaning of the book simply due to Hawthorne's duplicity. "All his reasoned
exposition is a pious fraud" (*P*, 318). Still, Lawrence praises the book
ecstatically as a "profound and wonderful book, one of the eternal rev-
elations. . . . It is far more profound than Dostoevsky and more perfect
than any French fiction" (*SM*, 154), though shortly before we were told
that Hawthorne was not, "at least in his greatest work, a realist or even
a novelist" (127). The characters are not even types. They represent the
human soul in its passional abstraction, as it exists in its first abstract
nakedness. *The Scarlet Letter* is a legendary myth. It contains the abstract
of the fall of the white race. It is the reverse of the myth of Eve, in the
Book of Genesis. The book scarcely belongs to the realm of art. It belongs
to the realm of primary or passional ethics and ethnology, the realm of
myth and the morality play (*SM*, 127). Its claim to be a historical romance
is entirely lost sight of.

The interpretation of Melville's South Sea romances is less far off the
mark. They are not only escapes to a paradise but also expressions of
hatred for the life of civilized man. Melville is saying, "The ugliest beast
on earth is the white man" (*S*, 147). But the chapter on *Moby Dick*, praising it as "a surprisingly beautiful book" (163), as "one of the strangest
and most wonderful books in the world" (172), is perverse in its allegorical misreading. The white whale is supposed to represent "our deepest
blood-consciousness," "the last phallic being of the white man" who is
hunted by "the maniacal fanaticism of our white mental consciousness"
(173), assisted by the other races: red, yellow, and black, Queequeg,
Tashtego, Daggoo. Why the white whale should or could represent the
phallic consciousness of the white man remains totally obscure. Nor can
one understand what is particularly "mental" about Captain Ahab's obsessive pursuit of the whale.

The last chapter, on Whitman, calls him "a very great poet" (*S*, 182),
"the first heroic seer to seize the soul by the scruff of her neck and plant
her down among the potsherds," saying "Stay in the flesh!" (184). But

Whitman is criticized and disparaged for his celebration of all-embracing sympathy. "He couldn't quite break the old maddening bond of the love-compulsion, he couldn't quite get out of the rut of the charity habit" (187). Whitman is addressed: "You've cooked the awful pudding of One Identity" (178). He reaches "an empty All-ness. An addled egg" (182), but this "last merging" is only death. The rejection of romantic merging with nature and the universe is an old theme of Lawrence. Wordsworth's poem on the primrose is ridiculed as "impertinence" and "bunk" (P2, 447–48), and Keats' nightingale never sang "a plaintive anthem" but was "Caruso at his jauntiest" (P, 44). But then in the Whitman essay Lawrence turns around and praises him for his "essential message, the Open Road" (S, 187), "the heroic message of the American future" (186), conceived of as a lonely journey away from mansions and too close association with other people. The message of Whitman seems identical with that of the Deerslayer. "Purified of Merging, purified of Myself, the exultant message of American Democracy, of souls in the Open Road, full of glad recognition, full of fierce readiness, full of joy of worship, when one soul sees a greater soul. The only riches, the great souls" (191).

These are the last words of a book that had an impact far beyond its claim to literary criticism. Examined as criticism, it will appear often perverse, insensitive, indiscriminating, lacking in all the virtues of scrupulosity, submission to a text, sympathy for a different mind. But it was not examined as literary criticism but praised without attention to detail because the book came at the crest of the wave against the Puritan and idealist tradition and because it ascribed to American literature a portentous significance at a time when American literature was still often seen as reflecting "the smiling aspects of life" or celebrating America as the symbol of progress, as the inheritor of dying Europe. Lawrence displayed its "power of darkness," the demonic underside. Hawthorne, Melville, Whitman, and even Cooper assume the role of prophets and even revolutionaries. Their meaning in historical context is forgotten or distorted. Lawrence imposed his own ideology on them, a world-view that it is unjust to label simply protofascist, for it is too personal a combination of irrationalistic motives, of vitalism, of messianic hopes for a new man, propped up by occult and pseudo-scientific notions. It appealed in the United States—because of its rejection of machine civilization and egalitarian democracy, and its call for a resuscitation of the flesh—to many who were worlds apart from Lawrence's social and political views: to William Carlos Williams, to Marius Bewley, to Richard Chase, and to Leslie Fiedler, who all found inspiration in Lawrence's book on America. If one reads in the mountainous literature heaping praise on Lawrence as the greatest English writer of the century, one marvels that all standards of accuracy of interpretation and fairness are abandoned in favor of the undeniable interest that his critical writings arouse as comments on his conceptions about sex, love, society, morals, and history, and as accompaniments to the novels, to which they often can be linked in intimate enmeshments: the Hardy study with *Women in Love*, *Studies in Classic American Literature* with *The Plumed Serpent*. Lawrence remarked once: "I always say, my motto is 'art for my sake' " (*L*, 860). This may be mistaken where his novels are concerned, but it is surely true of his criticism.

G. WILSON KNIGHT (1897–1985)

T. S. Eliot, the self-proclaimed classicist, had close associations with the critics who have to be called extreme romantics, G. Wilson Knight and Herbert Read. Eliot wrote a preface to *The Wheel of Fire* (1930) which launched Knight on his career of interpreting Shakespeare in a new way, and Herbert Read struck up a friendship with Eliot when he met him in 1917. He collaborated in editing Eliot's *Criterion* and published T. E. Hulme's *Speculations* (1924). But when Eliot proclaimed himself a "classicist in literature, a royalist in politics and an Anglo-Catholic in religion," Read retorted that he was a "romanticist in literature, an anarchist in politics and an agnostic in religion."[1] But this disagreement does not seem to have impaired their lifelong friendship.

Knight must be seen as coming from the whole tradition which interprets literature as myth, ritual, and symbol. In England the interest in primitive myths was stimulated by Sir James Frazer's *Golden Bough*, though Frazer himself was a good positivist who refused to read Freud. Eliot's *Sacred Wood* (1920) takes its title from a story in Frazer: the priest in the sacred grove has to be slain by his successor. The effect of Frazer's collection of myths from all over the world was paralleled by the work of a group of classical philologists in Cambridge who proved the ritual origins of Greek drama. Gilbert Murray (1866–1957), the translator of Euripides chastized by Eliot for his Swinburnesque style, is today the best known figure. In his *Hamlet and Orestes* (1914) the Hamlet story is said to have behind it "the prehistoric and world-wide ritual battle of Summer and Winter, of Life and Death which has played so vast a part in the mental development of the human race. And especially as E. K. Chambers has shown us in the history of medieval drama. Hamlet also like Orestes has the note of the Winter about him. Though he is on the side of right against wrong he is no joyous and triumphant slayer. He is clad in black, he rages alone, he is the bitter Fool who must slay the King. The whole tragic catharsis rests on the expulsion of evil in the ritual of spring. Tragedy is in origin Ritual Dance, a *Sacer Ludus*" (408—09). More immediately J. Middleton Murry's articles on Shakespeare acted on Knight "like an avatar" (see "J. Middleton Murry" in *NP,* 352). Knight besides knew the whole tradition of allegorical interpretations of Shakespeare. In his boyhood, he tells us (*NP,* 9), he read the *Commentaries* of G. G. Gervinus (see this *History* 3:211–12) and later he knew Colin Still's *Shakespeare's Mystery Play: A Study of 'The Tempest'* (1921; see *NP,* 11) which sees *The Tempest* as an analogy to pagan rites: initiation, ascent, fall, and redemption. Soon Knight was able to use the studies of Caroline Spurgeon, developed simultaneously with his own and summarized in *Shakespeare's Imagery and What It Tells Us* (1935). The book has been ridiculed because she tries, on the basis of imagery, to construct a portrait of the man Shakespeare and comes up with predictable results—Shakespeare was like a Victorian gentleman: healthy in body and mind, clean and fastidious in his habits, very sensitive to dirt and evil smells, a countryman through and through, a competent rider, a lover of animals, and so on. "By 1599 when he was five and thirty, Shakespeare has probably experienced heartburn as the result of acidity" (119).[2] This theme, pursued with naive glee, obscures, however, the valuable results based on a complete census of Shakespeare's imagery, to show (as she did earlier in *Leading Motives in the Imagery of Shakespeare's Tragedies,* 1930, and *Shakespeare's Iterative Imagery,* 1931) that individual plays are dominated by single images or clusters of images: sickness in *Hamlet,* animals in *Othello,* bird images in *Cymbeline,* and so on. One may doubt Caroline Spurgeon's delimitation of imagery which includes "any kind of simile as well as every kind of what is really compressed simile—metaphor" (5) and the often arbitrary classification of images according to their subject matter, but one should acknowledge that even the mechanical comparisons of Shakespeare with Bacon and Marlowe succeeded in bringing out the very different characteristics of these writers. Wilson Knight increasingly used her tables, statistics, and general method. She, in turn, while complimenting him for his "most profound and suggestive essay" on *Timon of Athens,* set off her method from his sharply: the gold-symbolism Knight finds dominating the play is only the theme talked about frequently while there is "only one image from gold throughout the play" (344–45).

Wilson Knight's method is different. He explained it many times, most influentially in the first chapter ("On the Principles of Shakespeare Interpretation") in *The Wheel of Fire.* There he clearly distinguishes interpretation from criticism. Criticism aims at judgment, at dividing the good from the bad. "Interpretation, on the contrary, tends to merge into the work it analyses; . . . it can recognize no division of 'good' from 'bad' " (*WF*, 1). "Criticism is a judgment of vision; interpretation a reconstruction of vision" (2). Interpretation means something special for Knight. Ordinary reading follows the time sequence, while his approach is "spatial," it looks at the work as a whole, for its "atmospheric quality" (4), for the "purely spiritual atmosphere interpenetrating the action" (5), for "the omnipresent and mysterious reality brooding motionless over and within the play's movement" (6). He develops this further. "The spatial, that is, the spiritual, quality uses the temporal, that is, the story, lending it dominance in order to express itself the more clearly: *Timon* is essentially an allegory or parable" (7). Consistently Knight has to reject any concern for intentions (8) and sources (9) or character which is "constantly entwined with a false and unduly ethical criticism" (10). Knight would like to dispense with ordinary moral standards. "The commentator must be true to his artistic, not his normal ethic" (11), or similarly "we must be prepared to modify our ethical response till it is in tune with our imaginative vision" (*IT,* 23). Knight thus intends to regard "each play as a visionary whole, close-knit in personification, atmospheric suggestion and direct poetic symbolism" (12).

On later occasions Knight repeats himself but also amplifies, modifies, and defends his method. In *The Imperial Theme* (1931), the theoretical chapter "On Imaginative Interpretation" rejects attention to character more sharply as "fatal" (19): "The action is not decorated with images: the images are the action. A play of Shakespeare is, as a rule, primarily imaginative, not psychological or didactic" (20). Knight argues then that while "the dramatic persons and their names change from play to play" (22) the symbols are actually not so variable. He reduces them to two opposites: music versus tempest, order versus disorder, both "changeless metaphysical realities" which he finds not only in Shakespeare but in "all tragic literature, all poetry" which "has its tempests of division, its unity of poetry's music." Finally "the ultimate dualism of joy and grief, good and evil, life and death, are unified within the harmonies of tragic intuition" (29).

In the introduction to the next book, *The Shakespearian Tempest* (1932), the main thesis is reaffirmed. "Shakespeare is differentiated from other poets by his peculiarly consistent use of images and symbols common to all" (*ST,* 5). Knight defends his use of symbolism unimpressed by arguments that this or that passage—such as Cleopatra floating on a barge—closely follows the account in Plutarch. Symbol in his view is "not a sign which 'stands instead of' something else" (14). A pure symbol has infinite relations. It is "fluent as the sea." It becomes a symbol when we start to interpret (14), a giveaway which seems to admit the complete subjective arbitrariness of the method. But Knight would not concede this, as "the tempest-music opposition in Shakespeare's system is fixed." "Plots vary, tempest persists." In *King Lear*, for instance, "the essence is to be considered the tempest, not the 'character' of the protagonist" (16).

In later years Wilson Knight felt constrained to defend his procedures against the emphasis on poetic language which came from both Leavis's *Scrutiny* and Bateson's *Essays in Criticism*. His interpretation, he repeats, is not verbal at all but spatial. "Its first interest is the structure, the pattern, the body of the work in question almost irrespective of the exact language used" ("The New Interpretation," *Essays in Criticism* 3 [1953]: 384), a defense made even more necessary as Knight had interpreted *Faust* and *Zarathustra* in translation, frankly admitting ignorance of German. Knight reasserts his shirking of all value judgments. "Literary criticism has always been my peculiar *bête noire* and for twenty-five years I have been offering something else in its place" (382), and even, "I am no more concerned with value distinctions than is a biologist studying the physiology of his subjects, butterfly and scorpion" (*Essays in Criticism* 4 [1954]: 220). Knight does not understand that even the simple selection of his symbols is an act of value judgment and that, in practice, he himself has constantly judged and ranked. *Timon of Athens* is consistently extolled as "a great and neglected play" (*CL*, 12), *Pericles* exhibits "the furthest reach of Shakespeare's poetic and visionary power" (16) and *The Tempest* is "the most perfect work of art and the most crystal act of mystic vision in our literature" (28). Knight not only ranks the plays of Shakespeare, he exalts the dramas of Byron to the sky and singles out a contemporary author, John Cowper Powys, as "among the three or four greatest authors in our literature" (*Essays in Criticism* 14 [1964]: 35). He cannot help being a critic. More and more Knight stressed "the imaginative response" which is "to lose one's egocentric mentality in a kind of self-annihilation before the objects" (*Essays in Criticism* 3 [1953]: 387). This emphatic surrender assumes more and more a mystical and later spiritualist and occult meaning. Sometimes the "space pattern" is described merely fancifully as "violently and dramatically active," as "a kind of vertical and oscillatory action" which implies a "Dionysian metaphysic" (*Essays in Criticism* 14 [1964]: 33). But this very un-Nietzschean metaphysic turns out to be spiritualism. "The business of great literature may be defined as the interweaving of human affairs with spiritualistic appearances. Phantasms of the dead, portents, resurrections and visitations" (*SD*, 316), "astral projection, out of body travel," (*BS*, 297), conversations with the dead as Knight claims to have spoken with his deceased brother, Jackson Knight.

At times Knight agrees that "poetry is, in hard fact, a temporal art, composed of sequences in logic and narrative, its spatial qualities being only spatial by metaphor. . . . Interpretation gives the poetry spatial projection, puts it, inwardly, on the stage of our imagination, produces for us" (*PP,* 82). This and similar passages show that Knight cannot be classed with authors who deny the temporality of literature, such as Wyndham Lewis attacking Bergson. Knight is unhistorical, aims at a timeless world of symbols and myths, but does not deny the temporal nature of verbal art. The individual works occur in time but history is a repetition of patterns, a Nietzschean eternal recurrence. Authority is vested in the interpreter who claims "prophetic vitality and significance, prophesies a Christian and poetic Renaissance" (*CR,* 3), based on a "new science of poetic interpretation" (4). Science here must mean the "poetic wisdom" proclaimed on the title page of *Christ and Nietzsche* (1948). It is symptomatic of all the later work of Wilson Knight: the flattening out of any distinctions, the reconciliation of everything with everything, the monotonous conclusion that the world is pervaded by dualisms—tempest and music, disorder and order, evil and good, darkness and light, tragic and comic, which are reconciled or rather abolished in immortality, infinity, mystery, the other world of ghosts. Literary criticism, including interpretation of texts, is left far behind. But I have "forfeited the right to critical judgment" as I "belong to twentieth century criticism which has rejected occult perceptions" (see "*Scrutiny* and Criticism" in *Essays in Criticism* 14 [1964]: 34).

It is fair to take a close look at Knight's early practice as critic. *The Wheel of Fire,* his best book, discusses characters, action, situations, and what A. C. Bradley called "atmosphere," the total mood or general impression of a play for which Knight seeks quite legitimately evidence in images, recurrent themes, and situations which assume, at least in some plays of Shakespeare, the role of symbols. Knight has done pioneering work in making us read Shakespeare's plays as poems, rejecting the realistic prejudices of the time and stage and seeing the work, the whole row of plays, as a totality which shows an inner evolution. But the detailed elaboration is often extravagant and even deliberately perverse. Thus the two essays on *Hamlet* attempt, contrary to all evidence of the text and the well-documented stage history, to turn things upsidedown. Hamlet, for Knight, is a figure of death (*WF,* 28), inhuman, a "Demon of cynicism," "a Madman," "an element of evil in the state of Denmark" (42), like Iago (29), like Dostoevsky's Stavrogin (39), while King Claudius is "a good and gentle king" (39), "wise and considerate" (48), "kindly, confident and fond of pleasure" (37), living in a court full of "healthy and robust life, good-nature, humour, romantic strength, and welfare" (35). The reversal is not worth refuting, as it ignores Hamlet's tragic heroism and the king's hypocritical criminality. It is justified in Knight's scheme by the dark-light contrast: the black-robed Hamlet represents love-cynicism and death-consciousness against an absurdly idealized court. A later essay, "Rose of May: An Essay on Life-themes in Hamlet" (in *IT*), develops the thesis even more extravagantly. The Ghost, a thing of darkness, is death and brings to birth "a death in Hamlet's soul" (*IT* 102). Claudius is "a kind-hearted and good king" (112). Finally Hamlet and Laertes, "death-consciousness and life-ardour, oppose each other." "A sense of tragic expiation concludes our baffling and indecisive vision. Each side wins, and loses" (124). "*Hamlet* Reconsidered" (added to new editions of *The Wheel of Fire* in 1947) acknowledges that the two *Hamlet* essays "are inadequate and their emphasis misleading." But the new essay, mostly devoted to such questions as Hamlet on the brink of insanity, the meaning of "To be or not to be," and the ritual of the final duel, does not correct the early perverse interpretation except implicitly-conceding Hamlet's goodness as "partly true" (*WF*, 316).

The other essays do not run so grossly against common sense. The essay on "The Philosophy of *Troilus and Cressida*" discusses the Platonic love philosophy in traditional terms. Knight concludes again with a dualism: "Immediate and personal experience, intuition, the infinite, the timeless; vs. the concepts of order and social system, intellect, the finite world, the time concept" (*WF*, 79). Troilus is divided. The essay is a curious exercise in schematics, far removed from the action of the play.

The essay "*Measure for Measure* and the Gospels" makes the play's central idea "And forgive us our debts as we forgive our debtors" (*WF*, 83) and the Duke a Christ figure. "He, like Jesus, moves among men suffering grief at their sins and deriving joy from an unexpected flower of simple goodness in the deserts of impurity and hardness" (90). Ronald M. Frye comments: "The interpretation translates Shakespeare out of dramatic and into theological terms—though not even a good theology but rather into sentimentalized and maudlin emotionalism."[3] No spatial approach is used or needed.

"The Othello music" works out the contrast between the highflown rhetoric of the Moor and the ugly cynicism of Iago. In the last scene "the Othello music itself sounds with a noble cadence, a richer flow of harmonies, a more selfless and universalized flight of the imagination than before" (*WF*, 131). "At the end Othello takes just pride in recalling his honourable service" (130). The attempts of Eliot and Leavis to denigrate Othello as a tragic hero are here rejected beforehand. It is all good character reading, though we may feel that the contrast between Iago's "spirit of negation, colourless, and undefined, attempting to make chaos of a world of stately, architectural and exquisitely coloured forms" (131) is overdrawn. Desdemona is seen in her domesticity and femininity but is needlessly considered a poetic symbol "equated with the Divine Principle" (120). The storm is called a symbol of grace (123), thus reversing the usual association between tempest and evil, disorder and disaster.

"Brutus and Macbeth" is in part a straightforward comparison of these two characters, pointing out the similarities of their divided minds, and in part a study of imagery: storm, blood, and animals. We are told that "the interpenetration of the protagonist with his environment is a supreme act of poetry" (*WF*, 152) in both *Macbeth* and *Julius Caesar*. The prophecies in both plays allow Knight to say that "the future is thus shown as existing within the present and the time sequence has a secondary reality only" (152), a doubtful argument for the spatial approach. "*Macbeth* and the Metaphysics of Evil" sees the very different (from *Julius Caesar*), atmosphere and ethos of the play, "the mesmeric, nightmare quality of style" (161), the darkness, the horror, the disorder. This is hardly new. It is the kind of evocation practiced at least since Hazlitt. But more originally Knight sees a change. "Whilst Macbeth lives in conflict with himself there is misery, evil, fear: when at the end, he and others have openly identified himself with evil, he faces the world fearless: nor does he appear evil longer" (171). Knight speaks even of "a paean of triumph as the Macbeth-universe, having struggled darkly upward, now climbs into radiance" (174). This is presumably an instance of the reader abandoning his normal ethic.

"Lear and the Comedy of the Grotesque" makes a good case for the "macabre comedy" of *King Lear* (*WF*, 192). "The core of the play is an absurdity, an indignity, an incongruity" (184). "The end of Cordelia is horrible, cruel, unnecessarily cruel—the final grotesque horror in the play" (190), and he warns against "sentimentalizing the cosmic horror of the play" (192). The next paper, "The Lear Universe," elaborates this conception. "In face of the last scene any detailed comment of purgatorial expiation, of spiritual purification, is but a limp and tinkling irrelevance" (223). "The poet maintains the sense of universal injustice up to the last terrible moment of the tragedy" (211), but oddly, much in agreement with his whitewashing of Claudius, Knight thinks that "much is to be said for Goneril and Regan, and Edmund is most attractive" (194). He is given a noble, an essentially tragic end, Regan and Goneril "die, at least, in the cause of love—love of Edmund" (190), a complete misreading of the situation: the deadly hatred of the sisters killing each other, the dastardly Edmund facing his deserved punishment.

The essay " The Pilgrimage of Hate: An Essay on *Timon of Athens*" has done much to draw attention to this neglected play. Knight who professes not to judge calls it "the most masterfully deliberate of Shakespeare's sombre tragedies" and "the archetype and norm of all tragedy" (*WF*, 240–41). "For this play is Hamlet, Troilus, Othello, Lear, become self-conscious and universal; it includes and transcends them all" (259). The sudden reversal from love to hate is for Knight "a tragic moment so swift, so clean-cut, so daring and so terrible" (242) as nowhere else in all Shakespeare. "This unswerving majesty is a greater thing than the barbaric fury of Othello, or the faltering ire of Lear" (243). "Life and death have interchanged their meaning for him, and he now voices that paradox which is at the heart of all tragedy" (255). The restoration of *Timon of Athens* to eminence became Knight's lifelong concern. He himself acted Timon both in Toronto and Leeds and constantly used it as the star example for his proposal expounded in *Principles of Shakespearian Production* (1936, renamed *Shakesperian Production*, 1968). Contrary to the common assumption that Knight's theories of spatial form require a static, untheatrical staging of Shakespeare's plays and are merely bookish fancies, Knight had practiced poetic acting and speaking and devised scenery which is apparently rather similar to that of the stylized productions of Herbert Beerbohm-Tree or Edward Gordon Craig. A book of photographs, *Symbol of Man* (1979), shows Knight as an actor, nearly nude, in Shakespearean roles to illustrate an elaborate theory of bodily expressions, derived from the system of François Delsarte and Rudolf Steiner's "Eurhythmie," an occult-inspired scheme of dancing.

The Wheel of Fire concludes with two essays: "Symbolic Personification" and "The Shakespearian Metaphysic," in which the "metaphysics of symbolism" (209) is reduced to a rigid schematism. Knight distinguishes "the transcendental unreality of the *Macbeth*-experience, from the pure realism or naturalism of *Lear*, and the transcendental realism of *Antony and Cleopatra*" (293–94). The third is thus the sum of the first two. "The three modes are related to Evil, Hate, Love, or fear, knowledge, and recognition of Reality in the widest and profoundest implications of the word" (294). One wonders whether this is metaphysic and how we distinguish these realisms and unrealisms.

I have described every essay in *The Wheel of Fire* in order to forestall the objection that only a few highlights, either good or bad, were picked out and to obviate the necessity of describing the many books which followed in Knight's extremely productive career. Every book exemplifies the same methods and comes to the same monotonous results. Some passages revive simply the old evocative method. What, we may ask, is achieved by saying that "the style of *Othello* is like a large glowing coal; that of *Macbeth* like the sparks from an anvil; *Lear* is a rocket, *Timon,* like phosphorus churned to flame in a tropic ocean? That of *Antony and Cleopatra* is like a thin, blazing, electric filament, steadily instinct with keenest fire" (*IT,* 204)? Other essays collect, often consulting a concordance, instances of words or phrases of supposed significance: thus in discussing *Antony and Cleopatra* we are given a list of words with thin or feminine vowel sounds which is not even accurate, as "fire, slime, Nile, variety" and others were always pronounced with an "aj" and not an "i" (201). We are then treated to long lists of references to "gold" and "empire," to geographical names, to mentions of sea, horses, "wealth, power, military strength, and material magnificence" (218) which is followed by a list of erotic images which elsewhere in the same paper are described rather oddly. "The sensuous is not presented sensuously: the poet's medium purifies all it touches as though all were thinned yet clarified from a new visionary height" (200). After the love-theme Knight treats the theme of music and stresses the peculiarly "transcendental humanism," whatever that oxymoron may mean, of the play. "Thus we shall advance towards knowledge why and in what sense this play is not merely a story of a soldier's fall, but rather a spelled land of romance achieved and victorious: a paradisal vision expressed in terms of humanity's quest of love" (227).

Other essays manage, at least on occasion, to convey the mood or atmosphere of a play, often in striking picturesque terms. Thus *Coriolanus* contrasts with the "wide universalism" of *Antony and Cleopatra.* "We are limited by city walls. And cities are here metallic, our world constricted, bound in hard walls; and this constriction, with suggestion of hardness, is rooted deep in our theme" (*IT,* 156), or even more picturesquely phrased, "These two, Volumnia and Coriolanus, have loved parochially, provincially, among the gray slated roofs, the pipes and conduits, the stony roofs and walls, of this metallic, urban, exclusive setting" (191).

The second method, the accumulation of themes and words, dominates most of the later books which go beyond the original concentration on Shakespeare. There are essays on Lilly, Webster, Ford, and of course on Marlowe, who in Knight's fervently patriotic writings during the war appear to point "unmistakably to Nazi Germany" because of his sadism (*PA,* 143) just as the concourse of fallen angels in *Paradise Lost* plotting revenge "is not unlike a National Socialist gathering" (144); Hitler resembles Milton's Satan, "Satan's various leaders, the violent Moloch, crafty Belial, Mammon and Beelzebub, have rough counterparts in Hitler's following" (145). A whole little book, *The Olive and the Sword* (1944), is devoted to Shakespeare as the "poet of royalism" (a reprint in *SF*, 8). "Kingship is golden. Shakespeare's work is royally alive in our time" (*SF*, 90). Knight describes all his wartime labors as "using Shakespeare to define the meaning of the Crown, for us, today" (274).

The book on Alexander Pope, *Laureate of Peace: On the Genius of Alexander Pope* (1954; reprinted as *The Poetry of Pope*, 1965) seems to me in spite of some extravagancies the most sober, text-oriented of the later books. The interpretation of *The Essay on Man* (first in *The Mutual Flame*, 1939) could be developed and substantiated in Maynard Mack's edition; the comments on Byron's obsession with Pope or on *The Temple of Fame*, which lends itself to the "spatial" approach, are often illuminating though Knight obfuscates much by claiming that Pope "offers what is perhaps the most valuable of all insights: a coherent romanticism." This is reached through (i) a sense of ever-springing life in nature, the continual miracle of existence, and (ii) a dominating sense of the cosmic whole" (*PP*, 46). But why the resolution of the good-and-evil antinomy should be considered also central to Knight's interpretations remains a puzzle, as neither the Stoics nor Cicero were exactly romantic.

New also is the detailed application to the English romantic poets. Particularly great claims have been made for Knight's interpretation of *Kubla Khan*. The dome is read as a symbol of wholeness reconciling the opposites of heat and cold, sun and ice. The garden and the "deep romantic chasm" display another range of dualisms; natural, artificial, indefinite versus precise, sacred versus profane, inchoate versus structured, and so on. Kubla Khan himself becomes God (*SD*, 93). The same technique of listing contrasts and their reconciliation is applied to Wordsworth (mainly on *The Borderers*), Shelley, and Keats. The three books on Byron vary: *Lord Byron's Marriage* (1957) is a well-researched argument about the reasons for Byron's separation. It was not apparently the accusation of incest but homosexuality and sodomy. *Lord Byron: The Christian Virtues* (1952) is an extravagant celebration of his personality, his religion, and his ethics, while *Byron and Shakespeare* (1966) collects evidence for Byron's interest in Shakespeare, claiming that Byron was "Shakesperian drama incarnate." He was "by turn or simultaneously Hamlet, Puck, Macbeth, Falstaff, Antony, Timon and Prospero" (*BS*, 13). Knight reaches heights of absurdity when he repeats his earlier saying that "Byron is the next Promethean figure in Western History after

Christ" and defends this by asking: "Could any test for such a claim be more reasonable than that the new Messiah should, in our renaissance era, be an incarnation, involving, as *our religion does not,* both sex and politics, of Shakespearian drama? That is what I show Byron to have been" (22). "Byron sums and surpasses the great figures of the past and is a hinge towards the future, pointing on to Ibsen and Nietzsche" (19). Knight, no doubt, knows Byron's life and work intimately and conveys some of the fascination he exercised even with his superstitions, astral or soul projection, clairvoyance, ghosts, and magic. But Knight shows also an appalling insensitivity to the gulf between Shakespeare and Byron and no sense of the shoddiness and derivativeness of much of Byron's verse and dramas. The concern for the occult and magic motivates also Knight's admiration for two contemporary writers: John Cowper Powys, to whom he devoted a whole book (*The Saturnian Quest,* 1964), and Francis Berry, whom he considers "the greatest of all who have written within the present century" (*NP,* 476). But these eccentricities and the occult streak should not obscure the power of his early Shakespearean interpretations which have strongly influenced later critics such as L. C. Knights, Robert Heilman, and his own student in Toronto, Northrop Frye.

HERBERT READ (1893–1968)

Herbert Read has written so much (there are at least eighty book titles in his bibliography) on so many subjects ranging from poems, autobiographies, novels, books on art and art education and on individual artists such as Cézanne, Paul Klee, and Henry Moore, to literary criticism. The criticism, only a fraction of his activity, passes through violent transformations: from an early participation in the imagist movement through an allegiance to the classicism of T. E. Hulme, Pound, and Eliot, to a conversion to romanticism which included advocacy of *surréalisme* and flirtations with many incompatible philosophies—Nietzsche, Bergson, Croce, Santayana, and occasionally Marxism and even Neo-Thomism. The books contain essays reproduced sometimes, in changed form, from earlier collections. They shift and display often disconcerting contradictions and appeal to often transient authorities. The form of presentation also changes from long argumentative essays to a mosaic of little vignettes or reviews, all well phrased, lucid, and straightforward, "sincere," as Read cultivates sincerity as the guiding principle of his life and thought. One could dismiss him as an eclectic, a designation he accepted gladly (*TM,* 3).

Still, it is possible to define his basic outlook, at least in the phase of his most influential writings: *Wordsworth* (1930), *Form in Modern Poetry* (1932), *In Defense of Shelley* (1936), *Collected Essays in Literary Criticism* (1938), *A Coat of Many Colours* (1945), culminating in *The True Voice of Feeling* (1953), which summarizes much of his earlier production. Read calls "the rehabilitation of romanticism an adequate description of his aims" (*CELC*, 123), a clear repudiation of his early interest in Thomism and Julien Benda, the detractor of Bergson to whom he had devoted a little book a few years earlier (1930). Romanticism for Read means all art that is "essentially irrational" (134), the "true voice of feeling" in Keats's phrase. It follows that art is an expression of personality which Read sharply distinguishes from character and is written in a condition of trance (111). Read for a time became an advocate of surrealism, and poetry appears as a "mediator between dream and reality" (115). Personality requires sincerity, which must not be confused with spontaneity, the main argument of the title essay of the late *The Cult of Sincerity* (1968). While art is irrational and the process of creation unconscious, Read very early found what he considered a rational tool of criticism: psychoanalysis, at first derived from Freud and later from C. G. Jung, with his emphasis on the collective unconscious and the archetypes of human imagination. The early essay "Psycho-analysis and Criticism" (1924) (in *RR*, 83–106) is still very hesitant about the value of psychoanalysis for criticism (86) and the book on Wordsworth is preoccupied with a psychological explanation of Wordsworth's decline as a poet, which is hardly technically Freudian and Jungian. Read argues that Wordsworth had a morbid sense of guilt and remorse for his affair with Annette Vallon, which finally led to an atrophy of feeling drying up the sources of his poetic powers. While Read succeeds in establishing the pervasive mood of remorse, it remains unclear how Wordsworth could compose his greatest poetry years after his return from France and why his poetic powers declined only after some twelve years. The long essay *In Defense of Shelley* (1936) directed against Eliot's disparagement rather reflects back unfavorably on Shelley's character, as Read argues for Shelley's narcissism, which then developed into an unconscious homosexuality. This, in turn, explains his preoccupation with the theme of incest. More convincingly Read defends the coherence of Shelley's philosophy: the combination of Godwin and Plato (*TVF*, 259) which Shelley did not find incompatible.

These feeble psychoanalytical defenses of Wordsworth and Shelley were more and more displaced in Read's writings by attempts to reformulate an organic aesthetics, largely derived from Coleridge. Organic form is conceived as "the natural effect of the poet's integrity" (*TVF*, 9).

Read, in difference from many Coleridge students who exalt Coleridge's originality, is well aware of Coleridge's dependence on Schelling and August Wilhelm Schlegel. He even prints a translation of Schelling's oration "Concerning the Relation of the Plastic Arts to Nature" (1807) (in the appendix to *TVF*, 323–64) which is the model of the piece called "On Poesy and Art," often cited as if it were Coleridge's central statement of theory. Read applies or at least shows how the theory would apply to Wordsworth and Keats, Hopkins, Whitman, and D. H. Lawrence as he wants to trace an alternate tradition to Eliot's classical line. "There is," he argues, "not one literary tradition, but many traditions." His own age is neither romantic nor classical (*CELC*, 122). At times Read replaces the classical-romantic dichotomy with the imagistic versus metaphorical. Shakespeare, Shelley, and Blake are imagists; Dryden, Pope, and Wordsworth are metaphorical poets (107), a division which cuts across the classical-romantic. Read felt strongly his old ties to imagism, to Hulme whom he grossly overrates, to Pound, and also to metaphysical poetry understood in Eliot's sense as "an emotional apprehension of thought" (71), which he conceives oddly enough as a "fairly 'hard' " and even a "necessarily 'dry' process" (86–87). In this context Read defends obscurity in poetry, Mallarmé's and Valéry's as positive value. The poet must invent words and create images; he "must mishandle and stretch the meaning of words" (100). "A poem has a necessary and eternal existence: it is impervious to reason, and if it has no discoverable meaning it has immeasurable power" (100).

Fortunately most of Read's practical criticism shows hardly any trace of this kind of obscurantism. He can be an essayist in the tradition of Hazlitt or the much admired Bagehot, soberly discussing the mind and ethos of many prose-writers. He rarely gets technical, though an early book was devoted to *English Prose Style* (1928). There we get a survey of traditional topics of rhetoric with the warning that "all modes of rhetoric become proofs of original genius only so far as they are modified by a predominant passion in the writer" (215). The "constructive expression of prose" is contrasted with the "creative expression of poetry." In poetry, in terms which seem derived ultimately from Croce, "thought is the word and the word is the thought" (x–xi). Read fears "the danger in the narrow drift of technical research, the analysis of means of expression" (*CELC*, 125). In his discussion of Laurence Sterne's *Tristram Shandy*, sympathetic to a fellow Yorkshireman, Read says nothing whatever of its techniques or composition or self-reflexivity which earned recent attention as the first example of a novel on novel-writing. Read is only interested in his attitude and his analysis of feelings which make him the "precursor of all psychological fiction" (264). Also the essay on Swift is mainly concerned with trying to define his dominant tone, which Read finds to be "sardonic" rather than cynical, satiric, or ironic (206). Several highly laudatory essays on Henry James praise the late phase and "the subtlest ethical intelligence of our time" applied in *The Golden Bowl* (*TM*, 197). Read's tolerance and appreciation is very broad: it ranges from Malory to Henry Miller, whom he finds significant as he always defended rebellion, anarchism, and Max Stirner, though he himself lived like a country gentleman in Yorkshire and accepted a knighthood.

But Read felt himself to be primarily a poet and wrote most enthusiastically on poets. He helped to revive interest in the English romantic poets, commenting well on Wordsworth's *Prelude,* the odes of Keats, and Shelley's *Prometheus Unbound.* He did much to excite interest in Hopkins, whose metrical theories and experiments he admired, and was a good commentator on Yeats, Pound, and Eliot as well as American poets. He can, for instance, closely examine the two versions of Yeats's poem "The Sorrows of Love" and argue for preferring the original text to the radical revision (*CMC*, 208), or he can sharply protest against divorcing American poetry from English, believing in "a big Anglo-Saxon total" (281).

Basically Read is a critic well in the tradition of the nineteenth century: expounding an organic aesthetics more clearly than Coleridge himself could and an immediate expression of feeling disapproving of what he felt to be unaesthetic, abstract "wit-writing," the poetry of the eighteenth century, and simply anything which seemed to him excogitated, derivative, reproducing an abstract pattern. This is why he advocated free verse, which seemed to him the only sincere form for modern poetry (*CELC*, 109), and that is why he wants personality and believes in inspiration as the necessary "intermittency of genius" (*FMP,* 19). But while these theories and preferences seem highly individualistic, Read is very conscious of the social mission of art: he sounds like his much admired master Ruskin or often like William Morris. He can cite Georg Lukács and think that Marx and Freud worked to the same end (*CMC*, 218): the integration of man. Like Croce he minimizes the distinction between the arts. He draws parallels between English poetry and painting, aligning Wordsworth with Constable, Keats with Turner (*IDS*, 236ff.), and argues against Lessing's *Laokoon.* There is only one imagination, "whether painting or poetry does not matter" (*TM*, 173). Sympathy is Read's watchword as critic (*CMC*, 326) and sympathy for him means the rejection of rationalism both in poetics and philosophy. A whole paper is devoted to a refutation of Descartes's dualism (*CELC*, 183) and the praise of Kierkegaard's "Innerlichkeit" (*CMC*, 248) and the interest in existentialism chime in. Sympathy widens and becomes social and universal in Read's voluminous writings on *Art and Society* and *Education through Art,* where literature is only one item in generous, often utopian schemes of making art again, as he believed it should be, an essential factor of human happiness.

CHRISTOPHER CAUDWELL (1907–37)

It may surprise that I discuss Christopher Caudwell (pseudonym for St. John Sprigg) in this context. *Illusion and Reality* (1937) is considered the first important document of English Marxism. There is no doubt of Caudwell's loyalty to the Communist party. He worked in the Poplar (East London) branch from 1935 until December 1936 before joining the International Brigade in Spain where he was killed in the defense of Madrid. But his book which made him famous posthumously is, in spite of its Marxist frame and rhetoric, as aesthetics and literary criticism part of the movement which, with I. A. Richards, considers poetry "irrational" (*IR,* 129), full of "internal symbolism of reference to emotional attitudes" (131), "concrete, subjective" (131), a "kind of inverted dream" (213). Caudwell's theory of the birth of poetry is a phantasy about the origins of art reviving the old myth of the original unity of the arts: dance, poetry, and music created to make the crops grow. "In the collective festival where poetry is born, the phantastic world of poetry anticipates the harvest and, by so doing, makes possible the real harvest" (69). "Only by means of this illusion can be brought into being a reality which would not otherwise exist. Without the ceremony phantastically portraying the granaries bursting with grain, the pleasure and delights of the harvest, men would not face the hard labour necessary to bring it into being" (30). Poetry and production, illusion and reality are united as they would be again in the Socialist Utopia. With the rise of bourgeois capitalism a new kind of poetry devoted to the "bourgeois illusion of freedom" arose and the individualistic novel became the rival of originally collective poetry. Caudwell's attempts to draw parallels between the stages of economic development (primitive accumulation, the industrial revolution) and the phases of English poetry are crude and insensitive. Shakespeare appears as "an official of the court or of the bourgeois nobility" (76). Caliban is "the bestial serf—and a 'free' spirit who serves only for a time—Ariel, is the apotheosis of the free wage-labourer" (79). "Pope perfectly expresses the ideals of the bourgeois class in alliance with a bourgeoisified aristocracy in the epoch of manufacture" (86). Keats "is the first great poet to feel the strain of the poet's position in this state of the bourgeois illusion, as producer for the free market" (94). The gulf between these abstractions and a sense of the concrete individuality of these poets is immense.

The two later books, *Studies in a Dying Culture* (1938) and *Further Studies in a Dying Culture* (1949) are even more purely ideological. The essay on Bernard Shaw shows that he was a bad socialist; the one on H. G. Wells that he was a vague Utopian; the one on T. E. Lawrence that he was no hero and the one on D. H. Lawrence that he was a self-contradictory Fascist "who appeals to the consciousness of men to abandon consciousness" (*SDC,* 59). The second book is about general themes: history, psychology, philosophy, and "Beauty" which parodies the aesthetics of I. A. Richards. "Beauty is a state of the bourgeois" (80). In 1970 another manuscript, *Romance and Realism: A Study in English Bourgeois Literature* was unearthed which contains more straight literary criticism than any of the preceding volumes. It predictably condemns Kipling as an imperialist but shows sympathy and understanding for Hardy and surprisingly for the later novels of George Moore. Only on occasion does Caudwell return to the Marxist clichés: Tennyson's *In Memoriam* mysteriously shows "how rapidly the industrial petty bourgeois class has started to decay" (73).

One must admire the wide-ranging reading of this young man, his devotion to his cause, and the ambition of a grand synthesis of physics (Einstein, Heisenberg), psychology (Freud, Jung), sociology (Durkheim, Lévy-Bruhl), economics (Marx) and literary history. But the synthesis did not succeed. It hardly could or can. Motifs and ideas clash unreconciled and unreconcilable. Many years were to pass before a more sophisticated Marxist criticism took root in England.

5 : THE INNOVATORS

THE GREAT CHANGE in the theory and practice of English criticism was accomplished by T. S. Eliot, I. A. Richards, and their disciples F. R. Leavis and William Empson in the twenties and thirties of this century. It would be erroneous to think that it was accomplished suddenly or that the victory was complete. The careers of the critics whom we discussed as the Bloomsbury group and as the New Romantics overlap. William Butler Yeats lived till the eve of the Second World War. The doctrines of the innovators were prepared, at least as polemical pronouncements and slogans, before the First World War by T. E. Hulme, Ezra Pound, and Wyndham Lewis. Their radicalism and break with the English tradition must at least in part be due to their backgrounds. T. E. Hulme was a rebellious son of a Staffordshire pottery manufacturer; he was sent down from Cambridge and spent some years in western Canada as a lumberjack before returning to London in 1908. Ezra Pound was born in Hailey, Idaho, but grew up in Philadelphia, Pennsylvania; he studied Romance philology at the university, held a job at Wabash College (Crawfordsville, Indiana), but was dismissed and came to England in the same year to seek his fortune as a poet and journalist. Wyndham Lewis, the son of an American and an Englishwoman, was born on their yacht in the harbor of Amherst, Nova Scotia; he tried to make his way in the London art world from 1910 on. T. S. Eliot, born in St. Louis, Missouri, a Harvard graduate and almost Ph.D. in philosophy, remained or had to remain in England after the outbreak of the war in 1914. They were all outsiders, but they should not be called an avant-garde, as only Ezra Pound was an organizer. T. E. Hulme stood alone, however gregarious he was in his life.

The reaction against the Victorian tradition, particularly its later phases—the Pre-Raphaelites and Swinburne—was nothing new. The so-called Georgian poets, who under the editorship of Edward Marsh published five anthologies of *Georgian Poetry* (1911–22), rejected both the aestheticism of the 1890s and the high-minded didacticism of the Victorians. In practice, they limited the themes of poetry to the nature of the English countryside, to children, to animals, and to the land of dreams. They remained within the orbit of late romanticism, oddly untouched even by symbolism.

"Imagism" was the new slogan in 1912 and "vorticism" in 1914. The theories proclaimed are extremely simple and even trite. "Image" seemed a great discovery: the poet is to evoke visual images without rhetoric. Precision of observation is needed. But an effect can be achieved only by metaphor and analogy. Free verse is recommended as a break with tradition. "Vorticism" was an even more ephemeral slogan, using a term derived from Descartes to add dynamism and movement to the image. It is a version of what in Germany would be called expressionism. Neither imagism nor vorticism could play any role in a history of literary criticism—at most in a history of literary coteries.

These writers never used the terms "modernism" or "modernist," which were imposed on them only by hindsight. Robert Graves (*TLS*, October 1, 1954) could write "Pound-Eliot modernism of the twenties is already dated as a stream-lined pogo-stick with decorative motifs from Tutan-Khaman's tomb" and in 1960 Harry Levin published a lecture "What *was* Modernism?" (reprinted in *Refractions*, 1968). There was a short-lived review, *The Modernist: A Monthly Magazine of Modern Arts and Letters,* in 1919 which reprinted articles by G. B. Shaw, Theodore Dreiser, Hart Crane, and Georges Duhamel in the first issue but mainly propagated the Russian Revolution. In 1927 Robert Graves and Laura Riding published *A Survey of Modernist Poetry* which was mainly devoted to a defense of the typographical vagaries of E. E. Cummings and only incidentally referred to *The Waste Land.*

"Modernism," "modernist," and "modern" are terms all derived from the Latin *modo,* meaning "today," and used by everybody who felt that he was bringing or wanting something new or disapproved of novelty. There were polemics between *antiqui* and *moderni* in thirteenth-century scholasticism. All French literary histories treat the *Querelle des Anciens et Modernes* in the late seventeenth century at length. In England it instigated "The Battle of the Books" in which Jonathan Swift played a part as partisan of the ancients. One can argue that the distinction "classical–romantic," formulated by the brothers Schlegel (preceded by Schiller's similar double "naive–sentimental") are restatements of this debate. Baudelaire in 1863 celebrated "modernity," the "ephemeral and fleeting beauty of modern life." In Germany, about 1887, the variant form "Die Moderne" was used as a slogan by writers whom we would today have to characterize as naturalists. In Spanish, the Nicaraguan poet Rubén Darío

had used the term "modernismo" since 1888. It became firmly established as a label for the most diverse authors such as Unamuno, Valle
Inclán, Azorín, and many others. There was also the widely noted "modernism" movement in Roman Catholic theology, which was suppressed
by an encyclical of Pope Pius X in 1907. An Englishman, George Tyrrell,
was a prominent exponent, and the Baron von Hügel, who lived most
of his life in England, had close relations with the movement. T. S. Eliot
wrote a strongly sympathizing review of a collection of his *Letters* under
the title "An Emotional Unity" for the *Dial* (84 [1928]: 109–12) discussing the movement. I can only guess that Eliot avoided the term because
of the danger of confusion. Certainly Eliot never defined the term. It
became a widely used label in the fifties with the paradoxical contrasts
to "postmodernism" (what is after "today"?) and "contemporaneous."
Joyce and Eliot belong to modernism, Beckett to postmodernism, and
writers such as the Angry Young Men are merely contemporaneous. It
is best to avoid this mare's nest. Criticism was a matter of very distinct
individuals: T. E. Hulme, Ezra Pound, Wyndham Lewis, and T. S. Eliot.
We shall consider them one by one.

T. E. HULME (1883–1917)

First we need to distinguish between the activity and printed writings of
T. E. Hulme during his lifetime and the posthumous reputation estab-
lished after the publication of printed and unprinted manuscripts called
Speculations (1924), edited by Herbert Read. Only much later did Sam
Hynes reprint the early writings as *Further Speculations* (1955) with an
American university press.

In his own time, Hulme played a rather obscure role in the founding
of imagism. Pound later dismissed it, saying that Ford Madox Hueffer
was more important; he called F. S. Flint's "History of Imagism" (1915),
which made much of Hulme, "bullshit." Flint there credits Hulme, apparently correctly, with proposing the first Poets' Club in 1908. But this
proves nothing about the ideas; the club was a gathering place for poets
who shared at most a general dissatisfaction with the present state of
poetry. Nothing is proved about the origin of the slogan "image" and
imagism (which Pound also spelled *imagisme*). Hulme gave a lecture on
"Modern Poetry" supposedly in 1908 and again in 1909, but the surviv-
ing version dates from 1914 and was printed only in 1938. Hulme
printed five little poems under the ironic title "Complete Poetical Works"
in Orage's *New Age* in January 1912 and must have allowed Pound to
reprint them in an appendix to his *Ripostes* in the same year.

In 1910 Hulme published a series of articles about now largely forgotten philosophers Ernest Belford Bax, Richard Burton Haldane, and Jules de Gaulthier in the *New Age* and then in 1911–12 a series of articles on Bergson, also in the *New Age*, which were good expositions obviously accepting Bergson's philosophy in toto. Hulme also translated and published Bergson's *Introduction to Metaphysics*. In the same year his interests shifted to modern art. He wrote a laudatory review of an exhibition of the cubist sculptor Jacob Epstein and in 1914 a series of articles on English post-impressionist and cubist artists, commenting on exhibitions and pictures. He also translated Georges Sorel's *Reflections on Violence* (1916) with an introduction published earlier, in 1915, in the *New Age*. The war changed Hulme's life. He wrote war notes about his experiences in the trenches and polemical articles against Bertrand Russell's pacifism. He was killed in battle in Flanders on September 28, 1917.

These bibliographical details are important for answering the much debated question of the influence of Hulme on Pound and Eliot. Pound knew Hulme but quickly dissociated himself from him and later minimized his role. "Mr. Hulme is on his way," he complained, "to mythological glory. The Hulme notes, printed after his death, had little or nothing to do with what went on in 1910, 1911, or 1912" (Pound, "This Hulme Business," in *Townsman* 2 [January 1939]). Pound claimed for himself the invention of the word "imagism" but acknowledged, "I made the word—on a Hulme basis—and carefully made a name that was not and never had been used in France specifically to distinguish us from any of the French groups catalogued by Flint in *The Poetry Review*." There we heard of unanimism and futurism, but also of paroxysme, impulsionisme, néo-paganisme, and other ephemeral groups. Eliot did not remember even having met Hulme (letter to Sam Hynes, 1934), but he certainly read him, as he quotes his translation of Bergson's *Introduction to Metaphysics* and the poem "The Embankment" very early in "Reflections on *Vers Libre*" (*New Statesman*, March 3, 1917) and says in "The Function of Criticism" (1923), "The poems of T. E. Hulme only need to be read aloud to have immediate effect" (*Selected Essays* [1932, rpt. 1950], 32). Ronald Schuchard has recently shown convincingly that Eliot expounded in Oxford Extension Lectures (actually given in remote Ilkley in Yorkshire in the autumn of 1916) a view of poetry identical or at least strongly reminiscent of Hulme's. But merely on the basis of Eliot's syllabus for the course discovered by Schuchard, no proof of Hulme's influence can be established. It is sufficient to account for Eliot's views from the sources that he himself assigned among readings, Maurras and Lasserre and his Harvard teacher Irving Babbitt. It seems likely that

Eliot read the *New Age* and thus "Notebook of T. E. Hulme" (December 9, 1915–February 10, 1916), an earlier version of "Humanism and the Religious Attitude," printed in *Speculations*. When Read published *Speculations*, Eliot hailed the book in the *Criterion* (April 1924) as "a work of very great significance. In this volume he appears the fore-runner of a new attitude of mind which should be the twentieth-century mind, if the twentieth century is to have a mind of its own." Since then Hulme has attracted biographers and a large body of comment wherever English criticism is discussed, which seems to me totally out of proportion to the quality and originality of his writings on literary matters.

Michael Roberts, whose sympathetic, expository book (1938) was the first full-length study of Hulme, makes many admissions that are far more damaging than he seems to realize. "A hostile critic might say that Hulme's sole merit was that he could read French and German. He was not an original thinker, he solved no problems" (12). "There is scarcely a single statement in Hulme that is not borrowed" (117). In philosophy, Hulme has merits as a propagandist, translator, and expounder of Bergson and Georges Sorel. He was one of the Englishmen impressed by Lasserre, the *Action française,* and the whole French antiromanticism. Though less systematically, he later showed an awareness of new German philosophical and aesthetic trends: he speaks of the neo-Kantianism of Hermann Cohen, of the so-called Marburg school, he has read and paraphrases something of Wilhelm Dilthey and Max Scheler, he knows the beginnings of phenomenology in Husserl, and he uses Wilhelm Worringer's *Abstraction und Einfühlung* (1908) to justify his artistic tastes. Hulme wanted to write a book on modern theories of art, which in addition to Bergson and Croce would have emphasized the German theoreticians— "this astonishing and intensely interesting literature entirely unknown in England" (*S,* 262)—centering on Theodor Lipps, "the greatest writer in aesthetics" (*S,* 264). But it is hard to see how these different motifs of thought could have been assimilated into anything else except some kind of superior *reportage.* His adherence to the philosophy of Bergson cannot be reconciled with the abstract classicism Hulme's taste demanded. He himself seems to have been worried about this. In 1911 he wrote:

> I noticed early this year that M. Pierre Lasserre, . . . one of the most interesting of the group, had made an attack on Bergson. I was very much in sympathy with the anti-romanticism of his two books, *La morale de Nietzsche* and *Le Romantisme français,* and I wondered from what point of view exactly he was attacking Bergson. I was in agreement with both sides, and so I wondered whether there was any real

inconsistency in my own position. When I was in Paris, then, last
April I went to see Lasserre and talk to him about it. (Roberts, 18)

Roberts does not record the outcome, if any, of this discussion. It seems
to me that there could not have been any: one cannot believe in a highly
irrational philosophy of flux and at the same time believe in ethical ab-
solutes, classicism, order, and abstract geometrical art.

But it is best to look at the more strictly literary and aesthetic pronouncements by Hulme. There are only a few documents that have any
bearing on our main interests: "Modern Art and Its Philosophy" (1914),
"Romanticism and Classicism," "A Lecture on Modern Poetry," and
"Notes on Language and Style." Each must, I think, be discussed separately. "Modern Art and Its Philosophy" is, as Hulme himself points out,
"practically an abstract of Worringer's views" (S, 82). It seems to me
totally incompatible with Hulme's Bergsonism, but it satisfied a personal
need of his taste. Hulme found in Worringer a defense for his interest
in abstract art: in Egyptian art, in Byzantine mosaics (he must have
visited Ravenna), and in Epstein, whom he knew personally and greatly
admired. The thesis of the paper is that of Worringer's book; there are
two kinds of art: one vitalistic, based on sympathy or empathy with nature and living forms—organic—and the other abstract, abstracting, geometrical, "searching after an austerity, a monumental stability and
permanence, a perfection and rigidity which vital things can never have"
(9). Hulme sympathizes with abstract art and hails its reemergence: its
"desire for austerity and bareness, a striving towards structure and away
from the messiness and confusion of nature and natural things" (96). It
is an exposition and a plea for a kind of art disparaged and neglected
by vitalistic, organistic art, produced by the Greeks, the Renaissance, and
the German classics.

Things became much more complex when Hulme writes on "Romanticism and Classicism." He starts, as he himself indicated, with the antiromanticism of Maurras and Lasserre (S, 114); he interprets
romanticism in the general political sense of the French antiromantics,
endorsing, for example, the view that "romanticism has made the revolution. They hate the revolution, so they hate romanticism" (115). Romanticism is conceived to be simply optimistic liberalism, belief in
progress, and so on, just the theories that most of the great romantics
hated most. Romanticism, in this view, is a lower form of the Enlightenment—something that can be possibly found in Rousseau, Hugo, or
Shelley, but surely not in the Schlegels, or any German romantic, or
Leopardi, Chateaubriand, Vigny, Blake, Wordsworth, or Coleridge. Ro-

manticism, according to Hulme, is "spilt religion" (118), a sentimental trust in human nature, a yearning for the vaguely infinite. Against this Hulme poses classicism, which implies a belief in original sin, in the stability of human nature, the impossibility of progress, and lack of interest in the vague infinite. The contrast is pinned then to the Coleridgean distinction between imagination and fancy. Hulme does not, however, come to grips with Coleridge's own distinction but fastens on Ruskin's later development of the terms to disparage imagination as a solemn yearning for the vague and to recommend fancy. Fancy is preoccupied with the finite; fanciful poetry is dry and hard. Beauty, Hulme pleads, "can be in small, dry things" (131). "The great aim is accurate, precise and definite description" (132). The aim of art is to catch the "exact curve" of the thing, complete "sincerity"—"the fundamental quality of good art without dragging in the infinite or serious." "I prophesy that a period of dry, hard, classical verse is coming" (133). A visual concrete language is the aim, which makes the reader see a physical thing. But this "making the reader see" cannot be achieved by simple description. "It is only by new metaphors, that is, by fancy, that it can be made precise" (137). So far, so good—one can speak of a theory of imagism, but then suddenly an astonishing attempt is made to recruit Coleridge and Bergson into the camp of this "classicism": Hulme argues that this classical art is still somehow vital, "intuitive," organic, though "vital"—or "organic"—is "merely a convenient metaphor for a complexity of a different kind, that in which the parts cannot be said to be elements as each one is modified by the other's presence, and each one to a certain extent is the whole" (138–39). But this is, of course, a false interpretation of Coleridge. "Organic" in Coleridge surely implies a metaphysics, a concept of creative imagination, and I cannot see how Bergsonian "intuition" can be brought in to defend such a "classicism." The bridge seems to be provided by the implied concept of the "characteristic," in which the artist seizes intuitively, a notion acceptable to Hulme, Bergson, and most romantics. The essay is of great interest as a statement of aversion to a complex of ideas that Hulme quite unhistorically calls "romantic" and as a prophecy of an imagistic, unemotional, fanciful poetry of hard, dry things. But it is hardly a piece that can be recommended as a full and fair discussion of the issue.

We come nearer to Hulme's concrete taste in the "Lecture on Modern Poetry." It starts out with a repudiation of the metaphysical claims of poetry. "A reviewer writing in the *Saturday Review* last week spoke of poetry as the means by which the soul soared into higher regions, and as a means of expression by which it became merged into a higher kind of reality. Well, that is the kind of statement that I utterly detest" (*FS*, 67). Hulme states boldly, "I have not a catholic taste, but a violently personal prejudiced one. I have no reverence for tradition" (68), and then explains his views: "Poetry no longer deals with heroic action, it has become definitely and finally introspective and deals with expression and communication of momentary phases in the poet's mind. It was well put by Mr. G. K. Chesterton in this way—that where the old dealt with the Siege of Troy, the new attempts to express the emotions of a boy fishing" (72). Hulme himself recognizes that what he demands here is something like impressionism in painting. He remembers that "the first time [he] ever felt the necessity and inevitableness of verse, was in the desire to reproduce the peculiar quality of feeling which is induced by the flat spaces and wide horizons of the virgin prairie of western Canada" (72). What poetry is after is the precise image: "This method of recording impressions by visual images in distinct lines does not require the old metric system" (73). Hulme disapproves of chanting, hypnotic verse. "Regular meter to this impressionistic poetry is cramping, jangling, meaningless, and out of place. Into the delicate pattern of images and colour, it introduces the heavy, crude pattern of rhetorical verse" (74). The differentia between poetry and prose is not meter but imagery. With a reversal of the usual terminology, Hulme argues that "the direct language is poetry, because it deals in images. The indirect language is prose, because it uses images that have died and become figures of speech" (75). "Images are born in poetry. They are used in prose, and finally die a long, lingering death in journalists' English. Now this process is very rapid, so that the poet must continually be creating new images, and his sincerity may be measured by the number of his images" (75). "This new verse resembles sculpture rather than music; it appeals to the eye rather than to the ear" (84). But who can ever measure sincerity by the number of images, and why should impressionist poetry resemble sculpture rather than painting?

These ideas can be supplemented by aphorisms in the "Notes on Language and Style." Much says the same as the "Lecture." Poetry should be visual, "each word must be an image *seen*, not a counter" (*FS*, 28). "Poetry is neither more nor less than a mosaic of words, so great is exactness required for each one" (87). But poetry must be metaphorical. "Never, never, never a simple statement. It has no effect" (87). Astonishingly enough, metaphor leads Hulme to recommend analogy, and analogy to a hint of a romantic metaphysics of symbolism and correspondences. "It is not sufficient to find analogies. It is necessary to find those that add something to each, and give a sense of wonder, a sense of being united in another mystic world" (88). The "Notes" contain assertions much in the style of late nineteenth-century aestheticism. Poetry "must be absolutely removed from reality" (94, 99). "Poetry is not for others, but for the poet"; "expression builds up personality"; poetry comes "in moments of ecstasy," "with the jumps, cf. love, fighting, dancing" (99–100). "The literary man deliberately perpetrates a hypocrisy, in that he fits together his own isolated moments of ecstasy," some of them "perhaps brought on by drink." The last entry is "All theories are toys" (100), and it would be easy to conclude on this note. All theories were toys to Hulme, but it is both more charitable and more accurate to say that Hulme was a young man groping for a view of the world, with a definite taste in art for which he was trying to find defenses. There seems to me an undeniable contradiction between his Bergsonism and his "classicism," but as in Eliot, the classicism is only an ideological superstructure: the taste is for the imagistic, the "characteristic," the "sincere," the fanciful, and that is really not incompatible with Bergsonism, whose metaphysics Hulme had embraced with such conviction.

EZRA POUND (1885–1972)

T. S. Eliot has paid extravagant homage to Pound, not only the poet but also the critic. In editing a collection of his *Literary Essays* (1954) he called Pound's literary criticism "the most important contemporary literary criticism of its kind" (x), "the *least dispensable* body of critical writing in our time" (xiii), comparing it with the essays of Dryden, the prefaces of Wordsworth, and *Biographia Literaria* as among the notable contributions of poets to criticism. Eliot's cautious qualification "of its kind" shows that he well understood the limitations of Pound's criticism. He defines it elsewhere as "advocacy of a certain kind of poetry: it is an assertion that poetry written in the immediate future must, if it is to be good poetry, observe certain methods and follow certain directions" (*Poetry* 68 [1946]: 328). It must be seen in the setting of its time, as advice to poets (and, I would add, to Pound himself), as a repudiation of the immediate past and an appeal to a new selective tradition. Pound himself assigned only a modest role to criticism. Once he distinguishes two functions: "1. Theoretically it tries to forerun composition, to serve as gunsight, though there is, I believe, no recorded instance of the foresight having *ever* been of the slightest use save to actual composers. . . . 2. Excernment. The general ordering and weeding out of what has actually been performed. . . . The work analogous to that which a good hanging committee or a curator would perform in a national Gallery or in a biological museum" (*LE*, 75). In practice, however, Pound did not believe that advice to the poets is unprofitable: he lavishes it in his early writings and his letters to his younger contemporaries. But most of his critical books serve the second purpose: exhibition, pointing out, selection. "I am for say 80 per cent exhibit and 20 per cent yatter," "Critics to be judged far more by their selections than by their palaver" (*PE*, 148), or, in a different tone: "A lot of my prose scribbling is mostly 'There digge!' plus belief that criticism shd. consume itself and disappear" (*L*, 261). The critical question is always "Gentlemen, are those verses worth reading?" or answering "a friend's question who approaches one's bookshelf asking 'What the deuce shall I read?'" (*LE*, 240, 306). The judgment will be professedly personal. "In the end the critic can only say 'I like it,' or 'I am moved,' or something of that sort. When he has shown us himself we are able to understand him" (56). Thus the only "really vicious criticism is the academic criticism of those who make the grand abnegation, who refuse to say what they think, if they do think, and who quote accepted opinions; these men are the vermin, their treachery to the work of the past is as great as that of the false artist to the present. If they do not care enough for the heritage to have a personal conviction then they have no licence to write" (56). Pound fulfilled this critical function: he says constantly in most decisive and abrupt terms what he likes and what he detests.

Pound cares little for the history of criticism. While Eliot reacted primarily against the critics who preceded him—Arthur Symons, Walter Pater, John Addington Symonds, and others—Pound rejected the poetry of his time, the Georgians and the Victorians, precisely because he himself had started writing in the style of Browning and the Pre-Raphaelites. Pound thinks "the evil done by St. Beuve [*sic*] is considerable and incalculable. It has allowed every parasite and nitwit to present himself as a critic, and thousands of essayists incapable of understanding a man's work or his genius have found opportunity in a discussion of wash lists" (*PE*, 3; cf. 87). But this is only a parodistic protest against the abuses of the biographical approach. Of all the critics, Pound seems to admire only Remy de Gourmont, who was obviously very dear to his sense of life. He calls him "Confucian, Epicurean, a considerer and entertainer of ideas" and speaks of his "complicated sensuous wisdom" (*LE*, 340–41). He even thinks that "de Gourmont's ultimate significance may not be less than Voltaire's" (*Fortnightly Review* 104 [1915]: 1164). But in all the three essays devoted to de Gourmont we see no attempt to expound or discuss his ideas on criticism, and even the longest essay consists merely in a string of unrelated quotations culminating in a letter to Pound from de Gourmont, which is then contrasted, in its politeness, with a letter from the editor of the *Quarterly Review*, Lord Prothero, in which he refuses to publish Pound because he had been associated with *Blast* (*LE*, 356–58). Pound's personal grievance overrides any interest in his subject. Clearly, de Gourmont's literary cosmopolitanism struck a sympathetic chord in Pound. He always emphasized the idea of *Weltliteratur*, going so far as to deplore "the crime perpetrated in American schools by courses in 'American literature.' You might as well give courses in 'American chemistry,' neglecting all foreign discoveries" (218), ignoring here the problem of nationality and the difference between scientific progress and poetic expression. T. S. Eliot hit the nail on the head when he said that "perhaps if Pound had stopped at home, he might have become a professor of comparative literature" (*Poetry* 68 [1946]: 330). Pound had studied Romance philology at the University of Pennsylvania under H. A. Rennert, the biographer of Lope de Vega, and Wickersham Crawford, a specialist in the Spanish Golden Age. His indiscriminate contempt for American "learneries" has a touch of sour grapes. Pound all his life sounds like a teacher and professor manqué. He adopted an international view when he called for "a universal standard which pays no attention to time or country—a Weltliteraturstandard" (*L*, 24f.), or when he described the history of English poetry as "a history of successful steals from the French" (*Future* 2 [1917]: 10). This internationalism buttresses Pound's emphasis on translating and the role of translations in history, to which he devoted many articles, unearthing little-known Elizabethan translations or early Latin translations of Homer (see *LE*, 227–75). It was startling to hear that Gavin Douglas's translation of the *Aeneid* was "better than the original" (35) or that Golding's translation of Ovid's *Metamorphoses* is "possibly the most beautiful book in our language" (238n.). Pound, in spite of all his wide-ranging interests in often remote corners of the history of poetry, has a completely unhistorical approach to its study. He believes that poetry is "always the same, the changes are superficial" (*Egoist* 2 [1915]: 11) and that "what we need is a literary scholarship which will weigh Theocritus and Yeats with one balance" (*SR*, 8), since "all ages are contemporaneous" (8). At the end Pound must conclude, "The value of criticism in proportion to actual making is less than one to one hundred. The only critical formulations that rise above this level are the specifications made by artists who later put them into practice and achieve demonstrations" (*Pavannes and Divagations* [1918], 231).

Thus theory of literature—poetics—plays only a minor role in Pound's thinking. Mostly it is "specification" for practice, elementary and often vague or very general advice, which served its purpose in a context but does not justify such claims as Christoph de Nagy's that "Pound would be a very great critic, even if he had only written his conceptualized poetics" (*Ezra Pound's Poetics*, 19). The early manifestos such as "Don't" in *Poetry* (March 1913) amount only to recommending "direct treatment of the thing," economy of words, and "composing in the sequence of the musical phrase," which were all very well as a rejection of Victorian rhetoric and regular metrics but seem today hardly more than truisms. The definition of the "image" is more interesting, since it deviates from the accepted meaning of image as a visual picture. "An 'image' presents an intellectual and emotional complex in an instant of time" (*LE*, 4). The term *complex*, Pound tells us, is used here in a technical sense employed by the newer psychologists such as Hart. Dr. Bernard Hart, the author of *The Psychology of Insanity* (1912), defined "complex" as a system of "emotionally toned Ideas operating unobserved in the mind, which caused random traces of thought to return continually to one object or feeling." Still, it remains unclear how Pound or anybody else could present such complexes in an instant of time. Pound, as far as I know, did not take up this pretentious formulation. It draws attention, however, to the fact that imagism must not be identified with a recommendation of visual imagery, though Pound in many other contexts seems to mean little more. Imagism changed easily into vorticism with "vortex" breaking sharply with anything that could be interpreted as visual impressionism. Vorticism has even been described as "Expressionism, English Style."[1] But both image and vortex remain slogans, as does the ideogram suggested to Pound by his reading of Ernest Fenollosa's *The Chinese Written Character as a Medium of Poetry* (1919, known to Pound in manuscript since 1913). Image, vortex, ideogram are simply schemata to allow Pound to defend the technique of montage, the "sufficient phalanx of particulars" (*Cantos*, 74) of which the *Cantos* are an ample display. The literature on Pound has, with incredible solemnity, seen all kinds of philosophical implications in his shifting statements. Walther L. Fischer has brought up Chinese correlation logic;[2] William Fleming has made Pound out to be a Cartesian,[3] and Christine Brooke-Rose sees affinities with Husserl's phenomenology,[4] while Hugh Kenner seems to consider Pound a mystic for whom the word is the thing.[5] All this seems to me quite unnecessary. Pound is obviously a totally unphilosophical and untheoretical mind: he never pretends to such knowledge. In his sweeping way, he can say that "philosophy since Leibnitz (at least since Leibnitz) has been a weak trailer after material science, engaging men of tertiary importance" (*LE*, 76), men, apparently, such as Hume, Kant, and Hegel. But also Aristotle (spelled sometimes in Pound's puerile jocularity as Arry Stotl) is vituperated as "master of those that cut apart, dissect and divide. Competent precursor of the card-index. But without organic sense" (*GK*, 343); and he can refer to the "crap like Bergson" in disparaging the importance of T. E. Hulme ("This Hulme Business," *Townsman* 2 [1939]: 15). There is more point in seeing Pound as a modern Stoic. He quotes the Stoics with approval when they say "reality existed only in the particular"; "universals were to them subjective concepts formed by abstraction" (*GK*, 123). Pound is, if he has to be pinned down to a philosophical position, a naive realist and even a sensualist who, in his imagism, wants to combine a concern for the concrete multifarious world of the senses with a belief in the need of man's expressing emotion. "Poetry is the statement," he can say, "of overwhelming emotional values, all the rest is an affair of cuisine, of art" (*Little Review* [1918]: 23). But cuisine, art, apparently disparaged here, plays a great role in Pound's critical writings. He pays constant attention to meter, to stanzaic forms, and is, admittedly, often preoccupied with technical invention to a degree that lays him open to the charge of divorcing form from content. But he does remember, on occasion, that "emotion is the organizer of form" (*New Age* 16 [1915]: 350) or that an "intentness on the quality of the emotion to be conveyed makes for poetry" (*LE*, 285). This sounds almost like Croce. Pound's saying that "poetry is a sort of inspired mathematics, which gives us equations, not for abstract figures, triangles, spheres, and the like, but equations for the human emotions" (*SR*, 14) was considered by Mario Praz "the starting point of Eliot's theory of the 'objective correlative.' "[6]

But mostly Pound preaches, surprisingly, a version of realism in the sense of an accurate representation of reality. Art is for Pound a science just as chemistry is a science. "The arts give us a great percentage of the lasting and unassailable data regarding the nature of man, of immaterial man, of man considered as a thinking and sentient creature" (*LE*, 42). Good art is accurate art. "Bad art is inaccurate art. It is art that makes false reports," or, similarly, "the arts give us our data of psychology, of man as to his interiors, as to the ratio of his thought to his emotions, etc. The touchstone of an art is its precision" (43, 48). One may wonder how such a ratio could possibly be established but cannot deny Pound's sympathy for a scientific naturalism. He quotes the preface to the Goncourts' novel, *Germinie Lacerteux*, several times with approval (416f.). Accurate art means for Pound also that art cannot be immoral. "Good art cannot be immoral. By good art I mean art that bears true witness, I mean art that is most precise" (44). At times, Pound defends an art-for-art's-sake position, denying any immediate social role to art. "Now art never asks anybody to do anything, or to think anything, or to be anything. It exists as the tree exists" (46). But this position is often abandoned or modified by a recognition of the broad linguistic and finally social effects of literature. "It has to do with the clarity and vigor of 'any and every' thought and opinion. It has to do with maintaining the very cleanliness of the tools, the health of the very matter of thought itself" (21). This follows from Pound's belief in the mot juste, which he derives from Flaubert, from his constant insistence on living, colloquial speech in rhythms close to those of the spoken language, "with its eye turned on the object— austere, direct, free from emotional slither" (12). It was advice that Pound ascribed to Ford Madox Hueffer but could have very well have discovered for himself in his revulsion against the rhetoric of his time.

Pound insists on a classification of kinds of poetry to which he recurs many times: melopoeia, "wherein words are charged with musical property"; phanopoeia, which is "a casting of images upon the visual imagination"; and logopoeia, "the dance of the intellect among words" (*LE*, 25). If thought of as a rigid division, the theory would contradict all that we know of the poem as organism. But the distinctions do roughly correspond to the main strata of a work of art. Much of Pound's interests are in the sound-stratum, in rhythms, rhyme, and sound patterns. He conceives of the sound of poetry as closely allied to music. "Poets who are not interested in music are, or become, bad poets. I would almost say that poets should never be too long out of touch with musicians. Poets who will not study music are defective" (437). "Poetry," Pound insists, "must be read as music and not as oratory" (437). But while Pound's whole interest in poetry that was written to be sung, such as Provençal poetry or Elizabethan songs, and his interest in music were lifelong and far from merely theoretical (he composed music himself), still he does not seem to have had a proper grasp of the actual relationship between poetry and music, nor any technical understanding of modern metrics. The fact of his reliance for Italian metrics on an old school-text picked up in a Sicilian hotel tells the story. Pound has an oddly amateurish side to his knowledge of the craft, which is, of course, in practice often redeemed by his ear.

Phanopoeia is another name for imagery. It means definiteness of presentation, not mere description (*LE*, 6f.). It presumably would include metaphor, which Pound distinguishes sharply from the symbol, as he did not wish to approve of symbolism, a trend that seems to him mystical and given to suggestion, to "mushy technique," to vagueness rather than his cherished precision.[7]

The last, logopoeia, is least discussed directly. But Pound always plays up to the role of the intellect in art. In the amusing review of A. E.

Housman's lecture on "The Name and Nature of Poetry," called "Mr. Housman at Little Bethel," Pound exclaims: "Saxpence reward for any authenticated case of intellect having stopped a chap's writing poetry! You might as well claim that railway tracks stop the engine" (*LE*, 71). Laforgue seems the only example of logopoeia Pound can think of in poetry. It must mean something more than the mere dance of the intellect: it seems to mean something like the contextual modification which Cleanth Brooks calls "irony," "employing words not only for their direct meaning but taking count in a special way of habits of usage, of the context we *expect* to find with the word, its usual concommitants, of its known acceptances, and of ironical play" (25). Pound finds a fourth element in poetry, "architectonics" or "the form of the whole" (26), but he does not think it indispensable or central. "Major form," he admits, "is not a non-literary component. But it can do us no harm to stop for an hour or so and consider the number of very important works of world-literature in which form, major form, is remarkable for absence" (394). He cites the *Iliad,* Aeschylus' *Prometheus Bound,* Rabelais, Lope de Vega, and Flaubert's *Bouvard et Pécuchet.* "The component of these great works and the indispensable component is texture" (395), not structure. It is not farfetched to suggest that this serves as a defense of the loose overall form of the *Cantos.*

This seems to be all one can find in Pound's writings which could conceivably be called poetic or literary theory. It seems meager enough but was for Pound sufficient to justify a very dogmatic taste which cannot be argued about, since Pound lacks analytical skill and critical vocabulary. His essays are largely anthologies of passages connected by apodictic pronouncements and value judgments which divide the whole history of poetry into good and bad poems according to criteria that are either very elementary (simplicity versus rhetoric, clarity versus fogginess) or unexplained and possibily unexplainable. A short survey of his opinions may demonstrate this.

All Pound's essays and little pedagogical books—*How to Read* (1931) and *ABC of Reading* (1934)—fulfill one function: "All criticism," Pound quotes I don't know whom, "is an attempt to define the classic" (*LE*, 214). Certainly Pound's is, at least, a naming of the classics, a ranking, an excluding and including. Among the Greeks Pound cares only for Homer and Sappho, among the Romans for Catullus, Ovid, and Propertius. "I am chucking out Pindar, and Virgil, without the slightest compunction" (28). Pindar is called "the prize windbag of all ages" (*L,* 87), and Virgil a "second-rater, a Tennysonianized version of Homer" (87). We are to laugh at Aeneas' being called "a stick who would have contributed to the

New Statesman (*LE*, 215) and at the anecdote about a sailor who thought that Aeneas was a priest and not a hero (*ABC*, 44).

In the Middle Ages Pound admires the Anglo-Saxon *Seafarer*, "fit to compare to Homer" (*LE*, 64), which he translated or rather paraphrased. He likes *Beowulf*, the *Cid*, which he prefers to the *Chanson de Roland* (*SR*, 66), the Icelandic sagas, and he admires Provençal poetry and what is derived from it. Cavalcanti occupied Pound for many years: he devoted translations, commentary, and finally an edition to his favorite, though, to judge from the opinions of both Italian and foreign specialists, Pound's efforts yielded little to advance scholarship. Dante, of course, is Pound's great admiration, and he does know some of the *Minnesänger*: Heinrich von Morungen and Walther von der Vogelweide. Villon, to whom he devoted a lively chapter in the *Spirit of Romance*, appeals to him most directly. He is "the hardest, the most authentic, the most absolute poet of France" (*ABC*, 104). Thus the selection from the Middle Ages seems wide and on the whole judicious. Only Petrarch is disparaged as "miles behind Ventadorn and Arnault Daniel. An excellent author for an Italian law student seeking to improve his 'delivery' " (*SR*, 166n.). Chaucer is praised only perfunctorily as "an enrichment, one might say, a more creamy version of the 'matter of France' " (*LE*, 28) in Pound's early writings, but in the *ABC of Reading* the praise becomes hymnical. Chaucer is played up against Shakespeare: "Chaucer had a deeper knowledge of life than Shakespeare. He understands the intellectual con-quests of Europe . . . in a way that Will Shakespeare probably did not" (*ABC*, 99, 101). We are told that "Chaucer's culture was wider than Dante's, Petrarch is immeasurably inferior to both." "You would not be far out if you chose to consider Chaucer as the father of *litterae humaniores* for Europe" (103).

Pound feels very ambiguous toward the Renaissance and particularly toward Elizabethan literature. "Since Lamb and his contemporary critics everything has been based, and absurdly based, on the Elizabethans, who are a pastiche. They are 'neither very intense nor very accomplished' (I leave Shakespeare out of this discussion)" (*LE*, 216), he adds cautiously, though Pound deplores that "English opinion has been bamboozled for centuries by a love of the stage, the glamour of the theatre, the love of bombastic rhetoric" (*ABC*, 99) in preferring Shakespeare to Chaucer. The general argument runs this way: "After Villon, and having begun before his time, we find this *fioritura*, and for centuries we find little else. Even in Marlowe and Shakespeare there is this embroidery of language, this talk about the matter, rather than presentation. I doubt if anyone ever acquired discrimination in studying 'the Elizabethans' " (*LE*, 29).

But Pound had an intense interest in the Elizabethan translators and seems to have changed his mind about Donne. In *How to Read,* which classifies writers into inventors, masters, diluters, and "men who do more or less good work in the more or less good style of the period," Donne is placed among this last group (23), but in the *ABC of Reading* he is called "the one English metaphysical poet who towers above the rest" (*ABC,* 140), and "The Ecstasy" is reprinted and praised as "Platonism believed." The conclusion seems, however, completely misinterpreted when "bodies" in the last line is glossed as "atoms" (140).

Pound's pet aversion, his *diable noir,* is Milton. The main point of accusation is that "Milton got into a mess trying to write English as if it were Latin" (*LE,* 40), or in more violent terms: "He tried to turn English into Latin; to use an uninflected language as if it were an inflected one, neglecting the genius of English, distorting its fibrous manner, making schoolboy translations of Latin phrases: 'Him who disobeys me disobeys.' . . . I am leaving apart all my disgust with what he has to say; his asinine bigotry, his beastly Hebraism, the coarseness of his mentality, I am dealing with a technical matter. . . . Milton is the most unpleasant of English poets. . . . His popularity has been largely due to his bigotry. . . . His real place is nearer to Drummond of Hawthornden than to 'Shakespeare and Dante' whereto the stupidity of our forebears tried to exalt him" (238). The comparison with Dante is preposterous. "Milton resembles Dante in nothing: judging superficially, one might say that they both write long poems which mention God and the angels, but their gods and their angels are as different as their styles and abilities. Dante's god is ineffable divinity, Milton's god is a fussy old man with a hobby. Dante is metaphysical, where Milton is merely sectarian" (*SR,* 155–56). Macaulay compared, fully as unjustly, the frozen monstrous Satan in Dante's *Inferno* with the titanic sufferer of Milton to the obvious detriment of Dante.

The other sin on Milton's ledger is the reference to Shakespeare's "woodnotes wild," for which Milton is called "the dog-eared Milton who passed on that driveling imbecility about woodnotes so dear to the Wordsworthian epiglottis" (*LE,* 72), a phrase which earns Milton elsewhere the charge of "gross and utter stupidity and obtuseness" (*ABC,* 103). He can speak of "Laurence Binyon's sad youth poisoned in the cradle by the abominable dogbiscuit of Milton's rhetoric" (*LE,* 201), or in a new variation tell us that "Milton is the worst sort of poison. He is a thoroughgoing decadent in the worst sense of the term. . . . He is bombast, perhaps of a very high order, but he is the worst possible food for a growing poet, save possibly Francis Thompson and Tasso" (216f.). The difference between Eliot's and Pound's criticism could hardly be better illustrated than by these quotations. They seem to agree in substance about the danger of Milton's influence; disregarding the crudity of Pound's deliberately offensive vocabulary, Eliot argues his case, while Pound merely asserts it.

Pound, unlike Eliot, has no use for Dryden. He protests that he has "never told anyone to read Dryden," that he does not want "Johnnie Dryden dug up again. Mr. Eliot's endeavours having served only to strengthen my resolve never, never again, to open either John Dryden, his works or any comment upon them." But no reason is given anywhere except to speak of the "outstanding aridity," the "platitude and verbosity" of this "lunkhead," unless we think that an allusion to the first syllable of his name is an argument (*LE*, 70; cf. *PE*, 139). There is little on Pope, though in quoting some verses from the *Essay on Criticism* Pound complains of "abstract statement and easy meter." "The texture of the lines is seen to be prose texture as soon as the rhyme dazzle is removed" (*ABC*, 166). The translation of Homer is commended mildly. "He has at least the merit of translating Homer into *something*" (*LE*, 250), though in a letter Pound speaks of Pope's "boring unity of surface" (*L*, 274). Pound comes closest to defining Pope's position when he says that Pope is "really the Elizabethan satirical style, more or less born out of Horace, and a little improved or at least regularized" (*LE*, 287). The only other eighteenth-century English poet Pound appreciates is Crabbe, whom he praises for "realism and spoken language" (276; *L*, 115). Dr. Johnson's "Vanity of Human Wishes" is praised as "the apogee and top notch of that mode" but is then dismissed as "by and large buncombe." Both "London" and "The Vanity of Human Wishes" are "facile, not really thought at all" (*GK*, 179–81). In general Pound thinks that "in a highly superior and accomplished way the whole of 18th century literature was a cliché," a form of "intellectual gongorism" with gongorism defined as "excess attention to high-colored detail" (180).

Pound has no use for the romantics; Wordsworth gets a measure of praise, very Poundian praise indeed. "The cult of the innocuous has debouched into the adoration of Wordsworth. He was a silly old sheep with a genius, an unquestionable genius, for imagisme, for a presentation of natural detail, wild fowl bathing in a hole in the ice, etc., and this talent, or the fruit of this talent, he buried in a desert of bleatings" (*LE*, 277; cf. *L*, 90). Pound objected to Wordsworth's advocacy of the common language. "He so busied about the ordinary word that he never found the time to think about *le mot juste*" (*LE*, 373).

One would expect Pound to be more sympathetic to Byron. He couples him with Musset as a romantic and careless writer of the same degree of relative goodness and badness. "Byron is rather more snap, a good satirist and a loose writer," but his technique is "rotten" (*L,* 134).

Pound seems to have changed his mind about Shelley. In the early *Spirit of Romance* (1910), a comparison with Dante seemed to him not unreasonable. "He is in sort, a faint echo of the Paradiso, . . . Shelley resembles Dante afar off, and in a certain effect of clear light which both could produce" (*SR,* 155f.), but later "The Sensitive Plant" is called "one of the rottenest poems ever written, at least one of the worst ascribable to a recognized author. It jiggles to the same tune as *a little peach in the orchard grew.* Yet Shelley recovered and wrote the fifth act of the *Cenci*" (*LE,* 51; cf. 305).

There is almost nothing on the other romantics: Blake is once called "dippy William" (*LE,* 72), and Keats is said to have "very probably made the last profitable rehash of Elizabethanism" (216). Pound must allude to the line in *Lamia* "Do not all charms fly at the mere touch of cold philosophy?" when he praises Keats for seeing that poetry "need not be the packmule of philosophy" (292).

Among the early nineteenth-century poets Pound admires Landor most. He praises him for a "hardness which is not of necessity 'rugged,' " though he thinks that Landor is "from poem to poem, extremely uneven" (*LE,* 286). The *ABC of Reading* contains a whole little anthology of Landor's shorter verse, but it is impossible to discover why Pound would speak of "a whole culture" in Landor (*L,* 89) or go so far as to say that "a set of Landor's collected works will go further toward civilizing a man than any university education now on the market" (*LE,* 344).

Pound is usually considered unfriendly to the Victorian poets. But this is not quite true. The references to Tennyson are jeering in tone, but they dwell rather on the cramping influence of Victorian respectability. "When he began to write for Viccy's ignorant ear, he immediately ceased to be the 'Tennyson so muzzy that he tried to go through the fireplace,' the Tennyson with the broad North accent, the old man with the worst manners in England (except Carlyle's), the Tennyson whom 'it kept the whole combined efforts of his family and his publishers to keep respectable' " (*LE,* 276). Pound repeats that Tennyson, "personally the North-Country ox, might very well take refuge from his deplorable manners in verbal *pâtisserie*" (290). The standard of good manners is odd to come from Pound.

The poet who appealed most to Pound was obviously Browning. In a letter in French to René Taupin he falls suddenly into German. "Und überhaupt stamm ich aus Browning. Pourquoi nier son père?" (*L,* 218). Browning is called "the soundest of all Victorians," the best of the Victorians (*LE,* 276, 277). Browning "has no French or European parallels. He has, indubitably, grave limitations, but *The Ring and the Book* is serious experimentation. He is a better poet than Landor who was perhaps the only complete and serious man of letters ever born in these islands" (33). Pound recommends *Sordello,* quotes from it, and ridicules "Victorian half-wits who claimed that the poem was obscure" (*ABC,* 191). "The most interesting poems in Victorian English are Browning's *Men and Women* or if that statement is too absolute, let me contend that the form of these poems is the most vital form of that period of English" (*LE,* 419). Obviously Pound himself learned from the dramatic monologue.

It is more surprising that Pound is very soft on Swinburne. He tries to rescue him from the ultra-respectable portrait in Gosse's *Life.* We should be thankful for "any man who kept alive some spirit of paganism and of revolt in a papier-mâché era." "The rhythm-building faculty was in Swinburne, and was perhaps the chief part of his genius" (*LE,* 293). But Pound says, more or less as Eliot did, that "he neglected the value of words as words, and was intent on their value as sound." "There is a lack of intellect in his work" (292). But this seems to be belied by Pound's conclusion. "There is, underneath all his writing, a magnificent passion for liberty. . . . The passion not merely for political, but also for personal liberty is the bedrock of Swinburne's writing. The sense of tragedy, and the unreasoning cruelty of the gods, hangs over it. He fell into no facile solution for his universe. His belief did not desert him. No, not even at Putney" (294). Pound pays a backhanded compliment to Swinburne's translations from Villon. "Swinburne's Villon is not Villon very exactly, but it is perhaps the best Swinburne we have" (36).

Rossetti is appreciated mainly for his translations. "Rossetti's translations were perhaps better than Rossetti, and his *Vita Nuova* and early Italian poets guide one to originals, which he has now and again improved" (*LE,* 36; cf. 193). Pound acknowledges Rossetti's influence on his own early translations rather ruefully. "My early versions of Guido (Cavalcanti) are bogged down in Dante Gabriel and Algernon" (194).

Pound does not comment on any nineteenth-century American poet at any length except Whitman. One would expect that the early Pound steeped in the Pre-Raphaelites and troubadours would have ignored or rejected Whitman, but actually Pound felt a deep kinship with Whitman, though he recognized his "crudity which is an exceeding great stench" and calls him "disgusting." "He is an exceedingly nauseating pill, but he accomplishes his mission." Whitman, Pound claims, is what Dante is to Italy, "the first great man to write in the language of the people." "Honour him for he prophesied me while I can only recognise him as a forebear of whom I ought to be proud" (*Selected Prose*, 145–46). This was written in 1909 when Pound was barely beginning his rise to fame. He repeated this estimate a few years later in general reflections on America ("Patria Mia," published in Orage's *New Age*, 1913). Whitman sounded the "American key-note," "a certain generosity; a certain carelessness, or looseness, if you will: a hatred of the sordid, an ability to forget the part for the sake of the whole, a desire for largeness, a willingness to stand exposed.

> Camerado, this is no book;
> Who touches this touches a man."   (*Selected Prose*, 123)

But it was only in *Canto* 82 that Pound paid him again tribute, quoting "O throat! O throbbing heart!" from "Out of the Cradle Endlessly Rocking" in a celebration of *Gea Terra*.

On the whole, Pound's taste is much more ninety-ish, even *fin de siècle*, than it might appear. For instance, he gives an extremely sympathetic account of Lionel Johnson. He recognizes that he cannot be shown to be in accord with our "present doctrine and ambitions. His language is a bookish dialect, or rather it is not a dialect, it is curial speech and our aim is natural speech, the language spoken." But Pound admires his pure imagism and calls his verse "small slabs of ivory, firmly combined and contrived" (*LE*, 362f.). He praises the effect of neatness and hardness and thinks he might even have taken a place in *Weltliteratur* if Gautier had not written before him (368).

Pound sees the beginnings of the new movement, the "prose tradition in verse," in Ford Madox Hueffer. He finds him revolutionary, because of his insistence on clarity and precision. A poem, "On Heaven," is called in 1914 "the best poem yet written in the 'twentieth-century fashion' " (*LE*, 373). What Pound quotes sounds to me no better than anything by Coppée. Hueffer must have impressed Pound by his person: the collection of rather flaccid articles, *The Critical Path* (1911), does little more than expound the trite demand that "what we so very much need to-day is a picture of the life we live" (*P*, 33).

The relations with Yeats were also personal. For a time, Pound served as Yeats's secretary, and Yeats sought his advice even on individual words in his poems.[8] Pound praised the later Yeats, beginning with *Responsibilities* (1914), for becoming gaunter, seeking a greater hardness of outline (*LE*, 379), but very early he thought of Yeats as "a sort of great dim figure with its associations set in the past" (*L*, 121), historically important as providing a link between imagism and symbolism (*L*, 218). But Pound's deeper influence on Yeats seems doubtful.[9]

Pound's most enduring merit may be the encouragement he gave to younger contemporaries. He was one of the first to give favorable reviews to the early collections of Robert Frost (*LE*, 382f.), he welcomed with impetuous enthusiasm William Carlos Williams, an old friend from Philadelphia days (*LE*, 389–98), and we all know of Pound's help to T. S. Eliot in cutting *The Waste Land*. Eliot wrote before the original manuscript was discovered: "I should wish the blue penciling on it to be preserved as irrefutable evidence of Pound's critical genius" (*Poetry* 68 [1946]: 330). Pound gave Eliot several generous reviews: one on *Prufrock* in the *Egoist* in 1917 (*LE*, 418–22) and one more grudging on the criticism under the title "Mr. Eliot's Solid Merit" in *Polite Essays* (1937). Later Pound became increasingly estranged from Eliot; he disliked his caution, "the method of increasingly guarded abstract statement" ("Criterionism," *Hound and Horn* 4 [1930]: 114), and had no use for his religion. But he came to his funeral from Italy.

Pound's views of poets other than English ones are much more erratic and selective. French poetry between Villon and Gautier does not exist for him. Gautier is his great admiration: he "achieved hardness" in *Emaux et camées* and "hardness" for Pound is "nearly always a virtue" (*LE*, 285). After Gautier comes Tristan Corbière, who seems to Pound the greatest poet of the period, "hard-bitten, perhaps the most poignant poet since Villon, in very much Villon's manner" (282); Rimbaud, "a vivid and indubitable genius," and Laforgue, "the most sophisticated of all the French poets" (281), "an incomparable artist" (282). "Laforgue conveys his intent by comment, Corbière by ejaculation, as if the words were wrenched and knocked out of him by fatality; by the violence of his feeling, Rimbaud presents a thick suave colour, firm, even" (*Instigations* [1920]). The silence about Mallarmé and even Baudelaire is surprising, as is the uncritical enthusiasm for contemporary French poets now almost forgotten, such as Max Elkamp, Albert Mockel, André Spire, and Arcos. The praise of Francis Jammes was lavish until Pound decided that he "went *gaga* over Catholicism."[10]

I shall not press the case against Pound as a critic by citing his opinions about German literature. He has no use for anything between the *Minnesänger* and Heine. "After Villon one can, I think, skip everything down to Heine" (*L*, 88). Pound early translated a few of Heine's poems (see Demetz, "German Studies"), and praised his "absolutely clear palette" (*LE*, 216). Goethe remained a stranger. "His lyrics are so fine, so unapproachable—I mean they are as good as Heine's or Von der Vogelweide's—but outside his lyrics he never comes off his perch. We are tired of men on perches" (217). The silence on other poets must be ascribed

to Pound's limited knowledge of the language and to an increasing distaste for German politics and scholarship (though Pound admired Leo
Frobenius enormously).

What shall one say of Pound's dismissal of the "Rooshuns"? "All right;
let a man judge them after he has encountered Charles Bovary; he will
read them with a better balance" (LE, 40). Perhaps, Pound's dismissal
was not quite wholesale. In the essay on Remy de Gourmont Pound draws
a parallel to Turgenev's *Nest of Gentlefolk* which shows an intimate knowledge of and admiration for this novel, read in French translation (*Selected
Prose*, 414).

Pound is less interested in prose than in poetry, and what he says about
the main novelists is hardly worth recording. He does not care for Balzac.
He recommends Stendhal and praises Flaubert, *Madame Bovary* and *Trois
Contes*, especially *Un Coeur simple*, which contains "all that anyone knows
about writing" (*L*, 89). But Pound dislikes *Salammbô* and calls it "dull and
tedious" (*L*, 93), "an old charade in fancy clothes" (*ABC*, 74). But there
are two novelists on whom Pound wrote more extensively than on any
other author: Henry James and James Joyce. The long piece on James
is the most sympathetic and detailed essay Pound ever wrote. He even
makes brief shots at characterization, saying, for instance, that "his emotional centre is in being sensitive to the feel of the place or to the tonality
of the person" (*LE*, 306). He praises James's sense of the differences of
national civilizations (298) and admires James as a hater of tyranny, a
friend of human and personal liberty (296). Much of the essay consists
of a grading of the novels and stories, from which it is obvious that Pound
cares most for the early middle James, for *Washington Square*, *Portrait of
a Lady*, and, oddly enough, *The Sacred Fount*. Pound dislikes the late
James, who should not have "so excessively cobwebbed, fussed, blathered,
worried about minor mundanities" (311). Pound resents also "the shreds
of Back Bay and Buffalo [a confusion with Albany?], the midweek-prayer
meeting point of view," for instance in the essay on Baudelaire, "an
egregious slip" (307). Some of Pound's judgments on individual works
are eccentric: why should he say that the "obscenity of the *Turn of the
Screw* has given it undue prominence" (326) or consider *The Aspern Papers*
inferior (320) or give away the whole case for James by saying "one
wonders if parts of Kipling by the sheer force of content, of tale to tell,
will not outlast most of James's cobwebs" (324)? Pound has a very personal interest in James's problem of the expatriate American in Europe.
He commends *The American Scene*, a book "no serious American will
neglect," and is fascinated by James's memoirs, *The Middle Years*, describ-

ing his arrival in England. "Only an American who has come abroad will ever draw all the succulence from Henry James's writings" (332).

Pound did not discover Joyce but he encouraged him and helped him more than anyone else. Before he met him in Sirmione on Lake Garda in 1920, Pound had written on *Dubliners*, on *Exiles*, and on *A Portrait of the Artist as a Young Man* in wholly laudatory terms. The review of *Dubliners* (1914) praises the "freedom from sloppiness," "the clear hard prose," his lack of Irishness. "It is surprising that Mr. Joyce is Irish. One is so tired of the Irish or 'Celtic' imagination (or 'phantasy' as I think they now call it) flopping about. Mr. Joyce does not flop about. He defines" (*LE*, 399f.). "He writes as a contemporary of continental writers. . . . He is not ploughing the underworld for horror. He is not presenting a macabre subjectivity. He is classic in that he deals with normal things and with normal people" (461). Similarly, an article entitled "The Non-Existence of Ireland" states that Joyce "writes with no trace of morbidity. The sordid is there but he does not seek for the sordid. He has the sense of abundant beauty. . . . We can be thankful for the clear, hard surfaces, for an escape from the softness and mushiness of the neo-symbolist movement, and from the fruitier school of neo-realists" (*New Age* 16 [1915]: 452; repr. in *P/J*, 32ff.). The praise of *Portrait of the Artist* is almost identical: the novel is the nearest to Flaubertian prose, "hard, clear-cut, with no waste of words, no bundling up of useless phrases, no filling in with pages of slosh" (*P/J*, 88f.). But Pound sees now the scope of Joyce more clearly, "the reach of his writing from the fried breadcrusts and from the fig-seeds in Cranley's teeth to the casual discussion of Aquinas" (*LE*, 411). "On almost every page of Joyce you will find just such swift alternation of subjective beauty and external shabbiness, squalor, and sordidness" (412). With *Ulysses*, which Pound propagated and defended tirelessly against charges of obscenity and attempts at its suppression, the criticism becomes more concrete in its praise. Pound objects to the view that Joyce can write only about himself. "Joyce has created his second character (Bloom); he has moved to the creation of the complementary figure" (416). Molly is defined as "an earth symbol, a coarse-grained bitch, not a whore, an adultress. . . . She says ultimately that her body is a flower; her last word is affirmative" (407). An article in French, "James Joyce et Pécuchet," makes much of the parallels with Flaubert's *sottissier* and tries to show that the novel has the form of a sonata: theme, countertheme, recontre, development, finale (in *Mercure de France* [1922]; repr. in *P/J*, 200–11). But even in the most laudatory review Pound expresses some reservations about the parallels to the *Odyssey*. "These correspondences are chiefly his own affair, a scaffold, a means of construction, justified by the result, and justifiable by it only. The result is a triumph of form, in a balance, a main scheme, with continuous interweaving and arabesque" (*LE*, 406). The mild reservation becomes in time, for reasons that still seem obscure, a strong rejection: "I don't care," Pound wrote in 1931 in the *New Review*, "a damn about the metaphysics and the correspondences and the allegorical and the anagogical and the scatological parallels of his opus. . . . I respect Mr. Joyce's integrity as an author in that he has not taken the easy path. I never had any respect for his common sense or for his intelligence. I mean general intelligence, apart from his gifts as a writer" (*P/J*, 239). Pound intensely disliked *Finnigans Wake* for its "curlicues." "I cannot see that Mr. Joyce's later work concerns more than a few specialists" (251). "Joyce has sat within the grove of his thought. He mumbles things to himself, he has heard his voice on the phonograph and thought of sound, sound, mumble, murmur. Three decades of life have been lived since he began writing, of the last two he has learned almost nothing" (256). A letter then says: "I am through with this diarrhea of consciousness" (257). In a radio talk from Rome, after Joyce's death, the praise of *Ulysses* as a "mine of rich comedy" is again high but now Cummings's novel *Eimi* and Wyndham Lewis's *Apes of God* are played up as worthy successors (267). Lewis was Pound's old comrade in arms of vorticism, and Pound has praised *Tarr* as the "most vigorous and volcanic English novel of our time, Lewis is the only English writer who can be compared with Dostoievsky" (*LE,* 424). Possibly one cannot take Pound's dismissal of the Russians literally: he intends this comparison as praise.

This last quotation and many earlier ones raise again the question of the extent to which Pound's pronouncements can be taken seriously. Many certainly are not to be. Pound constantly wants to shock, exaggerate, overstate quite deliberately, as he does not mind considering himself something like a barker in front of his show. He defends almost any means to attract attention. He plays the role of a pedagogue with special glee, in the little books *How to Read* and *ABC of Reading,* in the cranky *Guide to Kulchur,* and in personal letters such as those to Iris Barry, who is given advice not so much on how to read as on what. One may be repelled by many crude jocularities and coarse insults. One must often agree with Yvor Winters, who calls Pound "a barbarian on the loose in a museum" (*In Defense of Reason* [1947], 480). Often the pretense to scholarship turns out to be unfounded: certainly the Chinese obsession based on the fantastic theories of Ernest Fenollosa (see Kennedy, "Fenollosa, Pound") is an example of pretentious ignorance. So are often the condemnations of authors and whole periods of literature, which one suspects are often made on the basis of casual impressions and secondhand reports. The cocksureness on almost every topic is overwhelming but, one must admit, achieved what Pound wanted to achieve—a revolution in taste.

Pound (and T. S. Eliot) broke resolutely with the rhetorical tradition and defined a new taste: in the novel, for the objective novel of Flaubert, James, and Joyce; in poetry, for direct, simple, often visual, prosaic or apparently prosaic verse. There was genuine merit in Pound's fight against English provincialism, however erratic his selection from many literatures may be. There was finally great merit in Pound's generous support of new writing. It was a rare critical flair which made him the champion of Robert Frost, William Carlos Williams, Marianne Moore, T. S. Eliot, and James Joyce. If one of the functions of criticism is the discovery of new talent, a prediction of the new course of literature, then Pound was an important critic in his time.

WYNDHAM LEWIS (1882–1957)

Wyndham Lewis was closely associated, ideologically and personally, with Hulme, Pound, Joyce, and Eliot. He shared their French type of anti-romanticism; he had read Benda, Maurras, Lasserre, and others and imbibed a violent distaste for Rousseauistic primitivism and for the whole philosophy of flux: for Bergson and Bergsonism, and for the belief in progress and history. He joined their claim that a new "classical" art was being created: "classical" meaning severe, hard, and even coarse. It meant, in Lewis's practice as an artist, cubism (but not abstract art) or its variety for which he accepted Pound's term "vorticism." Lewis founded a magazine, *Blast,* of which only two numbers appeared in June 1914 and July 1915. Pound published in between an essay on vorticism in the *Fortnightly Review* on September 1, 1914. The war interrupted everything (Lewis served at the front). Vorticism was dead, although Pound claimed George Antheil to be a musical "vorticist" as late as the twenties. The slogan "vortex" and the manifestos and aphorisms by Lewis, "Our Vortex," are only bombastic proclamations of complete independence and novelty and wild generalizations about national characteristics. A distaste for Marinetti, his "sentimental rubbish about Automobiles and Aeroplanes" (*OA,* 49), and an attack on English humor define the position only a little better than such sayings as that we are "Primitive Mercenaries in the Modern World" and "Our Cause is—No-man's" (27).

Only after the war can Wyndham Lewis be said to have written literary criticism. *The Lion and the Fox* (1927) is an ambitious study of Shakespeare with scholarly pretensions. It sketches the relations between Italy and Tudor England and emphasizes and exaggerates the influence of Machiavelli, largely drawing on secondary sources such as Eduard Meyer's pioneering research. All this introduces an interpretation of Shakespeare's heroes in terms of Machiavelli's metaphor for the necessity of the Prince to combine the virtues of the lion and the fox. Lewis, however, does not keep to this scheme and even admits that "it is impossible to make a fox-hunter of him [Shakespeare]; and he shows no tendency to wish to be a lion" (*LF,* 178). Rather, Lewis interprets Shakespeare, using Frazer's *Golden Bough,* as a "public executioner," whose "impassibility was the professional mask of a hangman" (145). His tragic protagonists "are struck down always by the puniest weapons; always by deceit, but quite ordinary deceit" (188). Othello, Cordelia, and Timon are his examples. Lewis belongs to the long line of critics who imagine that they can single out the voice of Shakespeare. Lewis concludes that Shakespeare was "the adversary of life itself" and "his works a beautifully impersonal outpouring of fury, bitter reflection, invective and complaint" (160)—an apt characterization of Lewis's own criticism, except that his was nothing if not personal. He developed more and more a self-destructive tendency of making enemies of his friends and allies.

All of Lewis's later criticism of his contemporaries can be described as invective, satire, and even personal abuse. Lewis has a basic justification developed at great length in *Time and Western Man* (1927). Western civilization is in disarray; the worship of Time and the flux of history fostered by the philosophies of Bergson and Croce, Spengler and Whitehead, is the root of all evils, as it is in literature, where it brought about the inordinate prevalence of introspection, psychology, and finally the "stream of consciousness." Against the internal method, against "telling from the inside" (*MA,* 145, 127), Lewis exalts the eye, the external point of view and hence satire, where "the eye is supreme" (127). He considers satire the only possible modern art, the art he practiced himself in his novels. These simple convictions allow Lewis to attack practically all his contemporaries, including his friends, often in virulent terms. One should grant, however, that Lewis has not only a sharp tongue but a sharp eye for defects and lapses and a great verbal inventiveness in characterizing, ridiculing, and often abusing his victims.

Gertrude Stein seems to him the arch-Bergsonian. She is an easy target. Her "thick monotonous prose-song" is compared to "a cold, black suet-pudding" and "a sausage of by-the-yard variety" (*TWM,* 78). She made a clown of Hemingway by teaching him her babytalk—"an infantile, dull-witted, dreamy stutter" (*MA*, 27). In contrast to Merimée's "rude, crude, naked force in men and women," Hemingway depicts "futile, clown-like, passive and above all purposeless figures. His world of men and women is (in violent action certainly), completely empty of will" (21–22). They are "wooden-headed, loutish and oafish marionettes" (29), speaking a low-class pidgin English. Still, Lewis recognizes the art of Hemingway and concludes with a double-edged compliment. "The expression of the soul of the dumb ox would have a penetrating beauty of its own, if it were uttered with genius—with bovine genius (and in the case of Hemingway that is what has happened)" (40). "Steining," as Lewis calls it, is not his only aversion. He disapproves of all irrationalism, primitivism, child worship, whether upperclass and refined, or crude, dark, and mystical. Bloomsbury seems to him derivative from the aesthetic movement presided over by Oscar Wilde (171). Lewis had quarreled bitterly with Roger Fry and feels like taking "the cow by the horns" in attacking the "shrinking and tittering," "a little old-maidish" Virginia Woolf (169). He criticizes the essay "Mr. Bennett and Mrs. Brown" (1924) for posing artificial dilemmas: as if there were no other novels than those of Arnold Bennett, Galsworthy, and H. G. Wells. Much later Lewis still referred to "the quite second-rate, although pleasant and delicate literary output of Mrs. Woolf, the original female counterpart of the Führer Lytton" (*ES*, 93). The source of this decadence is in Proust and Henry James, both having the mind's eye, the time-eye that "looks equally upon the past and present but perceives the actual scene a little dimly" (*MA*, 145). In the essay on James, Lewis makes no effort to criticize "the great disembodied romances," the "twilit feminine universe—of little direct action and of no gross substance at all" (149) but rather comments on the juvenile James's "snobbish" reviews of Trollope. He interprets James in terms derived from Van Wyck Brooks's *Pilgrimage of Henry James* as a refuge from American barrenness (which he finds even in the landscape along the Eastern coast), who fled too late to Europe to shed the American disembodied abstractness.

In 1934 it was still unusual to pay attention to Faulkner. Oddly enough, Lewis does not see that at least *The Sound and the Fury* might support his aversion to the worship of the flow of time; he discusses Faulkner as "a bold bustling romantic writer, of the 'psychological' school" (*MA*, 58) and "a very considerable moralist—a moralist with a corncob" (64), who believes in fate, which "seems to be with him a scientific notion, centered in heredity" (57). "His novels are, strictly speaking, clinics. Destiny weighs heavily upon every figure which has its being in this suffocating atmosphere of whip-poor-wills, magnolias, fire-flies and water-oaks (not to mention the emanations of the dark and invariably viscid earth). And the particular form that destiny takes is race. Whether it is Christmas or Sartoris, it is a matter of fatality residing in the blood" (49). Lewis recognizes the poetry in Faulkner clashing with the violent melodramatic action and complains, for instance, of a description of "moonlight [which] seeped into the room impalpably, refracted and *sourceless*" (45), collecting then other obsessive uses of "sourceless" in other novels besides *Light in August.* But at least in the instance quoted, it seems well-observed: moonlight might appear so diffused that its source is not apparent.

Faulkner worshipped the dark gods of tragedy. D. H. Lawrence is worse in his worship of the dark gods of Mexico. *Mornings in Mexico* is elaborately ridiculed in a long section of *Paleface* (1929). Lawrence's "abdominal raptures about the Mexican Indian" (*Rude Assignment,* 204) seem to him merely the absurd extremes of a celebration of mindlessness, community (which Lewis equates with communism), feminism, of the "invitation to suicide addressed to the White Man" (*P,* 193). Lewis hardly discusses the novels: *Sons and Lovers* is "an eloquent wallowing mass of Mother-love and Sex-idolatry. His *Women in Love* is again the same thick, sentimental, luscious stew" (*P,* 180). Later Lewis referred to Lawrence as "that novelist of genius" (*Rude Assignment,* 106). Sherwood Anderson, particularly *Dark Laughter* (1926), is easily dismissed as "Sherwood Lawrence," a joke derived from H. L. Mencken (*P,* 198). Anderson invites us "to merge in the 'dark' juicy matrix of Mother Nature in colossal, direct, 'soulless' abandons" (*P,* 212).

The aversion Lewis had conceived against anything that could be connected with the worship of time and history induced him to criticize his old friends Ezra Pound and James Joyce. Lewis makes some acknowledgment of Pound's "personal kindness" and "generous and graceful person" (*TWM,* 38). He remembers his association with *Blast* but then solemnly announces that he has to "repudiate his association with Pound" (41), apparently annoyed by an interview of Pound in which he suggested that music should be played in a factory and by his turn toward music and the promotion of George Antheil. Pound is now disparaged as a man living in the past, a "person without a trace of originality" (69), as "a great intellectual parasite," "a great time-trotter" (71) who consorts only with the dead. Some of the *Cantos* are criticized for their horseplay, "their thick facetiousness of the rollicking slap-on-the-back order" (74). Pound seems to him a child, a primitive: "Some inhibition has prevented him from getting that genuine naif (which would have made him a poet) into his work. There, unfortunately, he always attitudinizes, frowns, struts, looks terribly knowing, breaks off, shows off, puffs himself out, and so obscures the really simple, charming creature that he is" (74).

The attack on Joyce is more surprising. They had been drinking companions in Paris in the early twenties. One could argue that Joyce tried to do precisely what Lewis postulated: to conceive experience on a simultaneous plane, to escape from the nightmare of history. *Ulysses* is the prime example of spatial form. But in *Time and Western Man*, a whole long chapter, "An Analysis of the Mind of James Joyce," makes *Ulysses* a "time-book." Joyce is "very strictly of the school of Bergson-Einstein, Stein-Proust" (89). Joyce's method of telling from the inside "lands the reader inside an Aladdin's cave of incredible bric-à-brac in which a dense mass of dead stuff is collected, from 1901 toothpaste, a bar or two of Sweet Rosie O'Grady, to pre-nordic architecture" (91). *Ulysses* appears as "the very nightmare of the naturalistic method," reminding us of a "gigantic victorian quilt or antimacassar" (91–92). Lewis also makes specific criticisms of Joyce's characters. Stephen Dedalus is a "really wooden figure" (97). Bloom is "not even a Jew most of the time but his talented Irish author" (101), and, the most unkind cut of all, Joyce is "steeped in the sadness and the shabbiness of the pathetic gentility of the upper shopkeeping class, slumbering at the bottom of a neglected province" (77). Some attempts are made to suggest Joyce's antecedents in Gertrude Stein, the Elizabethan Thomas Nash, and for the staccato sentences, quite plausibly, in the speeches of Jingle in *The Pickwick Papers*. In spite of these often malicious criticisms, Lewis sees Joyce as "a genial and comic writer of the traditional English school—in temper, at his best, very like Sterne" (76). He recognizes Joyce's technical virtuosity, his meticulous craftsmanship, though "the homeric framework" seems to him "only an entertaining structural device or conceit" (104). Lewis of course dismisses the charge of obscenity. Joyce is respectable, even conventional, dated, obsolete. To read him "is like listening to a contemporary of Meredith or Dickens (capering to the Elizabethan hornpipe of Nash perhaps—as interpreted by Miss Stein)" (109). It seems obtuse to call *Portrait of the Artist as a Young Man* "a rather cold and priggish book" (75) and to dismiss *Dubliners* for "its small neat naturalism" (100). *Ulysses* is seen wrongly as the climax of naturalism, as an outpouring of mere stuff and matter, as "a record diarrhoea" (92), but a soft variety of naturalism, flabby, vague in "its Bergsonian fluidity" (103).

Lewis's critical principles are very simple: independence, freedom of the artist, distaste for the contemporary scene. Hence the necessity of satire, which means the external approach, the visual, the concrete. It implies a disapproval of introspection, of depth psychology, of stream-of-consciousness. In the comments on the literary criticism of T. S. Eliot and I. A. Richards in *Men Without Art* (1933), however, the ostensibly classical Lewis criticizes Eliot's impersonality theory as he does Richards's idea of "disbelief." Lewis was a highly personal author, strongly committed to his causes. Impersonality seems to him scientific, even behaviorist. He chides Eliot for "confusing scientific values with art values" (*MA,* 75). Lewis sees that Richards's view that there is in Eliot "a complete severance between his poetry and *all* beliefs" (*Science and Poetry* [1926], 64–65) must be mistaken, as is the reduction of all assertions in poetry to "pseudo-statements." Eliot could not possibly even then be described as "the man with absolutely no beliefs whatever" (*MA,* 76). Lewis with some irony depicts the reluctant disagreements between Eliot and Richards and argues then that Richards propounds a new art-for-art's-sake theory or "stylists' evangel," however disguised (78). Lewis ignores Richards's deep commitment to the social use of poetry, even if one dismisses the salvation by poetry proclaimed by Arnold as foolishness (94).

One could add other pronouncements of Lewis to this list. He commented admiringly on George Orwell's *Animal Farm,* and *1984* found his approval, while he dismissed the earlier writings. He admired Camus, whom he preferred to Sartre; he detested Malraux. He defended Matthew Arnold as a poet (in *TLS,* 1954; reprinted in *ES,* 179–83). He attacked Shaw and ridiculed the Sitwells. All his pronouncements are clear, pungent, and often witty and perceptive, though doctrinaire in their assumptions of an uncompromising traditionalism, ideological classicism, and hatred for Bergsonism. But the effect of Lewis's criticism was greatly impaired by the prolixity of his main critical books, *Time and Western Man* and *Men Without Art*; sharp formulations are drowned in dreary polemics and often nit-picking verbal disputes. To this one must add Lewis's bad reputation for his political opinions, such as the early praise of Hitler (1931) and the pugnacious attacks on former friends and sundry enemies. Hemingway revenged himself in *A Movable Feast* ([1964], 108–10), Joyce punned elaborately in *Finnegans Wake,* Virginia Woolf shows her hurt in her *Diary,* Lawrence expressed his contempt in essays and letters, Leavis called him "boring and brutal." Only Eliot, who had met Lewis in 1915 and went on a tour of France with him in 1920, remained an admirer, though they quarreled over the rejection of a manuscript of Lewis's in 1925. But Eliot continued the benevolent relationship, and in 1938 Lewis painted two excellent portraits of Eliot; after Lewis's death Eliot wrote a laudatory obituary (in *Hudson Review* [Summer 1957]: 167–71). More recently, Lewis has found new admirers and defenders beginning with Hugh Kenner in 1954. Lewis deserves to be restored to a position in the group that includes Hulme, Pound, and Eliot, but it seems unlikely that his oeuvre of some fifty volumes can ever achieve the prominence of either Eliot's or Pound's.

6: T. S. ELIOT (1888–1965)

T. S. ELIOT is by far the most important critic of the twentieth century in the English-speaking world. His influence on the taste of his time is most conspicuous: he has done more than anybody else to promote the shift of sensibility away from the taste of the "Georgians" and to revaluate the major periods and figures of the history of English poetry. He reacted most strongly against romanticism, he criticized Milton and the Miltonic tradition, he exalted Dante, and Jacobean dramatists, the metaphysical poets, Dryden, and the French symbolists as "*the* tradition" of great poetry. But Eliot is at least equally important for his theory of poetry, which buttresses this new taste and which is much more coherent and systematic than most commentators and Eliot himself have allowed. His concept of "impersonal poetry," his description of the creative process, which demands a "unified sensibility" and should end in an "objective correlative," his justification of "tradition," his scheme of the history of English poetry as a process which led to the "dissociation" of an originally unified sensibility, his emphasis on the "perfection of common speech" as the language of poetry, his discussion of the relationship between ideas and poetry under the term "belief"—all these are crucial critical matters for which Eliot found memorable formulas, if not always convincing solutions.

Eliot's significance as a theorist is somewhat obscured by his constant denial of interest in aesthetics and of an ability for systematic thinking. He can say that he is too well aware of his "incapacity for abstruse reasoning," and therefore that he has "no general theory of [his] own" (*UP,* 143) and assert that "the extreme of theorising about the nature of poetry, the essence of poetry if there is any, belongs to the study of aesthetics and is no concern of the poet or of a critic with my limited qualifications" (149–50). He does not want to indulge in "speculations about aesthetics, for which [he has] neither the competence nor the interest" (Stallman, 110; suppressed in *OPP* reprint). It is hard not to find such self-disparagement and confession of ignorance and dilettantism

excessive in a man who devoted years to the professional study of philosophy. His Harvard thesis on F. H. Bradley (published as *Knowledge and
Experience in the Philosophy of F. H. Bradley,* 1963) and two articles on Leib-
niz (in *The Monist,* 1916, reprinted with the thesis) must be considered
very competent contributions to technical philosophy. But it is not merely
humility which makes him disparage a concern and ability to erect a
general theory. It is a genuine conviction that ultimate questions are
beyond the reach of intellect and that attempts to define poetry must
fail. "Criticism, of course, never finds out what poetry is, in the sense of
arriving at an adequate definition" (*UP,* 16). "There are," he believes,
"surprisingly few things that can be said about poetry; and of these few,
the most turn out either to be false or to say nothing of significance"
(*Criterion* 13 [1933–34]: 153).

While this suspicion of abstract philosophical aesthetics seems genuine
enough, it should not conceal the fact that Eliot has been constantly
working at a general theory and, from the very beginning of his career
as a critic, has had a theory in the back of his mind. There are, one must
admit, certain tensions and some contradictions in his major positions.
That his point of view or at least emphasis shifted on several problems
after his "conversion" is undeniable. But there is a continuity between
his earliest articles on criticism and the views he expounded in his Extension lectures given in 1916–19 which is far greater than is usually
admitted (cf. Schuchard, "Eliot and Hulme in 1916"). On some figures
and issues Eliot changed his opinions between 1922 and 1925, but essentially his theories can be treated as having a clear, coherent pattern,
though some internal contradictions persist. It is true that he has the
habit of approaching his problems from different angles, of suddenly
dropping an argument, of dealing with issues piecemeal, of concealing
or not realizing interconnections, of making obiter dicta without apparent proof or support, of producing quotations without drawing any consequence from them. In spite of his late denials that his criticism is a
"design for a massive critical structure" (*CC,* 14, 19), it does imply, read
as a whole and with due regard to context in each instance, something
like a system defining or describing the central issues of poetic theory.
Eliot might be rightly annoyed and even puzzled by the success of the
two phrases, "dissociation of sensibility" and "objective correlative" (*CC,*
19; *OPP,* 106), and he can with good conscience plead as early as in his
dissertation that "the true critic is a scrupulous avoider of formulae: he
refrains from statements which pretend to be literally true. He finds fact
nowhere and approximation always. His truths are the truths of experience rather than of calculation" (*KE,* 164). He can rightly voice irri-

tation at "having my words, perhaps written thirty or forty years ago, quoted as if I had uttered them yesterday" (*CC*, 14) or even criticize his own earlier writings for "the occasional note of arrogance, of vehemence, of cocksureness or rudeness, the bragadoccio of the mild-mannered man safely entrenched behind his typewriter" (14) or exclude three essays from a reprint of *Essays on Elizabethan Drama* (1964) as "embarrassing by their callousness, and by a facility of unqualified assertion which verges, here and there, on impudence" (vii). But nothing can prevent the student surveying the whole of Eliot's work from seeing the inner cohesion, the pattern in the carpet of his thinking. He will make allowances for Eliot's habit of writing for special occasions, for periodicals, for the exigencies of lectures and introductions, for the context of polemics at specific times, but also for a defective theory of criticism.

Eliot thinks of his criticism largely as that of a poet "always trying to defend the kind of poetry he is writing" (*OPP*, 26). His criticism, he avers, is "workshop criticism" (107), "a by-product of my private poetic work-shop" (106). His own theorizing has been "epiphenomenal of [his] taste" (*CC*, 20). But this, as I shall argue, cannot be true, for Eliot's taste is often in little relation to his theory. One can even speak, at times, of a conflict between the ideology and the actual literary preferences, though he sees himself that "for literary judgment we need to be acutely aware of two things at once: of 'what we like' and 'what we ought to like' " (*EAM*, 109). But mostly Eliot generalizes from the conviction that his criticism is a defense of his poetry (which it is in part with all poet-critics) and on occasion seems almost to forget that there have been other critics than poets. He reflects, for instance, on the relationship between schol-arship and criticism by contrasting the scholar "concerned with the understanding of the masterpiece in the environment of its author" with the practitioner who "seeks of what *use* is the poetry of this poet to poets writing today? Is it, or can it become, a living force in English poetry still unwritten? So we may say that the scholar's interest is in the per-manent, the practitioner's in the immediate" (*OPP*, 147). But making criticism serve only temporary ends while scholarship serves the per-manent seems a specious conclusion based on a false dichotomy. It per-vades Eliot's reflections on criticism.

Eliot distinguishes three types of criticism (*BTCP*): so-called creative criticism, really "etiolated creation" of which Pater serves as a frightening example; historical and moralistic criticism, represented by Sainte-Beuve; and criticism proper, poetic criticism. The first Eliot dismisses contemptuously with the words, "It does not count." Eliot considered Arthur Symons and Walter Pater "incomplete artists" who sought illegitimate satisfaction of creative urges in criticism. Oddly enough, in 1956 Eliot professed not to remember "a single book, or the name of a single critic, as representative of the kind of impressionistic criticism which aroused my ire 36 years ago" (*OPP*, 108)—which would put the "ire" into the year 1923, while the comments on Symons and Pater date from 1920.

The second type, historical criticism, is, according to Eliot, really not literary criticism at all, although it is frequently praised by him. At times, he seems to recommend every kind of factualism. "Scholarship, even in its humblest form, has its rights ... *fact* cannot corrupt taste" (*SE*, 33). But Eliot's compliments to scholars such as Herbert Grierson and W. P. Ker should not disguise the fact that he separates scholarship from criticism. Such critics (even Sainte-Beuve) should be called historians, philosophers, or moralists.

Thus the only genuine criticism is that of the poet-critic who is "criticising poetry in order to create poetry" (*SW*, 14). Eliot, however, somewhat modifies this statement. He admits that "at one time I was inclined to take the extreme position that the *only* criticism worth reading were the critics who practised, and practised well, the art of which they wrote" (*SE*, 31), but later he merely asked the critic to have some experience in composing poetry. It is merely "to be expected that the critic and the creative artist should frequently be the same person" (*SW*, 14). He shifts then the argument by saying that only poet-critics are of use to other poets, hardly noting that criticism is not written only for poets and their practical use. Even the statement that "the important critic is the person who is absorbed in the present problems of art, and who wishes to bring the forces of the past to bear on these problems" (*SW*, 33) seems unduly restrictive. But it is a description which fits the series of English poet-critics, Dryden, Johnson, Coleridge, and Matthew Arnold, of which Eliot says, with some mock modesty, that "it is into this company that I must shyly intrude" (*CC*, 13). Eliot allows only one exception: Aristotle (*SW*, 9–10, 14), whose success as a theorist and critic seems quite inexplicable in Eliot's scheme.

Criticism, in Eliot's theory, is left with little to do. He rejects both interpretation and judicial criticism, though it is hard to see how criticism could function without either interpreting or judging. Interpretation seems to him only a pretense at conveying some insight into another author, but "instead of insight," he protests, "you get a fiction." Interpretation is legitimate only "when it is not interpretation at all, but merely putting the reader in possession of facts which he would otherwise have missed" (*SE*, 32), or even more extravagantly we are told that "*qua* work of art, the work of art cannot be interpreted; there is nothing to interpret. . . . For 'interpretation' the chief task is the presentation of historical facts which the reader is not assumed to know" (142). Usually the dismissal of interpretation in favor of the information of a commentary is not that wholesale. Eliot rather voices a profound skepticism as to the possibility of any single interpretation or its permanence in history. As early as the dissertation he tells us that "every interpretation, along perhaps with some utterly contradictory interpretation, has to be taken up and reinterpreted by every thinking mind and by every civilization" (KE, 164) and as late as 1956 Eliot doubts whether "just one interpretation of the poem as a whole, must be right" (OPP, 113). In practice, however, Eliot did much to recommend interpreters, though even in the laudatory introduction to G. Wilson Knight's Wheel of Fire (1930) he speaks of interpretation as a necessary evil, a makeshift, a compensation for our imperfections. "If we lived [the work of Shakespeare] completely we should need no interpretation" (WF, xix) is Eliot's unhelpful conclusion. It sounds like saying, "If we were God, we would need no theology."

While in "all interpretation there may be an essential part of error" (WF, xix), judgment is expressly forbidden. "The critic must not coerce, and he must not make judgments of worse and better" (SW, 10). Judgment arises somehow from "elucidation" which seems obscurely different from "interpretation." The critic "must simply elucidate; the reader will form the correct judgment for himself" (SW, 10). But Eliot could not have meant the rejection of both interpretation and judicial criticism literally; he seems rather to protest against subjective and arbitrary interpretations and against the dogmatic ranking of authors. He can show his annoyance at Joseph Margolis's reading of Prufrock in John Wain's collection Interpretations (1955), ridiculing it as belonging to the "lemon-squeezer school of criticism" (OPP, 113) and complaining that "taking the machine to pieces" impairs his enjoyment of the poems analyzed (114). It is an old complaint which may be justified in particular cases but was countered by Eliot himself when he spoke early of the aim of criticism as "the return to the work of art with improved perception and intensified, because more conscious enjoyment" (SW, 11–12).

But the interdiction of judgment and ranking is completely belied by Eliot's practice. Ranking, judging, was the secret of his success and appeal as a critic. One wanted to hear that Crashaw was "a finished master" and Keats and Shelley "apprentices with immense possibilities before them" (FLA, 120), that Campion was a greater poet than Herrick, Dryden than Pope, or that, after Shakespeare, Marlowe, Jonson, and Chapman belong to the first class of Elizabethan and Jacobean dramatists while Middleton, Webster, and Tourneur rank second, and Beaumont and Fletcher with Shirley third. The essay on Ford argues then that he had to be placed with the third group, though slightly higher than Beaumont and Fletcher (*SE*, 204). And as to approbation one cannot be more emphatic than calling Middleton or a play of his "great" eight times on the same page (*SE*, 169).

Occasionally Eliot seems to recognize or at least to tolerate the theorist when he admits that "critical speculation, like philosophical speculation and scientific research, must be free to follow its own course" (*UP*, 143), but in general Eliot subordinates criticism to creation. "Criticism, by definition, is *about* something other than itself" (*SE*, 30). There is no autotelic criticism, no creative criticism, though once (in a 1926 review of Herbert Read and Ramon Fernandez), when he felt that the very existence of literature was in doubt, he said that "the distinction between the 'critic' and the 'creator' is not a very useful one. . . . In our time the most vigorous critical minds are philosophical minds, are, in short, creative of value" (*Criterion* 4:751). Eliot adopted the term "creator of values" which Remy de Gourmont had used for Sainte-Beuve, but he was speaking of the general critic, the philosopher, the apologist for the arts, and had not changed his mind about "poetic" or "creative" criticism.

Eliot's emphasis on the use of criticism for the poet, his skepticism about the value of aesthetics and interpretation implies a concept of the meaning of the work of art as something left to the reader, something indeterminate and even loose. "A poem may appear to mean different things to different readers, and all of these meanings may be different from what the author thought he meant" (*OPP*, 30). "The reader's interpretation may differ from the author's and be equally valid—it may even be better" (31). Nevill Coghill tells us about Eliot's reaction to a production of *Sweeney Agonistes*. He was "astonished" by it, as it ran completely counter to his own interpretation. Still, he "accepted" the production. To the question, "But if the two meanings are contradictory, is not one right and the other wrong? Must not the author's be right?" Eliot answered, "Not necessarily, do you think? Why is either wrong?"[1] This view corroborates Eliot's impersonal theory, the detachment of a work from the author's psyche, a rejection of the "intentional fallacy," and a knowledge of the process of history which has changed and enriched the meaning of works of art. Eliot is right in not wanting to lose this accrual of meaning: he has spoken well about "the several levels of significance" (*UP*, 153) at which Shakespeare can and has been taken by the various strata of his audience. Yet he does not seem to see that the divorce between work and audience cannot be complete, that there remains the problem of the "correctness" of interpretation which cannot be denied or shirked as it has been in much recent criticism. The apparent anarchy allowed in Eliot's theory of criticism runs strongly counter to his attempt to buttress his conception of tradition by objective standards, to his fundamental conviction that "we must assume, if we are to talk about poetry at all, that there is some absolute poetic hierarchy: we keep at the back of our minds the reminder of some end of the world, some final Judgment Day, on which the poets will be assembled in their ranks and orders. In the long run, there is an ultimate greater and less" (*GJD*, 5). But in Eliot's scattered reflections on the theory of criticism, little accounts for what he was engaged in himself so successfully, for his function in changing the taste of the time, in defining and evaluating the classic, in the "common pursuit of true judgment" (*SE*, 25), and in the description of the creative process itself as an impersonal event.

Eliot's conception seems to be this: the work of art is located "somewhere between the writer and the reader; it has a reality which is not simply the reality of what the writer is trying to 'express,' or of his experience of writing it, or of the experience of the reader or the writer as reader" (*UP*, 30). The poem "in some sense, has its own life. . . . The feeling, or emotion, or vision resulting from the poem is something different from the feeling or emotion or vision in the mind of the poet" (1928 preface to *SW*, x). "The difference between art and the event is always absolute" (*SE*, 19). A gulf between the individual experience and the poem is opened and it follows that the psychological process behind the poem cannot be a standard for the judging of poetry. "You cannot find a sure test for poetry, a test by which you may distinguish between poetry and mere good verse, by reference to its putative antecedents in the mind of the poet" (*UP*, 140). The way in which poetry is written, Eliot recognizes, is not any clue to its value (146). Tracing the poem to its origin is discouraged since that "has no relation to the poem and throws no light upon it" (*OPP*, 99). Creation is "when something new has happened, something that cannot wholly be explained by *anything that went before*" (112). Hence biographical criticism is considered irrelevant and Lowes's *The Road to Xanadu* (oddly enough treated as a novelty in 1956) is dismissed as "explanation by origins" in Coleridge's scraps of reading which leaves the poetry "as much of a mystery as ever" (*OPP*, 108). Poetry thus is not the "spontaneous overflow of powerful feelings." It might be the representation of something quite remote from the poet's personal experiences. "Emotions which he has never experienced will serve his turn as well as those familiar to him" (*SE*, 21; cf. *EAM*, 181).

Thus Eliot arrives at his "impersonal theory of poetry." "Poetry is not," he says in an often quoted passage, "a turning loose of emotion, but an escape from emotion; it is not the expression of personality, but an escape from personality" (*SE*, 21). "The more perfect the artist, the more completely separate in him will be the man who suffers and the mind which creates; the more perfectly will the mind digest and transmute the passions which are its material" (18). These sayings are preceded in "Tradition and the Individual Talent" by the comparison of the poet's mind to a "shred of platinum" which serves to form sulphurous acid from two gases but is itself unaffected, remains "inert, neutral and unchanged" (18). But surely this notorious metaphor must not be pressed too hard, and Eliot himself later thought it "a doubtful analogy" (*ASG*, 115). Eliot could not have thought of the poet as a "mere catalyst," a totally passive medium, though, in a passage rejecting the reduction of poetry to a mouthpiece of its time, to a mere social document, he reiterates that "in the greatest poetry there is always a hint of something behind, something in relation to which the author has been no more than the passive (if not always pure) medium" (*Criterion* 12:77). In the very same paragraph of "Tradition and the Individual Talent" the metaphor shifts, after all, to digesting and transmuting experience. The impersonality of the poet must, it seems, be taken to mean that poetry is not a direct transcript of experience, but it cannot mean that it is devoid of personal, almost physiognomic characteristics: otherwise we could not distinguish between the works of different authors and could not speak of a "Shakespearian" or a "Keatsian" quality. Eliot modifies his view himself when he recognizes that the "poet expresses his personality indirectly through concentrating upon his task which is a task in the same sense as the making of an efficient engine or the turning of a jug or a table-leg" (*SE*, 114), a small concession, for it would strain our ingenuity to discover the personality of the maker in an engine or a table-leg or even a jug.

But in practice, Eliot's criticism uses often a standard of personality which is not, of course, the anecdotal, empirical personality but the personality pattern emerging from the work itself. He values a body of work which shows a pattern, a "figure in the carpet," in Henry James's phrase, more highly than one that is purely discontinuous, a mere series of unrelated works. "There is," he says, "a relation between the various plays of Shakespeare, taken in order; and it is the work of years to venture even one individual interpretation of the pattern in Shakespeare's carpet" (*SE*, 231). That this pattern is one of personal evolution follows from another passage. "The standard set by Shakespeare is that of a continuous development from first to last, a development in which the choice both of theme and of dramatic and verse technique in each play seems to be determined increasingly by Shakespeare's state of feeling, by

the particular stage of his emotional maturity at the time" (193). The
Elizabethan dramatists are ranked in terms of personality, with Shakespeare at the top, and Marlowe, Jonson, Chapman, Middleton, Webster,
Ford, and Fletcher following in that precise order. Exactly the same standard is applied to the lyrical poetry of the time. Eliot contrasts Herrick
and Campion, admitting that from Herrick "we get the feeling of a
unifying personality" which we do not get from Campion's work. Yet
Eliot thinks that Campion is a greater poet because he is a "much more
accomplished craftsman" than Herrick (OPP, 46). Personality, it seems,
is only one criterion and not necessarily the decisive one.

    At times, Eliot seems completely to contradict the emphasis on imper-
sonality. There are passages in Eliot which ascribe to art a "cathartic"
effect on the author's personal suffering. We are told even that "we all
have to choose whatever subject matter allows [the poet] the most powerful and most secret release" (SPMM, xi), a sentence which seems to
ascribe to art a purgation of secret shame. Elsewhere he speaks of the
poet as "oppressed by a burden which he must bring to birth in order
to obtain relief" and describes "the moment of exhaustion, of appeasement, of absolution, and of something near annihilation which is in itself
indescribable" (OPP, 98) in almost sexual terms, a passage which repeats
a very early allusion to the poet's "painful and unpleasant business; it is
a sacrifice of the man to the work; it is a kind of death" (Athenaeum,
June 25, 1920, 842). At other times Eliot speaks of "personal and private
agonies" which the poet must struggle to transmute "into something rich
and strange, something universal and impersonal" (SE, 137). He seems
to have forgotten the passage quoted above which admits that these emotions might be experienced only in imagination. At other times Eliot
ignores the personal agonies and states bluntly that the "poet is tormented primarily by the need to write a poem" (UP, 138). While some
of these pronouncements are clearly irreconcilable, Eliot in general insists that there is a kind of impersonality, that the poet "out of intense
personal experience, is able to express a general truth; retaining all the
particularity of his experience, to make of it a general symbol" (OPP,
255). Poetry is always a transformation of emotion, a universalizing of
emotion, however personal it may have been originally.

    Eliot made several attempts to describe this difference between the
emotion in life and emotion transformed into art. He differentiates,
sometimes, between emotions and feelings (SE, 18) but uses the terms
often alternately, though in general "emotion" means something purely
personal, irrational, vague, and indistinct, whereas "feeling" is pervasive,
concrete, precise, almost the same as sensation or perception. This is the

drift of the passage that says that "great poetry may be made without the direct use of any emotion whatever: composed of feeling solely" (18). His praise of Canto XXVI (the Ulysses story) of the *Inferno* for having "no direct dependence on an emotion" (19) seems to imply this restricted use of the term. But elsewhere Eliot finds "a structural emotion" in a passage from Tourneur's *Revenger's Tragedy*. It reflects the "dominant tone" of the play, and this tone is "due to the fact that a number of floating feelings, having an affinity to this emotion by no means superficially evident, have combined with it to give us a new art emotion" (20). "Art emotion" and elsewhere "*significant* emotion" (22) are other versions of the same view that within poetry emotion is a very complex thing, whereas personal emotion may be "simple, crude and flat." The complexity of art emotion must not therefore be confused with the complexity of life emotion: the artist need not have new emotions but rather may express old emotions in a complex and concentrated form. Eliot praises Pound's verse for being "always definite and concrete because he has always a definite emotion behind it" (*CC*, 170), and the *Divine Comedy* is called "an emotional structure . . . an ordered scale of human emotions" (*SW*, 152). Massinger is criticized because he "dealt not with emotions so much as with the social abstractions of emotions" (*SE*, 215), and even Falstaff is in comparison with Jonson's characters described as "perhaps the *satisfaction* of more, and more complicated feelings: and perhaps he was, as the great tragic characters must have been, the offspring of deeper, less apprehensible feelings" (*SE*, 158).

These often contradictory or at least vacillating passages, phrased sometimes obscurely, seem to suggest that Eliot's concept of poetry is purely emotional both in its origin in the mind of the poet and in its effect on the reader. Here the dissertation on F. H. Bradley becomes crucial to an understanding of Eliot's views. Eliot then accepted the basic tenets of Bradley's philosophy though he criticized them on some points and modified them in a direction which can be best described as "realism" (in the philosophical sense) or even "behaviorism." In the dissertation Eliot rejects psychology and epistemology completely and dissolves the *cogito*, awareness, self-consciousness. As he phrased it in "Tradition and the Individual Talent," "I am struggling to attack the metaphysical theory of the substantial unity of the soul" (*SE*, 19). In the dissertation he replaces the Cartesian cogito or the Kantian subject with Bradley's "immediate experience," which precedes any division of subject and object and hence anything which is a personal state of mind, any personal emotion. But in his criticism Eliot avoids the term "immediate experience" and replaces it (as Bradley sometimes does) with "feeling" or "sensibility." The poet becomes the man who returns to this original immediate experience, to a unified sensibility by objectifying his feeling. Feeling and object cannot be distinguished, at least originally. In Bradley and in Eliot's dissertation this original state of immediate experience which only later divides into subject and object is a process applicable to all human beings. In Eliot's later critical theory it becomes a description of the poetic process and most often of the ideal poetic process. The poet ought to have a unified sensibility, he ought to pass from feeling to object as if there were no distinction between them. The great poets achieved this and Eliot can construe a history of English poetry on the assumption that this unified sensibility split up at the point he considers the beginning of the decadence of English poetry, and that he can devise a program for the restitution of this original unity. Eliot arrived at this view long before he found the famous formulas "dissociation of sensibility" and "objective correlative." The dissertation gives the clue without application to literature, though one passage discusses feeling when viewing a beautiful painting: "If we are sufficiently carried away, our feeling is a whole which is not, in a sense, *our* feeling" (*KE*, 20). Eliot holds the (to me incomprehensible) view that "so far as feelings are objects at all, they exist on the same footing as other objects. They are equally public, they are equally independent of consciousness, they are known and are themselves not knowing. And so far as feelings are merely felt, they are neither subjective nor objective" (24). More to our purpose Eliot asserts that "a distinction between feeling and object cannot be made by science" (27), for "immediate experience" is "nonrelational" and much wider than consciousness (28). Object and feeling are identified, and feeling is resolutely divorced from personal feeling. In the 1928 preface to *The Sacred Wood* "feeling or emotion or vision resulting from the poem" are comfortably lined up as interchangeable. "It is something different from the feeling or emotion or vision in the mind of the poet" (x). Eliot varies this theme without using the term "dissociation of sensibility" or "objective correlative." Thus in 1926 he contrasts Lancelot Andrewes's "emotion," which is "not personal, it is wholly evoked by the object of contemplation, to which it is adequate," with Donne, who is "constantly finding an object which shall be adequate to his feelings." Andrewes is a man "wholly absorbed in the object and therefore responds with the adequate emotion" while Donne is a "personality" whose sermons are a "means of self-expression" (*SE*, 327). Eliot had changed his mind about Donne. In 1917 he had contrasted him with Dostoevsky and Wordsworth as examples of writers who "attach the strongest emotions to definite tokens." In Dostoevsky "the emotion dissolves in a mass of sensational detail"; in Wordsworth "the emotion is the object and not human life"; "with certain poets (e.g., Donne) the emotion is definitely human, merely seizing the object in order to express itself" (*Egoist* 4:118). The theory behind this puzzling passage presupposes that the "emotion," somehow divorced from the personality of the poet, is human, presumably "universally human," and that it seizes the object in order to express itself—*itself* and not the poet. The process seems obscure, but so is all creation, not only in Eliot's poetry.

This unified sensibility, which in the passages hitherto adduced is identified with immediate experience or feeling, is in other developments described as the whole of man's mind, as containing both thought and feeling. Ideas enter into literature; they are to Eliot one of the main sources of poetry. They cannot, of course, remain mere philosophical doctrines, mere abstract statements. "Poetry can be penetrated by a philosophical idea, it can deal with this idea when it has reached the point of immediate acceptance, when it has become almost a physical modification" (*SW*, 147). "Physical modification" seems an alternative phrase for "sensation," and actually Eliot, either because of a failure to distinguish the two meanings or deliberately, exploits the ambiguity of the term "sensibility" and conceives this fusion of thought and feeling as equivalent to a fusion of thought and sensation. The metaphysical poets represent this fusion to perfection. In Chapman he finds "a direct sensuous apprehension of thought, or a recreation of thought into feeling, which is exactly what we find in Donne" (*SE*, 272). "A thought to Donne was an experience; it modified his sensibility." In contrast, "Tennyson and Browning are poets, and they think; but they do not feel their thought as immediately as the odour of a rose" (*SE*, 273). The phrasing has shifted: the "odour of a rose" now exploits the ambiguity of the English word "feel." The poet must both feel and sense his thought. But elsewhere the emphasis is not on the union of feeling and thought but on perception, and particularly on vision. The praise of Dante is, in part at least, a praise of his success in assimilating ideas to his vision. "Dante, more than any other poet, has succeeded in dealing with his philosophy, not as a theory (in the modern and not the Greek sense of that word) or as his comment or reflection, but in terms of something *perceived*" (*SW*, 155). The fusion of intellect and emotion or the transformation into pure vision are primarily terms to describe the process of assimilating ideas, beliefs, and philosophies into poetry in a unified sensibility which satisfies Eliot's and man's yearning for wholeness and integrity.

The ideal fusion of intellect and emotion becomes the nucleus of Eliot's view of the history of English poetry and a scheme for which he found

the phrase "a dissociation of sensibility" (*SE*, 274), suggested by de Gourmont's analysis of Laforgue's mind (*Promenades littéraires*, 1:105–06). To
put it in simple terms: poets up to the seventeenth century thought and
felt and saw together but in the seventeenth century a fatal split occurred.
After the triumph of scientific rationalism, poets only thought (as they
did in the eighteenth century), and, with the romantic reaction, they
only felt. In the later nineteenth century there seems to be, in Eliot's
scheme, a return to thinking, or rather a confusion (and not fusion) of
thought and feeling which Eliot disparagingly calls "rumination." What
is needed today is reintegration (*UP*, 84–85). Eliot suggested at first that
this split was "aggravated by the influence of the two most powerful poets
of the century, Milton and Dryden" (*SE*, 274), but later he recognized
that the process was much more complex and profound and could not
be accounted for in purely literary terms. "We must seek the causes in
Europe and not in England alone" (*OPP*, 153) is his cautious conclusion
which seems nearer the truth than the attempts of others such as Cleanth
Brooks to foist the dissociation on Hobbes or of L. C. Knights to find it
first in Bacon. One may doubt, as Frank Kermode has argued (in *The
Romantic Image*), whether the seventeenth century was the turning point
or even whether such a process ever took place.

In the unpublished Clark lectures (1926), to judge by a recent report,[2]
Eliot pushed the supposed dissolution back to the age of Dante and
Cavalcanti. The idea itself is an old one. In the debate about Eliot's
scheme anticipations as far back as Sir Joshua Reynolds's lectures were
cited and a long list of poets and critics in the nineteenth century can
be compiled saying something similar.[3] The idea was not confined to the
English tradition. Lichtenberg, the eighteenth-century aphorist, appealed to a saying of Addison's: "The whole man must move at once,"
and as late as the early 1900s Hugo von Hofmannsthal quoted Addison
as formulating his classical ideal.[4]

But while Eliot speaks of unified sensibility, of union of thought and
feeling, he still insists that poetry is not knowledge or even a kind of
knowledge. The poet is no philosopher and no thinker. There is a notorious passage saying that "in truth neither Shakespeare nor Dante did
any real thinking" (*SE*, 136). Eliot must mean that the poet does not
philosophize in any systematic manner, but he goes further, denying the
very possibility of the philosopher-poet. "For a poet to be also a philosopher he would have to be virtually two men; I cannot think of any
example of this thorough schizophrenia, nor can I see anything to be
gained by it: the work is better performed inside two skulls than one"
(*UP*, 99). True, the poet in Eliot's scheme uses ideas but he will be the

better poet if he uses ideas that are not his own. Eliot elaborates a scheme of the relation between poetry and philosophy which distinguishes three types of relationships. There is, first, the poet who takes over a finished system of philosophy, such as Dante and Lucretius.The second type is the poet who "accepts current ideas and makes use of them" (Z, 103) in an unsystematic, eclectic fashion. The prime examples are Shakespeare and Donne. Shakespeare has a "rag-bag philosophy" (WF, xviii). Donne "merely picked up like a magpie, various shining fragments of ideas as they struck his eye, and stuck them about here and there in his verse" (SE, 138–39). The third type, the union of philosopher and poet, seems most undesirable to Eliot. His examples are Goethe and in other contexts Blake and Yeats. It is a curious scheme, the opposite of what one could argue if one assumed the creativity of the human mind. One could say that poetry and philosophy were never further apart than when Dante took over a system without changing. The true collaboration between philosophy and poetry occurred when there were poet-thinkers such as Empedocles in ancient Greece or Ficino and Bruno in the Renaissance, or Goethe, Schiller, and Hölderlin in Germany. But not for Eliot: in his view, truth is something given, static, impersonal. Eliot does not admit that the poet might "feel" his own ideas. An external standard of truth is applied from outside the work of art. "The truest philosophy is the best material for the greatest poet; so that the poet must be rated in the end both by the philosophy he realizes in poetry and by the fullness and adequacy of the realization" (Z, 106).

Art with the later Eliot is considered a preparation for religion. "It is ultimately the function of art, in imposing a credible order upon ordinary reality, and thereby eliciting some perception of an order in reality, to bring us to a condition of serenity, stillness, and reconciliation; and then leave us, as Virgil left Dante, to proceed toward a religion where that guide can avail us no further" (OPP, 87).

Earlier Eliot defended a view emphasizing the autonomy of art, the "integrity of poetry," constantly arguing against the confusion of art and religion, art and morality, against Matthew Arnold and the American humanists, but later he advocated a double standard of criticism: artistic on the one hand and moral-philosophical-theological on the other. "In an age like our own . . . it is the more necessary . . . to scrutinize works of imagination, with explicit ethical and theological standards. The 'greatness' of literature cannot be determined solely by literary standards; though we must remember that whether it is literature or not can be determined only by literary standards" (EAM, 93). This widely quoted passage assigns to literary criticism a mere preliminary sifting between art and non-art and leaves to moral and theological considerations the decision about "greatness," as if morality and theology were ingredients merely added to minimal aesthetic value. The earlier admission of an act of "validating" or "aesthetic sanction for thought" (*Z*, 106–07) seems to leave at least something for literary criticism, while the passage on greatness grants almost everything to the rating of philosophies according to their truth, which with Eliot means their conformity to Catholic tradition, to what he called orthodoxy. To accept Eliot's dichotomy of "greatness" and "artness" means giving up an organic point of view, establishing a new divorce of form and content.

Eliot arrived at this position also because he approached the question of the relation between literature and ideas not through the works themselves, the way ideas enter into literature, but because he became entangled in the problem of "belief." Very early (1916) Eliot admitted that "aesthetic rapture is not dependent upon any particular theory about the world" (*International Journal of Ethics* 26:285), and he decided sensibly that "you are not called upon to believe in Dante's philosophical and theological views," for there is "a difference between philosophical *belief* and poetic *assent*" (*SE*, 243). Obviously the range of literature accessible to us would be narrowed if we had to agree with the beliefs of every poet we read. We would have trouble with Homer, Aeschylus, and Virgil, and perhaps with Neruda, Mayakovsky, and Brecht.

But Eliot soon abandoned this position. A note to the second Dante essay grants "that I cannot, in practice, wholly separate my poetic appreciation from my personal beliefs" and suggests that "one probably has more pleasure in the poetry when one shares the beliefs of the poet" (*SE,* 257). This is still a modest and sound generalization from the empirical fact that we are not always able to reach the state of disinterested contemplation that poetry demands. Later, however, Eliot broached the question again in connection with Shelley, by whose ideas he feels "affronted," whose beliefs excite his "abhorrence." He formulated a new, widely quoted, conclusion. "When the doctrine, theory, belief, or 'view of life' presented in the poem is one which the mind of the reader can accept as coherent, mature, and founded on the facts of experience, it interposes no obstacle to the reader's enjoyment, whether it be one that he can accept or deny, approve or deprecate" (*UP,* 96). The terms are carefully chosen to allow the paradox of "enjoying" something which you "deprecate" and "deny" (as Eliot denies, say, Lucretius and Seneca) but not something which you "abhor" and consider incoherent, immature, and not founded on the facts of experience (for example, Shelley). One can reply that coherence is an aesthetic as well as a logical criterion, that the maturity of a work of art is its inclusiveness, its awareness of complexity, and that the correspondence to reality is registered in the work itself. An incoherent, immature, "unreal" poem is a bad poem aesthetically. In the late essay on Goethe (1955) Eliot propounded a slightly different solution. He still adheres to the double point of view. He defends Hans Egon Holthusen, a German critic of strong religious commitment, for enjoying the poetry of Rilke while rejecting his philosophy but argues, on the other hand, that the philosophy implied in a poem must be "tenable," must not "strike us as wholly vile" and appear "sheer nonsense" (*OPP*, 225). Eliot now relies on the term "wisdom," which he requires of all great poetry. It is the right union of form and content, feeling and intellect, philosophy and poetry, a new magic formula which seems as liable to ideological abuse as "orthodoxy" or as bafflingly vague as "greatness." It is precisely because one agrees with Eliot that one cannot leave behind one's personality that the whole problem of belief in the sense of acceptance of an author's ideas should be dismissed as a purely empirical problem of the reader's state of mind varying from man to man and age to age. It is not susceptible of a theoretical solution.

In Eliot this problem is frequently related to and even sometimes confused with the very different question of the poet's belief in his own ideas, with the whole question of "sincerity." Eliot propounds the hypothetical case that Dante composed for relaxation Lucretius' *De Rerum Natura* as a Latin exercise after completing the *Divine Comedy* (*SE*, 255). Our capacity of enjoying either poem would be, Eliot argues, mutilated. But even if we accept this odd mental experiment, a standard of sincerity seems quite beyond investigation, proof, or use. The worst poetry of the world is adolescent love poetry, agonizingly felt by its perpetrators; bad religious poetry by sincere believers fills libraries.

Eliot himself saw that we can never find out what Dante privately believed and felt (*Dial* 82 [1927]: 242). He draws a distinction between Dante's belief as a man and his beliefs as a poet (*SE*, 255) and later between beliefs as *held* and beliefs as *felt* (*UP*, 136), with the obvious demand that the poet should feel rather than merely hold his beliefs. On occasion he speaks of "something more profound and more complex than what is ordinarily called 'sincerity' " (*SE*, 194) and adopts the term "genuineness" (*OPP*, 51), which avoids the fallacy of the psychological term "sincerity." At times he seems to admit the irrelevancy of the whole question when he argues that one cannot distinguish between the sincerity of the beliefs of Dante, Crashaw, and Christina Rossetti, while the "important distinctions between them arise within this framework of acceptance of certain common dogmas" (*Enemy* 1 [1927]: 16). Sincerity seems to me a psychological problem which is critically irrelevant. Strength of belief has no relation to successful art.

Eliot is a much more satisfactory critic when he forgets about sincerity, the mare's nest of "belief," and the mysterious creative process, and turns his attention resolutely to the work of art as a describable object, a symbolic world which is amenable to analysis and judgment. He found the term "objective correlative" for this symbolic world which he thought of as continuous with the feelings of the poet, objectifying and patterning them. The objective correlative is anticipated and varied in many forms without the term: when Eliot says that "literature is a presentation of feeling by a statement of events in human actions or objects in the external world" (*SW*, 58) or that "the strongest writers make their feeling into an articulate external world" (*Dial* 71 [1921]: 216). But the term "objective correlative" is prominently used only in the *Hamlet* essay of 1919. It occurs, with a very different meaning, in Washington Allston's *Lectures on Art* (1850) but was more likely suggested by Santayana's use of "correlative objects"[5] and in general fits with Bradley's account of "feeling," which, "while it remains a constant basis, nevertheless contains a world which in a sense goes beyond itself."[6] "The only way of expressing emotion in the form of art," states Eliot in the *Hamlet* essay, "is by finding an 'objective correlative'; in other words, a set of objects, a situation, a chain of events which shall be the formula of that *particular* emotion; such that when the external acts, which must terminate in sensory experience, are given the emotion is immediately evoked" (*SE*, 145). The term here seems to mean simply the right kind of situation, the right plot, or a set of symbolic objects in a play or a novel which motivates the emotion of the characters in the play or novel. Eliot gives the example of Lady Macbeth sleepwalking as a successful "objective correlative," showing a "complete adequacy of the external to the emotion" (145). But the discussion of *Hamlet* runs into obscurities. "Hamlet (the man)," he tells us, "is dominated by an emotion which is inexpressible, because it is in *excess* of the facts as they appear" (145); but it is not clear to whom: to us or to Hamlet. Apparently Eliot means that Hamlet's disgust with life (which is very well expressed) is not fully motivated by the marriage of his mother and the suspected murder of his father. But why should it be inexpressible and how, if it were, could anybody know about it? And why should not the hasty incestuous marriage of his mother and the murder of his father be sufficient motivation for his despair and disgust? Why should there not be a tragic hero who reacts excessively to the situation in which he is placed? Is this not often the very presupposition of tragedy in general and, if we think of Lear, Othello, Romeo, or Coriolanus, of Shakespearean tragedy in particular? Perversely, Eliot, in this essay, applies his view of Hamlet to Shakespeare himself. "And the supposed identity of Hamlet with his author is genuine to this point: that Hamlet's bafflement at the absence of objective equivalent to his feelings is a prolongation of the bafflement of his creator in the face of his artistic problem." Eliot introduces, at this point, his theory of catharsis, the poet's self-purgation through art. "Hamlet is up against the difficulty that his disgust is occasioned by his mother, but that his mother is not an adequate equivalent for it; his disgust envelops and exceeds her" (145). (One could add that it includes all sex, all life, and himself.) "It is thus a feeling which he cannot understand; he cannot objectify it, and it therefore remains to poison life and obstruct action." "In the character Hamlet it is the buffoonery of an emotion which can find no outlet in action: in the dramatist it is the buffoonery of an emotion which he cannot express in art" (146). But the reflections on vague, adolescent, objectless feelings which follow do not make this much clearer. One must conclude with Eliseo Vivas: "The assumption that we can criticize the play *Hamlet* by comparing the emotion expressed in the play with Shakespeare's emotions, or that through the play we can discover the emotions that went into it, is a confusing illusion."[7] But even though Eliot's analysis of Hamlet seems mistaken and to speak of *Hamlet* as "a failure" seems odd, as Eliot himself later recognized,[8] we need not reject the term "objective correlative" as a convenient phrase for the right kind of devices, situations, plots, and objects which motivate the emotion of a character in a play or a novel, or even, as Eliot used it more broadly, simply as the "equivalent" of the author's emotion, the successful objectivation of emotion in a work of art.

How concretely is this objective construct analyzable? Eliot in approaching a work of poetry thinks of it, first of all, as language. In all kinds of contexts, from his earlier writings to his late, Eliot repeats, "Literature must be judged by language, it is the duty of the poet to develop language" (*Egoist* 5 [1918]: 55), "to preserve, and even restore, the beauty of a language" (*OPP*, 22). The language of poetry, Eliot asserts over and over again, must not "stray too far from the ordinary everyday language which we use and hear" (29). It should be "one's language as it is spoken at one's own time" (*New English Weekly* 15 [1939]: 28). Thus praise is bestowed on the poets who restored poetry to an approximation of spoken language. Dante's language is called the "perfection of a common language" (*SE*, 238), and Dryden "restored English verse to the condition of speech" (*JD*, 13). But these widely quoted pronouncements must not again be taken too literally as a prescription of colloquialism.

"We should," admitted Eliot in an essay on Dr. Johnson in 1944, "recognize that there should be, for every period, some standard of correct poetic diction, neither identical with, nor too remote from current speech" (*OPP*, 185). In discussing Hopkins, Eliot defends his language, which is only apparently remote from speech. "But Hopkins does give the impression that his poetry has the necessary fidelity to his way of thinking and talking to himself" (33), a very different standard from the implied comparison with the speech current in a specific society. On the other side are the poets who corrupted language or rather elaborated its musical possibilities. Eliot's main target is Milton, who subjected the language to "a peculiar kind of deterioration" (138). His language is artificial, conventional. "It is not so unfair, as it might at first appear, to say that Milton writes English like a dead language" (141). Eliot's so-called recantation of 1947 is largely an argument that when he and his friends started to write, they found it necessary to return language to colloquial speech and thus, as poets, to oppose the dangerous influence of Milton. Today the revolution has been accomplished. We are now in a period of the elaboration of the language and poets can afford to pay attention to the experiment of Milton. But the judgment of Milton remains unchanged.

Eliot applied the same standard of speech as words not merely heard but a presentation of objects, as things seen, to the history of English prose. Eliot ranks low Sir Thomas Browne and Jeremy Taylor, in whom he finds only "common sententiousness in reverberating language," a "language dissociated from things, assuming an independent existence" (*PV*, 6–7). He disapproved of the poetic prose of the nineteenth century, of the "orgy," "the open licence" of Carlyle, of Ruskin's and Pater's "exaggerated" styles (*Vanity Fair*, July 1920, 51, 98), and while he admired Joyce for different reasons, he thought of the later Joyce, author of *Finnegans Wake*, as an eccentric similar in this respect to another "blind musician," Milton, who "exploits the musical resources of the language to the utmost" (*OPP*, 157). I can only allude to Eliot's long struggle for the right kind of diction on the stage. In 1926 he suggested that "the recognized forms of speech-verse are not as efficient as they should be: probably a new form will be devised out of colloquial speech,"[9] and all his plays are an attempt to fulfill this prediction.

The whole relation between poetry and prose bothers Eliot greatly, for he wants to defend prosaic style in poetry (as in Dryden or Dr. Johnson) and yet reject poetic prose à la Pater. On the one hand he seems to advocate a blurring of distinctions, a mixture of genres, and on the other hand he wants to widen the gulf between prose and poetry. Eliot gets involved in terminological difficulties: he defends Dryden as a poet and not a mere "versifier," but later, in praising Kipling, he tries to establish a category, "verse," and speaks of Kipling's poetry as "great verse." "While speaking of Kipling's work as 'verse' and not as 'poetry,' I am still able to speak of individual compositions as poems, and also to maintain that there is 'poetry' in the 'verse' " (*OPP*, 251). Eliot is unable to make up his mind as to the differentiae between poetry and prose. He rejects the oldest solution: the identification of poetry and verse. "Good poetry is obviously something else besides good verse; and good verse may be very indifferent poetry." But he concedes that "versification brings something which is not present in prose, because it is from another point of view than that of art, a superfluity, a definite concession to the desire for 'play' " (*PV*, 4). He finds the distinction between poetry and prose very obscure. He suggests that "we have three terms where we need four. We have verse and poetry on the one hand and only prose on the other. The other difficulty follows from the first: that the words imply a valuation in one context which they do not in another. 'Poetry' introduces a distinction between good and bad verse; but we have no word to separate bad prose from good prose. As a matter of fact, much bad prose is poetic prose, and only a very small part of bad verse is bad because it is prosaic."[10] As other passages show, Eliot has two different criteria for poetry: praising St. John Perse and his prose poetry he sees the poetic as the "logic of imagination," as a series of images, and elsewhere he grants that "the work of poetry is performed by the use of images: by a cumulative succession of images each fusing with the next; and by a rapid and unexpected combination of images apparently unrelated" (*FLA*, 138). "Logic of imagination" seems to mean here merely some coherence and order in the sequence of images, which can hardly be identified with what in his dissertation he spoke of as the "connections in really great imaginative work felt to be bound by as logical necessity as any connections found anywhere" (*KE*, 75).

But in other contexts Eliot defends rather the poetry of statement, poetry which proceeds without imagery or with little imagery, that of Dryden, Goldsmith, and Crabbe. Here the criterion of poetry is precision, closeness to the object, a virtue which Eliot calls "living speech." Goldsmith and Johnson write "verse which is poetry partly because it has the virtues of good prose," endorsing a saying of Ezra Pound (which goes back to Victor Hugo and D'Alembert) that "verse must be at least as well written as prose." [11] Eliot is convinced that "it is bad when poetry and prose are too far apart" (*JD*, 43). But when Eliot ponders the problems of the long poem and the drama, another criterion, that of "intensity," is introduced. "There must be transitions between passages of greater and less intensity. . . . The passages of less intensity will be in relation to the level on which the total poem operates, prosaic" (*OPP*, 32). In the *Divine Comedy*, the *Odyssey*, and the *Aeneid*, Eliot finds "the movement toward and from intensity which is life itself" (*PV*, 5), and in reflecting on the right kind of language for poetic drama he defines poetry as "the language at those dramatic moments when it reaches intensity" (*OPP*, 92). Intensity is a vague word apparently meaning an emotional heightening, a tensing of tone. It is a doubtful criterion for poetry, for it would lead to the isolation of purple passages, to Poe's argument against the very possibility of a long poem, to the "poetic moments" of Saintsbury or to the whole dichotomy of poetry and literature as we find it in Croce. Usually Eliot appeals to our intuition as the final arbiter. "We should not be able to recognize poetry . . . unless we had an innate idea of poetry in general" (*UP*, 19) seems a sound enough insight into the common situation that we know something by experience without being able to define its proper criterion of application. But this is a gesture of resignation due to Eliot's refusal to discuss poetry either in terms of fictionality or in terms of its sound-structure.

This does not mean, however, that Eliot ignores the problem of sound and meter. He only refuses to recognize it as the essential distinction between poetry and prose. He often reflects sensitively and sensibly about metrical problems: the history of English blank verse, the amalgam of different metrical systems in English, or "on the contrast between fixity and flux," "the evasion of monotony which is the very life of verse" (*CC*, 187), though he professes never to have been able "to retain the names of feet and metres" and dismisses the study of metrics as like the study of anatomy, which "will not teach you to make a hen lay eggs" (*OPP*, 27). But beyond often detailed comments on individual metrical or sound effects Eliot uses the terms rhythm and music. Rhythm is a vague general term with him, "It is the real pattern in the carpet, the scheme of organization, of thought, feeling and vocabulary, the way in which everything comes together" (*Dial* 75 [1923]: 595). It is a "highly personal matter. It is not a verse-form. It is very uncommon" (*SPMM*, preface). It precedes somehow the actual poem (*OPP*, 38), and sometimes it is a national characteristic as in Dunbar and Whitman (*Criterion* 14 [1935]: 611). But it is never analyzed or used concretely.

"Music," while not so indefinite, is also a very broad term in Eliot. It is not merely the sound-pattern in poetry. Eliot doubts whether "verbal beauty is ever beauty of pure sound" (*PV*, 7). He sees that sound and meter are implicated in the whole structure of the poem. Music in poetry is a "musical pattern of sounds and a musical pattern of secondary meanings of the words which compose it, and these two patterns are indissoluble and one" (*OPP,* 33). Before this statement, Eliot described what he means by the "music of the word." "It is at a point of intersection: it arises from its relation first to the words immediately preceding and following it, and indefinitely to the rest of the context; and from another relation, that of the immediate meaning to that context to all the other meanings which it has in other contexts, to its greater or less wealth of association" (32). Thus Eliot sees words as having contextual meanings within a poem and meanings within the whole linguistic system. But it is regrettable that Eliot obscures this fine insight by calling a semantic phenomenon, the interplay of meanings, "music," though he well understands the difference between poetry and music and draws the usual parallel quite cautiously (38). "Musical qualities" are sometimes used as equivalent to "auditory imagination" (a term derived from Théodule Ribot), which is not simply the poet's sense for sound and meter but something much broader, "a feeling for syllable and rhythm, penetrating far below the conscious levels of thought and feeling . . . sinking to the most primitive and forgotten. . . . It works through meanings . . . and fuses the most ancient and the most civilized mentality" (*UP,* 118–19). At times Eliot expresses a sense of the limits of poetry in terms of its striving toward music. "We touch the border of those feelings which only music can express. We can never emulate music, because to arrive at the condition of music would be the annihilation of poetry, and especially of dramatic poetry" (*OPP,* 87). He expressly denies that there can be nonsense poetry. Edward Lear's is a "parody of sense," and a poem which is "gibberish and has not meaning, is no poem," but "merely an imitation of instrumental music" (*OPP,* 29–30).

Thus the term music suggests the frontiers of poetry and consciousness: the contact of the poet with what we call, since Jung, "the collective unconscious." Eliot cites the work of Caillet and Bédé on the relation of the symbolist movement to the primitive psyche with apparent approval (*UP,* 148n.). Yet it is inconceivable that Eliot could really accept an irrationalistic mysticism. He rejects the fashionable primitivism of our time (see *Nouvelle Revue Française* 14 [1927]: 670–71) and doubts the main assumptions of Jungian symbolism. "What does [Herbert Read] mean by unconscious symbols? If we are unconscious that a symbol is a symbol, then is it a symbol at all? And the moment we become conscious that it is a symbol, is it any longer a symbol?" (*Criterion* 4 [1926]: 756). In discussing French symbolism Eliot considers it an injustice to isolate these poets from poetry in general. He gives an entirely unmystical description of the meaning of symbol. "In poetry it is the tendency of the word to mean as much as possible ... to mean as many things as possible, to make it both exact and comprehensive and really to *unite* the disparate and remote, to give them a fusion and a pattern with the word, surely this is the mastery at which the poet aims, and the poet is distinguished by making the word do more *work* than it does for other writers."[12] Symbol is simply the rightly charged word and not a pointing to the supernatural. Rather Eliot thinks of art often as ritual. Parodying Pater he said that "all art emulates the condition of ritual" (*Dial* 75 [1923]: 597), and in all his proposals of the mid-1920s for the renewal of poetic drama ritual is the key concept. "The stage—not only in its remote origins, but always—is a ritual and the failure of the contemporary stage to satisfy the craving for ritual is one of the reasons why it is not a living art" (*Criterion* 1 [1922–23]: 305). Even myth, on which he draws constantly as a poet, is recommended only as a method, a technique and device, as a "way of controlling, of ordering, of giving shape and a significance to the immense panorama of futility and anarchy which is contemporary history" unfolded in *Ulysses* (*Dial* 75 [1923]: 480). But Eliot does not identify poetry with myth-making or the search for the original myth. We are nearest the center of Eliot's view when he tells us that "the artist is more primitive, as well as more civilized than his contemporaries" (*Egoist* 5 [1918]: 105). The artist is both old and new: he has or should have the unified sensibility which reaches from the most elementary response to the highest intellectual abstractions. He contains all history which is the essence of his universality.

Eliot has a difficult and possibly contradictory concept of history, development, and the poet's relation to it in mind. On the one hand, he seems to hold an almost Hegelian view of history. Each age is completely integrated, and the poet is a mere mouthpiece of his age. Speaking of Dante he says that "the great poet, in writing himself writes his time" (*SE*, 137) but apparently cannot help writing his time. In the defense against Paul Elmer More's accusation that there is a cleavage between Eliot's correctly classical criticism and his perversely modernist poetry, Eliot endorses the strange view that in a chaotic age poetry must be chaotic. The situation cannot be altered by any effort. "At the moment when one writes, one is what one is, and the damage of a lifetime, and of having been born in an unsettled society cannot be repaired at the moment of composition" (*ASG*, 30). Sometimes, however, a distinction is drawn. The business of the poet is to express the culture in which he lives and to which he belongs, not to express "aspiration toward one which is not yet incarnate." But Eliot hastens to add: "This is not, of course, meant to imply that the poet has to approve the society in which he lives: to express an actual culture, and to approve a social situation, are two quite different things. This expression of his culture, indeed, may set the poet into violent opposition to a social situation which violates that culture" (Stallman, 108). While Eliot emphasizes the right of the poet to disagree with the powers that be, though not with the deep-seated assumptions of one's culture, he can praise the Elizabethans for their anachronisms, for accepting their age uncritically. "They were in a position to concentrate their attention to their respective abilities, upon the common characteristics of humanity in all ages rather than upon the differences" (*SE*, 202). A lack of historical and critical sense, conformity, is here valued as a condition of universalizing art, of an art which could be called "classical."

This "timelessness" is what Eliot means by classicism and tradition. Eliot has a double standard, a double conception of time. On the one hand, he recognizes the necessities of a time and often judges works of literature according to the contribution to the "progress" of language and poetry, and on the other hand, he affirms an eternal standard. He disclaims "literary Pyrrhonism," though he sees the vicissitudes of reputations, and their relations to specific needs and affinities of an age (*GJD*, 7). In "Tradition and the Individual Talent" (1919) Eliot defined this interplay memorably. Tradition "involves, in the first place, the historical sense . . . and the historical sense involves a perception, not only of the pastness of the past, but of its presence; the historical sense compels a man to write not merely with his own generation in his bones, but with a feeling that the whole of the literature of Europe from Homer and within it the whole of the literature of his own country has a simultaneous existence and composes a simultaneous order. This historical sense, which is the sense of the timeless as well as of the temporal and of the timeless and the temporal together, is what makes a writer traditional" (*SE*, 14). What Eliot here calls "the historical sense" is not what has been traditionally called so. He rejects deterministic historical causation, he is not a relativist, but he rather understands that the absolute is in the relative: yet not finally and fully in it. It seems misleading of J. C. Ransom to label Eliot "the historical critic" (*The New Criticism*, 1941). Rather, Eliot wants the critic to see literature "not as consecrated by time, but to see it beyond time; to see the best work of our time and the best work of twenty-five hundred years ago with the same eyes" (*SW*, xiv). All works of art are conceived as still somehow present, "the existing monuments form an ideal order among themselves, which is modified by the introduction of the new (the really new) work of art among them. . . .

Whoever has approved this idea of order, of the form of European, of English literature, will not find it preposterous that the past should be altered by the present as much as the present is directed by the past" (*SE*, 15). While the figure of the past is being constantly redrawn, the order constantly rearranged, it still remains a simultaneous order. As Eliot was to say in *Little Gidding*: "History is a pattern of timeless moments."

The consequences of Eliot's view of tradition are obvious. They are, in part, negative: they justify the distrust of mere personality, novelty, and originality. "The poem which is absolutely original is absolutely bad" (*SPEP*, x). They discourage revolution, individualistic indulgence of any kind. Positively Eliot recommends that the poet be well-read and even learned in the history of poetry, that he conform, though not completely or passively. "True originality is merely a development" (ibid.).

What is put theoretically in terms of tradition assumes concrete meaning when tradition is defined by Eliot as *the* tradition and described as classical. Eliot declared himself "classicist," "royalist," and "Anglican" in the preface to *For Lancelot Andrewes* (1928), a statement which he later came to call, somewhat ruefully, "injudicious." He did not recant but rather objected to the interpretation that the "three subjects are of equal importance" to him and that he "believes that they all hang together or fall together" (*ASG*, 29). Eliot's version of classicism is not merely another version of French academic classicism, for he does not worship the French golden age like Nisard and Brunetière. He was hardly interested in the French classics, though he made laudatory allusions to Racine's *Athalie*, "a very great play indeed" (*OPP*, 176), and wrote an essay on Pascal which is, however, quite properly not literary.

Eliot's admiration for the Greek and Roman classics seems quite general and theoretical. He admits candidly that he is "among those who have not remembered enough of the classical languages to read the originals with ease" (*CC*, 159). But Eliot has, as his plays show, a close acquaintance with Greek tragedy in translation and early took an almost professional interest in Seneca, mainly as background for his thorough study of Elizabethan drama. The one ancient author on whom Eliot has commented extensively and most sympathetically is Virgil. He contrasts the world of Virgil with that of Homer as "a more civilized world of dignity, reason and order." Although he considers Virgil's sensibility "more nearly Christian than that of any other Roman or Greek poet," he decides that it is not quite true to say that Virgil was "*anima naturaliter Christiana*" (*OPP*, 130). Virgil was no mystic; he lacked love in Dante's sense. The comments on Virgil are the only ones which vibrate with affection for a classical author who is seen in terms of his "characteristic peculiarly sympathetic to the Christian mind" (121) as making a "liaison between the old world and the new" (123). Even the fourth *Eclogue,* though Eliot recognizes that it does not prophesy the coming of Christ, is considered a "symbol" of Virgil's peculiar station (123). At times antiquity seems hardly valued on its own terms but only as a preparatory stage for Christianity.

Nor can one say that Eliot is particularly drawn to the age of English neoclassicism. "My own opinion is, that we have no classic age, and no classic poet in English" (*OPP,* 59). Eliot is cool to Pope, "a master of miniature" (*SE,* 296), while Swift excited his horrified admiration. In a comparison with Ben Jonson, Eliot calls "the last chapter of the *Voyage to the Houyhnhnms* a more terrible satire than anything Jonson ever wrote, yet it can move us to pity and a kind of purgation. We feel everywhere the tragedy of Swift himself . . . the terrible personality in his work which came out of deeper and intenser emotion" than Jonson's (*Dial* 85 [1928]: 68). This is the tenor of later comments about "the terrible sincerity of Swift's vituperation of the human race"[13] or "the progressive cynicism of the mature and disappointed man of the world . . . who hated the very smell of the human animal."[14] Eliot's criticism of Milton is a criticism of neoclassical taste: of the artificial language, the sonorous rhetoric, the melodrama. Only Dryden appeals to Eliot strongly for his use of the spoken language, his satiric power, and his criticism. Though Dryden is consistently praised for having "established a *normal* English speech, a speech valid for both verse and prose" (*JD,* 2), Eliot admits that "with all his intelligence, Dryden had a commonplace mind. . . . He lacked a large and unique view of life; he lacked insight, he lacked profundity" (*SE,* 300, 302). In general the eighteenth century is disparaged also for its "limited range of sensibility, and especially in the scale of religious feeling" (*OPP,* 60). Only Dr. Johnson is exempted for the precision of the verse of the two Juvenalian satires, its urbanity, certainty, and ease,[15] and is highly valued as a critic and moralist. In passing we are told to our surprise that "I place *The Deserted Village,* higher than any poem by Johnson and Gray" (*OPP,* 181), and Crabbe is recommended as "a very good poet . . . but you do not go to him for magic" (49).

All this seems to indicate that Eliot's taste cannot be described as classical or neoclassical. The classics are, however, the wellspring of tradition. The lecture *What Is a Classic?* (1944) expounds a view very similar to Sainte-Beuve's, though Eliot assures us that he had not read Sainte-Beuve's essay of the same title for some thirty-odd years (*OPP,* 53). "The blood-stream of European literature is Latin and Greek—not as two systems of circulation, but one, for it is through Rome that our parentage to Greece must be traced" (70). Implicitly the conception, prevalent particularly in Germany, that Rome should be bypassed and that one should go directly to Greece is rejected. Rome is, in Eliot's view, the indispensable link in the chain of tradition. He lauds the "continuity of the impulse of Rome" and identifies the classical tradition with the Christian tradition and specifically with the Roman and Catholic tradition, which is also politically authoritarian (*Criterion* 4 [1926]: 22). Eliot stresses the "need of the cultural unification of Europe," which can grow out only of the old roots, "the Christian faith and the classical languages." "These roots are, I think, inextricably intertwined" (*CC*, 160).

At times, Eliot includes Germany in the unity of European culture, defined as both Christian and classical. But he denies that Goethe is a universal classic, finds him "a little provincial" (*OPP*, 67), and even thinks that "he dabbled in both philosophy and poetry and made no great success of either; his true role was that of the man of the world and sage—a La Rochefoucauld, a La Bruyère, a Vauvenargues" (*UP*, 99). Earlier Eliot called the "Hymn to Nature" "nonsense" and "dismal as a rural sermon," apparently unaware that its authorship was denied by Goethe (*Nation and Athenaeum* 44 [1929]: 527). In any case this prose hymn today ascribed to Johann Christoph Tobler is derivative of Shaftesbury's address to Nature in *The Moralists* and hardly says anything more shocking than what the ancient Stoics taught. Later, in a speech delivered in Hamburg in 1955, Eliot recanted his low opinion of Goethe. He includes him now with Dante and Shakespeare among the great European classics and finds in him "wisdom" which is not merely the worldly wisdom of a La Rochefoucauld. Eliot had read the book *Man or Matter* by Ernst Lehrs, who interprets the scientist Goethe absurdly as a forerunner of Rudolf Steiner's occult "anthroposophy." Eliot now finds Goethe less representative of his age than he thought before, more universal, almost above his age like Blake. Lehrs unfortunately is a fantastic and uncritical interpreter. In the lecture Eliot shows no interest in the works of Goethe, though he says that he has come to prefer the second part of *Faust* to the first. But the new admiration for Goethe has a certain air of unreality and even cultural diplomacy about it. Germany, in 1955, was to be readmitted to European civilization.

We must recognize that Eliot's classicism is a matter of cultural politics rather than of literary criticism. It is clearly derived from Irving Babbitt and the French antiromantic polemicists: Lasserre, Seillière, and Charles Maurras. Eliot acknowledged that Maurras's *L'Avenir de l'intelligence* (1905) exerted a great influence on his intellectual development (*Nouvelle*

Revue Française 9 [1923]: 619–25) and defended Maurras in his conflict with the Vatican. Eliot's booklet on *Dante* (1929) is dedicated to Maurras. In Maurras we find the identification of the classical with the Roman tradition, and the view (surely false, especially outside France) that romanticism *is* revolution and that the two are both moral and aesthetic anarchy. In the French Eliot found the idea of an authoritarian tradition, of order, and the heritage of Rome. He accepted their general attack on romanticism as a cultural phenomenon but not their concrete literary tastes, which are hardly applicable to English literature. Eliot calls modern classicism a "tendency toward a higher and clearer conception of Reason, and a more severe and serene control of the emotions by Reason," and cites then the names Sorel, Maurras, Benda, Hulme, Maritain, and Babbitt (*Criterion* 4 [1926]: 5) as indicating the drift. It is surely symptomatic that all these names are those of ideologists with no poet among them, unless one takes the few little imagistic poems by Hulme seriously. Eliot did take them seriously when he commented that Hulme had "the great advantage of a creative gift," though compared with Maurras, Sorel, and Lassere, Hulme was "immature and unsubstantial." Eliot saw the problem himself. "The weakness from which the classical movement in France has suffered is that it has been a critique rather than a creation. . . . A new classical age will be reached when the dogma, or *ideology* of the critics is so modified by contact with creative writing, and when the creative writers are so permeated by the new dogma, that a state of equilibrium is reached" (*Criterion* 2 [1924]: 232). But this synthesis did not and could not happen. Classicism with Eliot remains an ethical and religious ideal: "the classicist, or adult mind, is thoroughly realist, without illusions, without day-dreams, without hope, without bitterness, and with an abundant resignation" (*Criterion* 1 [1923]: 39). The aesthetic implications of order and form are minimal when he contrasts classicism and romanticism as "the complete and the fragmentary, the orderly and the chaotic" (*SE*, 26). In 1934 he thought that the distinction "should not be taken too seriously" (*ASG*, 25), and in 1961 he found "that the terms have no longer the importance to me that they once had" (*CC*, 15).

Actually Eliot's view of the English romantic poets is by no means uniformly unfavorable. He admires Blake, though the exact reason remains rather obscure. He praises him for preserving a "mind unclouded by current opinion" (*SE*, 306) but also complains that Blake lacked a "framework of accepted and traditional ideas which would have prevented him from indulging in a philosophy of his own" (308). Eliot seems to take away with one hand what he had given with the other. But the apparent contradiction can be resolved: Blake could have been what he was only because of his loneliness and this loneliness caused his eccentricity.

The poetry of Wordsworth and Coleridge is never discussed by Eliot in any detail. Eliot refers to the "exaggerated repute" of *Kubla Khan* (*UP*, 146) and calls the *Ode on Intimations of Immortality* a "superb piece of verbiage" (*Dial* 83 [1927]: 260). But the criticism of both Wordsworth and Coleridge interests Eliot much more. Eliot called *Biographia Litteraria* "one of the wisest and silliest, the most exciting and most exasperating books of criticism ever written" but ascribes to it a great historical importance. "He brought out clearly the relation of literary criticism to that branch of philosophy which has flourished amazingly under the name of esthetics" ("Experiment in Criticism," 70 [1929]: 227), a novelty, one should add, only for the English-speaking world. He quotes Coleridge's description of the imagination as reconciling opposites with approval as a justification of metaphysical wit (*SE*, 278) but rejects Coleridge's distinction between imagination and fancy (*UP*, 77) and the phrase "the willing suspension of disbelief," apparently not understanding that Coleridge speaks of theatrical illusion and not of Eliot's belief in a poet's doctrine (95).

It seems somewhat surprising that Eliot admires Byron, whom he interprets as a belated Scotch Calvinist with a sense of damnation. He praises particularly the last cantos of *Don Juan* where Byron found a genuine emotion, hatred of hypocrisy (*OPP*, 205). Still, Eliot thinks Byron's commonplace language indicates a "defective sensibility," as his "callous masquerade of cynicism" shows an "uninteresting mind and a disorderly one" (201).

Keats is considered a great poet. Eliot thinks the odes—"especially perhaps his *Ode to Psyche*—are sufficient to justify his reputation." Eliot, however, professes not to understand what is meant by "beauty is truth, truth beauty" and calls the line "a serious blemish on a beautiful poem" (*SE*, 256). Eliot found "traces of a struggle toward unification of sensibility" in the second *Hyperion* (*SE*, 174), but kept his doubts about the poem (*UP*, 100). He admired the letters as "certainly the most notable and the most important ever written by any English poet" (100) and quotes the letter to Benjamin Bailey (November 22, 1817): "Men of Genius as great as certain Chemicals operating on the Mass of neutral intellect—but they have not any individuality, any determined character." It must have impressed Eliot as an anticipation of his own preference for "impersonality" and struck him as "classical" rather than "romantic."

The one poet who is singled out for adverse criticism among the English romantics is Shelley. Eliot's objections are mainly ideological: Shelley's atheism, his hatred of kings and priests, his views about free love offend him. He calls him "humourless, pedantic, self-centered and sometimes almost a blackguard" (*UP*, 89). But he criticizes Shelley also as a poet: for a confused image (*SE*, 292) or for a stanza of "The Skylark" whose astronomy seemed to him obscure (*Dial* 84 [1928]: 247). The *Cenci* is called only a "reconstruction" of Elizabethan tragedy (*SW*, 55; cf. *JD*, 35–36, and *OPP*, 34), and *The Defence of Poetry* is considered inferior to Wordsworth's *Preface* (*UP*, 93). Eliot has on occasion a good word for "The Triumph of Life" because it shows, like Keats's *Hyperion*, "traces of a struggle toward unification of sensibility" (*SE*, 274) and contains "some of the greatest and most Dantesque lines in English verse" (*CC*, 130). Eliot, in writing an introduction to Leone Vivante's *English Poetry* (1950), admits that Vivante's chapter brought him "to a new and more sympathetic appreciation of Shelley" (x).

Eliot's rejection of romanticism is thus aimed rather at Tennyson and Swinburne, Pater and Morris, and at the Georgians, Rupert Brooke and John Drinkwater, than at the actual romantics. But even the relation to Tennyson had its ups and downs. In 1918 he made a double-edged defense of Tennyson as a careful technician. "And Tennyson," he adds, "had a brain (a large dull brain like a farmhouse clock) which saved him from triviality. The subject given (airy fairy Lillian) he took lightly, but as a serious study in technique" (*Egoist* 5 [1915]: 43). But in 1936 he wrote a rather bland introduction to an edition of the *Poems*, which praises him for "the finest ear of any English poet since Milton" for his "abundance, variety and competence" and objects only to the *Princess* as dull and *Maud* as unreal. "I should," he concludes, "reproach Tennyson not for mildness, or tepidity but rather for lack of serenity" (*EAM*, 175, 181). Swinburne, however, is singled out as the example of the poet for whom "the object has ceased to exist, because meaning is merely the hallucination of meaning, because language has adapted itself to an independent life of atmospheric nourishment" (*SE*, 313). In Swinburne meaning and sound are one thing, or rather there is only sound and the meaning is so general as to evaporate. But surprisingly Eliot admires Swinburne as a student and appreciator rather than critic of the Elizabethan dramatists and thinks that "his judgment, if carefully scrutinized, appears temperate and just" (*SW*, 17). Eliot obviously reacted also against Whitman, complaining of "the large part of clap-trap in his content" (*SPEP*, xi), and while acknowledging him to be a "great prose writer" considered him "spurious in pretending his prose was a new form of verse" (Nebraska lecture [1960], 206). Eliot becomes only satirical and even violent when he discusses Gilbert Murray's Euripides translation as a "vulgar debasement of the eminently personal idiom of Swinburne" (*SW*, 66) or when he ridicules John Drinkwater for boasting of his purely English ancestry (*Vanity Fair*, November 1923, 44) or when he dismissed Edgar Lee Masters, Carl Sandburg, and Vachel Lindsay as "commonplace and conventional minds" (ibid., 118).

One cannot thus describe Eliot's poetic taste and the lineage he construes for his tradition in terms of a simple opposition of classicism and romanticism. In spite of the ideological superstructure of classicism, Eliot's taste belongs to a line which could be called medieval-baroque-symbolist. The styles have enough in common to make his preferences consistent and clear. There is no need to discuss Eliot's relation to Dante, who seemed to him the greatest poet in all history, "the most European, the least provincial" (*CC*, 134). Eliot's view of Dante is somewhat partial but it brings into focus several basic conceptions of his literary theory: the emphasis on visual imagination, on the spoken language, on a body of accepted thought and the emotional structure which has absorbed and transformed abstract ideas. Dante seems the only medieval author who interested Eliot deeply, though he voices a liking for Malory and Villon, and he referred to Guido Cavalcanti and Richard of St. Victor.[16]

I use the term "baroque" to label all art reacting against the Renaissance standards of beauty while preceding the establishment of neoclassicism. Eliot seems not particularly interested in the Renaissance as such. He nowhere discusses any of its prominent poets in detail until he comes to the Elizabethan dramatists, Marlowe and particularly Shakespeare. In two long papers which could be called Eliot's contributions to English historical scholarship (rather than criticism), Eliot studied the translations of Seneca and "Shakespeare and the Stoicism of Seneca" (*SE*, 65, 126), admiring the handling of blank verse: its freedom, its nearness to common speech, flexible and powerful at the same time. He sees the Elizabethan playwrights as working within ill-defined conventions and argues persuasively that the weakness of Elizabethan drama is "not its conventions but its lack of conventions" (112). The details of Eliot's criticism seem often open to question. One can hardly describe *The Jew of Malta* as a "farce," even though it be "the farce of the old English humour . . . which spent its last breath in the decadent genius of Dickens" (123). Nor can one be convinced by his interpretation of Othello's last speech as an attempt at "cheering himself up," "a terrible exposure of human weakness," a kind of *bovarysme*. It is not true that "Othello has ceased to think about Desdemona, and is thinking about himself" (130–31). Eliot fails to convey the mood and result of Othello's self-accusation. Othello makes his last speech preparing his suicide, diverting attention from pulling the dagger against himself. Nor can one accept the interpretation of *Hamlet* which relies far too heavily on J. M. Robertson's unverifiable speculations. It seems symptomatic that Eliot thought *Antony and Cleopatra* and *Coriolanus* Shakespeare's "most assured artistic successes" (144). He obviously cared far more for the Jacobean and Caroline dramatists to whom he devoted some of his finest essays: Ben Jonson, Thomas Middleton, Thomas Heywood, Cyril Tourneur, John Ford, Philip Massinger, and John Marston. Eliot's involvement with Jonson, Middleton, Tourneur, and Marston, their "hatred of life," and their words, "a network of tentacular roots reaching down to the deepest terrors and desire" (155), have done much to reestablish them in favor with the theater and with criticism.

Eliot's championing of the metaphysical poets proved even more influential, although taste for Donne was no novelty: Coleridge, Saintsbury, Gosse, and others had admired Donne in the nineteenth century, and Grierson edited the critical edition in 1912. Eliot did not define or describe the nature of metaphysical poetry in any new way, for the idea of "unified sensibility" or "felt thought" goes back at least as far as the Rev. Alexander Grosart, nor did he even try to define the nature of the "conceit." Eliot rather makes the case for intellectual poetry and states the lesson for our own time. Poets in our civilization "must be difficult. The poet must become more and more comprehensive, more allusive, more indirect, in order to force, to dislocate if necessary, language into his meaning. It is not sufficient to 'look into our hearts and write.' One must look into the cerebral cortex, the nervous system, and the digestive tracts" (*SE*, 275–76).

Eliot is generally considered the herald of Donne's fame. In the key essay, "The Metaphysical Poets" (1921), he uses examples from Donne to illustrate "a direct apprehension of thought, or a recreation of thought into feeling" (*SE*, 272), and Donne is expressly singled out: "A thought for Donne was an experience: it modified his sensibility" (273). An almost wholly laudatory early review (*Nation and Athenaeum* 33 [1923]: 331–32) and remarks on his seeing "the thing as it is" (*Egoist* 4 [1917]: 118) testify to Eliot's early enthusiasm. But about 1926 he must have changed his mind, possibly under the influence of Mario Praz's book on Donne and Crashaw.[17] The Clark lectures, partly available in the French translation of a comparison between Dante and Donne, draw an elaborate contrast between their conceptions of love obviously in favor of Dante. Eliot makes literal-minded objections to images in Donne's "Ecstasy," because he misinterprets the tone and point of the poem, which I, following Pierre

Legouis, consider a sophisticated invitation to physical love.[18] But this criticism of Donne is mild compared to what followed: Donne appears as the example of the poet merely playing with ideas. "I could not find either any 'mediævalism' or any thinking, but only a vast jumble of incoherent erudition on which he drew for purely poetic effects. I found it quite impossible to come to the conclusion that Donne believed anything" (*SE*, 138–39). Soon afterward Eliot drew another comparison unfavorable to Donne, this time with Lancelot Andrewes. Donne has "a little of the religious spellbinder, the Reverend Billy Sunday of his time, the fleshcreeper, the sorcerer of emotional orgy" (320). It is then rather surprising that Eliot contributed to Theodore Spencer's celebratory *A Garland for John Donne* (1930), where he bestows praise upon Donne as a reformer of the English poetic language but finds in him "a manifest fissure between thought and sensibility," thinks his influence on his own time overrated, and predicts that his sermons "will disappear as suddenly as they appeared" (*GJD*, 8, 19).

Eliot rates George Herbert more highly as a great master of language, as a sincere devotional poet, as an anatomist of feeling, and as a man who, in his short life, went further along the road to humility than Donne (*Spectator*, 1932, 360–61). *The Temple* is praised as a continuous religious meditation with a planned, intellectual framework (*OPP*, 45). "The emotion of Herbert is clear, definite, mature and sustained" (*Dial* 83 [1927]: 263). These views are repeated in a colorless pamphlet on Herbert which Eliot wrote as late as 1962. It is introduced by a biography and filled with long quotations but tries also to set off Herbert against Donne, "a difference between the dominance of intellect over sensibility and the dominance of sensibility over intellect" (17). Compared with Herbert, Henry Vaughan is considered minor. He is neither a great mystic nor a great poet, but a forerunner of Wordsworth and Lamb in his love for one's childhood, a mood for which Eliot has little use (*Dial* 83 [1927]: 259–63).

Though the essay on Marvell seems to be written also around quotations (twenty-seven from seventeen poems of eleven authors in three languages), it had much greater impact. Eliot took Marvell resolutely out of the then-usual grouping with Bunyan and Milton as a "Puritan" and proclaimed his best verse "the product of European, that is to say, Latin culture," a verdict fully confirmed since by scholarship which has established Marvell's contacts with French and neo-Latin poetry. Eliot succeeds in characterizing Marvell in memorable phrases: "the tough reasonableness beneath the slight lyric grace," "the bright, hard precision," "an equipoise, balance and proportion of tones," and "the wit which is fused into the imagination" (*SE*, 279, 285, 288, 282).

Eliot also admired Crashaw very highly. He finds intellectual pleasure even in the entirely preposterous images of Crashaw. He endorses Mario Praz, who puts Crashaw "above Marino, Góngora, and everybody else as the representative of the baroque spirit in literature" (*SE*, 250).

Cowley interests Eliot as showing the new scientific spirit. He gives occasion for a summary of Eliot's admiration for seventeenth-century poetry as the most "civilized" age of English poetry. Eliot admires its wit, "a kind of balance and proportion of intellectual and emotional values" (*Seventeenth Century Studies*, 1938, 242), and relates wit to "other meanings of the word, and even to that which connotes mirth—though there especially perhaps, to what is most alien to our age, holy mirth" (*Nouvelle Revue Française* 9 [1926]: 525). Wit, not to be confused with cynicism, implies a "constant inspection and criticism of experience. It involves, probably, a recognition, implicit in the expression of every experience, of other kinds of experience which are possible" (*SE*, 289). It seems here almost a synonym of what the New Critics called irony.

In Eliot's history of poetry, the eighteenth century and the romantic age appear as ages of disintegration, dissociation into intellect and feeling. The reconstitution of the original unity was attempted by the French symbolists and, Eliot hopes, by his own work, by Pound, Joyce, and Marianne Moore. Eliot, however, rejects the professed poetic theories of the French symbolist movement: their mystical or occult assumptions, their emphasis on suggestiveness, their striving for musicality (*PV*). In linking Mallarmé to Poe, Eliot lumps them together, charging them with not believing in the theories they invented, calling them mere technicians who wanted to "expand their sensibility beyond the limits of the normal world" (*Nouvelle Revue Française* 9 [1926]: 525). Eliot could not conceive of the poet as a decipherer of the hieroglyphics of nature or accept the Swedenborgian or Schopenhauerian metaphysics of the French poets. He rather thought of them as the discoverers of new techniques and as men of a new sensibility. Baudelaire is to him "by far the greatest of the French symbolists" (*Criterion* 9 [1930]: 357), whereas Laforgue was only a "minor successor" (*SE*, 376).

The "minor successor," Jules Laforgue, was, however, far more important for Eliot's own poetic development. Eliot freely acknowledges his influence on his early poetry (*CC*, 22, 126), but in his published writings has little to say about him. Most of his scattered remarks make rather strong reservations. He complains of "unassimilated fragments of metaphysics, and of sentiments floating about" in his work (*Egoist* 5 [1918]: 69) and even says that he "remains imprisoned in his own adolescence" (*SPEP*, viii). But in the still unpublished Clark lectures given at Cambridge, England, in 1926 and in the Turnbull lectures at Johns Hopkins University in 1933, which are quoted in recent books by Edward Lobb and Ronald Bush and in an article by Michele Hannoosh, Laforgue is discussed at some considerable length. In the Clark lectures, Laforgue and Baudelaire are seen as the first poets who revived the problem of Good and Evil and thus succeeded in recombining thought and feeling and establishing a moral order. Even Baudelaire's "Satanism—the cultivation of Evil is a derivative or an imitation of the spiritual life" (Hannoosh, 168), a theme developed in the essay on Baudelaire (1930). Laforgue "had an innate craving for order; this is that every feeling should have its intellectual equivalent, its philosophical justification, and that every idea have its emotional equivalent, its sentimental justification."[19] In the Turnbull lectures, this is repeated in a more religious phraseology. Laforgue seeks "salvation" so that thought and sensibility would work together for a "fullness of life." Laforgue's irony comes from the "war between the feelings implied by his ideas, and the ideas implied by his feelings."[20] Laforgue is "at once a sentimentalist daydreaming over the *jeune fille* at the piano with her geraniums, and the behaviourist inspecting her reflexes" (Lobb, 42) in the light of his reading of Schopenhauer and Hartmann. Eliot defines Laforgue's irony as self-irony and thus the expression of suffering. Eliot praises Laforgue for his technical innovations from which he profited but considers him "much below Corbière and Rimbaud as an artist" (Hannoosh, 173–74). His final failure is ascribed to the fact that the philosophers on which Laforgue drew were not pure thinkers (as Thomas Aquinas was for Dante) but were corrupted by feeling, were poetical. Or alternatively, Eliot suggests that Laforgue really did not believe in them and thus remained divided, *dédoublé*.

In an early essay (*Criterion* 9 [1930]), a review of Arthur Symons's 1927 translation of Baudelaire, Eliot condemns Symons's translation and his comments for making Baudelaire a figure of the nineties, of a naughty religion of vice. Symons does not understand the highly traditional character of Baudelaire's verse, with its Racinian strictness, and he does not understand his mind: his lucidity, and his Christianity. Eliot agrees with Charles Du Bos that Baudelaire was "essentially a Christian, born out of his due time, and a classicist, born out of his due time" (*EAM*, 73). The later essay (1930) is much more critical. Eliot admits that "the view—that Baudelaire is essentially Christian—needs considerable reservation."

Baudelaire's Christianity is "rudimentary or embryonic." Eliot sees the disorder of his life and dismisses "his prostitutes, mulattoes, Jewesses, serpents, cats, corpses" as "machinery which has not worn well" (*SE*, 372), as "romantic detritus" (371). Still, he is "the first counter-romantic in poetry" (372), admired for his fundamental sincerity, for his sense of sin in the permanent Christian sense. "He was at least able to understand that the sexual act as evil is more dignified, less boring, than as the natural, 'life-giving,' cheery automatism of the modern world" (377), a theme congenial to Eliot's temperament.

Eliot has little to say about Rimbaud and Mallarmé. He at first preferred the "sincere prose" of Rimbaud to "the laboured opacity of Mallarmé (which fades colourless and dead)" (*New Statesman*, May 19, 1917, 158). I do not know what Eliot could mean when he referred to Mallarmé's "mossiness" (*CC*, 170) and see some contradiction in his praise for Mallarmé's language experiments to his usual emphasis on colloquial language in poetry. He tells with evident approval that "every battle he [Mallarmé] fought with syntax represents an effort to transmute lead into gold, ordinary language into poetry" ("Prose and Verse," in *Chapbook* 22 [1921]: 3–10), and "Note sur Mallarmé et Poe" praises his brilliant critique of Poe's "to purify the dialect of the tribe." Mallarmé by his peculiar syntax turned the accidental into the real. Even though he, like Poe and Donne, did not believe in his theories, he achieved the reality by incantation, which insists on the primitive power of the word (*Nouvelle Revue Française* 14 [1926]: 524–26). In the unpublished Turnbull Lectures (1933), Eliot developed this, quoting from Mallarmé's "M'introduire dans ton histoire" the lines "tonnerre et rubis aux moyeux" to show that poetry is incantation as well as imagery. " 'Thunder and rubies up to the wheelhub' cannot be seen, heard, or thought together, but their collocation brings out the connotation of each word" (quoted in Bush, 176). The lines "Garlic and sapphires in the mud / Clot the bedded axle-tree" in "Burnt Norton" show that Eliot had learned Mallarmé's lesson. But whatever Eliot's practice may have been, as late as 1958 in the preface to Valéry's *Art of Poetry*, Eliot strongly reasserted against Valéry's sharp contrast between poetry and prose inherited from Mallarmé that "the norm of a poet's language is the way his contemporaries talk" (xvi–xvii). He had other even deeper disagreements with Valéry. He praised him for "the reintegration of the symbolist movement into the great tradition,"[21] for his impulse toward classicism, and for his theory of impersonality. Eliot plays down the question of Valéry's philosophy and praises *La Pythie* and *Le Serpent* as unique poetic expressions of states of mind rather than as abstract statements. Later Eliot discussed the theory of "pure poetry," which he considers as "a goal that can never be reached," for subject matter cannot be completely eliminated from poetry. Valéry is seen as the "most self-conscious of poets," for whom "the act of composition is more interesting than the poem which results from it" (*CC*, 39–40). While Eliot admired the "marvel of introspection" (*Quarterly Review* 2 [1947]: 213) performed in Valéry's essays on the gestations of his poems and expounded the merits of his poetic theory in some way parallel to his own—the emphasis on "brain-work," upon the study of prosodic and stanzaic forms and upon structure (*AP*, xv)—he disagrees with Valéry's sharp distinction between poetry and prose and looks with some detachment on his concept of the poet. "The tower of ivory has been fitted up as a laboratory—a solitary laboratory" (*AP*, xxi). Valéry's description of his procedure in preparing for a poem as "cleaning up the verbal situation," he considers, "in plain English, eyewash" (*AP*, xxii). This is still respectful irony, but when it comes to Valéry's world-view Eliot becomes positively savage in his reaction. He complains at first of Valéry's extreme skepticism. "It might be thought that such a man, without believing in anything which could be the subject of poetry, would find refuge in a doctrine of 'art for art's sake,' but Valéry was much too sceptical to believe even in art" (*CC*, 39). But later the skepticism is seen as sheer egoism. "It would seem that the one object of his curiosity was—himself. He reminds us of Narcissus gazing into the pool" (*AP*, xxiii). In an obituary Valéry is condemned as a "profoundly destructive, even nihilistic mind," though Eliot continued to admire his intelligence and some of his poems (*Quarterly Review of Literature* 2 [1947]: 213).

A certain distance from the main figures of French symbolism is paralleled by Eliot's detached view of W. B. Yeats. An early article, "A Foreign Mind" (*Athenaeum*, July 4, 1919), treats him as "not of this world," as "a cause of bewilderment and distress." "His mind, extreme in egoism, and, as often with egoism, remains a little crude." The crudity, as in Joyce, would be excusable if it were motivated by powerful feeling, but "the fault of Mr. Yeats's is that it is crude without being powerful" (552). Eliot consistently objected to Yeats's "somewhat artificially induced poeticality" (*ASG*, 48) and resented his attempt to "take heaven by magic" (*UP*, 140). Yet he recognized Yeats's triumph in extricating himself from the Celtic twilight. "Yeats began to write and is still [in 1933] writing some of the most beautiful poetry in the language, some of the clearest, simplest, most direct" (140). In a lecture given at the Abbey Theatre in 1940, Eliot seemed oddly noncommittal considering the festive occasion. He pointedly tells us that Yeats did *not* influence his early poetry: that "the kind of poetry I needed, to teach me the use of my own voice, did not exist in English at all; it was only to be found in French" (*OPP,* 252) and that "there are aspects of Yeats's thought and feeling which to myself are unsympathetic" (262). But he describes Yeats's struggle to become a character, a personality who would be still universal. "In beginning to speak as a particular man he is beginning to speak for man" (256). He praises Yeats's role in the development of the Irish theater as "the expression of the consciousness of a people" (261) and as an antidote to the plays (mainly Shaw's) that are "ephemeral tracts on some transient social problem." Eliot sees Yeats's plays as allied to his own ambition for poetic drama, though he finds *Purgatory* not "very pleasant," and can reflect on Yeats as "a poet of middle age," endorsing the view that Yeats's lines about "lust and rage" in his old age are "not very pleasant" (257)—odd adjectives to come from Eliot. Still, he could call Yeats "the greatest poet of his time" (*Criterion* 14 [1935]: 672).

The contemporary poet who meant most to Eliot was Ezra Pound. Eliot's view of Pound is so strongly determined by their personal association that it cannot be properly discussed in this context. Pound's surgical operation on *The Waste Land* has now been fully revealed in the edition of the drafts. We know of Eliot's somewhat double-edged dedication of the poem to Pound, "il miglior fabbro." It implicitly compares Pound to Arnaut Daniel and Eliot to Dante (*Purgatorio,* XXVI, 116). Very early Eliot wrote on Pound: a little book anonymously in 1917 and two reviews in 1918 and 1919. Later he introduced *Selected Poems* (1928) by Pound and did a great service to Pound's reputation as a critic by publishing and introducing his *Literary Essays* (1954). The first booklet is largely written around quotations but sets the tone of many later pronouncements: the emphasis on Pound's learning ("one of the most learned of poets" [*CC,* 166]), on the definiteness and concreteness of his verse (170), for which he quotes Ford Madox Hueffer saying that "poetry consists in so rendering concrete objects that the emotion produced by the objects shall arise in the reader" (181), another anticipation of the "objective correlative." Slightly later Eliot described Pound's method as the "historical method" in terms reminiscent of "Tradition and the Individual Talent." "As the present is no more than the present existence, the present significance of the entire past, Mr. Pound proceeds by acquiring the entire past; and when the entire past is acquired, the constituents fall into place and the present is revealed. Such a method involves immense capacities of learning and of dominating one's learning and the peculiarity of expressing oneself through historical masks." Pound's method is "not archeology or pedantry but one method, and a very high method of poetry" (*Athenaeum,* October 24, 1919, 1065).

In 1928 Eliot pays tribute to Pound's "complete and isolated superiority" as "a master of verse form. . . . No one living has practised it with more success. I make no exception of age or of country, including France and Germany." He records his conviction that Pound's verse has "steadily improved, and that the *Cantos* are the most interesting of all." But he now allows a false distinction when he confesses that as for "the meaning of the *Cantos,* that never worries me and I do not believe I care," and even more strongly: "I confess that I am seldom interested in what he is saying, but only in the way he says it." Actually Eliot does comment on the philosophy: he calls it "a little antiquated" and speaks of "a steamroller of Confucian rationalism (The Religion of a Gentleman, and therefore an Inferior Religion) which has flattened over the whole" (*Dial* 84 [1928]: 4–7). Also later Eliot admits that he is "doubtful about some of the *Cantos*" and finds in them "an increasing defect of communication" (*Poetry* 68 [1946]: 326–38). By then Eliot's estimate of Pound had largely concentrated on his early stimulus as a critic. In 1936 he spoke of his criticism as "the greatest literary influence of the century up to the present time" and complained that "the central importance of Mr. Pound's criticism has not yet been fully recognised" (*Criterion* 16: 668). In the fervent personal tribute of 1946 Eliot tells of Pound's blue-penciling of *The Waste Land* as "irrefutable evidence of Pound's critical genius." Pound created "the situation in which for the first time there was a 'modern movement in poetry' in which English and American poets collaborated, knew each other's works, and influenced each other." "Pound's critical writing is almost the only contemporary writing on the Art of Poetry a young poet can study with profit. It forms a corpus of poetic doctrine." But Eliot rejects the view that Pound's "eventual reputation will rest upon his criticism and not upon his poetry (I have been paid the same compliment myself). I disagree. It is on his total work that he must be judged." Eliot even defends what he recognizes are the "irritatingly biased" and irreverent judgments of Pound by pleading that they must be seen in their proper setting as polemical weapons of use to young poets (*Poetry* 68 [1946]: 326–38). In 1954 Eliot edited a selection of Pound's *Literary Essays* which brought them out of the backfiles of magazines again into public view and most strongly stated Pound's claim for an exalted position in the history of criticism. Eliot calls Pound's criticism "the least dispensable body of critical writing of our time" (xiii), "the most important contemporary criticism of its kind" (x), making Pound "more responsible for the XXth Century revolution in poetry than any other individual" (xi). Only minor reservations are voiced: "The limitation of Pound's kind is in its concentration upon the craft of letters, and of poetry especially" (xii). Eliot again alludes to Pound's "impatience" and to "irritating and sometimes disputable knocking about of accepted valuations in Latin and Greek literature" (xiii). He could not have shared Pound's contempt for Virgil. The two friends had drifted apart in politics and religion but Eliot always clung to Pound's early lessons: the emphasis on the image and on colloquial speech, and simply on the arduous art and craft of poetry.

The other comments on modern poets, such as the introductions to the poems of Harold Monroe and Marianne Moore, chime in, but we are not prepared for Eliot's enthusiasm for Kipling's verse. It fits with Eliot's interest in spoken language, in verse which, like Dryden's, could be charged with being prosaic, and with one rather surprising side of Eliot's taste: for the music hall, the popular song, and the ballad. But the attraction of Kipling goes beyond this: he feels him to be "the most inscrutable of authors," with a "queer gift of second sight," of "transmitting messages from elsewhere," and again, as in Pound, he finds in him the "historical imagination," a "dizzy sense of the nearness of the past," and approves a nationalism which is "an awareness of grandeur and of responsibility" (*OPP*, 241, 243). The multiple motivation of Eliot's championing of Kipling is comprehensible but may seem today a defense of a lost cause.

Almost all of Eliot's critical writings concern poetry or criticism. Poetry includes the drama, which Eliot thought of as poetic drama, which he tried to revive in practice and defend in theory, pursuing "a kind of mirage of the perfection of verse drama, which would be a design of human action and of words, such as to present at once the two aspects of dramatic and musical order" (*OPP*, 87). He wrote extensively on the possibilities of poetic drama and in *Three Voices of Poetry* (1953; *OPP*, 89–102) tried out something like a genre theory: making the lyric the first voice overheard by the reader (a description reminiscent of John Stuart Mill's concept of poetry), the dramatic monologue, the poet speaking through a mask, the second voice, and the drama with imaginary characters speaking the third voice. But always, also in that paper, Eliot insists on all three voices being present in the drama. Earlier he had objected to Middleton Murry's view that "drama is the highest and fullest form of poetry." "There is a great deal that is high and full poetry that will not go into that form. . . . I do not see how we can assert that it is a higher and fuller form than that used by Homer or that used by Dante" (*Criterion* 15 [1936]: 709). Eliot consistently upheld the unity of poetry.

But the novel seems to have remained outside his critical interests. There is no treatise or even paper on the novel among Eliot's critical

writings, and he shows no interest in what today is awkwardly enough
called "narratology." But he commented much more frequently and extensively than the collected volumes of essays show on novels and novelists. In a review of Saintsbury's *History of the French Novel,* Eliot expresses
doubts about Saintsbury's preference for Balzac over Stendhal and elaborates a contrast between Balzac and Dostoevsky which considers Balzac's
atmosphere as "the highest possible development of the atmosphere of
Mrs. Radcliffe" while Dostoevsky, "even when he tells of even more un-
imaginable things," remains in contact with the actual. "The 'aura' is
simply the continuation of the quotidian experience of the brain into
seldom explored extremities of torture." Eliot sides with Stendhal and
Flaubert, who "suggest unmistakably the awful separation between potential passion and any actualization possible in life. They indicate also
the indestructible barriers between one human being and another" (*Athenaeum,* May 30, 1919, 392–93).

Eliot's main concerns among novelists were Henry James and James
Joyce. James appealed to him first, as he did to Pound, as the expatriate
American, the "Citizen of two countries" (as the inscription on James's
tomb proclaims). The note "In Memory" (*The Egoist* 5 [1918]) says even,
"I do not suppose that anyone who is not an American can *properly* appreciate James." Eliot thinks rather surprisingly that James was not a
good literary critic and that as a novelist he was the first to make "a social
entity of which men and women are constituents" the hero of a novel.
Eliot notes James's lack of ideology and abstract philosophy in an often
quoted and misunderstood passage: "He had a mind so fine that no idea
could violate it," contrasting "thinking with our feelings with corrupting
our feelings with ideas." "James is maintaining a point of view, a viewpoint untouched by the parasite idea. He is the most intelligent man of
his generation" (*Egoist* 5 [1918]: 2). One must know the vocabulary of
the early Eliot: the praise of intelligence and of thinking and the condemnation of abstract "ideas" which are somehow lifeless, divorced from
sensibility and particularity. James naturally raises the whole question of
America and Americanness for Eliot. He relates James immediately to
Hawthorne, considering his relation to the Victorian novel "negligible"
(ignoring George Eliot) and the influence of Balzac "not good." James is
seen as positively the "continuator of the New England genius" which
Eliot always interpreted (also much later) as a spiritual triumph over an
uncongenial environment, as "growing on a granite soil" (*Little Review* 5
[1918]: 53). In a later comment Eliot emphasizes that Henry James's
books form a complete whole. "One must read all of them, for one must
grasp, of anything, both the unity and the progression." James did not

try to make character portraits as usually expected in the English novel. If he was "romanticizing English society he did it possessed with the vision of an ideal society and thus was far from blind to the failings of actuality." Eliot concludes: "James did not provide us with 'ideas,' but with another world of thought and feeling. For such a world some have gone to Dostoevsky, some to James; and I am inclined to think that the spirit of James, so much less violent, with so much more reasonableness and so much more resignation than that of the Russian, is no less profound, and is more useful, more applicable for our future" (*Vanity Fair,* February 1924).

Joyce, whom Eliot met first in Paris in 1920, is for him the model of the fiercely independent artist. He protested against the suppression of *Ulysses* and an insensitive obituary in the *Times* and constantly asserted Joyce's greatness. *Ulysses* is "a book quite as Irish in material as a book can be, but a book so significant in the history of the English language that it must take its place as a part of the tradition, of that language. Such a book not only realises untried possibilities in a language, but revivifies the whole of the past" (*Vanity Fair,* November 1923, 118). But I am not aware of any closer discussion, except that once Eliot takes "The Dead" from *Dubliners* to contrast this story with stories by Katherine Mansfield and D. H. Lawrence. Joyce, he tries to show, is "the ethically most orthodox of the more eminent writers of this time" (*ASG*, 38). The words on the last page of the story—"His soul had approached that region where dwell the vast hosts of the dead"—make Joyce a religious writer in contrast to the "heretic" Lawrence. The characters of Lawrence's "In the Shadow of the Rose Garden" betray "no respect, or even awareness of moral obligations and seem to be unfurnished with even the most commonplace kind of conscience" (37). Still, Lawrence is considered "a very much greater genius, if not a greater artist, than Hardy" and then lambasted for a lack of sense of humor, "an incapacity for what we ordinarily call thinking," and for "sexual morbidity," but also praised for "an extraordinarily keen sensibility and capacity for profound intuition—intuition from which he commonly drew the wrong conclusions" (58). Eliot, however, recognizes his spiritual struggle. "No man was less a sensualist" (60), and the *Fantasia of the Unconscious* he finds unanswerable as an indictment of the modern world. These harsh comments in *After Strange Gods* are anticipated or developed in different contexts and in different tones. Thus in 1927 Eliot referred contemptuously to his "Tin Chapel Atheism" (*Criterion* 6:179). In a French article Lawrence is labeled a "demoniac, a natural and unsophisticated demoniac with a gospel." "The love-making of Lawrence's characters—and they do nothing else—" seems to him like "some hideous coition of protoplasm" (*Nouvelle Revue Française* 27 [1927]: 164), while a later essay admitted that Lawrence was an "investigator of the religious life," a kind of "*contemplative* rather than a theologian," who arrived at a "religion of power and magic," which is finally "only a religion of autotherapy."[22] In commending a study of Lawrence by Father William Tiverton (a pseudonym for Martin Jarrett-Kerr), Eliot seems to have come to a more favorable conclusion. He still thinks of him "as an ignorant man in the sense that he was unaware of how much he did not know" but calls him now a "man of fitful and profound insights" reaching for a "fundamental truth." "Without being a Christian, he was primarily and always religious."[23] Eliot sums up his relation in a late lecture (1962): about Lawrence "my mind will, I fear, always waver between dislike, exasperation, boredom and admiration." Eliot tells of his readiness to appear for Lawrence's defense in the trial of *Lady Chatterley's Lover* (in 1960) but reiterates his antipathy on the ground of what seems to him Lawrence's egotism, a "strain of cruelty, and a failing in common with Thomas Hardy—the lack of a sense of humour" (*CC*, 24–25). I cannot see that Eliot was ever deeply influenced by Lawrence as has been asserted. He did not care for him as a great novelist: Lawrence "never," he says, "succeeded in making a work of art" (*Criterion* 10 [1930–31]: 769). He praises "magnificent descriptions here and there" (770), some dialogues, and a story, "Two Blue Birds," "which has no relation to Lawrence's own emotional disease" (770). He took Middleton Murry's psychoanalytical diagnosis of a "mother-complex" as proven. Eliot often complained of bad writing in Lawrence. He always thought of Lawrence rather as "a false prophet" (769), a "medicine man" of a strange religion. At most he could sympathize with his criticism of modern civilization.

Eliot saw Lawrence also as a symptom of the decay of Protestantism, of the disappearance of God for which Hardy serves as another example. He calls Hardy "a powerful personality uncurbed by any institutional attachment or by submission to any objective beliefs" (*ASG*, 54). His extreme emotionalism seems to Eliot a symptom of decadence (55). Eliot simply has no use for modern agnostic or atheistic pessimism or even optimism, as witness his disparaging remarks about Meredith. "Most of Meredith's profundity is profound platitude" (*Egoist* 5 [1918]: 114).

Eliot avoided comments on immediate contemporaries, though his preferences are very clear. He admired Wyndham Lewis, a personal friend, and compared *Tarr* to Dostoevsky, though he sees that Lewis is "impressively deliberate, frigid . . . perhaps inhuman would be a better word than frigid" (*Egoist* 5 [1918]: 105). He was greatly impressed by

Djuna Barnes's *Nightwood*, which he felt fulfilled his ideal of a prose which "has the prose rhythm that is prose style, and the musical pattern which is not that of verse." He calls it a work of creative imagination, not a philosophical treatise, and finds in it "a quality of horror or doom very nearly related to that of Elizabethan tragedy" (*Criterion* 16 [1937]: 561, 564). One sees how Eliot could link the book with some of his preoccupations—prose style and Jacobean tragedy—but one cannot help thinking that they blinded him to its failings.

Inevitably we have to come back to some central issues raised by this survey of Eliot's theories and opinions. One must distinguish between three elements: Eliot's theory of literature, which as a matter of course widened to a concept of politics and religion; Eliot's practical criticism, his opinions of writers, his taste; and Eliot's practice as a poet. It would be foolish to deny that these three activities of his mind (one mind, after all) were not interrelated, but it is impossible, as this survey demonstrates, to conclude that they all cohere in a seamless web. Each in its own compartment coheres and has its continuity but one cannot gloss over the fissures between the three. Eliot often says that his criticism is a defense of his practice, is "workshop criticism," but this seems true only on a very general level. He can justify, by his theory, his attempt to keep out his person from his writing, though he hardly succeeded in doing so completely. He can defend his use of colloquial contemporary speech, though much of his poetry obviously deviates from it widely. He can argue for ritual drama and emphasize visual imagery, but his theories do not grapple at all with the actual style and character of his own poetry, and, on the other hand, his theories and concrete opinions far exceed in their application and applicability a mere defense of his poetic practice. If they were mere rationalizations of his practice, they would be of little interest except to students of Eliot's poetry. But surely they want to be and are much more: they claim to be exemplary and they have made many converts. It is sufficient to refer to two distinguished American critics, Allen Tate and Austin Warren. But this relationship between Eliot's theory and practice is a difficult problem outside the scope of this discussion, which aims at metacriticism and must avoid the danger of submerging in a history of poetry. It would lose its focus.

Eliot also said that his theories are "epiphenomenal to his taste." But this also is true only in part. As our survey of Eliot's literary opinions shows, his taste runs often counter to his theories. There is a tension between his preferences for Dante or the metaphysicals and Jacobean dramatists and the French symbolists or even Pound and Joyce, and the literary theory with its emphasis on impersonality, tradition, classicism, order, and reason. On some points Eliot recognized the conflict himself and modified his theories accordingly. The doctrine of impersonality, of objective or objectified feelings, collided with his deep-seated concern for personality and finally for the soul and its salvation. At first Eliot accepted a "total scepticism, an uncynical disillusion" which he found in Bradley (*SE*, 398). He rejected all metaphysical systems "which are condemned to go up like a rocket and come down like a stick," the whole structure "a faquir's show for a penny" (*KE*, 168). The ego is dissolved into immediate experience, and immediate experience is "at either the beginning or end of our journey, annihilation and utter night" (*KE*, 31). But this very resignation and agnosticism (though Eliot would not have liked this term associated with Thomas H. Huxley) seems to have allowed Eliot to embrace Catholic Christianity boldly and literally. Eliot came to believe in the soul, its unity, its immortality, and seems like Hamlet to have feared the after-life. I do not think we can know when exactly Eliot embraced this conviction, but it must have antedated his public conversion by at least ten years. In literary criticism, however, Eliot long resisted the pressure of his new beliefs, partly because he kept, even in his latest stage, a clear consciousness that poetry is not religion and never can replace religion (as Arnold and I. A. Richards hope). From the point of view of literary criticism, it seems a pity that Eliot came to identify the idea of tradition with orthodoxy (*ASG*, 31–32) and that his criticism more and more became a testing of conformity with fixed dogma. The "supervision of the tradition by orthodoxy" (67) which he demanded and practiced made him smell "diabolical influence" everywhere and compile a "primer of Modern Heresy." He looked complacently upon those who refuse to choose between Rome and Canterbury on the one hand and Moscow on the other (Communism was for him a religion) and who refuse to applaud his glorification of an earlier stage of British culture. Still, it seems to me an error to say that Eliot "declined" as a critic after his conversion. He used his gifts as well as ever. But his interests shifted away from literary criticism and thus he was apt to use literature as documents for his Jeremiads on the modern world. He embraced a double standard which dissolves the unity of a work of art as well as the sensibility which goes into its making and the critical act itself. He thus weakened (on behalf of what he felt to be higher interests) the impact of his achievement as a literary critic. Taken in its early purity his literary criticism seems to be very great indeed.

7: I. A. RICHARDS (1893–1979)

IN 1937 I wrote an article, in Czech, for the quarterly of the Prague Linguistic Circle[1] in which I reported on the Cambridge group of literary theorists: I. A. Richards, W. Empson, and F. R. Leavis. I gave a descriptive account of Richards's views up to and including *Coleridge on Imagination* (1934) and made the reservations which seemed necessary to anybody committed to a fundamentally structuralist approach. While I praised Richards's skill in disentangling the sources of misreading of poetry and welcomed his attention to poetic language, I dismissed his psychology and criticized his views on the mode of existence of a literary work of art. Though I reread Richards on several occasions I did not change my opinion and his lecture "Emotive Language Still," which he gave at Yale in 1949,[2] confirmed my view that rumors of Richards's repudiation of his earlier teachings were quite unsupported by public evidence. About the same time, in another paper, "Emotive Meaning Again,"[3] Richards said that "in rereading *Principles* . . . I am more impressed by its anticipations of my later views than by the occurrence of anything to retract. I changed my vocabulary and my metaphors somewhat . . . to present much the same views again" (*SI*, 53n.). Richards must have known what he was talking about.

Since then many years have passed. Richards published another collection of papers, *Speculative Instruments* (1955), which reprints some older pieces but contains much that is new; two slim volumes of his own poems, *Goodbye Earth and Other Poems* (1958) and *The Screens and Other Poems* (1960), which contain prose commentaries and a lecture, "The Future of Poetry"; and scattered lectures and articles among which two, published in the records of a conference on *Style in Language* (1960), are of particular interest.

Here I am inevitably faced again with the figure of Richards. John Crowe Ransom in *The New Criticism* (1941) begins his chapter by saying: "Discussion of the new criticism must start with Mr. Richards. The new criticism very nearly began with him," and Stanley Hyman, in *The Armed*

Vision (1948), echoes the claim that Richards "created modern criticism in the most literal sense." I thus reread his books, and also read, for the first time, some of his early scattered papers and some later pronouncements. I read a long book by W. H. N. Hotopf, *Language, Thought and Comprehension: A Case Study of the Writings of I. A. Richards* (1965) and an excellent book by Jerome Schiller, *I. A. Richards's Theory of Literature* (1969). I hope that I cannot be suspected, as Richards does suspect his critics, of not having read his books (*SI*, 44) and that I shall not confirm his "sad conviction that when you are refuting a view you become too busy to see what it is" (76).

Richards, first, rejects the view that there is an "aesthetic mode or aesthetic state" or "aesthetic emotion" (*PLC*, 11, 15) and argues that "when we look at a picture, or read a poem, or listen to music, we are not doing something quite unlike what we were doing on our way to the Gallery or when we dressed in the morning" (16), or as he formulates abstractly: "The world of poetry has in no sense any different reality from the rest of the world and it has no special laws and no other-worldly peculiarities" (78). But this total abolition of the difference between art and life, between different kinds of behavior—looking at pictures, listening to music, walking to the Gallery, dressing or, to continue in this vein, eating breakfast, doing sums, and so on—cannot satisfy the aesthetician who must, in one way or another, aim at a definition of the specificity of art. Richards sees the problem and, after fumbling with a definition of the difference between ordinary experiences and those due to art as being ascribable to "a greater number of impulses which have to be brought into co-ordination with one another" (110), arrives at his famous definition of the effect of art: "the resolution, inter-inanimation, and balancing of impulses" (113). "Impulses" is a wider term including stimuli which induce in us "attitudes," "imaginal and incipient activities or tendencies of action" (112).

Richards's theory is thus a restatement of the affective theory of art which can be traced back to Aristotle's catharsis and has its immediate ancestors in the tradition of psychological aesthetics in Germany, England, and the United States. We find Richards's precise vocabulary in Ethel D. Puffer's *Psychology of Beauty* (1905), which speaks of the "equilibrium of impulses," and in Wilbur M. Urban's *Valuation* (1909), which belabors the "balance of impulses" within a theory of value. Richards's term for the resulting repose and union, "coenaesthesis," comes from James Ward's *Psychological Principles*. Ward was one of the Cambridge professors active in Richards's undergraduate years. Ultimately the relationship to the whole enormous literature on *Einfühlung* (Lipps, Vernon Lee, and others) is obvious and it, in turn, derives from Dilthey, Robert Vischer, Fechner, and Lotze. In Dilthey, or rather a phase of Dilthey, the anticipations of Richards's theory are particularly striking, though it seems unlikely that Richards would have known these texts. Hugo Münsterberg, to whom Ethel Puffer acknowledges a great debt, is probably an intermediary. In any case, whatever the immediate sources, Richards's central psychological theory is not original with him: its impact is due to the fact that he used it for a modern defense of poetry and was able to apply it more concretely to literary criticism than any of his predecessors. They remained general psychologists, or abstract philosophers, or, like Ethel Puffer, contaminated their aesthetic with sentimental rhetoric.

But was Richards ever able to describe this balancing of impulses more clearly in relation to literature? I doubt it. The only attempt to describe this process is an odd reformulation of the Aristotelian catharsis: "Pity, the impulse to approach and terror, the impulse to retreat, are brought in tragedy to reconciliation" (PLC, 245). This seems a grossly inadequate account even of pity and terror not to speak of their purging. It can be treated only as a metaphor for what is Richards's persistent claim for the effect of poetry: it orders our minds (CI, 227), it makes them more highly organized, and thus makes us happier and healthier.

In terms known to all defenders of art, and particularly to Wordsworth and Shelley, Richards tells us that "the enlargement of the mind, the widening of the sphere of human sensibility, is brought about through poetry" (PLC, 67); that poetry gives us a "shock of discovering how alive with new aspects everything whatever is" (PC, 254); that poetry, owing "to the closeness of its contact with reality," becomes "a powerful weapon for breaking up unreal ideas and responses" (251) or that "it stretches our minds"[4]—all defensible and sensible claims. But then also more extravagantly Richards asserts that poetry "makes a fuller and completer life more easy"[5] and that "it will remake our minds and with them our world" (CI, 229). He deplores that "not a tenth of the power of poetry is released for the general benefit, indeed not a thousandth part" (PC, 321). In a late lecture "The Future of Poetry" (1960) Richards endorses Shelley's peroration on "the poets as the unacknowledged legislators of the world" (Screens, 106) and chides me for having said that "it must be obvious today that this kind of defense of poetry defeats its own purposes" (this History, 2:125). But Richards does not attempt to refute my argument in the next two sentences which he does not quote: "Poetry loses its identity completely in a loose synthesis of philosophy, morality and art. What can be ascribed to all three together or to any one of the other two will not be seriously credited to poetry alone." This is precisely true of Richards's own defense of poetry. Poetry for Richards is "capable of saving us"; it "is a perfectly possible means of overcoming chaos" (*SP,* 95), because in Richards, as in Shelley and in the Neoplatonic tradition, poetry has become identified with myth and religion or rather, in Richards, with myth deprived of its ancient claims to truth and religion stripped of revelation, doctrine, biblical history, and any claim to knowledge. Richards thus revives Matthew Arnold's hope for poetry: "What now passes with us for religion and philosophy will be replaced by poetry" (*Essays in Criticism,* 2nd series [1888], 2). It seems hardly necessary to say that this is an impossible and undesirable goal: men will not give up philosophies, ideologies, and religions for anything remotely resembling poetry in any known form.

More soberly, Richards defends the value of poetry with an argument for a transference from poetry to the other activities of man. The cultivation of poetry is a school of sensibility. Obtuseness in poetic matters implies disabilities in sensibility. Bad taste in poetry reflects unfavorably on our total personality. "A general insensitivity to poetry does witness a low level of general imaginative life" (*PC,* 320). But Richards himself admits that "a man who is stupid with poetry" need not be "stupid with life" (319) and if "stupidity" may be limited to matters of the intellect, he elsewhere pointedly asks, "How truthfully can anyone affirm that students of the humanities are in general more excellent human beings than others?" (*SI,* 98). The two arguments have plausibility only if we take the civilizing function of poetry in the widest and highest sense to include the mythology of Homer, the theology of Dante, the ethics of Shakespeare, and if we focus on the long-range social effect. It can hardly be proved or analyzed but can be presumed, though it would be impossible to isolate it. If we think of the poets there is ample evidence that Richards's view of poetry as an ordering of the mind and as the making of a perfect human being is false: there were madmen, suicides, scoundrels, and many horribly unhappy and disorganized men even among the great poets.

Richards can arrive at such extravagant hopes for poetry because he holds an optimistic, individualistic view of man and his ideals. The healthy mind, a free organization for which "conflicts between different impulses are the greatest evil" (*SP,* 42), is his aim for himself and others. "Man is not a thing to be pushed about, however kindly or beneficently. He is a spirit who learns . . . by exercising the freedom which is his being" (*SI,* 63). There is, Richards believes, no conflict between this individualism and a concern for humanity. He calls himself a "pedagogue" and all his interests in Basic English (invented by C. K. Ogden, his close collaborator), in the United Nations, and so on testify to his love for mankind and its well-being. But this well-being is conceived in terms of utilitarianism, with little feeling for tragic experience or sense of history, and with only a slight interest in social conflict and none in anything which could be called transcendental.

All this has little to do with literary criticism, or apparently so. But the main consequence of Richards's emphasis on the elusive impulses, appetencies, and attitudes was that Richards, in theory at least, was cut off from the object of art, the poem. The psychologism embraced by Richards simply denies the objective structure of a work of art. "The whole state of mind, the mental condition *is* the poem" (*PC*, 204). There is nothing out there. Beauty is "not inherent in physical objects, but a character of some of our responses to objects" (*PLC*, 164). A statue "can produce a certain state of mind. It is this state of mind which matters and which gives its value to the statue" (163). This theme of subjectivity is developed in regard to all aspects of the poem. Words in poetry are "free to mean as they please," "free to waltz about with one another as much as they please" (*SI*, 150). Hence Richards drew the conclusion that poetic language is, by definition, ambiguous (or better, plurisignificant), "liquid," "fluid," "resourceful," open to many diverse and even conflicting interpretations as Richards's pupil William Empson demonstrated in *Seven Types of Ambiguity*, in a way which Richards apparently later felt to be a little "overwhelming" (*SI*, 184). What is true of words and poetic language is true also of meter. "Metre is a part or aspect of the self-organization of the mind" (*CI*, 118). "Its effect is not due to our perceiving a pattern in something outside us, but to our becoming patterned ourselves" (*PLC*, 139). Images and metaphors imply no compulsion on our part to visualize. People differ radically on this point and there is no reason why they should react uniformly. Tragedy happens also in our mind: it gives us joy but "this is not an indication that 'all's right with the world' or that 'somewhere, somehow, there is Justice'; it is an indication that all is right here and now in the nervous system" (246). The romantic poet's concept of an "active universe" has nothing to do with nature as studied by science: it is a mere projection of the poet's mind onto nature, an animistic superstition (*CI*).

The bridge to the work of art collapses completely. At times Richards draws the logical consequences. "The balanced poise" achieved by art "can be given by a carpet or a pot or by a gesture as unmistakably as by the Parthenon, it may come about through an epigram as clearly as through a Sonata. . . . The balance is not in the structure of the stimulating object, it is in the response" (*PLC*, 248). Thus it is "less important to like 'good' poetry and dislike 'bad' than to be able to use them both as means of ordering our minds" (*PC*, 349). These passages justify the view that poetry, in Richards, is reduced to mental therapy, to a harmless drug where the character of the object (a pot, a carpet, a gesture) or the quality of the object (good or bad poetry) ceases to matter. The door is opened to complete anarchy in criticism, as the only standard is the needs of the person using bad or good poems, pots, carpets, and gestures, to achieve "mental health" (*PLC*, 248). One wonders why people built Parthenons, painted enormous frescoes, composed symphonies, wrote lengthy epics, if they could have achieved the same results by making pots, carpets, and, easiest of all, gestures. From the point of view of critical theory which conceives its aim as "the common pursuit of judgment," no greater aberration and abdication can be conceived. Judged as psychological aesthetics Richards has managed to describe in different terms the unity in multiplicity, the blocking off from overt action, and the restful satisfaction of aesthetic experience, all characteristics well known in traditional Kantian aesthetics. But who has ever observed the "very complex tide of neural settings" (135) or knows anything of "distorted impulses" or "convulsions" caused by stimuli (263) or would be able to relate these creatures of science fiction to a concrete work of art? Happily this is only one aspect of Richards's theory.

The psychological account of the aesthetic experience is combined with a theory of language expounded in his and Ogden's *Meaning of Meaning* (1923). It brought the new suspicion of language and the confusions caused by its use into focus and analyzed the different aspects of verbal meaning acutely. In difference from the linguists and philosophers who had concerned themselves with the problem of meaning, Richards and Ogden thought also about meaning in poetry and the peculiar status of poetic language. They solved it by making a simple distinction: there are "two totally distinct uses of language: the referential and the emotive" (*PLC*, 261). Poetry uses, or rather is, emotive language. Thus "it ought to be impossible to talk about poetry or religion as though they are capable of giving 'knowledge.'" "A poem has no concern with limited and directed reference. It tells, or should tell us, nothing" (*MM*, 158). Richards argues that truth and doctrine have no place in poetry and that didactic verse is necessarily of low value (*PLC*, 75–76). He shares Tolstoy's view that poetry is the communication of feelings, though he does not, as Tolstoy does, limit their range to good feelings promoting the brotherhood of man. Poetry in Richards is radically cut off from philosophy, ideology, doctrine, and knowledge of any kind.

Richards consistently tries to face the problem of the cognitive value
of poetry with his psychological approach, by discussing "belief," that is,
the question whether the reader is required to believe in the poet's professed doctrines and ideas, and, on the other hand, whether a poet needs
to have or convey a set of ideas or doctrines. He rightly answers both
questions in the negative but exaggerates the justified distrust of intellectual doctrine in poetry to a complete rejection of any implied world-
view. Thus he proclaims that "we must free poetry from entanglement
with belief" (*SP*, 96), asserts that "we need no beliefs, and indeed must
have none, if we are to read *King Lear*" (72), and criticizes Yeats and
D. H. Lawrence for their doctrinal commitments which he considers ar-
chaic and superstitious. He hopes for a poetry without any doctrinal
commitment: he thought he found such a poem in T. S. Eliot's *The Waste
Land* which, supposedly, "effects a complete severance between his poetry and *all* beliefs" (76n.).

Richards, however, modified his position sometimes by introducing a
distinction between "emotional" and "intellectual" belief (*PC*, 278).
Donne's sonnet "At the round earth's imagined corners" may be given
"the fullest emotional belief while withholding intellectual belief" (278);
but this is apparently an inferior attitude. The "poem requires *actual
belief* in the doctrine for its full and perfect imaginative realization" (272–
73). A little further on we are required to give "emotional belief" to
Shakespeare's "The Phoenix and the Turtle" (270), but then a few pages
later Richards modifies this again and says sensibly that "the idea is
neither believed nor disbelieved, nor doubted nor questioned: it is just
present" (275) and that "the question of belief or disbelief, in the intellectual sense, never arises when we are reading well" (277). The whole
mare's nest seems due to Coleridge's striking phrase on "the willing
suspension of disbelief," a formula originally derived from Moses Men-
delssohn's discussion of theatrical illusion. There its meaning is clear
enough: we must suspend our everyday disbelief that in sitting in a chair,
in a theater, we witness events in, say, Alexandria at the time of Antony
and Cleopatra, and we might argue that the same problem arises in
reading. We must not disbelieve in elves, dragons, centaurs, and the
phoenix, though it is hard to see why this is necessary for understanding,
enjoying, and even composing a poem about "The Phoenix and the Turtle." Shakespeare might very well have known that there is no such bird
and still have composed the poem, just as many other poets wrote about
giants and fairies, Leda and Daphne, without believing in their historical
existence. Nor is it true that we need not bring any beliefs to a reading
of *King Lear*: we need not believe in the historical truth of the plot but

we must believe in the distinction between right and wrong, gratitude and ingratitude, cruelty and charity. Nor is Eliot's *The Waste Land* "severed from all beliefs" (however negative), nor does Yeats's or Lawrence's poetry require for our understanding a belief in the phases of the moon or the dark gods of the blood. The whole theory which worries a psychological problem varying from person to person, the exact degree of conviction as to the reality and truth of poetic statements, is an attempt to dissolve the old problem of poetic truth: the relation of poetry to reality, its claim to knowledge which cannot be disposed of either by simply rejecting old-fashioned "revelation" theories or by reducing the question to an issue of degrees of credulity or feelings of certitude. One can very well uphold a resolutely secular view of poetry without accepting the sharp dichotomy of intellect and feeling, object and subject, which Richards embraces.

This psychologism is put to so severe a strain that Richards himself felt the necessity of overcoming it by an appeal to some standard. One occurs in the discussion of badness in poetry (*PLC*, 199ff.) where he makes a distinction between an unsuccessful communication of a valuable experience exemplified by a little imagistic poem by H. D., "The Pool," and a successful communication of a trivial experience illustrated by a sonnet of Ella Wheeler Wilcox. But surely the distinction drawn by Richards is unverifiable: how can anyone know that H. D.'s experience has some value and what value for whom and when and why that experience is not communicated in the poem, which is our only source for that experience? How can anyone prove that Mrs. Wilcox's poem "reproduces the state of the mind of the writer very exactly" (201)? Actually Richards criticizes the poem, the supposedly successful communication, well enough: its confused imagery, "the heavy regular rhythm, the dead stamp of the rimes, the obviousness of the description, the triteness of the close," all observable traits in the text which have nothing to do with the supposed "appeasement of the restless spirit" achieved by Mrs. Wilcox. Richards's observations suggest that a critical reader would be annoyed and irritated by the poem rather than achieve the "equilibrium of impulses" Richards postulates.

Nor is the second attempt to go beyond the psychic equipoise much more successful. Richards distinguishes four meanings of the word *poem*: "the artist's experience, such of it as is relevant, the experience of a qualified reader who made no mistakes, an ideal and perfect reader's possible experience, and our own actual experience" (*PLC*, 225). Richards rejects the first and fourth definitions, as he recognizes that the artist's experience is unique and unrepeatable, and as our own actual experience cannot be the standard for the reading of a poem—for the reason that it varies from individual to individual and would lead to the conclusion that there are as many poems as readers and readings. Richards decides that "we cannot take any single experience as the poem: we must have a class of more or less similar experiences instead." This class will be "composed of all actual experiences, occasioned by the words," which do not differ within certain limits from "the original experience of the poet" (226). Richards cannot tell, however, how we could determine this class and the limits of the deviation from the poet's experience which he himself recognizes to have been unique. "The standard experience," he concludes, "is the relevant experience of the poet when contemplating the completed composition" (227). But in a note Richards seems to admit the difficulties of this solution. "The poet might be dissatisfied without reason. Coleridge thought *Kubla Khan* merely a 'psychological curiosity' without poetic merits, and may have been justified in some degree. If he was not, it is his dream experience which we should presumably have to take as our standard" (227n.). The word "presumably" shows that Richards himself was not contented with this paradoxical solution. The attempt to find the mode of existence of a work of art in the inaccessible psychic state of its author, whether during the act of creation or during an act of contemplating the finished composition, or even in the anarchic variety of any number of readers' responses, leads to potentially absurd conclusions. Richards's solution fails because it conceals highly doubtful dogmas. He assumes that the equilibrium of a reader of good poetry is more valuable than the equilibrium of an illiterate or unpoetic person who does not "need" poetry. It remains unclear why a more complex organization of impulses should be better than a less complex one and how a system of balances can be said to contribute to the growth of the mind. Nor is it clear that poetry is communication of specific emotional experiences of an author and that reading a poem enables us to have an identical or very similar experience.

Richards cannot extricate himself from the maze created by the idea of "sincerity," a specialty of the tradition of English criticism. He sees some of its difficulty, as he is by taste and training suspicious of the "spontaneous overflow of powerful feelings." He sees that the feelings in a poem "need not be actual personal 'real, live feelings,' they may be," he admits, "imagined feelings" (*PC,* 280). He disapproves of the saying that "poetry should come from the heart, i.e., the poet is unpacking his heart in words" (*CI,* 208). He sees that "sincerity" is associated with spontaneity, with Rousseau's romantic fiction, the "natural man," but he still concludes: "Whatever it is, it is the quality we most insistently require in poetry" (*PC*, 282). It remains for him "a criterion of excellence in poetry" (298n.) but he tries to redefine it, to give it a special meaning for which he appeals to passages from Confucius which are none too clearly related to Richards's thought and vocabulary. Sincerity, we finally make out, is "nothing but the desire for self-completion" (285), "obedience to that tendency which 'seeks' a more perfect order within the mind" (288). It is our old friend "the ordered mind": a poem is "sincere" and hence valuable if it helps us to "order our mind." As a test he suggests "something like a technique or ritual for heightening sincerity" (290), which turns out to be a list of themes for meditation on subjects such as "man's loneliness; the facts of birth and death, and its inexplicable oddity; the inconceivable immensity of the Universe; Man's place in the perspective of time; the enormity of our ignorance" (290). In the later editions Richards dropped the introductory advice: "Sit by the fire (with eyes shut and fingers pressed firmly upon the eyeballs) and consider with as full 'realization' as possible." A secular version of Loyola's exercises is propounded, which elicited T. S. Eliot's comment that Richards "tries to preserve emotions without the beliefs in which their history has been involved."[6] But Richards's list seems to be a good list of metaphysical and speculative problems to which religions have given their own answers. Still, meditating on them will not help us to judge poetry. Many have thought about these problems profoundly without being poets and there were fine poets who did not concern themselves with them. Richards's metaphysical pathos, his philosophical wonder, is apparent in such passages: it does not help literary criticism.

It contrasts oddly with his usual trust in science and the claim he makes for his criticism to establishing or at least preparing a science. Richards is, however, right when he protests against being called a "Behaviorist" (*SI*, 118). His point of view is rather that of British empiricism: his psychology comes from James Ward and G. F. Stout rather than from J. B. Watson. Still, in his early writings he makes many deferential gestures to neurology and its future advances (*PLC*, 170), comfortably relegating an epistemological problem to the "jungles of neurology" (120). On occasion he speaks in purely biological terms, equating the mind with the nervous system (83) and calling "mental events identical with neural events" (84), even producing a preposterous diagram (116) which depicts the eye and nerves leading in zigzags to attitudes from the words "Arcadia, Night, a Cloud, Pan and the Moon." Even in much later papers a collection of misreadings is called "of high significance for biology" (*SI*, 182) and is considered to be "of medical interest" (186). The early attempt to reduce thought to cause, to abolish the distinction between "awareness" and "causation" (*PLC*, 90) assumes an astonishingly naive theory of knowledge. But in the same book, we must not forget, Richards admits that "the relation between an awareness and what it is aware of" (89) is a mystery, as is the reason "why some events are conscious but not others" (86). Still, he can say that he writes on Coleridge "as a Materialist trying to interpret . . . the utterances of an extreme Idealist" (*CI*, 19) and agrees with "a metaphysical materialism which supposes that the mind is just certain ways of operation of the body" (60).

Richards thinks of his criticism as a science, a "new science" (*CI*, 43), at least as preparing, through experiment, the transformation of present-day criticism into a science (137); or as "a cooperative technique of enquiry that may become entitled to be named a science" (xii). Still, he is right in rejecting the accusation of "scientism" in the sense of a "belief in the universality of the scientific method" (*SI*, 48). Poetry in his wide sense is excluded from science and opposed to it and the defense of poetry, while carried on with weapons he considers scientific, is precisely aimed at reserving and preserving a special activity and its effect. Poetic language is emotive and is thus exempt from the scientific standard of correct reference and objective truth. But on the other hand Richards, after all, hopes for an ultimate total victory of science. "We have," he says in a late paper (1952), "to seek a way by which Value must unrestrictedly come into the care of Science" (145). "Fact would determine value, if the account could be encompassing enough" (16), and science will grow in time into "something which could satisfy the needs which the Religions more or less provided for," though this would require "considerable changes in the Rules of Scientific Evidence" (143).

In his later writings Richards has abandoned the neurological terminology and has adopted terms from the new information theory: "feedforward" and "feedback" (*SI*, 27), "message," "signal," "encoding," and "decoding," repeating his semantic scheme in a diagram with the new names. But finally he recognizes that the information theory is used to serve up the oldest of all fallacies which he calls "the vulgar packaging view"—the idea that the poet wraps his experience "in a neat and elegant verbal package" (*Screens*, 124). These are all attempts to bridge the gap between the two cultures—Richards, in general, adhering to the view that there are, at least in our time, two distinct realms: that of science and that of poetry, myth, and religion. While upholding the fundamental dichotomy he still tried to find something which would bridge the gulf. In the book on Coleridge he called science a myth: "All views of Nature are taken to be projections of the mind, and the religions as well as science are included among myths" (*CI*, 177). But the myth of science has, we must note, a special status. It has "the unrestricted claim upon our overt action," for example, "getting out of the way of motor-cars" (178) and much later he confirmed that "I hold, *and still do,* that science is true—i.e., that it says verifiable things" (*SI,* 55). It seems an odd idea to speak of "getting out of the way of motor-cars" as science! The term *myth* carries no disparagement and implies no contrast (56). All the cognitive and symbolizing activities of man are considered myths, an extension of the term which seems inadvisable. But on the other hand Richards insists that "science could not be the world government" (55), that "there are only rules of scientific behavior but no creed and no administrative headquarters, no court of last appeal, no focus of authority, for Science" (177). Slowly Richards had modified the original linguistic distinction between referential and emotive language to allow a certain overlap. In 1946 he devised a chart of the functions of science and poetry in which the same functions appear on both sides though in different order of importance. "Indicate" and "characterize" appear on the side of poetry as well as of science, below "appraise" and "influence" and the same function of poetry is now called "realizing" (*Yale Review* 39 [1946]: 110). But this recognition of the cognitive function of poetry is strangely disguised by the invention of a contrast between "the troth of poetry" and "the truth of science." The word "troth" (pronounced, he tells us, "trouth" [*SI,* 140]) seems to be suggested by Bacon quoting a Spanish proverb, "Tell a lie to find a troth," which Richards may have come across in Eneas Sweetland Dallas's *Gay Science* 2 (1866): 214, a now almost forgotten Victorian book on criticism. It seems an awkward device to replace the earlier term *pseudo-statements* which, Richards complains, has been misunderstood to mean "false statements," while he only wanted to say that statements in poetry are not statements at all, are neither true nor false, do not have "an assertorial clip" upon them. They are something like Meinong's "Annahmen," Vaihinger's "Als ob," or more probably like Bentham's "fictions" which had been studied by Richards's collaborator C. K. Ogden. Troths are "faiths, loyalties, resolutions, commitments and convictions." In our troths "we recover our control over the milieu and ourselves" (177–78). In short, troths order our minds. The term is another way of formulating Richards's central thesis: poetry may have no truth value but has a value for life—for the good, ordered life.

Poetry, however, for Richards may mean many things: in the widest sense all value judgment, religion, commitments, beliefs but also, bewilderingly, a specific kind of verse. Nor does he seem clear whether in defending poetry he is not defending the study of poetry and even simply

the use of emotive language. Richards must think that his theory applies
to all forms and kinds of imaginative writing. There are passages in
which he lists prose writers such as Henry James, Bunyan, Defoe, and
Swift on equal footing with poets (*PLC*, 211, 213), and in early years he
wrote on Dostoevsky and E. M. Forster. But genre questions hardly interest him nor is he concerned with historical types, movements, or traditions. In practice, all the emphasis is on the analysis of lyric poetry
and on attempts to discriminate among English poems and poets.

It is a paradox of Richards's work that here he can ignore the psychological jargon about "mental equipoise," "patterning of impulses," and
such metaphors of the mind as "an arrangement of many magnetic nee-
dles" (*SP*, 24) and still analyze poems as objects open to inspection. We
are never told so, but Richards does assume that we feel into objects (as
the theory of *Einfühlung* does), see in them not simply stimuli of our
desire or need for order but submit to impressions which we have to
grasp correctly and undistorted. Even the somewhat comic diagram with
the wiggly nerves can be translated into a fruitful analysis of the strata
of a poem: (1) the printed words; (2) the sounds imagined or voiced
which for unaccountable reasons Richards calls "images"; (3) the relatively free images, that is, visualizations evoked by the words;
(4) references; (5) emotions; and (6) affective-volitional attitudes. Richards is particularly effective in arguing against the divorce of sound and
meaning, meter and sense. His dummy stanza made up of nonsense
words in a pattern from Milton's "Ode on Christ's Nativity" (*PC*, 232) is
a convincing demonstration that "meter cannot be judged apart from
the sense and feelings of the words" (230). In analyzing metaphor Richards sensibly combats the doctrine that metaphors must be visualized
concretely. Metaphors, he argues, constitute meaning, a verbal device.
Tenor and vehicle (terms introduced by Richards to avoid the ambiguity
of "image") interact and cannot be confined to their resemblances. "The
disparities between tenor and vehicle" are "as much operative as the
similarities" (*PR*, 127). Also Coleridge's distinction between imagination
and fancy turns out to be, in Richards's interpretation, rather a typology
of metaphors than a distinction between faculties of the mind; it is the
contrast between a witty metaphor when there is only one point of contact
between tenor and vehicle as in Samuel Butler's lines, "And like a lobster
boil'd, the morn / From black to red began to turn," and an imaginative
metaphor such as Coleridge's favorite from *Venus and Adonis*, "Look, how
a bright star shooteth from the sky / So glides he in the night from Venus'
eye," where it is possible to discover more and more cross-connections
between the units of meaning. Coleridge's distinction between an "esem-

plastic" imagination and an associative fancy is used by Richards for what he insists is a purely descriptive typology of metaphors. Though he considers the distinction valid, Richards reduces it to a quantitative difference. "A counting of relations" (*CI*, 83) decides what is imagination and what is fancy and presumably even the degree of imagination. But the consequences of this interpretation are not drawn. Richards actually prefers fanciful, witty, "baroque" metaphors. This taste is supported by another typology he devised: the distinction between poetry of exclusion and inclusion—terms derived from Santayana.[7] In Richards "exclusion" means limitation to a specific mood or definite emotion (*PLC,* 249) while "inclusion" refers to complex poetry, permitting "heterogeneity," "rivalry and conflict" between feelings. One distinction between these two types of which Richards makes little became central in the theory of Cleanth Brooks: the test of irony. Exclusive or simple poetry cannot bear "an ironical contemplation" (250). Thus in spite of the psychological vocabulary about impulses, attitudes, and appetencies, Richards stimulated the analysis of poetic texts in terms of the interaction of words and the functions of imagery. From this comes his impact on the New Criticism which, though often adhering to his psychological vocabulary, showed little interest in his psychological speculations.

Richards's greatest and most beneficial influence was due to *Practical Criticism* (1929). It can be easily criticized adversely if we judge it as the scientific experiment it claims to be. There is little objective methodology used: there is no analysis in quantitative terms, nor is there even a proper method of questionnaire formulation, nor any kind of safeguard against what was clearly the danger of the situation, the reckless showing off by the "subjects" writing on the poems. Nor could Richards guard against obvious leg-pulling. But in spite of the uncontrolled documentation, the book manages to analyze the sources of misreadings and, convincingly, to prove the disorientation which affects students as soon as they are deprived of the prop of names, their authority, and their anchorage in history. The detailed classification of the sources of misreadings seems needlessly overlapping; some of the groups could be combined but, on the whole, the scheme is convincing. The plain sense of poetry turned out to be the first and major difficulty. Lack of sensibility (for instance, a misapprehension of the right rhythm of a poem) is the second source of misreading. Misinterpretation of figurative language is the third. The fourth is misunderstandings due to erratic personal associations. The fifth is the trap of stock responses, the sixth sentimentality, the seventh inhibitions, "hardness of heart," and the eighth the interference of doctrinal loyalties: religious, political, and philosophical prejudices. The

ninth is assumptions about poetic technique such as the requirement of
pure rhyme. And finally as the tenth source of failure are critical assumptions and prior demands on the nature of poetry. One could possibly reclassify these distinctions by grouping them as either deviations
into the too general, conventional, and trite (for which Richards uses the
term *stock responses*) or deviations towards the too individual, the arbitrarily personal.

The whole book assumes something which Richards's theory had
shirked: the correctness and validity of a specific interpretation, the objectivity of a structure of determination given by a poem. Richards must
believe that some or many of the readings of his students are dead wrong
and that many judgments and rankings of the poems for their aesthetic
quality are mistaken while his and some of his subjects' interpretations
and judgments are right. Why are some of the poems good and others
definitely bad? He cannot demonstrate this in terms of the "balance" of
his students or their mental "needs," yet he can do so by appealing to
the text, by showing that the imagery is confused, the rhythm jingling,
the theme trite and sentimental.

In a supplementary piece to *Practical Criticism,* "Fifteen Lines from
Landor" (1933), Richards faced the problem of correctness of reading
systematically for the first time. He reasserts his faith in subjective evidence: "A judgment seemingly about a poem is chiefly about its reader."
"An opinion about it . . . really tells us how it has been read under certain
mental conditions." Then Richards admits, "It may seem that on this
view the difference between a good and bad reading has gone; that there
is no sense left for 'correct' as applied to interpretations." "This would
be a mistake," he concedes and discusses various possible meanings of
the term "correct," deciding that the test for the correctness of any interpretation is "its internal coherence and its coherence with all else that
is relevant" (*SI,* 195–96). But how can he, on this psychological premise,
have access to a coherence theory? He himself continues: "But this is an
unnecessarily fictitious way of talking. We can say instead that this inner
and outer coherence is the correctness. When an interpretation hangs
together (without conflicting with anything else: history, literary tradition, etc.) we call it correct—when it takes into account all the items given
for interpretation and orders the other items by which it interprets them,
in the most acceptable manner." But what can "acceptable" mean in such
a theory? It seems that there is a problem behind such an adjective. "We
may not have 'the correct interpretation' of a passage and we probably
won't have it, and we might not recognize it for such if we had it; in this
our definition agrees nicely with the ordinary use of 'correct'—which

perhaps follows some such definition as 'co-responding' to what was in 'the poet's mind' " (196). In Richards's characteristic manner we are left up in the air, sent to an unknown and inaccessible state of the poet's mind, and even this gesture is hesitating, tempered with "perhaps."

Still, he had again to face the question of "correctness." He can on occasion speak, without qualm, of an "error" in interpretation (*SI*, 101) and of a "desire to read faithfully" (*PC*, 242). In the early writings Richards had made a sharp distinction between the technical and the critical part of a work of art and had ascribed little interest to the technical: form, unity, composition, expression, rhythm, stress, plot, character are given as examples of terms used as "though they stood for qualities inherent to things outside the mind" (*PLC*, 21); but they are only states of mind, experiences which Richards can describe in terms of stimuli, attitudes, and balances. Still, he came to recognize that there is the problem of "relevance of interpretation" (*SI*, 102), of "the mistake, the inadmissible interpretation" (*Style*, 242). He now concedes that "an appeal to some hypothetical events in Shakespeare's mind, or to equally hypothetical events in any reader's mind is not . . . propitious procedure," though oddly enough without giving any reasons he says "in a novel or play or sermon I would use such appeals unhesitatingly" (245). He struggles then to explain why an obvious misreading of a word in a sonnet by Shakespeare is mistaken: a knowledge of the English of Shakespeare's time and a knowledge of etymology is invoked as well as, more generally, "the over-all mutual relevance, a control of the whole over part" (249). The limitations that the system of a language imposes on any component, Richards now recognizes, "much resemble those that a society imposes on its members or those an organism imposes on its constituent cells" (250). This analogy is an old one in romantic criticism but, in Richards, it remains not only a metaphor comparing poem with man, beast, and plant but is conceived on the analogy of the human totality of mind and body, of a growing being within its society, language, and tradition. Richards once even hits on the "circle of understanding" known to any theory of interpretation since Schleiermacher. "The sovereign formula in all reading is that we must pass to judgment of details from judgment of the whole. It is always disastrous to reverse the process" (*PC*, 40). He does not, however, develop this insight further and stays with the organism analogy which, if pressed, leads, I think, to new errors: to an obscuring of the structure of the work of art which is not at all like a living being but is a coherent system of signs, norms, and values.

Nevertheless, the concept of organism, the parallel of poem and total man underlies Richards's critical standards and judgments. He appeals to the old standard of unity and harmony when he discusses E. M. Forster's *Howards End*. He objects to the conflict between the "survival theme," the half-mystical preoccupation with the succession of generations, and the sociological thesis, "the separation of people of vision and people of action."[8] The conflict "is the source of that elusive weakness which . . . disqualified *Howards End* as one of the world's greatest novels." The criterion of harmony is extended also to the postulate of a harmony with the trend of the time. Discussing Yeats and D. H. Lawrence, Richards objects that they are "inconsistent with the general development, a consideration of extreme importance in judging the value of a poet's work" (*PLC*, 197). On the other hand T. S. Eliot is praised for being on the main track, with the tide of the time (197n.). But all these three poets are still ranked as specialists and not as universalists, such as Shakespeare who appeals to human nature of all times.

Richards rejects historicism—the attempt to reduce poets and thinkers to "socio-economico-political products," to their presumed motivations whether studied by Freudian, Marxist, or propaganda analysis (*SI*, 82)—convinced as he is of the basic unity of mankind, the continuity of tradition from Plato to our time, of the convergence of the most alien civilizations, Chinese and English, and of the healing and civilizing power of poetry in the past and the future.

There is something gallant but also quixotic in Richards's great faith in the power of a general theory of language and poetry from which he expects "new powers over our minds comparable to those which systematic physical inquiries are giving us over our environment" (*CI*, 232). Nothing seems to point to such a future. Richards's theory of poetry as long as it is entangled in his psychology and operates with the simple concept of emotive language seems to me an impasse in criticism. But where he managed to look at texts, gave an account of misreadings, analyzed observable traits of a work of art, Richards found his way back to the organistic tradition of poetic theory descending from Aristotle through the Germans to Coleridge. But emphasizing these insights we assimilate him to something known before and deny what, after all, however extravagantly, was the stimulating novelty of his theory: the radical rejection of aesthetics, the resolute reduction of the work of art to a mental state, the denial of truth-value to poetry, and the defense of poetry as emotive language ordering our mind and giving us equilibrium and mental health.

"Perhaps," says Stanley Hyman, "more than any man since Bacon, Richards has taken all knowledge as his province, and his field the entire mind of man" (*The Armed Vision*, 315). But this seems wildly exaggerated;

Richards is, on the contrary, not a Bacon or a Hegel, or even a Dilthey or a Croce, but a specialist obsessed with one central idea, the critique of language which he has applied to many subject matters and which has led him into *Basic English, How to Read a Page, Mencius on the Mind,* and so on. He is not "the greatest and most important of practising literary critics" (ibid.). There is of course no reason why he should have gone outside of his chosen field of interest; still, he has not written on contemporary literature, has never attempted literary history or the characterization of any individual writer, and has not done any technical analysis of style. One could argue that Richards's lack of interest in the kind of stylistics practiced on the Continent (by the Russian formalists, the Czech structuralists, German *Romanisten* such as Leo Spitzer and Erich Auerbach) has rather widened the gulf between English and American criticism and developments on the Continent. Richards's few critical pronouncements on individual works are often demonstrably mistaken. The analysis of Hopkins's "Windhover," while meritorious as one of the first serious discussions of Hopkins, does not read the poem rightly as it ignores the address to Christ. The discussion of *The Waste Land* is refuted by the text and by Eliot's later development. The references to "Kubla Khan" seem quite unsound. The early article on "The God of Dostoyevsky" (*Forum* 78 [1927]: 97) misinterprets the thought completely when Richards concludes that Dostoevsky considered belief in a deity "inessential." But all of this hardly matters: the stimulus that Richards gave to English and American criticism (particularly Empson and Cleanth Brooks) by turning it resolutely to the question of language, its meaning and function in poetry, will always insure his position in any history of modern criticism.

8: F. R. LEAVIS (1895–1978) AND THE SCRUTINY GROUP

IN 1963, the name of F. R. Leavis appeared in many American newspapers. The *New York Times* carried his picture and a shocked report of a lecture at Downing College, Cambridge, delivered February 28, 1962, attacking Sir Charles Snow and his pamphlet *The Two Cultures and the Scientific Revolution.*[1] The violent tone of Leavis's criticism and the even more violently vituperative rash of letters answering Leavis in the British press caused an enormous sensation. Few commentators sided with Leavis: as far as I know only Lionel Trilling in an article, "Science, Literature and Culture: The Leavis-Snow Controversy,"[2] though deploring Leavis's "unexampled ferocity," saw that Leavis was right in dismissing Sir Charles's contrast between an old bad literary and a new good scientific culture. Still, Leavis damaged his case not only by the acerbity of his tone but by confusing the issue with a denunciation of the quality of Snow's novels. It is, however, not true that Leavis did not argue the case for literature at all. He not only denounced the emptiness of the "social hope" held out by Snow, but he tried to show, though briefly and obliquely, that men of letters such as Ruskin and Arnold came to grips with the social question and that imaginative novelists such as Conrad and Lawrence offered an ideal of life lived with self-awareness, intelligence, and responsibility totally inaccessible to the uncritical faith in hygienic and technological progress embraced by Sir Charles Snow. Unfortunately Leavis focused on the local English and even Cambridge issue of teaching literature and literary criticism, which he felt was endangered by the spread of scientific education and by the academic scholarship and criticism of the ruling professors of literature. Leavis was about to retire, at sixty-seven, from his lectureship, and he felt that his work and influence was being destroyed or discontinued. It was a parting shot, a bitter gesture of defiance.

Contrary to a widespread impression, Leavis did not and does not represent English teaching at Cambridge. Rather, he always struggled on the fringe of the university in opposition to the ruling group. For five years (1931–36) he was even denied a lectureship. In E. M. Tillyard's little book, *The Muse Unchained* (1958), which professes to give "an intimate account of the revolution of English studies at Cambridge," Leavis is pointedly ignored, though his periodical, *Scrutiny,* is condemned for its dogmatism and authoritarian tone (128–29). Leavis, in spite of official disapproval, succeeded in establishing a potent center of English studies at Downing College, which has carried his influence far and wide into English education through the agency of small but devoted groups of disciples. *Scrutiny,* which ran for twenty-one years, from 1932 to 1953, may not have been a financial success, but it became a widely noticed mouthpiece of the group. The Cambridge University Press reprinted the complete run of the nineteen volumes of the magazine. An anthology from *Scrutiny, The Importance of Scrutiny,* edited by Eric Bentley (1948), first attracted attention to the group in this country; paperback editions of Leavis's writings are penetrating into the remotest college bookshops of the United States, and the seven-volume *Pelican Guide to English Literature* (1954–61), edited by one of Leavis's disciples, Boris Ford, has sold at a tremendous rate. It is almost entirely written by former contributors to *Scrutiny* or personal pupils and represents Leavis's views most faithfully. A number of Leavis's closest associates have achieved academic status or at least reputation as critics: for example, L. C. Knights is well known for his pamphlet *How Many Children Had Lady Macbeth?* (1933), his book *Drama and Society in the Age of Jonson* (1937), a collection of essays, *Explorations* (1947), *Some Shakespearean Themes* (1959), and *An Approach to Hamlet* (1960). Derek Traversi, a Welshman in spite of his Italian name, the author of two well-known books on Shakespeare,[3] is another Leavisite. Martin Turnell's books, *The Classical Moment* (1946), *The Novel in France* (1951), *Baudelaire* (1953), and *The Art of French Fiction* (1959), constitute a large body of comment on modern French literature. An American student of Leavis, Marius Bewley, has written two books, *The Complex Fate* (1952) and *The Eccentric Design* (1959), on the tradition of the American nineteenth-century novel. There is even a Frenchman, Henri Fluchère, the author of *Shakespeare* (1948; Eng. trans., 1953) and *Laurence Sterne* (1961), who has had early associations with Leavis and sympathizes with his general outlook.

I mention these facts, which could be easily added to, in order to suggest that Leavis's own view of his utter failure and isolation is a case of grossly misplaced self-pity. It is undoubtedly true that Leavis suffered persecution: he was frequently treated with silent contempt or dismissed as a "cold intellectual." Leavis was, after all, reaping what he sowed. It would be childish to try to ascertain who, in each instance, began the fight. Leavis, no doubt, antagonized the older academic scholars and emphasized his differences from Eliot and what in England is called the school of "Christian discrimination"; he always rejected Marxism and its allies; and he has shown only contempt for the mass media of literary information—the *Times Literary Supplement,* the Third Program of the BBC, the Sunday papers, and the left-wing weeklies. He has also, with some perversity, underlined his differences from the American New Critics and from F. W. Bateson, the editor of the rival journal, *Essays in Criticism.* Leavis was a man with a chip on his shoulder, a man of strong convictions, and even resentments, of harsh polemical manners, who did not practice diplomacy and sometimes not even ordinary courtesy. He should have been pleased that, with all these handicaps of temperament and situation, he succeeded in establishing himself as the most influential English critic of this century after Eliot. There is a Leavis position, even an orthodoxy which can be described and criticized.

Leavis's initial views were a development of Eliot's insight and taste modified by some moral and generally cultural preoccupations reminiscent of Matthew Arnold. Leavis (as he is the first to acknowledge)[4] is deeply influenced by the early Eliot. His first major book, *New Bearings in English Poetry* (1932), can be described as an exposition, development, and application of Eliot's point of view: he starts with a sharp criticism of the Victorian and Georgian tradition, its conceptions of the "poetical," its escape into a dream world, its loss of touch with the intelligence of the age which led to the plight of poetry in the modern world as something inconsequential, as a polite amusement. In describing the situation at the end of the war, Leavis singles out for praise only the later Yeats, a few poems by Hardy, and something in Edward Thomas. He comes down hard on Rupert Brooke, A. E. Housman, and Robert Bridges, and then launches into an exposition of T. S. Eliot, commenting on *The Waste Land, Gerontion,* and *Ash-Wednesday* perceptively and sympathetically. The chapter on Pound is less favorable; but Leavis admires *High Selwyn Mauberley* as a great poem, while he is—very properly—uneasy about the *Cantos,* which "appear to be little more than a game—a game serious with the seriousness of pedantry" (*NB,* 155). The chapter on Hopkins was one of the earliest highly laudatory criticisms, a piece which seems to me still thoroughly convincing in its emphasis on Hopkins's integrity and novelty, in its concern to dismiss the attempts to reconcile Hopkins with Victorianism, and its lack of interest in Hopkins's metrical theory. He concludes, "A technique so much concerned with inner division, friction, and psychological complexities in general has a special bearing on the problems of contemporary poetry. He is likely to prove, for our time and the future, the only influential poet of the Victorian age, and he seems to me the greatest" (193). The love for Hopkins distinguishes Leavis from Eliot, and the last chapter shows Leavis's social concern— for the process of standardization, mass production, and leveling-down in literature, which became one of the major preoccupations of his periodical.

The second book of criticism, *Revaluation* (1936), can be described as an application of Eliot's methods and insights to the history of English poetry. It is, in a sketchy manner, the first consistent attempt I know of to rewrite the history of English poetry from a twentieth-century point of view. Spenser, Milton, Tennyson, the Pre-Raphaelites recede into the background; Donne, Pope, Wordsworth and Keats in part, Hopkins, the later Yeats, and T. S. Eliot move into the foreground. Leavis, more than Eliot, is concerned with establishing continuities: for example, on the seventeenth century he argues that the "line of wit" runs from Ben Jonson (and Donne) through Carew and Marvell to Pope. The chapter on Pope discovers his metaphysical descent; the chapter on Wordsworth makes much of the affinity with the eighteenth-century Georgic tradition. But the focus and tone of the chapters is rather various; the book, made up of articles, though making a whole, shifts in its preoccupations: the chapter on Milton is an attack on his style and verse pursuing Eliot's suggestions, while the essay on Pope strikingly shows how Pope was inspired by an ideal of a civilization in which Art and Nature should be reconnected and humane culture be "kept appropriately aware of its derivation from and dependence on the culture of the soil" (*R,* 80). Similarly, Wordsworth is discussed in terms of his "essential sanity and normality" (174), and Keats in terms of moral maturity, of his "tragic experience, met by discipline" (272). The one chapter which is almost entirely negative is on Shelley, whose poetry is called "repetitive, vaporous, monotonously self-regarding, and often emotionally cheap" (*IS,* 39). The general agreement with Eliot both in implied standards and in taste is obvious. But Leavis does not share Eliot's interest in Dryden; he is much more sympathetic to Pope; and Eliot has little of Leavis's interest in Wordsworth and Keats.

The third book, *The Great Tradition* (1948), is devoted to the English novel. Actually, it contains only essays on George Eliot, Henry James, and Joseph Conrad. The introduction justifies and somewhat expands this choice of the tradition. Leavis disparages the eighteenth-century novelists Fielding and Sterne,[5] and sees Jane Austen as the wellhead of the English novel. No detailed consideration is given to her because Mrs. Leavis had written several long articles on her for *Scrutiny,*[6] which presumably would find Leavis's endorsement. But he traces Jane Austen's influence on George Eliot and hence to James, who went to school to George Eliot, and there is no need to argue that Conrad comes, in part, from James. Leavis has little use for Thackeray, a "greater Trollope." He dislikes Meredith; he cannot bring himself to consider Hardy a major novelist; and he dismisses Emily Brontë's *Wuthering Heights* as a "kind of sport" (*GT,* 27). Most astonishingly he excludes Dickens, who seems not to have "total significance of a profoundly serious kind." "That Dickens was a great genius and is permanently among the classics is certain. But the genius was that of a great entertainer" (19). Leavis somewhat perversely picks out *Hard Times* as a neglected book and gives it a sympathetic reading that well isolates the wonderfully successful passages in a book which I cannot help feeling is, in general, a failure (227–48). The introduction also dismisses Joyce as a dead-end and praises, among recent novelists, only D. H. Lawrence, on whom Leavis had early written a sober little pamphlet (1930) and to whom he devoted a later book, *D. H. Lawrence: Novelist* (1955). Lawrence is to him "the great creative genius of our age, and one of the greatest figures in English literature," whom Leavis constantly and consistently defends for his fundamental intelligence and sanity, for his correct diagnosis of the ills of modern civilization. According to Leavis, "Lawrence belongs to the same ethical and religious tradition as George Eliot" (*DHL,* 18, 303, 204, 98, 104, 107)—the rural and nonconformist England. Leavis exalts *The Rainbow* and *Women in Love* as Lawrence's two greatest novels and keeps up a running fire against T. S. Eliot and other disparagers of Lawrence's creed or art. But Leavis's selection from Lawrence's other writings seems often extremely dubious: he extolls the dreary allegory, *St. Mawr,* or such a black-and-white fable as "The Daughters of the Vicar." He completely shirks discussing *The Man Who Died* and hardly comes to grips with Lawrence's politics or his peculiar "love ethic." *The Great Tradition* has its center in the essays on George Eliot, whom Leavis admires greatly and whom he helped to bring back from the comparative eclipse she had suffered. Leavis stresses George Eliot's later work, *Middlemarch,* parts of *Felix Holt,* and particularly *Daniel Deronda,* from which he would like to extricate the story of Gwendolen Harleth for separate publication and high appreciation.[7] The James essays emphasize the middle novels, in particular *The Portrait of a Lady,* and are sharply critical of the very late James. While in general it seems to me right to prefer the middle James, I find it impossible to dismiss *The Ambassadors* as brusquely as Leavis does and to give a reading to *The Wings of the Dove* and *The Golden Bowl* which not only sees James as losing his grip on reality but makes him morally obtuse and blind. The essays on Conrad extend the greatest admiration to *The Secret Agent* and *Nostromo* and disparage the early Malayan stories. *The Great Tradition* must be judged by the success of these essays, however much we may object to the harsh selectivity exercised among the books of Leavis's favorite writers; we must not be too put out by the sweeping dismissals of the first chapter.

The Common Pursuit (1952)—the title comes from Eliot's "Function of Criticism"—is a miscellaneous volume of essays. It reprints two widely noted but perverse essays: one on "The Irony of Swift" which makes Swift a purely destructive, though intense and powerful writer and ignores his implied religious and rationalist standards; and the piece on Othello, "Diabolic Intellect and the Noble Hero," which goes to the other extreme of Bradley's sentimental worship of the noble Moor. Othello appears as a brutal, obtuse egotist, sensual, stupid, and jealous, who even in his last speech indulges only in rhetorical self-deception. Scattered essays can be found in Bentley's anthology, in *Commentary*, the *Sewanee Review*, and elsewhere. They become either more shrill and strident, as the polemical article against T. S. Eliot's criticism ("T. S. Eliot's Stature as Critic"), or show rather new interests or shifts of interest. The introduction to Marius Bewley's *Complex Fate* (1952) is Leavis's fullest pronouncement on the American novel and its great tradition, which he finds in Hawthorne and James and to which he would like to link Mark Twain. Leavis disparages the frontier tradition which "derives an illicit respectability from the aura of Mark Twain" (*Complex Fate*, ix), and the whole attempt to exalt Whitman, Dreiser, and Scott Fitzgerald and their "Americanness" at the expense of what Leavis feels are the greatest and finest American writers: Hawthorne, James, and Mark Twain. It is only logical that Leavis also disparages Van Wyck Brooks for his uncritical nationalism and his interpretations of James and Mark Twain as defaulters from America.[8] Other new essays by Leavis are surprisingly mild and even conventional; thus an essay on *Dombey and Son*[9] is a quiet retraction (though not unreserved) of his earlier view of Dickens as a "great entertainer" outside the tradition of the English novel.

We come to better grips with Leavis's position if we abandon the attempt to describe his opinions and try to define his standards and methods. This is not easy, as Leavis himself constantly emphasizes his lack of interest in philosophical theory, in systematic defense and argument about principles, and recommends always a purely empirical textual approach to literary criticism.

I myself became the target of a *Scrutiny* piece, "Literary Criticism and Philosophy,"[10] in which I was selected as the occasion for Leavis's sharp discrimination between philosophy and literary criticism. I am several times called "a philosopher," presumably because I had written a book on *Immanuel Kant in England* (1931) and because I had tried to show that Leavis misunderstands the philosophy of the English romantic poets. I became something of a straw man to knock down, a role I do not relish, as I did not and do not hold the extreme intellectualist opinions he ascribes to me. I entirely agree with Leavis's general distinction between philosophy and poetry. It is not surprising, then, that my book *Theory of Literature* was reviewed in *Scrutiny* very unfavorably by an American follower of Leavis, Seymour Betsky.[11] He attempts to make me the propounder of a typically American, industrial, efficient, aridly theoretical ideal of scholarship. Leavis seems to have endorsed the review, as he chides F. W. Bateson for praising the book.[12] In the early piece, "Literary Criticism and Philosophy," Leavis emphasizes that they are two distinct and different kinds of discipline. The critic of poetry is the complete reader; the ideal critic is the ideal reader.

> Words in poetry invite us, not to "think about" and judge, but to "feel into" or "become"—to realize a complex experience that is given in the words. . . . The critic's aim is, first, to realize as sensitively and completely as possible this or that which claims his attention, and a certain valuing is implicit in the realizing. As he matures in experience of the new thing he asks, explicitly and implicitly: "Where does this come? How does it stand in relation to . . . ? How relatively important does it seem?" and the organization into which it settles is . . . not a theoretical system or a system determined by abstract considerations (*IS*, 32–32).

In a discussion with L. A. Lerner in the *London Magazine* (1955),[13] Leavis seems to have shifted his ground slightly. He was puzzled by a pronouncement of one of his contributors quoted against him. Geoffrey Walton had said that "too great a concern with fundamentals, to repeat a *Scrutiny* platitude, is ruinous to literary criticism."[14] Leavis recognized more explicitly that a critic is concerned with critical principles, with fundamentals, but still insisted that a discussion of fundamentals must not be philosophical. Criteria and grounds of criticism became Leavis's concern, though they are defined only in the actual process of criticism.

His main concern is always with the concrete. "I hoped, by putting in front of them [the readers of poetry] in a criticism that should keep as close to the concrete as possible my own developed 'coherence of response,' to get them to agree . . . that the map, the essential order, of English poetry seen as a whole did, when they interrogated their experience, look like that to them also" (*IS*, 33). Leavis sees criticism very much in terms of pedagogy. "It trains, in a way no other discipline can, intelligence and sensibility together, cultivating a sensitiveness and precision of response and a delicate integrity of intelligence" (*EU*, 34). While it implies an "appreciative habituation to the subtleties of language" (38), "everything must start from and be associated with the training of sensibility. It should, by continual insistence and varied exercise in analysis, be enforced that literature is made of words, and that everything worth saying in criticism of verse and prose can be related to judgments concerning particular arrangements of words on the page" (120).

This emphasis on the textual, even on the texture of the text in front of us, leads in Leavis to a complete dismissal of what is ordinarily called "literary history" or "scholarship." "There is no more futile study than that which ends with mere knowledge *about* literature. . . . The study of a literary text about which the student cannot say, or isn't concerned to be able to say, as a matter of first-hand perception and judgment—of intelligent realization—why it should be worth study is a self-stultifying occupation" (*EU*, 67–68). "Literary history" is called a "worthless acquisition; worthless for the student who cannot as a critic—that is, as an intelligent and discerning reader—make a personal approach to the essential data of the literary historian, the works of literature (an approach is personal or it is nothing: you cannot take over the appreciation of a poem, and unappreciated, the poem isn't 'there')" (68). Or similarly, "For the purposes of criticism, scholarship, unless directed by an intelligent interest in poetry . . . is useless" (*CP*, 9). In an interesting exchange with F. W. Bateson, Leavis argues that the distinction between literary criticism and literary history made by Bateson, the difference between opinion and fact, is extraordinarily uncritical. "What is this 'fact' of the 'dependence of Dryden's poetry on Waller's'?" he asks.

> I should like to see by what "sober evidence-weighing" Mr. Bateson would set out to establish it. The only evidence he specifies is "that provided by parallel passages"—by which, indeed, Dryden can be proved to have read Waller just as he can be proved to have read Cowley and Milton. But the most sober weighing can go no further, except in terms of critical judgements of a most complex and delicate order: "dependence" in any sense that can interest anyone interested in poetry . . . is still to be determined, estimated, defined, or poohpoohed. . . . Mr. Bateson as literary historian can have access to the work he proposes to deal with—to his most essential facts—only if he is sufficiently a critic; only by an appropriate and discriminating response to them; a response that is, involving the kind of activity that produces value-judgements. And these judgements are not, in-

sofar as they are real, expressions of opinion on facts that can be possessed and handled neutrally (*IS*, 21).

Only very rarely does Leavis make some concessions to theory: he admits that a "critique of criticism" is needed (*EV*, 132) and he occasionally discusses other critics. Aristotle's *Poetics*, he thinks, does not itself provide the means of making one a better critic. One must take a critical apparatus to it, to derive any benefit from it (133). Dryden's criticism he thinks much overrated: Dryden "showed strength and distinction in independent judgement, but I cannot believe that his discussion of any topic has much to offer us" (*IS*, 98). Leavis admires Dr. Johnson as a critic: he emphasizes his empiricism. "Johnson's recourse to experience is so constant and uncompromising and so subversive of Neo-classic authority that it is misleading to bring him under the Neo-classic head" (71). But he sees the defects of his sensibility (58), for example, in his treatment of Shakespeare, in his preference for the comedies (*CP*, 108), his bondage to the moralistic fallacy, his obtuseness to dramatic form. Leavis has hardly any use for Coleridge as a critic. He dismisses his aesthetics as a "nuisance" and comes to the conclusion that his "currency as an academic classic is something of a scandal" (*IS*, 86), but he recognizes the value of some of his reflections on meter and imagery, and the novelty of his literary opinions. The student, he declares bluntly, "will have no use at all for Hazlitt or Lamb" (*EV*, 133).

Arnold appeals to him most of the older English critics. He admires his plea for critical intelligence and critical standards and the statement of the idea of "centrality"; he defends the phrase about "criticism of life." "Arnold's phrase is sufficiently explained—and, I think, vindicated—as expressing an intention directly counter to the tendency that finds its comsummation in 'Art for Art's sake.' " Leavis, with his characteristic enmity toward theory, defends Arnold's lack of definition and explanation. His business was to evoke the criteria and not to define them. Similarly, he defends even the touchstones. "It is a tip for mobilizing our sensibility, for focussing our relevant experience in a sensitive point; for reminding us vividly what the best is like." Arnold may lack "the gift for consistency or for definition," but he has positive virtues: "tact and delicacy, a habit of keeping in sensitive touch with the concrete." Whatever his limitations, Arnold seems to him "decidedly more of a critic than the Sainte-Beuve to whom he so deferred" (*IS*, 89, 93, 95, 96, 98).

The defense of Arnold illuminates Leavis's central concern for the preservation of tradition. Leavis thinks of tradition primarily as literary and social, and he deplores Eliot's subordination of tradition to religion.

Leavis's point of view is not antireligious; nor is it purely aesthetic. In discussing Arnold, he quickly abandons him as a theological thinker but defends his concern for culture. "Many who deplore Arnold's way with religion will agree that, as other traditions relax and social forms disintegrate, it becomes correspondingly more important to preserve the literary tradition" (*IS*, 91). This attempt of criticism to preserve the literary tradition is necessarily secular. "Literary criticism must, in this sense [separable from any particular religious frame or bias] always be humanist; whatever it may end in, it must be humanist in approach, insofar as it is literary criticism and not something else" (*EV*, 19). But this humanism is emphatically not aestheticism. "I don't think that for any critic who understands his job there are any 'unique literary values' or any 'realm of the exclusively aesthetic.' But there *is*, for a critic, a problem of relevance, . . . an understanding of the resources of language, the nature of conventions, a specially developed sensibility" (*CP*, 114) which always precede concern for more remote sociological or cultural surrounding circumstances. Bateson, for example, is severely criticized for his sociological criticism. "The poem is a determinate thing; it is *there*; but there is nothing to correspond—nothing answering to Mr. Bateson's 'social context' that can be set over against the poem, or induced to reestablish itself round it as a kind of framework or completion, and there never *was* anything."[15]

While Leavis rejects sociological or religious criteria, Marxist or Catholic, he constantly returns to the moral, social, and vital implications of literature. While he rejects ordinary didacticism, he emphasizes that the critical act implies "moral discrimination, and judgement of relative human value" (*GT*, 29). He even asserts that the critic will be compelled to become "explicitly a moralist" (*IS*, 39). The method is described when Leavis defends his devastating analysis of a poem by Shelley ("That time is dead for ever, child"). "In the examination of his poetry the literary critic finds himself passing, by inevitable transitions, from describing characteristics to making adverse judgements about emotional quality; and from these to judgements that are pretty directly moral; and so to a kind of discussion in which, by its proper methods and in pursuit of its proper ends, literary criticism becomes the diagnosis of what, looking for an inclusive term, we can only call spiritual malady."[16] But also the social meaning of literature is precisely in these implications of health and disease, in a sound tradition of a good society. Literary tradition is, he admits, "largely a development of the language" (*EV*, 118), but this is involved in a cultural and social pattern. In a little book written with Denys Thompson, *Culture and Environment* (1933), and in Mrs. Q. D.

Leavis's *Fiction and the Reading Public* (1932), this thesis is pursued in sociological terms. It is a concern for the effect of mass production, standardization, leveling-down, advertising and its effects, the whole development of modern urban and industrial civilization, which is contrasted with the organic community of the English countryside and the communal life of earlier ages.

Mrs. Leavis analyzes concretely the different strata of English taste— high-brow, middle-brow, and low-brow—and accumulates a great mass of evidence for the successive deterioration of standards. In contrasting modern conditions with the past—the Elizabethan period, the eighteenth century, the Romantic Age—she always concludes that standards used to be higher and taste better. But in her exclusive regard for the "high-brow" she overlooks the genuine social function of much modest art and genuine craft and overrates the blessings of older ages. Classes whose tastes were simply not satisfied in earlier ages have become vocal today. Even though we may think that their voices are pretty raucous, speech seems better than silence, or mere inert acceptance of upper-class standards. But, of course, the Leavises deplore precisely this present lack of a central authority in criticism—the anarchy of values of our time—and propose to combat it by creating, at least, a small critical minority.

Leavis does constantly use a criterion of integration in a healthy society. For example, he describes Pope's concern for the "positive bases" or "the basic moral values of his civilization"; he praises Johnson and Crabbe for "bearing a serious relation to the life of their time" (*R,* 77, 83, 105) which is lacking in Gray and Thomson. He criticizes the Restoration for having no "serious relations to the moral bases of society" (113). With him, the poet has always an important social function. "The poet is at the most conscious point of the race in his time" (*NB,* 13), and literature is the "consciousness of the age" (*EV,* 119). Thus Johnson's feeling for a literary order is inseparable from a profound moral sense (*R,* 117), but this feeling is criticized, surely in too unqualified terms, as being one for a merely literary order which has lost a sense for social order, for Good Form, for a social code which is still overwhelmingly present in Pope. Dr. Johnson's manners may have been, at times, deplorably coarse, but his concern for social order is surely as intense as his regard for literary tradition.

Some of Leavis's pronouncements on tradition, on old society, even a social code, on order, and so forth, sound very conservative. The term "centrality" which comes from Arnold underlines this "humanism," the concern for "civilization" in an eighteenth-century sense, while other favorite terms—"maturity," "sanity," "discipline"—circumscribe the same

values. Just as, negatively, Leavis always disparages emotionalism, affla-
tus, rhetoric, he would say of some lines of Shelley that they are "dis-
tasteful, because there is strong feeling, and the feeling is false. It is false
because it is forced" (R, 237). "Shelley offers the emotion in itself, unattached, in the void, while Wordsworth's emotion seems to derive from
what is presented" (214). It is in Eliot's term, attached to some "objective
correlative."

But these standards are often modified in Leavis and possibly contradicted by a concern for life, for vitality. At times this merely means a
proper concern for reality, a distaste for aestheticism, an emphasis on
the empirical. The three great novelists Leavis admires most, George
Eliot, Henry James, and Conrad, "are all distinguished by a vital capacity
for experience, a kind of reverent openness before life, and a marked
moral intensity" (GT, 9). In the Keats essay the emphasis on life is also,
sometimes simply, anti-aesthetic. "Keats's aestheticism does not mean any
such cutting off of the special valued order of experience from direct,
vulgar living ('Live!—our servants will do that for us'), as is implied in
the aesthetic antithesis of Art and Life" (R, 257). But "life" assumes there
the more doubtful role of a criterion of health. "The 'Ode to a Nightingale,' " Leavis says strangely, "moves outwards and upwards towards
life as strongly as it moves downwards towards extinction" (246). Life,
with Leavis, becomes a dynamic, vitalistic force. The praise of Lawrence
even as a critic is thus justified. "He has an unfailingly sure sense of the
difference between that which makes for life and that which tends away
from health. It is this that makes him a so much better critic than Eliot"
(DHL, 311).

But it would be unjust to emphasize only these moral, social, and
vitalistic criteria in Leavis. He does, after all, start usually with an examination of the text, with aesthetic observations. But there he always
insists that all elements collaborate and are not really divorceable. In
criticizing Pound's distinctions between melopoeia, phanopoeia, and logopoeia, Leavis makes the point that melopoeia is quite inseparable from
meaning and from imagery, and that phanopoeia, imagery, is not merely
visual, still less a matter of seeing little pictures. "It may range from
incipient suggestion . . . to complete realization" (EV, 115). "Technique
can be studied and judged only in terms of the sensibility it expresses."
Otherwise it "is an unprofitable abstraction" (113). Still, Leavis, like Eliot,
in practice constantly values sharply visualized poetry, sensuous particularity, the lack of which he feels in Milton especially strongly. Like Eliot,
Leavis insists on language vitally related to common speech. Milton is
criticized for "renouncing the English language" (R, 52), while Hopkins,

"paradoxically as it may sound to say so, brought poetry much closer to living speech" (*NB*, 168). Poetry, however, must not flatter the singing voice, should not be merely mellifluous, should not, for example, give a mere general sense of motion. Incantatory poetry, remote from speech, is always disparaged. Milton treats language as "a kind of musical medium outside himself" (82); he "seems to be focussing rather upon words than upon perceptions, sensations or things." "He exhibits a feeling *for* words rather than a capacity for feeling *through* words" (*R*, 49–50). Language, while considered the immediate surface of literature, is thus only a surface leading to things, to objects, to reality. The linguistic interest in Leavis is strictly subordinate to his interest in what he would call life. Thus the emphasis on the text is somewhat deceptive. Leavis's observations on linguistic points seem often vague and imprecise or concern the effect of individual words or reflect on imagery;[17] he is not interested in stylistics or metrics and avoids all technical analysis of this kind. He is also quite uninterested in questions of technique of the novel. He will often speak about the "pressure behind words" (*R*, 56) or "the absence of controlling pressure from within" (*CP*, 57), which seems a mere gesture toward some indistinct feeling. Actually, he quickly leaves the verbal surface in order to define the particular emotion or sentiment which an author conveys. Like Croce, he is primarily interested in "sentiment" and hence soon becomes a moral and social critic.

There seems to me a contradiction between this emphasis on words and their final dismissal as servants whom you can only feel *through*, as there is a contradiction, or at least a tension, between Leavis's emphasis on civilized tradition, on humanism, and his advocacy of life for life's sake. It seems strange that he is able to admire (and I mean not passively but ardently) Eliot and Lawrence, though in later years he more and more turned against Eliot and exalted Lawrence to the position of the greatest English writer of the twentieth century. Leavis cares for Henry James, G. M. Hopkins, and Jane Austen on the one hand, and for Bunyan, Blake, and Mark Twain on the other. He cares for Pope and the "line of wit" as well as for the groping irrationalism of Lawrence. The central value, life, is an ambiguous term which shifts from meaning reality and truth to sincerity and even to a sense of community and oneness. On occasion life assumes even a religious coloring, either in the literal sense of religion meaning "relation, bond, allegiance," a sense with which "men and women know that they 'do not belong to themselves'" but are "responsible to something that transcends love and sex too" (*DHL*, 111). Elsewhere life means a feeling of "belonging in the universe," which seems to approximate Albert Schweitzer's "reverence for life":[18] it means

often simply courage, devotion, and finally optimism. In a curious paper
on tragedy (which puzzles me for for its ignorance of any theory of
tragedy besides Aristotle's and Santayana's), Leavis rejects *catharsis* as
purging of the passions, as the achieving of equilibrium, of "calm—all
passion spent." Tragedy rather has an exalting, exhilarating effect: it
enhances our sense of life, frees us from the limitations of ourselves,
makes us recognize value as in some way defined and vindicated by death
(*CP,* 132). Art thus always "ministers" to life, serves the spontaneous-
creative fullness of being. Artists who "do dirt on life" are disparaged:
Eliot, particularly in *The Cocktail Party,* shows attitudes of "disgust and
fear and rejection" to life;[19] Flaubert lacks compassion and trust in human dignity.[20]

I am, I fear, too much of a theorist not to feel strongly the ambiguity,
shiftiness, and vagueness of Leavis's ultimate value criterion, life. In its
implications and rejections it brings out the limitations of Leavis's concept of literature and the narrow range of his sympathies. Life for Leavis
is first of all simply realist art—not merely in a sense of copying or
transcribing a social situation, a dramatic, objective rendering of life, of
course, but as we find it in Shakespeare and the English novel of the
nineteenth century. In practice, Leavis has no sympathy for stylized,
conventionalized art, the art defined in Ortega's *Dehumanization of the
Arts.* This serious ideal of life makes Leavis also suspicious of art which
is merely playful, rococo, ornamental, aesthetic, formalistic in a narrow
sense, while his optimism makes him hostile to out-and-out pessimists
such as Hardy or Flaubert. Leavis's taste is rooted in nineteenth-century
critical realism, to which he manages to add the early poetry of T. S.
Eliot and a selection from the novels of D. H. Lawrence, *The Rainbow*
and *Women in Love* in particular. He is really deeply hostile to what could
be called modernism or avant-garde: to Joyce, Wyndham Lewis, Auden,
Dylan Thomas, to almost every author who has become prominent since
the 1930s. He clings, as I suppose we all do, to the discoveries of his
youth: Conrad, Lawrence, Hopkins, the early Eliot.

The emphasis on life in the sense of the concrete and immediate is
connected with Leavis's concern with the English provincial rural tradition which he apparently finds in Shakespeare, in Bunyan, in Jane Austen, George Eliot, and D. H. Lawrence, all countryfolk of a sort to which
the Londoners, Spenser, Milton, Dryden, provide a foil of learned urban
poetry. Life means also pedagogy, the concern for his students, for the
controversies of his university. It accounts also for what I cannot help
calling Leavis's provinciality and insularity. Besides English and American, he seems to have no interest whatever in another literature: I can

recall only a few highly laudatory references to Tolstoy and some critical remarks on Flaubert.[21] In *Scrutiny* he may have left French and German literature to the specialists, Martin Turnell and D. H. Enright. Leavis's gravest failing seems to me his distrust and even hatred for theory: his resolute, complacent, nominalistic empiricism, his worship of the concrete and particular at any price. But Leavis's standards *are* verbally formulable. In my letter printed in *Scrutiny* 5 (1937) (also in *IS*, 23), I sketched Leavis's ideal of poetry:

> Poetry must be in serious relation to actuality, it must have a firm grasp of the actual, of the object, it must be in relation to life, it must not be cut off from direct vulgar living, it should not be personal in the sense of indulging in personal dreams and fantasies, there should be no emotion for its own sake in it, no afflatus, no mere generous emotionality, no luxury in pain or joy, but also no sensuous poverty, but a sharp, concrete realization, a sensuous particularity. The language of poetry must not be cut off from speech, should not flatter the singing voice, should not be merely mellifluous, should not give, e.g., a mere general sense of motion.

All these phrases were quoted literally from *Revaluation*. In isolation, in a deliberately atomistic enumeration, they are "intolerably clumsy" (*CP*, 215), as Leavis complained in his rejoinder. I recognize that they assume their meaning only in a context, but they do represent implicit norms, an underlying scheme or pattern which is discoverable in every critic and which it is the business of a historian of criticism to describe and judge. The refusal to theorize has a paralyzing effect on Leavis's practice; it makes him reject the tools and concepts of technical analysis and be content with impressions or dogmatically stated feelings. He refers to the "complex rhythm organizing" *The Rainbow* without even attempting to describe it, or gropes to find terms for metrical or metaphorical effects in Donne which he can only sense but not name, or indulges in open contradictions when his feelings run counter to his unexamined presuppositions. Thus, we are told that "Johnson's abstractness here [in *The Vanity of Human Wishes*] doesn't exclude concreteness," since the style has "body," "a generalizing weight." Johnson's abstractions and generalities "focus a wide range of profoundly representative experience—experience felt by the reader as movingly present."[22] The struggle for expression, the entanglement in favorite words is painfully obvious in many passages of Leavis's tortuous and tortured writing, which, in its fierce clinging to the immediate, seems often to deny the life and light of reason. Empiricism, observation, sensitive submission to the objecte postulated as an ideal have been increasingly in conflict with the obscurantist vitalism preached by Lawrence and accepted by Leavis with uncritical adoration.

Still, whatever Leavis's limitations, he has succeeded in defining his taste, identifying that tradition he considers central, and imposing his judgment on his contemporaries. Leavis has accomplished what he set out to do: "A judgment," he tells us, "is a real judgment, or it is nothing. It must, that is, be a sincere personal judgment; but it aspires to be more than personal. Essentially it has the form: 'This is so, is it not?'"[23] A great many of our contemporaries have answered "It is so," and this is after all the success which every critic who is not merely a theorist, but a molder of taste, can hope for. Leavis has defined and given voice to a widespread taste and change of taste. I am convinced that he will preserve a position in the history of English criticism not far distant and even different from that of the much sweeter tempered Matthew Arnold.

THE LATER LEAVIS

Since I wrote, in 1963, the preceding essay on F. R. Leavis (first published in *Literary Views,* ed. Carroll Camden [1964]), Leavis published seven books which, in number of words, exceed all his earlier writings substantially: *Anna Karenina and Other Essays* (1967), *Lectures in America* (1969), *English Literature in Our Time and the University* (1969), *Dickens: The Novelist* (1970), *Nor Shall My Sword: Discourses on Pluralism, Compassion and Social Hope* (1972), *The Living Principle: 'English' as a Discipline of Thought* (1975), and *Thought, Words and Creativity: Art and Thought in Lawrence* (1976), to which we must add a few scattered essays such as "Justifying One's Evaluation of Blake" (in *William Blake: Essays in Honour of Sir Geoffrey Keynes,* 1973) and "Wordsworth: The Creative Conditions" (in *Twentieth-Century Literature in Retrospect,* ed. Reuben A. Brower, 1971). There are also items of interest in a collection of Leavis's letters to the press, *Letters in Criticism* (ed. John Tasker, 1974). Unsurprisingly, these books reaffirm, repeat, elaborate, and defend his earlier views sometimes literally, though I shall argue that there is a discernible shift of interest and emphasis and that we find new motifs not articulated in his earlier writings. Some of the new books reprint older pieces: *Anna Karenina* contains earlier essays from *Scrutiny* and the introduction to a selection from the *Calendar of Modern Letters* dating back to 1933. *Dickens: The Novelist* reprints the essay on *Hard Times* from *The Great Tradition* and the article on *Dombey and Son* from the *Sewanee Review* in 1962. *Nor Shall My Sword* reprints "Two Cultures: The Significance of C. P. Snow" and the defense from *Lectures in America,* and *The Living Principle* reprints the articles "Judgment and Analysis," "Imagery and Movement," "Reality and Sincerity," and "*Antony and Cleopatra* and *All for Love*" from *Scrutiny*. There is much overlapping and repetition as Leavis hammers in a few basic ideas with insistent eloquence and passionate urging.

In two of the new books, *Lectures in America* and *Dickens: The Novelist*, Q. D. Leavis (1907–1981) is listed as coauthor. From the date of their marriage (1929), Mrs. Leavis must have been a strong influence on her husband, as her own work was in turn shaped by his taste and ideology. Her contributions to *Scrutiny* show an independent mind and personal preoccupations; her early book *Fiction and the Reading Public* led logically to her writing about the finest critic of the English novel in the nineteenth century, Leslie Stephen (*Scrutiny* 7 [1939]) and to what she called "the sociology of the academic world" (*Scrutiny* 11 [1943]: 308n.), to acerbic criticisms of Walter Raleigh and other Oxford worthies. Her interests in the novel focused on Jane Austen's career ("A Critical Theory of Jane Austen's Writings," in *Scrutiny* 10 [1941] and 12 [1944]). She argues that Jane Austen incessantly revised and rewrote her early fictions. An elaborate reading of *Wuthering Heights* minimizes the mystical and metaphysical features in favor of the psychological characterizations (*LA*). Almost all of her work celebrates "the Englishness of the English Novel" expounded in a later essay (*Collected Essays*, ed. G. Singh, 1983). The nineteenth-century novel, which made a "great gain artistically by shifting from the picaresque tradition to a sociological unit" (313), is hailed as the moral mentor and model and the necessary criticism of English society. Q. D. Leavis praises the English aversion to aestheticism on the one hand and the suspicion of the doctrinaire in politics and religion, not concealing her dislike for what she considered technicians such as Virginia Woolf or dogmatic naturalists such as George Moore or Arnold Bennett. She fortifies her concept of a moral realism in solid essays on Dickens, George Eliot, and George Gissing and in excursions into the American novel, Henry James, and Edith Wharton as the heiress of Henry James (*Scrutiny* 7 [1938]). Q. D. Leavis, within her limits, contributed valiantly to the rehabilitation of the English novel.

F. R. Leavis is one of the many thinkers and publicists of our century who deplore the progress of machine civilization and recall the old organic community of preindustrial society with nostalgia. In his later writings Leavis is anxious to refute the charge of being a Luddite or simply a sentimental admirer of a nonexistent past. He over and over again asserts that there is no returning to the past but that "the memory of the old order must be the chief incitement towards a new" (*CE*, 97). He denies that he is unaware of the shady side of the good old times. "I have not been William Morris-ing, and I have proposed no ideal condition of humanity to be found in any past." Dickens alone would have made him aware of "the poverty, misery, oppression, and mismanagement that made Victorian England so very much other than a Utopia" (*NS*, 192). Still, in many contexts Leavis insists on the advantages of a preindustrial society, particularly for the health of literature which can draw on the sources of popular speech and culture. An essay on Bunyan's *Pilgrim's Progress* (1964) argues that Bunyan "had behind him—or rather, had around him and in him—that pervasive and potent continuity, a living culture" and a "language, a vehicle of collective wisdom and basic assumptions, a currency of criteria and valuations collaboratively determined" (*AK*, 41). Shakespeare is Leavis's other example of a poet rooted in popular speech with a creative power of language unmatched before or since. Leavis gets strangely indignant at T. S. Eliot's descriptions of the villagers in "East Coker" as "yokels, clumsy, gross, and incapable of spiritual or cultural graces," quoting, "Eating and drinking. Dung and death." "Yet it was they who created the English language . . . and made possible in due course Shakespeare, Dickens and the poet of *Four Quartets*" (*LP*, 196).

The dissolution of the old order is mirrored in the decay of literary culture which, Leavis recognizes, was and will be always a minority culture. He constantly urges the need of an "educated public," believes in a nucleus for it in the university, and particularly in an English school after his own heart which would be a school of criticism, a training of sensibility and understanding. All through his career Leavis has been intensely concerned with education, particularly at Cambridge. Though he has spelled out in some detail the persecutions and injustices he suffered at Cambridge (*EL*, 22; *LC*, 147–48) and has "no impulse or reason to see a model in Cambridge" (*NS*, 183), he constantly voices the hope for a new elite centered at the university. He rejects the term "elitism" as "a stupid word, perniciously so, because there must always be élites. . . . There are scientist élites, air-pilot élites, *corps d'élite*, and social élites (the best people) and the underprivileged masses know that professional footballers and BBC announcers are élites" (*NS*, 169). While Leavis has been charged by Aldous Huxley with "literarism" (opposed to "scientism"), Leavis is anxious to avoid the misinterpretation of "minority culture" as being reserved for literary criticism. He pleads rather for a collaboration between English and philosophy departments and his program of English studies focused on the seventeenth century was to be interdisciplinary, including political, social, and religious history. Leavis urges constantly the importance of what he calls "The Third Realm" (*LP*,

36), which is neither purely private nor public in the sense of scientific verifiability but is a communal collaborative enterprise of man, "culture," or what Hegel calls "the objective spirit." Thus Leavis recognizes only *one* culture. "It is obviously absurd to posit a 'culture' that the scientist has *qua* scientist" (*LA*, 14). But this culture is not literary culture, as Leavis does not believe in a separate realm of literature. "I don't believe in any 'literary values' and you won't find me talking about them; the judgments the literary critic is concerned with are judgments about life" (*LA*, 23). Ringingly he proclaims, "I think of myself as an anti-philosopher, which is what a literary critic ought to be. . . . 'Aesthetic' is a word I have little use for" (*TWC*, 34).

Leavis seems to deny that he is at all concerned with an aesthetic response and judgment. This is, I think, often true, particularly of his criticism of the novel, which merely pays attention to the author's discriminations and judgments about his characters. He seems to have forgotten his early endorsement of C. H. Rickword's "Note on Fiction," which says that "only as precipitate from the memory are plot or character tangible: yet only in solution have either any emotive valency," and even ignored his own admonition that "a novel, like a poem, is made of words" (*AK*, 228–29). Often Leavis has nothing to say about language or leaves the verbal surface very quickly content with some gestures toward its vitality, partly because he has hardly any descriptive (not to speak of analytical) tools at hand. He condemns linguistics and Wittgenstein's philosophy of language as useless for the literary student, assuming that "they postpone dealing at all seriously with meaning" (*LP*, 57).

Yet Leavis does some injustice to himself when he denies that he is concerned with literary values. It is notoriously difficult to pin him down as to his assumptions and criteria. Since writing the piece "Literary Criticism and Philosophy" (1937), expressly directed against my request for clarifications, he has reasserted his view that criteria can be defined only "in the actual process of criticism" and that defining them with precision would be "intolerably clumsy and ineffective" (*LC*, 48). He is always suspicious of theorists. Richards's *Principles of Literary Criticism*, he admits, had a liberating effect. "It released from the thought-frustrating spell of 'Form,' 'pure sound-value,' prosody and other time-honored critical futilities" (*EL*, 17), but Leavis considers Richards's "interest in literature not intense and never developed" and the pretensions of his theory "pseudo-scientific and pseudo-psychological" (*EL*, 17). Leavis, originally a great admirer of Eliot's criticism and obviously deeply influenced by his taste and method, later condemned his best-known theoretical essays ("Tradition and the Individual Talent" and "The Function of Criticism") as "pretentious, confused and unilluminating" (*NS*, 114). "Tradition and the Individual Talent" is called "pretentiously null as thought" (*TWC*, 16) and "confused and ambiguous" (*LP*, 186). But on occasion Leavis recognizes that there is an interplay of critic and theorist. Speaking of Coleridge he says, "If I cannot imagine a great master of such critical theory as matters who is not a great critic—a great critic in critical practice, neither can I imagine a great or considerable critic who is not very much concerned with critical principle."[24] Yet Leavis hardly follows his own recognition of a need for critical principles. He only admits that "one *has* to use key-words in special senses which one must rely on the context to define" (*LP*, 34). Quite early in describing *The Calendar of Letters* Leavis can say, "These 'standards of criticism' are assumed: nothing more is said about them; nothing more needed to be said" (*AK*, 221). Critical practice shows them. Leavis discovered a book, *The Knower and the Known* (1966) by Marjorie Grene (a disciple of Michael Polanyi, a chemist who became a philosopher best described as similar to Merleau-Ponty), from which he could quote that a standard is not "verbally formulable" (*LP*, 33) and where he could find a defense of "tacit knowing."

In my letter in *Scrutiny* 5 (1937), quoted above, I described Leavis's ideal of poetry, quoting literally from *Revaluation*. In his later writings Leavis avoided these terms and rather spoke of "realization," or "enactment," of "convincingness," and of "inevitability," all terms for successful art. More often, particularly in the criticism of poetry, Leavis appeals to the norm of "sincerity," a term obsessive in the history of English criticism which may easily become simply a moralistic criterion but can mean all kinds of good things such as "the sincerity that is of the whole being, and not merely of conscious intention" (*LA*, 15), something like Eliot's unified sensibility. Sometimes, gropingly, Leavis defines the great poet as having "the power of giving concrete definition (that is, of seizing and evoking in words and rhythms) feelings and apprehensions—the focal core with the elusive aura—that have seemed to him peculiarly significant elements in his private experience" (115). In more traditional terms he calls poetry "the product of a realizing imagination working from within a deeply and minutely felt theme" (*LP*, 155). The implied norm of poetry is often seen best by citing Leavis's rejections. He contrasts, for instance, Shakespeare's *Antony and Cleopatra* with Dryden's *All for Love*, showing how Shakespeare's description of Cleopatra on her barge "enacts meaning" while Dryden's parallel passage is merely "descriptive eloquence" (148). Or he argues that images are not merely visual and are not "plums in a cake" but "foci of complex life, inseparable from context" (106). He can sensitively contrast poems with ultimately aesthetic criteria when, for instance, he shows that one should prefer Wordsworth's sonnet "Surprised by Joy" to "It is a beauteous evening" (113–14). In theory Leavis knows very well "the difference between mere discursive thought and what we require of art" (103).

Yet often he passes quickly to a criticism of the world view propounded by the poet. In a very long and partly admiring discussion of *Four Quartets*, interspersed with compliments to Eliot as a "major poet" or a poet "greater than Yeats or Hardy" (*EL,* 136; also *LA,* 29) Eliot is criticized not simply for his religious views but for his conception of time. Leavis has become aware of what could be called Bergsonism, the whole philosophy of flux of Whitehead, Collingwood, and Samuel Alexander. Eliot is chided for wanting to deny time, since for Leavis "life is process, time is of its reality" (*LP,* 225). He must not voice the age-old yearning for eternity, the wish that "time may have a stop." Leavis construes a contradiction between Eliot's feeling of the inadequacy of language, his feeling for the need for ultimate silence, and, on the other hand, being a practicing poet, a creator of language. Eliot's profession of humility is interpreted as passivity, as a refusal of responsibility, as a denial of human freedom. Leavis has become a cosmic optimist, a strenuous believer in action, in universal responsibility, in the basic goodness of man. Eliot is disparaged for "his fear of life and contempt (which includes self-contempt) for humanity" (205) and in particular for his distaste for sex. "Eliot seems never to have been able to take cognizance of full human love between the sexes" (*LA,* 49). Eliot's poetry "hasn't a rich human experience behind it; it reveals, rather, a restriction; it comes, indeed, out of a decided poverty" (*EL,* 144), shows "an inner disorder and insecurity" (146), and "anguish of meaninglessness" (*NS,* 16). Leavis now sides with D. H. Lawrence, "a much greater writer" and "an incomparably greater critic than Eliot" (121).

Lawrence has become the standard of greatness and truth for Leavis, not that he cannot distinguish between his books on aesthetic grounds, disparaging *Lady Chatterley's Lover* as a "bad novel" (*AK,* 238) and *The Plumed Serpent* as a "disconcerting aberration" (*TWC,* 57). But in general, though Leavis sees that Lawrence is "a victim of the absence of any sharp boundary between his discursive thought and his fully creative art" (61), he extracts from him a creed which ignores or only gingerly alludes to Lawrence's obscurantist irrationalism, his occult leanings, or his nonsense about solar plexus, the dark gods and other fantasies. What Leavis admires and embraces is the worship of life which, in spite of its vagueness, he considers "a necessary word" (*NS,* 11ff.). It assumes, besides its obvious meaning, often a religious connotation in Leavis. The passage in the beginning of *The Rainbow* when Tom Brangwen discovers that he "does not belong to himself" but is "submissive to the greater ordering" takes on the meaning of religion, *re-ligio* in the etymological sense of "tie." Leavis uses words such as "beyond," "reverence for life" (with explicit reference to Albert Schweitzer), "responsibility" (almost in the sense of Dostoevsky's universal responsibility), a "sense of the mystery and unity of life" or, slightly differently phrased, "Life is intimately associated with 'wonder,' the 'unknown,' 'imagination,' 'religious' and 'responsible'" (*TWC*, 28). Leavis avoids, as far as I am aware, the word "God" and any commitment to a specific religious observance. Blake and Wordsworth become besides Lawrence patron saints of this creed, and oddly enough Dickens has become assimilated to this new tradition or rather "continuity," as Leavis now would not like to be identified with Eliot's concept (*NS*, 120), though he used "tradition" in the title of his book on the English novel. Blake seems to him more relevant today than Eliot. Eliot's old essay on Blake is criticized for the view that Blake would have been better off if he had been "controlled by a respect for impersonal reason, for common sense, for the objectivity of science" (*Selected Essays* [1932], 308) and is praised for extolling creativity and responsibility. Leavis quotes Blake's saying of his designs, "Though I call them Mine, I know that they are not Mine" (*LP*, 44), as if this were not merely a rephrasing of his belief in supernatural inspirations and even visitations and makes much of a distinction between "self-hood," conceived as narrowly individual, and "identity" which implies communal responsibility, participation in an all-human endeavor. The late essay on Blake (in *William Blake: Essays in Honour of Sir Geoffrey Keynes*, 1973) actually contains much straightforward literary criticism and even literary history. The *Poetical Sketches* are praised for the novelty of their recourse to Shakespeare's songs and their affinity to popular poetry, while Leavis minimizes the eighteenth-century associations. He strongly disapproves of making much of Blake's position in a history of mysticism, of his relations to Swedenborg or Boehme, and he dismisses the Prophetic Books as unsuccessful works of art (*William Blake*, 67). Leavis gives an explanation of Blake's failure which seems to me new. Blake needed an epic framework and in his time had to have recourse to the Fall of Man. He could only postulate an Apocalypse, an end of history, and thus, in Leavis's view, committed himself to determinism in contradiction to his usual assertion of human freedom and creativity. Leavis sympathizes with his revolt against Locke and Newton, the revolt against Cartesian dualism: he had read arguments against it in Michael Polanyi and Marjorie Grene (*LP*, 229).

Dickens, whom Leavis himself had called a "great entertainer" in *The Great Tradition* and had praised only for *Hard Times,* was later reinstated and exalted as second only to Shakespeare, as "one of the greatest creative writers" (*D,* ix). Dickens, like Blake, is a "vindicator of the spirit— that is, of life" (274) and "with Blake and Dickens" Leavis associates Lawrence, so that we have "a line running into the twentieth century" (275). As if Leavis had forgotten that he had called Dickens "a great entertainer," he now protests against this view loudly (29; also *EL,* 175), though in the Dickens book written in collaboration with his wife, who supplied the discussions of *David Copperfield, Bleak House,* and *Great Expectations,* he reprints the piece on *Hard Times* and the lukewarm essay on *Dombey and Son* unchanged. He then gives prominence to *Little Dorrit* as Dickens's best book, "supremely great" (*D,* 177) and simply "one of the very greatest novels" (213). Leavis rejects Edmund Wilson's supposed considering of Dickens's creative oeuvre "the uncontrolled product of childhood obsessions of experiences" (x) and is shocked by Santayana's view of Dickens as "a totally disinherited waif" as Leavis extols Dickens's roots in popular tradition (214). Still, the continuity Blake–Dickens–Lawrence seems an odd one based only on the vague, all-inclusive and, as Leavis admits, indefinable concept of life (224).

The original "Great Tradition" from Jane Austen to Joseph Conrad is not, however, forgotten. There is much new comment on the writers discussed there. George Eliot's *Adam Bede* rates an essay (*AK,* 49–58) which suggests antecedents and models for the novel in Scott, Hawthorne, Greek tragedy, Wordsworth and Shakespeare, as a literary historian might, and makes much of it as a document in social history. Henry James is discussed in several essays. *The Europeans* is described as a "moral fable" and a "comedy" and is well retold, though the affinity with Jane Austen suggested seems belied by James's own dislike for her (74). Also the essay on *What Maisie Knew* emphasizes its "high-spirited comedy" (80). Incidental remarks show that Leavis remained quite unrepentant about his ranking of the novels. *The Princess Casamassima* is called "a bad book" and *The Ambassadors* his "worst," a judgment which is incomprehensible to me. Conrad reappears in two essays: the one on the *Shadow-Line* contains a good defense against the reduction of Conrad's ethos to a "stolid application to duty" (98). The lesson the hero learns is far subtler and "can't be represented by any moral" (109). The essay on *The Secret Sharer* rejects a psychoanalytical reading and sees it as a straightforward lesson in "moral responsibility" (119). The young captain has no guilt feelings and decides that his double must be rescued from the law because it is right to rescue him.

The American novel enters somehow sideways into the great tradition, with Hawthorne as the ancestor of James and Mark Twain. *Huckleberry Finn* is praised as "one of the great books of the world" (*AK*, 121) and Leavis devotes an admiring essay to *Pudd'nhead Wilson* (121–37). Leavis disparages Whitman, Howells, Dreiser, Scott Fitzgerald, and Hemingway (*AK*, 153–54; *EL*, 180) and becomes more and more anti-American, not as he avows on personal or nationalistic grounds but for fear of Americanization, of "the American neo-imperialism of the computer" (*NS*, 206). Granting the agreement with his general horror of the evils of industrial civilization for which America becomes a symbol, one cannot help deploring his systematic disparagement of American scholarship on English literature. Edgar Johnson on Dickens, Gordon Haight on George Eliot, and Harry T. Moore on D. H. Lawrence are singled out by name (*D*, x) as not superseding the earlier English biographies, but usually a general charge is made that "even the most acclaimed critical work on English authors—Jane Austen, the Brontës, Dickens, George Eliot, D. H. Lawrence—betrays a disqualifying ignorance of the civilization out of which those authors wrote, and thus an inability to read them. The truth holds from Edmund Wilson downwards" (*EL*, 34 n.3; also *NS*, 185). It goes to absurd lengths when Leavis generalizes that "the currently applauded American writers" demonstrate "a depressing and often repellent poverty in the range of experience, satisfaction and human potentiality they seem to know of and to think all. As for the famed and flattered American criticis who write about the 'British-English' classics, they seem, judged by what they say about them, unable to read them" (*LP*, 52). Leavis is not only afraid that England will "become just a province of the American world" (*NS*, 159) but also fears Europe and Asia. He opposed Great Britain joining the Common Market and grumbles about the immigration of non-whites into England. His provincialism or Little Englandism is obvious also in his deliberate ignoring of other literatures than that written in English. Some of this reluctance may be due to genuine scruples about literature accessible only in translation. But if one excepts a few disparaging remarks on Flaubert, Mallarmé, and Valéry and a perfunctory tribute to Eugenio Montale,[25] the silence is deafening. There is only one exception, an essay on *Anna Karenina* (1967) which gives a sensitive and attentive reading of the moral issue of the book. As everybody noticed, Leavis sees the Levin-Kitty marriage as a foil to the Anna-Vronsky relationship but points out that the apparent norm of Levin's marriage is disturbed by his later development (*AK*, 14). Anna's conflict is not simply with society but she suffers from a sense of guilt growing from a "delicate inner pride" (22). But the essay seems to me marred by an obtrusive parallel drawn to a real-life situation, the D. H. Lawrence–Frieda relationship, and there is little point at this late date to belabor Arnold and Henry James for disparaging the art of Tolstoy.

Leavis has always been doctrinaire, convinced of his own rightness, which has been the privilege of most critics in history. He dismissed "pluralism" as "the right to be incoherent and opportunist" (*NS*, 165) and had no use for a historical relativism, as literature even of the remotest past must appeal to us now to be alive. But he also denies absolutism if we mean by it an appeal to fixed standards or a simple statement of personal authority. He always insists that criticism is a communal enterprise, "a common pursuit," appealing to the agreement of a public or at least a circle. The circle seems to have narrowed in later years, and more and more Leavis imposed his authority on pliant minds of friends and students. Certainly his totally negative attitude to almost every writer since the admirations of his youth, since Conrad and Lawrence, is glaring. Leavis has not a good word to say for Virginia Woolf (*AK*, 188), Auden or Spender (191), Aldous Huxley or Kingsley Amis, and is silent on every one of the British or American writers of the last decades who have received some attention. The later writings of Leavis are dominated by the debate, in Leavis's mind, between T. S. Eliot and D. H. Lawrence, and Lawrence has won hands down. Lawrence is exalted not only as the greatest novelist of the century but also for his "incomparable genius as a literary critic" (174), as "the finest literary critic of our time—as great a critic as there has ever been" (*TWC*, 32), a judgment which seems to me refuted by Lawrence's many perversities, shortcomings, and ignorances. Lawrence's judgments on the great Russian writers and the *Studies in Classic American Literature* (1923) with its wild generalizations on national psychology, history, and sexual typology should alone disqualify him. The admiration for Lawrence has blinded Leavis also in his discriminations among the works of Lawrence. The praise of *St. Mawr* or the discussion of "The Captain's Doll," "one of the supreme products of the genius" (43), which ignores its crude message seem to me obvious examples. The whole creed of D. H. Lawrence is refurbished and even made respectable as a sane rejection of machine civilization, as mildly mystical religiosity, as the preaching of a good marriage as a physical and spiritual union, and as an advocacy of an organic society. Lawrence is made over in Leavis's image. Leavis, in spite of all his defiance of the British Establishment and his abrasive polemical manners, is really a sensible critic with scholarly instincts who wants students to respond sympathetically to great literature. Leavis actually holds or implies a theory

of criticism which is not so different from Dilthey's or any other advocate
of understanding. He can say, "I realize the poem, but in realizing it I
have to assume both that it is independent of me and that minds can
meet in it" (*LP,* 53) and that in "reading a poem it is as if one were living
that particular action, situation or piece of life" (111). Quite rightly he
assumes valuation cannot be divorced from fact. Reading in Polanyi and
Marjorie Grene supported his earlier, almost instinctive insight into the
primacy of valuation. These values can be formulated as realism, optimism, the goodness of man, the morality of literature, the community
of a minority culture and eternal students sensitively responding to a
selection from English literature. Leavis is less of an outsider than in his
polemical fervor he would want to be: he fits well into the tradition of
English criticism, in the descent from Arnold, and his success among
English teachers and a wider public testifies to his increasing acceptance
which, within limits, has become even an orthodoxy. His early books
which elaborated Eliot's concept of the history of English poetry and his
exaltation of the Victorian novel (in spite of its exclusions or because of
them) have convinced, as has the singling out of *The Rainbow* and *Women
in Love* among the novels of Lawrence. But the later almost complete
rejection of T. S. Eliot and the uncritical exaltation of D. H. Lawrence
almost in toto seem eccentric. Still, even the latest writings preserve their
interest as expressions of a strong-willed personality, as a reformulation
and clarification of his earlier views and as testimony to a shift from the
so-called classicism of his Eliotic youth to a new romanticism, in which
Blake, the enemy of the enlightenment, Dickens, the "greatest of the
romantic novelists" (*D,* 276), and D. H. Lawrence appear as a new rival
tradition or continuity. Leavis's assertion, not unique to our time, of the
claims of culture against civilization, of a value-charged understanding
against scientific explanation, buttressed by a recognition of affinities
with some philosophers in the phenomenological and existentialist tradition, remain a necessary task for every humanist. In this sense, the
later Leavis has valiantly fought for the central concern of criticism.

9: F. W. BATESON (1901–1978)

IT MUST have been sometime early in 1935, when I was teaching English literature at Charles University in Prague, that my superior, Professor Vilém Mathesius, the founder and president of the Prague Linguistic Circle and the editor of its quarterly *Slovo a slovesnost* (Word and literature), gave me a little book, *English Poetry and the English Language*, for review. The review, published in the first volume of the new journal (1935, 229–31), hails the book as "formulating [I translate freely from the Czech] obviously quite independently, without the slightest knowledge of Russian formalism and other parallel movements on the Continent, a theory of literary history which is surprisingly similar. In a sketchy survey of the history of English literature he shows how this history would look according to his scheme. Bateson's book is another most interesting symptom of the crisis of methods in literary history and a new confirmation that the way out of the crisis (or at least one of the ways out) lies in close collaboration between literary history and linguistics. England—a conservative country also in literary historiography—comes to its methodological ferment apparently later than the rest of Europe. The picture which, in a rather too simplifying manner, Bateson draws of the state of English literary history corresponds to the picture of German or Czech literary history during the pre-war domination of positivism. According to Bateson the writing of literary history in the sense of Taine or Brandes has practically died out. 'The typical scholar,' he says in the preface, 'is today not strictly speaking a historian at all but an antiquary.'"

I then go on quoting or paraphrasing the contents of the book and conclude by expressing "my sympathy with its main theme: the close relationship between literary history and linguistics, the way the problem of literary historiography is seen clearly as the general problem of evolution, the way the difference between poetry and prose and the wholeness of a literary work of art is stated: all ideas with which formalism or structuralism is in full agreement. Also the objections to positivism in literary history, to philosophizing and sociologizing historiography, are convincing, though we must not forget that one can look at literature otherwise than as a history of the art of poetry. A history of literature from a philosophical point of view is entirely possible if we are conscious that we are neglecting the aesthetic function of literature. Bateson's basic thesis, the absolute subordination of the history of poetry to the history of language and the view that social influences can affect literature only through the language, seems to me, however, debatable. Bateson quite rightly refuses to see a meaningless series of irrational changes in the autonomous evolution of literature. He draws from this insight the conclusion that the evolution of literature is necessarily subordinated to the causal series of changes in the language. The evolution of literature in isolation is, however, not irrational either, but is just such a continuous organic series as is the series of changes in the language. Thus the necessity of an artificial distance between poetry and, say, the series of economic phenomena or the development of philosophical ideas disappears. Nothing is isolated and poetry—though it has its own evolution— is subject to direct interference by all other cultural phenomena. Poetry itself affects language, philosophy, and so on, a circumstance that Bateson surprisingly ignores. In short, Bateson has not understood the main idea of Hegelian dialectic, which would have prevented such a one-sided and artificial construct. Also the view that poetry is static is doubtful and derives from a mistaken understanding of the concept of the whole. There is a dynamic whole, a successive pattern (*Sukzessivgestalt*), a dialectical concept perfectly comprehensible if we only think of music, in which a temporal flow of sounds simultaneously establishes a clear pattern or whole. Bateson lacks theoretical, philosophical training and is hampered by his obviously total ignorance of analogous efforts on the Continent from which he could learn methods and theories. But just this independence and the somewhat headlong radicalism of his "Experiment in Literary History" adds to its value as a sign of the times. It reminds us of the almost mystical fact of convergence which is usually explained by the foggy term 'the spirit of the age.' It is after all quite comprehensible, if we realize that a similar state of problems leads necessarily to similar solutions, that certain questions which have everywhere become urgent require similar answers."

I have translated this review written so many years ago, wondering at its brashness and conceit (a collective conceit convinced of the inferiority of the empirical tradition) and also at the hopes there expressed for an internal evolutionary history of poetry, a hope that I have since treated with proper skepticism.[1] But the main point of my criticism, that the complete subordination of the history of literature to that of language and the idea that social influences affect poetry only through language, seems to me still well taken. Bateson himself changed his mind. In the epilogue to the third edition (1972) he grants that "the hypothesis was perhaps too tidy" (99). Actually many of his later arguments about the relation between literary history and linguistics amount to an almost complete repudiation of the early thesis. Linguistics, he argues in a paper contributed to a volume published on the occasion of my sixty-fifth birthday, *The Disciplines of Criticism,*[2] is irrelevant to literary criticism.

In the meantime Bateson wrote another book on the history of English poetry, *English Poetry: A Critical Introduction* (1950), which propounded a very different, equally striking theory. Long before the vogue of German *Rezeptionsästhetik* and similar reflections on the "fictive" or "implied" reader, Bateson stated boldly that "in the poet-reader *relationship* lies the essence of poetry" and that "without the reader's co-operation the poem might just as well not exist" (66). The reader thus "must be the poet's *alter ego*" (64). Bateson draws radical consequences from this insight. The reader or rather the ideal reader is "one of the more intelligent of the poet's original readers" (73). "The ultimate criterion . . . is what the poet meant to his contemporaries" (72), and "the meaning of a poem is the meaning that it had for the ideal representative of those contemporaries of the poet to whom the poem, implicitly or explicitly, was originally addressed" (76). Bateson thus resolutely embraces a view I call "historical reconstructionism," but he differs from other advocates of historicism who ask us to identify with the intentions of the author by proposing the audiences of the different periods as the standards of interpretation and evaluation. He does so by distinguishing the schools of English poetry (mainly on traditional stylistic grounds) and relating them to the then dominant social class. He lists six periods—lawyer's feudalism, the local democracy of yeomanry, the centralized absolutism of the Prince's servants, the oligarchy of the landed interests, and the present-day managerial state (113)—and selects texts to illustrate this sequence. Bateson assumes all the time that "poetry is the particular social order at its point of maximum consciousness" (261) and that the "historical-sociological approach alone provides the critic with a factual structure to which he can attach his perceptions and generalizations" (258). Poetry (and Bateson includes the drama and the novel) embodies, typifies, and somehow summarizes the society of its time. It is "simply the expression in language of the sense of social solidarity" (86). Wittily though arbitrarily, Bateson selects for example four heroines to represent four stages of English society. Alison, in Chaucer's "Miller's Tale," is regarded as "the

embodiment of the yeoman's philosophy of life, much as Shakespeare's
Cleopatra embodies the Renaissance idea, Millamant the Restoration's,
and Becky Sharp the nineteenth century" (134). Detailed interpretations
of poems by Wyatt, Milton, Waller, Gray, Keats, Wordsworth, and Tennyson fortify the scheme. It denies what would be J. S. Mill's definition
of poetry: "poetry is of the nature of soliloquy," "poetry is feeling con-
fessing itself to itself in moments of solitude."³ For Bateson the opposite
is true. For example Wordsworth's later poems failed "because they were
not addressed to anybody in particular" (211): Bateson believes that
"purely private emotion and reflection cannot get into poetry" (79), a
view that seems to deny the efforts of much romantic and symbolist
poetry to express the inexpressible, the most individual, the "interiority"
of man. Consistently Bateson almost completely ignores the adversary
relationship of many poets to their society, the whole problem of "alienation," and rather accepts the contrary romantic dictum: the Grimms'
das Volk dichtet (*Essays in Criticism*, 19:4). He rejects any inspiration theory
(14), does not believe in genius, considers hypnotic poetry undesirable
(29), and thinks that verbal music and "pure poetry" will not stand up
to close examination (52). This collectivist historicism is clearly akin to
Marxism though not in any orthodox version: the determining cause is
rather in a specific audience than in the economic base of the society,
and there is no prediction of the future and no prescription of a specific
style.

Bateson had to defend his view against F. R. Leavis, who argued that
reconstruction is impossible and undesirable and that the critic cannot
help judging by present-day criteria. This has been an issue in the exchange between Bateson and Leavis dating back to Leavis's review of
English Poetry and the English Language.⁴ Leavis then stated that a history
of English poetry "will be undertaken because the works of certain poets
are judged to be of lasting value—a value in the present" (13). Bateson
in his "Comment" understood this to mean that Leavis "will not allow
that there can be any such thing as literary history" (16), and proposed
then to distinguish between two types of propositions, one literary-his-
torical which says that "A derives from B" and one critical which can be
reduced to "A is better than B" or even just "A is good" (16). Leavis had
little trouble in demolishing this difference between supposed fact and
opinion. "Dependence," derivation, is not a fact. It requires "critical judgments of a most complex and delicate order." In *English Poetry: A Critical
Introduction* Bateson granted that there is no "hard-and-fast boundary"
between literary history and criticism but turned the tables on Leavis by
suggesting that "a strong case can be made for incorporating "criticism"

in 'history' " (252), a logical conclusion if all standards of judgment must be deduced from the historical situation. But Bateson was not satisfied with this claim. Later (*Essays in Criticism*, 14:12–13) he explicitly recanted. "I have only recently come to recognise," he says, that Leavis "was in general right." Bateson speaks of this even as "a medicine that took a good many years to work its cure" (19). He seems to have abandoned the historic position or rather sensibly concluded that "literary criticism and literary scholarship are complementary disciplines" (*SC*, vii).

Once he stated the contrast in new terms. Literary history is concerned with the art of literature, which is "historically determined, a mode of communication between the particular poet and his original readers or auditors that was right or wrong," whereas criticism is concerned with " 'life,' which thought it may evolve under pressure from a language and a society, is essentially a total continuum, a mirror of the ways of life, constantly available to all of us" (*Essays in Criticism*, 23:178). Bateson seems here to endorse Leavis's declaration that "the judgments the literary critic is concerned with are judgments about life,"[5] with the odd consequence that art is relegated to history. I cannot believe that Bateson could have seen this and could have seriously defended the position that criticism is only about life. Rather he accepted the distinction derived from E. D. Hirsch (itself derived from Gottlob Frege's distinction between *Sinn* and *Bedeutung*) between "meaning" and "significance," "meaning" being historically verifiable in the past, what Bateson calls also the "then-meaning" (*SC*, 188), whereas "significance" is contemporary relevance, implying a value judgment for the present.[6] Bateson is convinced that it is possible and valuable to recapture the original meaning of a work of art. He accepts the criterion of authorial "intention" and, in many contexts, rejects the "intentional fallacy" formulated by W. K. Wimsatt and Monroe Beardsley, which Bateson, I think, misinterprets to "forbid any attention to an author's other writings, his biography or the social order to which he belonged," an interdiction that Bateson labeled "obvious nonsense" (*ECD*, xv). Bateson produces examples which show the relevance of biography even for an interpretation of Chaucer's "Merchant's Tale" (88–91) and for an understanding of Housman's poems (100–14), in order to demonstrate "the fallacy of the Intentional Fallacy" (114). I need only allude to Bateson's *Wordsworth: A Re-interpretation* (1954) to show how strongly the private conflicts of a poet (which, however, have "a representative quality," 119) determined, in Bateson's eye, the nature and the value of the poetry. Bateson, in advocating the recovery of the original meaning, makes distinctions, at least, as to the desirability of communicating it to the readers of our time. He was a strong defender of modernization of spelling; he ridiculed the idea that we should, if we were consistently "historistic," "recite Blake and Keats with a Cockney accent" (*ECD*, 27), but he strongly endorsed (what Wimsatt would never have denied) that we need to recapture the original meaning of words, arguing, at length, against Empson's unhistorical, fanciful readings. Bateson constantly looked for constraints on the arbitrariness of interpretation in the literary tradition, in the conventions of genres, and ultimately in intellectual and social contexts. "As a result of the series of limitations imposed upon word-meanings, and word-associations at the various contextual levels, a final meaning begins to emerge. It can be called the correct meaning, the object as in itself it really is" (*Essays in Criticism* 3:18). This is the formulation in the programmatic essay "The Function of Criticism at the Present Time," where language and the original language is considered the object of critical concern, though "the final criterion of correctness is the awareness of the appropriate context" (19). In a note my and Austin Warren's *Theory of Literature* is criticized: "The central defect is the failure to realize the crucial role played by language in the literary object" (23n.).

Surprisingly, Bateson abandoned this emphasis on the continuity between language and literature as he discovered an argument against the importance of linguistics for literature. Most clearly in the paper "Linguistics and Literary Criticism," contributed to *The Disciplines of Criticism* (1968), Bateson modified his usual historicism by recognizing that "to become accessible to us critically, the literature of the past must in fact be translatable into the present tense" (7) and that a degree of "anti-historicism is the price that has to be paid for the continuing vitality of an English literary tradition" (8). He now uses the diagram that Saussure in his *Cours de linguistique générale*[7] calls "le circuit de la parole" to show that language is only a remote originating factor in critical response. The composition of a work of literature starts with an idea in the author's head, is then verbalized and transmitted by physical sounds to the ear of the receiver, who, in inverted order, transmits the physical sounds to be mentalized. Bateson appeals to Lessing's *Laokoön*: "in the moment of illusion we cease to be conscious of the means—that is, the words—which [the poet] employs for this purpose" (14). The argument is frankly psychological. Linguistics, whether historical or descriptive, breaks up the continuous process of reception and thus "can contribute little to the critical study of literature" (16). This new emphasis on the process of response, which is necessarily individual and subjective, yielded the main argument against the importance of linguistics for criticism in the exchange with Roger Fowler.[8] Linguistics is or claims to be a value-free descriptive science and thus has nothing to do with criticism. Criticism can be concerned only with style, which is conceived of not merely as a "superimposition upon speech" (*DC*, 10), but as an "inner vision" (*ECD*, 29) that precedes and transcends the linguistic origins. "It is the area of transcendence that is the primary concern of the scholar-critic" (*SC*, 79): "The ultimate function of style is to induce the symbolic condition in which words seem to assume the property of human things, 'significant' human situations or problems" (*SC*, 89). Earlier Bateson had alway focused on poetry: he gave a lecture on "The Novel's Original Sin" in which he states his conviction that the novel is "an inferior art-form" (*ECD*, 242). Its convention is "doing without conventions—one that minimizes the aesthetic distance between the world of art and the world of things" (247). It "deliberately confuses, or at least juxtaposes, two orders of reality: the world of art and the world of things" (243), a feature one would have expected to appeal to Bateson's usual dislike of aestheticism. But in the essay on style (*SC*, 78–100) the very fact that in the novel (and in prose, generally) words do not attract attention to themselves is considered an argument against the crucial role of words in literature. Bateson, to my mind, is right in doubting the critical value of much linguistic stylistics, and he is right, as I have also argued,[9] that literary criticism deals with strata of the work of art inaccessible to linguistic tools, but he must surely be mistaken in divorcing style from language so completely. I can sympathize with his resistance to what I call "linguistic imperialism" and the inflated claims for the new methods of linguistic analysis as relevant to literary study, but one cannot deny that the literary work is a verbal artifact, a "linguistic construct" (as Bateson had said in earlier years himself, for example in *Essays in Criticism* 7:474).

Bateson strongly objected to what he considered the implication of the term "artifact." He appeals to the undoubted fact that a work of literary art is assessible only as a temporal process and not as a structure existing in space: a conception he sees exemplified in the titles of such books as Cleanth Brooks's *Well-Wrought Urn* and W. K. Wimsatt's *Verbal Icon*. He argues that the parallel between a literary work and a speech-act, *parole* in Saussure's sense, "overturns the formalist position" (*ECD*, 11), or, more elaborately, that "to abstract from this human and temporal process 'the best words in the best order' after they have left the author and *before* they reach the auditor, and freeze them into an artificial spatial immobility is to treat *parole* as if it were *langue*. . . . This indeed, in the final analysis, is the Formalist Fallacy" (*ECD*, 11–12). But these formalists (and Bateson adds at times my own analysis of structure as a complex of stratified norms) would presumably answer that they recognize the temporal process of responding (reading or hearing) but do not think that succession is incompatible with structure, *Gestalt*. As I said in my old review of *English Language and English Poetry,* there is something that can be called *Sukzessivgestalt,* of which music yields the most obvious examples. Long ago Joseph Frank argued that the modern novel makes a conscious effort to achieve "spatial form" (*Sewanee Review* 53 [1945]), and more recently he has defended his view well in *Critical Inquiry* 5 [1978]). The point of my phenomenological analysis in my chapter "The Mode of Existence of a Literary Work of Art" in *Theory of Literature*[10] is precisely to define the ontological status of this elusive dynamic structure existing somehow between author and reader. Bateson misunderstands the phenomenological method when he considers the "ontological status a synonym for 'aesthetic' " (*Essays in Criticism* 19:428). This is contradicted by many statements of mine that the literary work must be thought of as an assembly of values, social, political, intellectual, moral, and what not, with the proviso that the dominance of the aesthetic function makes it a *literary* work of art. The ontological status cannot be identified with the aesthetic function. Defining the literary work of art as neither real (physical) nor mental nor ideal but a system of intersubjective norms achieves what must be considered a first step in any theory of a discipline: a definition of its object. Bateson is right, however, on one point in his criticism when he says that "to exclude statues from being works of art is obvious nonsense" (ibid.). My phrasing obscures the fact that I speak (as the context shows) only of the *literary* work of art, which as a language construct differs from a real, physical object such as a statue made of marble or bronze. Bateson, however, accepts my attempt to define the work of art as a system of intersubjective norms. He has his difficulties with the term "norms," which he thinks of as "a standard, a pattern, or type" (*CS,* 54), though they are conceived of in much more general terms as "structures of determination," a term from Husserl which in literature would include any constraints, however implied, conventions, traditions, and assumptions imposed by the text. The formula attempts to put theoretical limits on interpretation, surely one of the most urgent problems of literary study today, when total willfulness has been running riot, not only in France. Bateson has the same aim in mind. My appeal to "collective ideology" corresponds to his "intersubjective relationship" and "the controls against misuse provided by the relevant context" (*Essays in Criticism,* 430). But Bateson holds fast to what seems to me basically a communication theory and refuses to see the work of art hypostatized in any way: he fears aestheticism and cannot agree with the organic view of form (form understood as *eidos,* as totality and not as exterior husk).

"The organic metaphor cannot be taken very seriously" (*SC*, 61), he says, rightly I think, sensing its dangers if the parallel to living organisms is pushed too far. The "formalist" W. K. Wimsatt has seen this, too.[11]

Bateson remained in the empirical and finally psychological tradition. He constantly thinks of the inner processes in the mind of author and reader: the author's imagination, for which he likes to use the Coleridgean term "esemplastic" (an attempt to translate into Greek the German *Einbildungskraft*, misunderstood or punned on as *In-eins-Bildung*), and the reader's response, which aims at empathy and finally identification. But Bateson, who can speak of "the incorporation of the poem in one's own consciousness" (*English Poetry*, 60), tries to socialize this process by making the reader the spokesman of a group just as the poet is the representative of his time and nation. Bateson insists on the judicial function of criticism and denies that interpretation can be divorced from appreciation: "Value is also fact" (*SC*, 25). Judicial criticism must establish a canon, must distinguish between the good and the bad, presumably on aesthetic grounds. For Bateson, however, this judgment presupposes the power to discriminate "between what is good and what is less good in ordinary human behaviour" (*SC*, 66) and that requires some answer to the question of "what constitutes a Good Society" (*SC*, 16). Bateson is also a moralist and a social critic. One sees this in his disagreements with the two most eminent English critics of his time. T. S. Eliot, whom he calls "the best critic since Matthew Arnold," is chided not only for "dogmatism and recklessness of assertion" (*ECD*, 133) but also for "unsavoury class consciousness" and "sheer snobbery" in one of Bateson's last essays on "Criticism's Lost Leader."[12] Leavis, whose "moral fervour" and "total incorruptibility" Bateson admires, is criticized for his "reluctance to realize the democratic basis of his collaborative group." "Dr. Leavis was too much of a 'leader' and too little of a 'chairman' " (*Essays in Criticism* 14:20). Bateson thought of *Essays in Criticism* as a more democratic *Scrutiny*: he had like Arnold—and he called himself frankly an Arnoldian (ibid., 20:1)—the highest hopes not only for poetry but also for criticism. Not only does he expect criticism to increase our understanding of literature but also that "the trained reader will understand contemporary social processes better than his neighbours" (ibid., 3:153, 29). Bateson made many concrete proposals for a reform of the teaching of English, hoping that "the English School is destined to become the educational centre of the university in the English-speaking democracies" (ibid., 9:265). I cannot share these high hopes, remaining, as I do unrepentantly, a theorist and historian, but Bateson has at all points unerringly put his finger on the central issues, has asked the right questions and given answers, not always consistent or convincing to my mind, but always independent, honest answers which display the three Arnoldian virtues of "intellectual clarity, spiritual integrity and social conscience" (ibid., 3:2), which he hoped to foster with *Essays in Criticism*. My topic has precluded attention to his manifold activities as bibliographer, textual critic, editor, biographer, historian of trends, movements, and genres, and, most of all, as interpreter of specific poems. All will have to come to the conclusion that F. W. Bateson, though often a maverick, was a representative figure in English criticism of this century.

10: WILLIAM EMPSON (1906–1984)

WILLIAM EMPSON is unquestionably I. A. Richards's most gifted and most influential pupil. He was his student in Cambridge in 1928–29 (where he was then only 22 or 23) and wrote a thesis for the English Tripos which, obviously reworked and expanded, was published in 1930 as *Seven Types of Ambiguity.* Richards, in a somewhat condescending, avuncular reminiscence (in *Furioso* 1 [1940]) tells us that Empson "brought up the games of interpretation which Laura Riding and Robert Graves had been playing with the unpunctuated form of 'The expense of spirit in a waste of shame' (Sonnet 129). Taking the sonnet as a conjurer takes his hat, he produced an endless swarm of lively rabbits from it and ended: 'you could do that with any other poetry, couldn't you?' This was a Godsend to a Director of Studies, so I said 'you better go off and do it, hadn't you?' And, sure enough, after two weeks Empson produced a typescript of some 30,000 words." In a prefatory note to the finished book (of some 92,000 words) Empson says, "I derive the method I am using from Robert Graves's analysis of a Shakespeare sonnet, 'The expense of spirit in a waste of shame' in a *Survey of Modernist Poetry* (1928)." There in the third chapter, "William Shakespeare and E. E. Cummings: A Study in Original Punctuation and Spelling," Laura Riding and Robert Graves defend Cummings's deliberately odd punctuation and spelling by showing that the 1609 edition of the Sonnets punctuated quite differently (and much more lightly) than modern editions and that the old punctuation and spelling allow different interpretations. (Laura Riding and Robert Graves claim a word-by-word collaboration. Empson forgot about Laura Riding but rectified the omission in an errata slip.) They argue that "it is always the most difficult meaning that is the most final. (There are degrees of finality because no prose interpretation of poetry can have complete finality, can be difficult enough.)" (74–75). They write, for example, of the double meaning of the word "waste" as both "expense" and "wilderness" (79), of "alternate meanings acting on each other" and of "the intensified inbreeding of words" (80). Empson's

276 A HISTORY OF MODERN CRITICISM

method seems anticipated but the mere verbal analysis is insufficient to account for Empson's scheme. Empson is rather steeped in Richards's value theory, in his psychology of literary criticism, and his theory of meaning which allows and encourages multiple definitions as language is conceived as fluid and poetic language appreciated for being fluid.

Besides, everywhere we must assume Empson's adherence to Eliot's taste and historical assumptions, the exaltation of complex poetry and the idea of the dissociation of sensibility which puts the original union of thought and feeling into the time before the Civil War. Empson in a tribute to Eliot acknowledges: "I do not know for certain how much of my own mind he invented, let alone how much of it is a reaction against him or indeed a consequence of misreading him. He has a very penetrating influence, not unlike an east wind."[1]

Seven Types of Ambiguity is, however, hardly a systematic book. I remember when I came to the University of Iowa in 1939, I discovered that the library did not own the book. I ordered it and noticed that the librarian had the title put down as "*Seventy Types of Ambiguity.*" There is, I fear, some poetic justice in this slip. I have never been able to keep the seven types straight. In the preface to the second edition (1947), Empson says himself, "I claimed at the start that I would use the term 'ambiguity' to mean anything I liked, and repeatedly told the reader that the distinction between the Seven Types which he was asked to study could not be worth the attention of a profound thinker" (viii). One must not, however, take Empson at his word. The book would become merely a loose assembly of readings of passages from thirty-nine poets, five dramatists, and five prose writers (as somebody calculated). The passages are interpreted by a method which could be called "loose association," somewhat similar to the Freudian technique to elicit associations from a patient on the couch. The associations are, however, often the result of a search in the *Oxford English Dictionary* or the commentaries on Shakespeare's text. The first example in the book is an elaboration of the implications of a line of Sonnet 73, "Bare ruined choirs, where late the sweet birds sang." Empson defends the comparison

> because ruined monastery choirs are places in which to sing, because they involve sitting in a row, because they are made of wood, are carved into knots and so forth, because they used to be surrounded by a sheltering building crystallised out of the likeness of a forest, and coloured with stained glass and painting like flowers and leaves, because they are now abandoned by all but the grey walls coloured like the skies of winter, because the cold and Narcissistic charm suggested by choir-boys suits well with Shakespeare's feeling for the

object of the Sonnets, and for various sociological and historical reasons (the Protestant destruction of monasteries; fear of puritanism), which it would be hard now to trace out in their proportions; these reasons, and many more relating the simile to its place in the Sonnet, must all combine to give the line its beauty, and there is a sort of ambiguity in not knowing which of them to hold most clearly in mind (*STA*, 2–3).

Here an appeal is made to the possible contents of the minds of the readers in the Jacobean age (who might have feared puritanism and remembered the destruction of the monasteries early in the sixteenth century) but also to a modern theory that Gothic architecture is modeled on a forest, while the allusion to the "cold and Narcissistic charm" of choir-boys imputes specific feelings to the poet: his homoerotic relation to a younger patron. It is an all-inclusive play of fancy, uncontrolled and uncontrollable, flaunting the critic's ingenuity. It has been often attacked as irresponsible. Empson in a note to the third edition (xvi) admits that "it is a real puzzle how the mind can carry the right background ready as if dissolved . . . but we need only say that the more he does that the better."

The last poem discussed in the book, George Herbert's *Sacrifice*, presents a slightly different problem. Christ, hanging on the Cross, is speaking:

Oh all ye who pass by, behold and see;
Man stole the fruit, but I must climb the tree,
The tree of life, to all but only me.
     Was ever grief like mine?

Empson comments:

He climbs the tree to repay what was stolen, as if he was putting the apple back; but the phrase in itself implies rather that he is doing the stealing, that so far from sinless he is Prometheus and the criminal. Either he stole on behalf of man (it is he who appeared to be sinful, and was caught up the tree) or he is climbing upwards, like Jack on the Beanstalk, and taking his people with him back to Heaven. . . . Jesus seems a child in this metaphor . . . because he is evidently smaller than Man, or at any rate than Eve, who could pluck the fruit without climbing. This gives a pathetic humour and innocence . . . ; on the other hand, the son stealing from his father's orchard is a symbol of incest; in the person of the Christ the supreme act of sin is combined with the supreme act of virtue. (*STA*, 232)

Again one can object that this is sheer unnecessary fancy. "I must climb the tree" means only "I must ascend the Cross," and "must" here does not imply Christ's littleness or boyishness at all but merely refers to the

command of God. The tree is the tree of life because the sacrifice of
Christ returned immortal life to man. Herbert thinks in terms of medieval typology, of *figura* (as expounded by Erich Auerbach). Adam pre-
figures Christ. The Cross is the other tree. The Cross is the tree of life
to all mankind but is the tree of death to Christ himself. All the talk
about Jack on the Beanstalk, Prometheus, the son stealing from the father's orchard and committing incest is simply irrelevant. It can be defended only by Empson's disarmingly saying, a few pages earlier, "What
fun! all the Freudian stuff" (223). Rosemond Tuve, in *A Reading of George
Herbert* (1952), has brought a heavy battery of learning to bear on this
poem to show that there are liturgical phrases, Middle English and Latin
poems, devotional treatises, and so on which anticipate the general situation of Herbert's poem and that many details of the complaint of
Christ can be found long before Herbert in texts Herbert probably had
never seen, as well as in texts he might have known or knew for certain
as an Anglican priest. She wants to prove that Empson is mistaken in
speaking of Herbert's "method" and its uniqueness. Empson in his sly
rejoinder (*Kenyon Review* 12 [1950]: 735–38) quite rightly argues that no
amount of background study can solve the problem of poetic value; but
he seems mistaken when he ignores the problem of relevance, of the
correctness of interpretation. Here he goes completely astray.

Still, it would be entirely unjust to consider the book merely a string
of often far-fetched readings. Empson does attempt to construe a
scheme. He tries to arrange his ambiguities "in order of increasing distance from simple statement and logical exposition" (*STA,* 7) and later
actually introduces two more scales, "the degree to which the apprehension of the ambiguity must be conscious, and the degree of psychological
complexity involved" (48). What begins as a lexical investigation of puns,
double meanings, oscillations of one word between different senses, becomes often a probing into the author's psyche and into the presumed
conflicting attitudes a passage induces in a reader. Empson insists on the
critic's ability and even duty to draw conclusions on "conflicts supposed
to have raged within the author" and protests that denying him this task
"means striking at the very roots of criticism" (xiii). Much later, in the
introduction to his edition of *Coleridge's Verse* (1972), Empson, quite consistently, dismissed William K. Wimsatt's argument against the intentional fallacy. "If you accept this theory you have blinded yourself," he
states bluntly (14). Certainly, in *Seven Types of Ambiguity* Empson has no
qualms about ascribing psychological motives to poets. Wordsworth, we
are told, "frankly had no inspiration other than his use, when a boy, of
the mountains as a totem or father substitute, and Byron only at the end

of his life . . . escaped from the infantile incest fixation upon his sister which was till then all that he had got to say" (20). It seems, however, grossly unjust to say that Wordsworth had no other inspiration than the mountains of his boyhood—and Byron, Empson had to be told, did not meet his half-sister until he was 24.

Empson is often very positive about what went on in the mind of poets such as Donne, Herbert, or Hopkins. When Herbert, for instance, in "Affliction" concludes, "Ah, my dear God, though I am clean forgot, / Let me not love thee, if I love thee not," he is paraphrased jauntily as "Damn me, if I do not stick to the parsonage" (*STA*, 184), though Herbert asks God to accept only his sincere love. It may be described as an "ambiguity by tautology," but it was perfectly well understood even in Herbert's time, as Empson himself reports that Archbishop James Sharp died in 1679 with this couplet on his lips. He could not have thought it meant, "Damn me if I do not stick to the parsonage." The assumption of a dilemma in Herbert's life seems entirely gratuitous.

The free association method and the arbitrary depth psychology lead Empson often astray but where he sticks to explication he often throws light on a difficult text, and, as he claims rightly, on the nature of poetic language (*STA*, 80). Good convincing examples are the discussions of the song "Take, oh take thy lips away" from *Measure for Measure* (180–81), or of Keats's "Ode on Melancholy" (214f.).

The first chapter reflects well about rival theories of poetry: the idea that poetry is pure sound, or sound symbolism (quoting Richard Paget, *STA*, 15), that rhythm and meter make poetry are illustrated by a fine evocation of the effect of the Spenserian stanza and some sensitive comments on a sestina of Sidney, its "wailing and immovable monotony" (36). In the last chapter Empson more clearly than elsewhere defends his ideal of poetry as complexity, as tension. "The more prominent the contradiction, the greater the tension" (235). An evaluative scheme is involved: Empson sees the history of English poetry very much in the terms of Eliot, as culminating in the complexities of the late Shakespeare, of Donne, and of Herbert followed by a decline into the wit of Pope and the muddled emotions of Wordsworth or the vague verbalisms of Swinburne. But the overall effect of the book is that of a ragbag of verbal analyses which quickly deviate into assumptions about the psychological conflicts of the poets or simply run off into chaotic enumerations of all possible (and many impossible) associations which might be evoked in the mind of a reader—either contemporary with the author or more often in a sophisticated scholar of our time, with the *Oxford English Dictionary* open before him.

Empson's second book, *Some Versions of Pastoral* (1935), has much more
unity: its subject is the collapse of the pastoral relation between the swain-
hero and the sheep-people. It is again the theme of the loss of community, of the presumed original unity which underlies Eliot's concept of
history. Pastoral is used in a very wide sense: thus the first chapter discusses proletarian literature which Empson considers a covert pastoral.
But even proletarian literature is used in a much wider sense than the
usual one. So-called proletarian literature of the 1930s is dismissed as
"propaganda of a not very interesting kind." Proletarian art is pastoral.
The old pastoral implied "a beautiful relation between rich and poor"
(*SVP*, 11) but this relation has broken down, and the old pastoral has
been replaced by the mock pastoral, the comic variety at first. Both
versions, straight and comic, are based on a double attitude of the artist
to the worker, of the complex man to the simple one ("I am in one way
better, in another not so good"), and this may well recognize a permanent
truth about the aesthetic situation. "To produce pure proletarian art the
artist must be at one with the worker; this is impossible, not for political
reasons, but because the artist never is at one with any public" (15). The
essay begins with an amusing dissection of Gray's verses:

> Full many a gem of purest ray serene
> The dark, unfathomed caves of ocean bear;
> Full many a flower is born to blush unseen
> And waste its sweetness on the desert air.

> What this means . . . is that eighteenth-century England had no
> scholarship system or *carrière ouverte aux talents*. This is stated as
> pathetic, but the reader is put into a mood in which one would not
> try to alter it. . . . By comparing the social arrangement to Nature
> he makes it seem inevitable, which it was not, and gives it a dignity
> which was undeserved. Furthermore, a gem does not mind being in
> a cave and a flower prefers not to be picked. . . . The sexual sugges-
> tion of *blush* brings in the Christian idea that virginity is good in
> itself, and so that any renunciation is good; this may trick us into
> feeling it is lucky for the poor man that society keeps him unspotted
> from the World. (4)

This is considered "bourgeois ideology" though one could argue that it
is much older: simply an acceptance of social hierarchy, of the divinely
assigned or ordained status of every man whether in a Christian society
or any other stratified society.

The second essay, "Double Plots," is the most difficult to assimilate to
the general scheme. Examples are taken from the *Second Shepherd's Play,*
Troilus and Cressida, the first part of *Henry IV,* Dryden's *Marriage à la Mode,*

and Middleton's *Changeling*, always in order to show that the subplot, pastoral or comic, parodies the heroic main plot. Thus Falstaff takes the role of the sheep-people and parodies the King-hero. In the *Second Shepherd's Play* the sheep and the Christ-child are parallel. Even Cressida is somehow considered a version of the pastoral shepherdess.

The third essay analyzes (very much in the manner of *Seven Types of Ambiguity*) Shakespeare's Sonnet 94, beginning "They that have power to hurt and will do none." It shows the twist of heroic-pastoral ideas into an ironical acceptance of aristocracy, concluding after three paraphrases of the sonnet by assigning to Shakespeare what seems Empson's own peculiar wisdom about life, "the feeling that life is essentially inadequate to the human spirit, and yet that a good life must avoid saying so, is naturally at home with most versions of pastoral; in pastoral you take a limited life and pretend that it is the full and normal one" (*SVP*, 114). Literature gives us Utopia, but a limited Utopia.

The fourth essay discusses Marvell's "Garden" again in the manner of *Seven Types of Ambiguity*. The ideal simplicity is approached by resolving contradictions, of conscious and unconscious states, of intuitive and intellectual escape. The analysis of the poem is embedded in a framework which discusses the "magical view of nature" with the example of Coleridge's *Ancient Mariner* in mind, the difficulties of Donne's poem "Ecstasy," and the puns in a passage from *As You Like It*. Reflections about Homer and the Christian and modern concern for the conflict between freedom and necessity are followed by comments on such sayings as "Right is Might" and "Might is Right." Empson himself admits that "this talk about a hierarchy of levels is vague" (*SVP*, 145), but he sees the levels in the three sharply contrasted styles of the fourth, fifth, and sixth stanzas of Marvell's poem. I confess that I do not understand the interpretation of stanza 1 (123–24). The jargon, Richardsian in origin, about "balanced impulses" and "the principle of indeterminacy which no longer acts" seems in no relation to the text though Empson claims that "this idea is important for all the versions of pastoral, for the pastoral figure is always ready to be the critic" (124). I am unconvinced by the other readings. In stanza 6 the words "from pleasure less" are given two alternative meanings: either "from the lessening of pleasure" or "made less by pleasure" (i.e., the pleasure of the senses) is not even considered. The mind withdraws into its happiness from the higher pleasure of contemplation. Empson's dragging out the implication of the tide receding from the word "withdraws," telling us that "the *mind* is *less* now, but will return, and it is now that one can see the rock-pools" (125), seems to me sheer fancy.

I cannot see why the "melons" in stanza 5 are supposed to be an allusion to the apple in paradise and thus to the fall of man merely because "melon" comes from the Greek word for "apple." "All flesh is grass" is quoted to allegorize "I fall in grass" and the flowers which ensnare the poet "are the snakes in it that stopped Eurydice." But the fall on grass seems to me "a proper pastoral fall into the green grass, a fall comfortable and soft,"[2] and there is no need of snakes or Eurydice. The grapes are said to be "at once the primitive and the innocent wine; the *nectar* of Eden, and yet the blood of sacrifice" (*SVP*, 132), but it is unclear why the grapes should be a symbol of the Crucifixion in this context. This wonderful, charming, and witty poem has been smothered by erudition, related to Platonism, Neoplatonism, St. Paul, Bonaventura, and God knows how many other authors and concepts by several learned ladies such as Ruth Wallerstein, Rosalie Colie, Anne Bertoff and Marie-Sophie Røstvig. Empson gratuitously writes of something "very far Eastern" about it (119). But nothing except a very general knowledge of Platonism is necessary for an understanding of the poem. It should be read as a celebration of the contemplative life, away from women, in a garden with a hint of preparation for death, for the "longer flight" of a bird in stanza 7 which is the soul—surely not a difficult, remote, or new image.

The next essay takes up Richard Bentley's pedantic and often absurdly rationalistic emendations of *Paradise Lost* and uses them to criticize "Milton's world of harsh and hypnotic, superb and crotchety isolation" (*SVP*, 153). Satan is seen as a pastoral figure, the judge of creation from outside, while Adam and Eve are expelled from their pastoral paradise by God, for whom Empson reserves the adjective "appalling" (168), an idea later elaborated in his book *Milton's God* (1961). Robert Martin Adams, in *Ikon: Milton and the Modern Critics* (1955; repr. 1966), has shown how inaccurate Empson's use of Bentley and Zachary Pearce's pamphlet directed against him can be, how Empson ascribes his own ideas to the eighteenth-century commentators or misinterprets them grossly. But this seems a besetting sin of Empson and should not distract attention from his main argument.

The two concluding essays exemplify the decline of pastoral into mock-pastoral. *The Beggar's Opera* is seen as "a resolution of heroic and pastoral into a cult of independence" (*SVP*, 203). "The thieves and whores parody the aristocratic ideal, the dishonest prison-keeper and thief-catcher and their families parody the bourgeois ideal" (217). Empson exploits some passages to make much of the connection between "death and intoxication" which, he says, "gives a vague rich memory of the blood of the sacrament and the apocalyptic wine of the wrath of God" (247). He generalizes that "this clash and identification of the refined, the universal, and the low . . . is the whole point of the pastoral" (249).

The paper on *Alice's Adventures in Wonderland* (and also on *Through the Looking Glass*) makes many good points about parodies and allusions and the tone of comic primness and snobbery in the books. It reflects rather obviously on Dodgson's love for little girls. "He envied the child because it was sexless" (*SVP*, 260), but in the reading of the book Empson pushes Freudian allegorization very hard. "A fall through a deep hole into the secrets of Mother Earth" (271) is considered a description of the birth trauma. When Alice much later is cramped into the White Rabbit's hut, she is, according to Empson, "obviously in the foetus position" (271). The sea of tears in which she swims is earlier identified with "the amniotic fluid" (271). "She is a father in getting down the hole" (273; Empson seems to have forgotten about the more plausible birth trauma), "a foetus at the bottom, and can only be born by becoming a mother and producing her own amniotic fluid" (273), a summary which seems quite unnecessarily forcing a literal correspondence which is, after all, completely unprovable. But the paper is considered a classic of Freudian interpretation.

Empson's third book, *The Structure of Complex Words* (1951), seems to me his sanest and clearest. It is least appreciated because it is actually two books in one: much of it is simply lexicography and reflections about the meaning of individual words and recommendations on how to construct a dictionary. Details of the *Concise Oxford Dictionary* (such as its definitions of "rough" and "rude") are criticized. The other half of the book can be called literary criticism: an investigation of key words such as "wit" in Pope's *Essay on Criticism*, "all" in *Paradise Lost*, "fool" in *King Lear*, "dog" in *Timon of Athens*, "honest" in *Othello*, "sense" in *Measure for Measure* and in the *Prelude*, with many digressions and elaborations about the praise of folly in the Renaissance, or sense and sensibility in the eighteenth century, and so forth. The book is dedicated to I. A. Richards, "who is the source of all ideas in this book, even the minor ones arrived at by disagreeing with him." Surely, however, the disagreement is not only minor. Empson in the introductory chapters tries to demolish Richards's emphasis on the emotive meaning of words and to argue that emotive meaning cannot be divorced from referential meaning. He also sensibly disposes of the problem of belief by saying that "we imagine some other person who holds them, an author, or a character, and thus get a kind of experience of what their consequences (for a given sort of person) really are" (*SCW*, 9). Empson then tries to get away from what he now feels to be the purely personal and localized sense of ambiguity and introduces the idea of "equation," which assumes that in a certain period words are ambiguous, or have different equal meanings. Ambiguity refers to a single passage, to a poet's creative act; equation is a collective linguistic effect. "The stock assumptions of the period are being fitted out by the context with simple equations in its pet words," though Empson admits that "in any given period some of the possible equations in a word will be in common use and others used rarely if at all; while some could not affect opinion anyway" (73). The essay on Pope's wit and on sense in *Measure for Measure* are ingenious exercises in such an investigation. I am not convinced by the new conclusion that ambiguity must be based on equations to be effective. Equations may be, after all, due to individual invention. The two early books are precisely open to the charge that they do not realize this clearly. "Fool in Lear" seems to me Empson's most successful application of a simple close reading. The forty-seven uses of the word in the play, its shifts from "natural" and jester to madman and finally to Lear calling Cordelia "my poor fool," are made the springboard for a sensitive interpretation of the play's meaning; the scene by scene analysis is surprisingly similar to Bradley's discussion in *Shakespearean Tragedy* but comes, not surprisingly, to a different conclusion. Empson strongly disapproves of Christianizers: he sees the play in terms of its background in cosmic horror. Lear "the scapegoat who has collected all this wisdom for us is viewed at the end with a sort of hushed envy, not I think really because he has become wise but because the general human desire for experience has been so glutted in him; he has been through everything" (157). But for this conclusion no study of the word "fool" was needed. Empson has here and elsewhere in the book become simply a literary critic who pays attention to the situation, the plot, and the general meaning. He recognizes himself the limitations of his method: "To pretend that every long poem has one key word which sums up all of it would of course be absurd" (74).

A late paper, "Rhythm and Imagery in English Poetry" (1961),[3] formulates most clearly his basic assumptions. The second half is an attack on imagism, on the whole idea that thinking can be done by visual images. "The belief that poetry positively ought not to mean anything is still very strong. . . . I have met people," Empson says, "in the course of my profession who actually hold these delusions; and are prepared to show me that my poetry too, like all poetry, is merely a collage of logically unrelated images. I think just the opposite: arguing in verse seemed to me a wonderfully poetic thing to do" (49). "The Imagist account of the human mind makes it totally subhuman, subcanine for that matter, the

mind of a blackbeetle" (50). "Ezra Pound himself is a very bad judge of
imagery; because he is such a clever man and has such natural good
feelings, that he actually hasn't had to do any conscious thinking for fifty
years or so" (50). Empson rejects the revolt against reason and comes
close to refuting his earlier purely verbal interests: he comments perceptively on a passage in *Winter's Tale* (see 51–52). The story is suddenly
recognized as overriding the image (and the single word). While Empson
has done much to exalt verbal analysis he has, I think, done damage to
criticism by his neglect of the form of a play, or a poem, of its overall
structure, its totality. Here, at least, he sees that verbal analysis is not
enough, that the situation, the fable, the story shapes the verbal surface.
As Elder Olson argued against Empson, "Shakespeare's profoundest
touches are a case in point. 'Pray you, undo the button' and 'The table's
full' are profound . . . we shall not explain them by jumbling the dictionary meanings of 'button' and 'table,' but by asking among other things,
why Lear requested the unfastening of a button and why Macbeth
thought the table was full."[5] Empson himself moved away from his early
preoccupations with words in the book on *Milton's God* and in many later
scattered articles.

   Milton's God (1961) excited much angry reaction for its attack on Christianity or rather on the idea of eternal damnation. Its flippant jeers at
Milton's concept of God and jokes about the sex-life of the angels should
not obscure the literary interest of the book. To be just one must distinguish three different issues not always distinguished by either Empson
or his critics. One is the attack on Christianity in general which is irrelevant to any concern with criticism. Another is the analysis and frequent
ridicule of Milton's personal theology, and last, there is a strictly literary
criticism of the poem itself. Empson makes something of a case for Milton's theology. Milton, he argues, "succeeds in making [God] noticeably
less wicked than the traditional Christian one" (*MG,* 11). "That this
searching goes on in *Paradise Lost,* I submit, is the chief source of its
fascination and poignancy" (11). Empson praises Milton for having "cut
out of Christianity both the torture-horror and the sex-horror" (269),
that is, for glossing over the physical horror of the Passion and singing
the joys of Adam and Eve's prelapsarian sex. The root of Milton's power
is "that he could accept and express a downright horrible conception of
God, and yet keep somehow alive, underneath it, all the breadth and
generosity, the welcome to every noble pleasure, which had been prominent in European history just before his time" (276–77). But usually
Empson pursues Milton's God relentlessly for the whole scheme of redemption, for his "craving to torture his son" (246), indignantly voicing

"cold horror at the 'justice' of God" (268), and often ridiculing him as "a pompous old buffer" (184), "a jovial old ruffian" (124), for his "mean-minded, Quilp-like malignity" (156), or for his indifference to the fate of the damned at the Last Judgment like "a cat shaking a drop of milk from his paw" (271). Most outrageously he speaks of Milton's God as "astonishingly like Uncle Joe Stalin; the same patience under an appearance of roughness, the same flashes of joviality, the same thorough unscrupulousness, the same real bad temper" (146). There seems no point in arguing with Empson's interpretation, which does not heed his own belief that "the central function of literature is to make you realize that other people act on moral convictions different from your own" (261)—and moral convictions surely should include religious and philosophical convictions. But elsewhere Empson refuses to take a historical point of view, to imagine what it meant to Milton to make an epic of the account in Genesis which he must have believed to be literally true. Empson firmly rejects the view that the "first business of the literary critic is to sink his mind wholly into the mental world of the author," as he believes that "the critic ought to use his moral judgment" (200). He does so from an entirely alien point of view which he himself identifies with Bentham's principle "that the satisfaction of any impulse is in itself an elementary good, and the practical ethical question is merely how to satisfy the greatest number" (259). Empson treats a work of imaginative grandeur as a treatise, as a versified *De Doctrina Christiana*.

Fortunately, occasionally something critical emerges from the argumentation against the scheme of redemption. Empson sees the poem extravagantly as "horrible and wonderful: I regard it as like Aztec or Benin sculpture, or the novels of Kafka" (*MG*, 13). He sides with Blake and Shelley in his admiration for Satan, though he recognizes that Milton could not have been of the Devil's party and sees Satan's deterioration and degradation. He admires the scenes in Paradise and tries to defend Eve (as he defends Delilah in a special chapter). He rejects the view of Eliot and Leavis that Milton lacked visual imagination (as he never believed in imagism, which he calls "nonsense" [29]) nor does he sympathize with their strictures against Milton's style. But literary criticism has become only a secondary concern: Empson has become an amateur theologian surprisingly upset by issues a good atheist should not and need not worry about.

Milton's God was Empson's last book, though he continued to publish papers and reviews for another twenty years. Empson, who died on April 15, 1984, had arranged for a collection of his later essays, which came out posthumously under the title *Using Biography* (1984). The book

is ostensibly held together by the use of biography, by the polemical aim
of refuting "the Wimsatt law which says that no reader can ever grasp
the intention of an author" (vii). But this is a gross distortion of the
meaning of "the Intentional Fallacy." Wimsatt never dreamed of forbid-
ding the use of biography and history and used them all the time himself.
Empson's new book contains essays of no or little interest for literary
criticism, particularly a very long article which argues against Fred S.
Tupper writing in *PMLA* (1938) that Andrew Marvell was legally though
clandestinely married to his housekeeper. Also the paper devoted to a
tract by John Dryden ascribed to him only in 1745 which voices deist
sentiments is only of interest to specialists trying to trace Dryden's shifts
of religious allegiance. Even the paper "Natural Magic and Populism in
Marvell's Poetry" is largely concerned with Marvell's character as a citizen
and politician, commenting on some of the satires (very sure about which
individual lines are by Marvell) and only quickly defends his old reading
of "The Garden" against the comments of Pierre Legouis, the French
biographer of Marvell. The other papers can be called literary criticism.
The much admired piece on Fielding's *Tom Jones* argues that *Tom Jones*
has to be taken seriously as expounding a "theory about ethics" (133)
which is "humanist, materialist, recommending happiness on earth"
(134) while seeing no conflict with Christianity. Tom Jones's love affairs
are condoned because they are not mere indulgences of the sexual appetite but are motivated by a "mutuality of impulse," by benevolence and
affection. Tom Jones never makes love to a woman unless she first makes
love to him (137). Empson buttresses this sensible conclusion with an
elaborate theory of "double irony." "Single irony presumes a censor; the
ironist (A) is fooling a tyrant (B) while appealing to the judgment of a
person addressed (C). For double irony A shows both B and C that he
understands both their positions" (131). Fielding "has imaginative sympathy for both codes at once," a statement which allows Empson to reas-
sert ambiguity, moral ambiguity, and even relativism and to reflect: "It
strikes me that modern critics, whether as a result of the neo-Christian
movement, or not, have become oddly resistant to admitting that there
is more than one code of morals in the world, whereas the central purpose of reading imaginative literature is to accustom ourself to this basic
fact" (134). Empson reflects well on Fielding's shifting concept of honor,
on incest, prudence, and benevolence, but underrates (as C. J. Rawson
has shown)[6] Fielding's "emphatic explicitness" and overstates the evasive
irony. Rawson argues convincingly that Fielding restates a then widespread doctrine with an anti-Hobbsian point which he calls "benevolist
hedonism," where self-love and social love are conceived as one.[7] Another

paper, "Variants for the Byzantium Poems" of W. B. Yeats, attempts to interpret the two poems, "Sailing to Byzantium" and "Byzantium," as "science fiction narrative," though Empson has to admit that the symbolist method prevents this (185). Empson argues elaborately from the variants often in opposition to the earlier students, Curtis Bradford and Jon Stallworthy, ridiculing the view that Byzantium is meant to be paradise or that the poems take place in the presence of God (173). No biography is needed except a knowledge of Yeats's distaste for aging, amply documented in other poems. Also the review of the facsimile edition of the original manuscript of Eliot's *Waste Land,* while praising the suppressed Dickensian sketches, does not illuminate the poem by telling something about his family's opposition to his staying in England and Eliot's "grouse about his father" (197). It is elementary psychoanalysis.

The final papers on Joyce are obviously meant to be the climax of the book. "The Ultimate Novel" dates from 1982 and seems to be Empson's last or almost last piece of writing. It goes back to older pronouncements about Joyce. They all protest against the view of Hugh Kenner who made Joyce over "into a nag and scold and a man devoted to God" (203). Empson shows, convincingly I think, that Stephen at the end of *The Portrait of the Artist as a Young Man* has to be taken seriously when he voices his ambition "to forge in the smithy of my soul the uncreated conscience of my race." Smithy, the sword *Nothung,* Wagner's *Ring,* Shaw's socialist reading of Ibsen and Wagner are brought in to buttress the view that Joyce and his hero felt to be another liberator (205). Empson comments that "to maintain that the author intended to jeer at the whole sequence, and dropped hints so that the reader could join him in this activity seems to me to betray a degree of mean-mindedness positively incapacitating for a literary critic" (209). Empson rejects Kenner's view that "the fit reader is intended to enjoy the hopeless fatuity of the thought of Bloom and Stephen" and argues, drawing on Richard Ellmann's biography for details, that Joyce never made his peace with Christianity. It is "more sensible to blame him for an obsessional hatred of the religion" (213). "The Ultimate Novel" propounds an odd thesis about its continuation which Empson considers the solution of the question of what the book is all about, claiming that "if you are not interested in the answer to the great question-mark at the end of *Ulysses* you have no real interest in the book" (229). But it is trivializing criticism to reduce it to speculations about the presumed continuation of *Ulysses.* It is like looking for the picture under the frame. Empson argues with passion and ingenuity that Bloom offers his wife Molly to Stephen, and that he then hopes, stimulated by watching the two copulate, to beget a son on Molly.

Joyce thought at that time "the happy triangle a noble idea" (223). Empson constantly simply identifies the action of the novel with Joyce's own experiences. He complains "at present there is a thick fog blanketing such questions, a general movement among American critics towards formalism or unrealism. Wimsatt's law is a powerful means of destroying all literary appreciation" (225). Empson is right saying, "Joyce is always present in the book—rather obsessively so, like a judge in court" (225), but that cannot mean that the Bloom offer (that is, the fictional Bloom offering the favors of Molly to Stephen) was "never actually made: it would have been, or something very like it, but a miracle happened instead. He saw Nora passing in the street—otherwise he would have lost his real self" (253). But *Ulysses* was composed years after Bloomsday (June 14, 1904); whatever the amount of realistic details, names, streets, pubs, features of men and women, the book is fiction, a construct which should not be reduced to mere language as it achieves the creation of a second world, analogous to our own, but not simply identical with actual events.

Confusion between fiction and reality is also the oddest feature of much of Empson's later criticism which contains often as perceptive interpretations as any of his early books. In discussing Coleridge's *Ancient Mariner* he can argue that "the albatross is shot for food, a soup is made and drunk, and later only the externals of the albatross were hung around the Mariner's neck." It would be easier to do. The Polar Spirit has then some excuse for killing the whole crew but Empson does not believe that there were two hundred of them ("The Ancient Mariner," *Critical Quarterly* 6 [1964]: 301). In an edition of *Coleridge's Verse: A Selection* in collaboration with David Pirier (1972) we are told that the Spectre ship is a slave ship because it is called "plankless," and Empson wonders why the nature spirit should be a seraph. He looked up "seraph" in the concordance to Coleridge's poems and found that in a poem dating from 1796 the bride of the Prince Regent, imagining him before she met him, had "shaped a seraph form and named it Love." Empson comments: "Come now, if Prinny could be seraph, surely a nature-spirit could be. That settles the matter" (46). The jocularity and learned pedantry obscures the genuine insight of a critic who is fundamentally very rational and even rationalistic, believing that poetry "shares the fundamental logic with prose discourse" (103). Empson in this edition rather pursues his old quarrel with Christianizers and allegorizers. The poem, he argues, is not an allegory of redemption through suffering, but rather the Mariner suffers from neurotic and imaginary guilt. "The story is, at most only a parody of Redemption" (38). The Mariner "has been framed by the supreme powers" (40). The thesis, however, cannot convince, though Empson brings in Coleridge's theological opinions at the time of composition, when he professed to be a necessarian. Empson fails to understand the dreamworld of a supernatural ballad.

One can sympathize with the arguments of some scattered essays. Empson shrewdly criticizes Helen Gardner's edition of *Donne's Elegies and the Songs and Sonnets* (1965) for its occasional efforts to tone down the erotic or even obscene implications of some of Donne's poems (such as preferring the reading "they" to "he" in "To his Mistris Going to Bed"). Empson has a better grasp of the tone of many texts than other scholars bent on fitting them into a preconceived scheme of morality. He rejects, for instance, Clifford Leech's view that in Webster's *Duchess of Malfi* "the author and the first audience were jeering at the Duchess for her carnal lust." The Duchess is rather the heroine and the moral of the play is not that the Duchess was "wanton but that her brothers were sinfully proud" (82) as Webster was "sensational about the Roman Catholic southern Europeans." (See "My Eyes Dazzle" in *Essays in Criticism* 14 [1964]: 80–86.) Empson is at his best when the polemical purpose is only incidental, as in the two essays on Ben Jonson's *Volpone* and *The Alchemist* (*Hudson Review* 21, 1969 and 22, 1970). Volpone is characterized convincingly as "powerful and sinister" (653), as "the opposite of a miser because his occupation and his delight is to cheat misers as they deserve" (654). He is right in saying that "we are expected to feel a basic sympathy for him" (656). "Mosca and Volpone are right, as well as clever and brave to cheat the grandees of Venice" (657). Empson even defends the attempt to rape Celia and Volpone's expressions of lavish generosity to her, his glowing enthusiasm for jewels and classical charades in fancy dress. Volpone's final confession is interpreted as his preferring "to be wronged under his own high name" as he has nothing anymore to live for (664). Empson rejects the moralizing interpreters who expect us to feel only contempt for every character in the play, with Volpone the most loathsome. He argues convincingly that "this is wholly out of context with the basic tone of the work," but Empson seems mistaken when he speaks of a final pardon for Volpone. In the play Volpone is condemned to "lie in prison, cramped with iron" and he is removed from the stage in chains. Only at the very end does the actor playing Volpone come forward to address the audience, saying that

Though the fox be punished by the law,
He yet doth hope there is not suff'ring due
For any fact which he hath done 'gainst you.

The actor merely pleads, conventionally, that he hopes not to have offended the audience.

> If there be, censure him; here he doubtful stands
> If not, fare jovially, and clap your hands.

Empson and not the moralizing school (if there is one on *Volpone*) is unable to face the actual ending of the play. The cruel punishment of Volpone should not obscure his magnificence and Ben Jonson's sympathy for his grand gestures and rhetoric.

The essay on *The Alchemist* argues similarly that it depends, like *Volpone*, upon "a rogue-sentiment" (531). Sir Epicure Mammon, however absurd, is generous-minded. His love of luxury is somehow admirable and even Kastril can be defended as a type "terrified that he may fail to die in proper style" (600). As well, the moral of the play concerns "matters of vanity or social advantage, which readily distract the characters from their nonetheless oppressive duty of monetary gain" (608), besides being an obvious warning against superstitious belief.

Empson has been called "the chief English literary critic of the century" by Frank Kermode. He has the merit of developing and widely propagating the concept of ambiguity. In spite of fanciful and farfetched associations he has increased our understanding of complex, mainly metaphysical poetry and the stylistic devices which make for its success. The idea of the fluidity of language has, however, pushed farther than Empson ever did, helped to bring about the theories now current which see nothing but the "undecidable" in poetry. They ultimately lead to complete skepticism and hence to the destruction of scholarship and rational enquiry. The genre concept of the Pastoral in Empson's expanded sense is also an ingenious device to marshal texts into a continuity of history, basically Eliotic in its assumptions, in spite of the Marxist phraseology. With the *Structure of Complex Words*, his most substantial book, Empson broke away from the emotionalism of the doctrines of I. A. Richards and returned to a rationalistic and utilitarian view of language which allowed him to discuss new texts, dramas, epics, and novels in terms of plots and ideas inaccessible to his earlier preoccupations with single words and diction. Empson arrived at a view of literature which makes its discourse indistinguishable from that of any other communication and literary criticism from any discussion of motives and morals. There is not much theory in Empson. Philosophically he seems nearest to the ordinary language philosophy and not as has been claimed to Husserlian phenomenology. He remains a practical critic, an unsurpassed though often willful and eccentric reader of poetry, and in his later writings, a shrewd commentator on plots and situations in Shakespeare, Ben Jonson, Marvell, Milton, Fielding, Coleridge, Yeats, and Joyce. But he rarely discusses a work of art as a whole or judges as a literary critic with some aesthetic values in mind. Basically he is a very secular moralist.

BIBLIOGRAPHIES AND NOTES

INTRODUCTION

NOTES TO PAGES xv–xxiv

1. George Saintsbury, *History of Criticism,* 3rd ed. (1908), 1:36.

2. R. S. Crane, "J. W. Atkins's *English Literary Criticism: 17th & 18th Century," University of Toronto Quarterly* 22 (1953); repr. in *The Idea of Humanities* (1967), vol. 2.

3. Georg Hegel, *Werke* (Theorie-Werkausgabe) (1971), 18:16, 19, 37, 20, 55, 57, 24.

4. Erich Auerbach, "Wellek's *History of Modern Criticism," Romanische Forschungen* 67 (1967): 387–97.

5. Bernard Smith, *Forces in American Criticism: A Study in the History of American Literary Thought* (1939), vii.

6. Ernst Gombrich, *In Search of Cultural History* (1969), 31.

7. See René Wellek, "The Fall of Literary History," in R. Koselleck and Wolf-Dieter Stempel, eds., *Geschichte: Ereignis und Erzählung* (1973), 430–36.

8. Morris R. Cohen, *The Meaning of Human History* (1947), 102.

9. W. B. Gallie, *Philosophy and the Historical Understanding* (1958), 153ff.

10. John Passmore, "The Idea of a History of Philosophy," in *History and Theory: Studies in the Philosophy of History,* vol. 5 (1965), 1–31.

11. I. A. Richards, *Coleridge on Imagination* (1934), 232.

12. Passmore, "The Idea of a History of Philosophy," 31.

13. Thomas Kuhn, *Structure of Scientific Revolutions* (1970), 200.

14. Kenneth Percival, "The Applicability of Kuhn's Paradigms to the History of Linguistics," *Language* 52 (1976): 285–94.

SELECT BIBLIOGRAPHY: SYMBOLISM IN ENGLISH

W. B. YEATS

The Works of William Blake, ed. Edwin John Ellis and W. B. Yeats. 3 vols. (1893). Cited as *WWB.*

Letters to the New Island, ed. Horace Reynolds (1934).

The Oxford Book of Modern Verse, chosen by W. B. Yeats (1936). Cited as *Oxford.*

On the Boiler (1938).

W. B. Yeats and T. Sturge Moore: Their Correspondence, 1901–1937, ed. Ursula Bridge (1953).

The Letters of W. B. Yeats, ed. Allan Wade (1955). Cited as *L*.

The Autobiography of William Butler Yeats (1958). Cited as *A*.

Mythologies (1959).

Essays and Introductions (1961). Cited as *EI*.

A Vision (1961). Cited as *V*.

Explorations (1962). Cited as *E*.

Letters on Poetry from W. B. Yeats to Dorothy Wellesley, introduction by Kathleen Raine (1964).

Uncollected Prose, collected and edited by John P. Frayne. 2 vols. (1970–76). Cited as *UP*.

The huge literature on Yeats often discusses the aesthetics and the criticism in passing. A few such works are listed here, as well as several general books on Yeats and studies dealing with the spread of symbolism to England (which include material on Symons and Moore).

Ruth Z. Temple. *The Critic's Alchemy: A Study of the Introduction of French Symbolism into England* (1953). The fullest and best work on its subject.

Frank Kermode. *Romantic Image* (1957). Discusses both Yeats and Arthur Symons.

Giorgio Melchiori. *The Whole Mystery of Art: Pattern into Poetry in the Work of W. B. Yeats* (1960). Comments well on Yeats's symbolism.

Enid Starkie. *From Gautier to Eliot: The Influence of France on English Literature, 1851–1939* (1960). The treatment of symbolism is rather thin.

Edward Engelberg. *The Vast Design: Patterns in W. B. Yeats's Aesthetic* (1964). Most rewarding.

Thomas R. Whitaker. *Swan and Shadow: Yeats's Dialogue with History* (1964). Fullest on Yeats's views of history.

Richard Ellmann. *Eminent Domain: Yeats among Wilde, Joyce, Pound, Eliot, and Auden* (1967). Most instructive.

Cleanth Brooks. "William Butler Yeats as a Literary Critic," in *The Disciplines of Criticism*, ed. Peter Demetz et al. (1968), 17–42. Excellent for the literary opinions.

Frank Lentricchia. *The Gaiety of Language: An Essay on the Radical Poetics of W. B. Yeats and Wallace Stevens* (1968). Makes good points.

Denis Donoghue. *W. B. Yeats* (1971). Comments well on Yeats's symbolism.

Harold Bloom, *Yeats* (1972).

Richard Ellmann. *Golden Codgers* (1973). Has a chapter on "Discovering Symbolism."

Robert Snukal. *High Talk: The Philosophical Poetry of W. B. Yeats* (1973). Good on symbol and symbolism and on Yeats's knowledge of philosophy.

Vinod Sena. *W. B. Yeats: The Poet as Critic* (Macmillan/India, 1980). Not seen.

NOTES

1. Review of Tennyson's *Poems* (1831) in *The Writings of Arthur Hallam*, ed. T. H. Vail Motter (1943), 190; reprinted in full in 1893 in *The Poems*, ed. R. Le Gallienne.

2. Ellmann, *Eminent Domain*, 66 (a letter to Lady Gregory, January 3, 1913, not in *L*).

ARTHUR SYMONS

Studies in Two Literatures (1897).

Studies in Prose and Verse (1904).

The Romantic Movement in English Poetry (1909). Cited as *RM*.

Figures of Several Centuries (1916).

Dramatis Personae (1923).

Collected Works, 9 vols. (1924).

The Symbolist Movement in Literature, reprinted with an introduction by Richard Ellmann (1956). Cited as *SM*.

Max Wildi. *Arthur Symons als Kritiker der Literatur* (1929). A good Swiss dissertation.

Roger Lhombreaud. *Arthur Symons: A Critical Biography* (1963).

John M. Munro. *Arthur Symons* (1969).

GEORGE MOORE

Confessions of a Young Man (1888). Cited as *YM*.

Impressions and Opinions (1891). Cited as *IO*.

Avowals (1919). Cited as *A*.

An Anthology of Pure Poetry (1924). Cited as *PP.*

Conversations in Ebury Street (1924). Cited as *ES*.

Collected Works, Carra edition, 21 vols. (1922–24).

Malcolm Brown. *George Moore: A Reconsideration* (1955). Contains a chapter on "The Craftsman as Critic," reprinted in *The Man of Wax: Critical Essays on George Moore*, ed. Douglas A. Hughes (1971).

Georges-Paul Collet. *George Moore et la France* (1957). Includes a bibliography of early articles and writings about Moore.

Jean-C. Noel. *George Moore: L'homme et l'œuvre* (1966). A huge (706 pp.) *thèse* that pays little attention to the criticism; it contains an elaborate bibliography.

NOTES TO PAGES 18–22

1. *IO*, 95–102, esp. 97–98: "Two Unknown Poets"; Moore quotes Rimbaud's "Ma Bohème" as "never before published," though he must have copied it from *La Revue Indépendante* (January–February 1889); see Rimbaud, *Oeuvres*, Pléiade ed., 663.

2. See Milton Chaikin, "The Composition of George Moore's *A Modern Lover*," *Comparative Literature* 7 (1955): 259–64.

3. *IO*, 43, 16; cf. *CES*, 73; in *Conversations* Moore reproduces an early article on Balzac (1889) with some changes and reprints a French lecture, "Balzac et Shakespeare" (1910), reprinted earlier in *Avowals* (1919); see *CES*, 67–93.

SELECT BIBLIOGRAPHY: ACADEMIC CRITICS

THE HISTORY OF ENGLISH STUDIES

Stephen Potter. *The Muse in Chains: A Study in Education* (1937). Flippant.
E. M. W. Tillyard. *The Muse Unchained: An Intimate Account of the Revolution in English Studies at Cambridge* (1958).
D. J. Palmer. *The Rise of English Studies: An Account of the Study of English Language and Literature from Its Origins to the Making of the Oxford English School* (1965). Solid.
Chris Baldick. *The Social Mission of English Criticism, 1848–1932* (1983).

COLLINS, RALEIGH, QUILLER-COUCH

J. Churton Collins. *Ephemera Critica* (1901).
Life and Memoirs of J. Churton Collins Written and Compiled by His Son L. C. Collins (1912).

Sir Walter Raleigh. *The English Novel* (1894).
———. *Milton* (1900).
———. *Wordsworth* (1903).
———. *Shakespeare* (1907).
The Letters of Sir Walter Raleigh (1879–1922), ed. Lady Raleigh, with a preface by David Nichol Smith. 2 vols. (1926).

Sir Arthur Quiller-Couch. *On the Art of Writing* (1916). Cited as *AW*.

————. *On the Art of Reading* (1920).

————. *Oxford Book of English Verse* (1900).

————. *The Poet as Citizen* (1934). Cited as *PC*.

————. *Studies in Literature*. 3 vols. (1919, 1922, 1929). Cited as *SL*.

F. Brittain. *Arthur Quiller-Couch: A Biographical Study* (1947).

A. C. BRADLEY

Shakespearean Tragedy (1905). Cited as *ST*.

Oxford Lectures on Poetry (1909). Cited as *OL*.

A Miscellany (1929). Cited as *M*.

Ideals of Religion (1940). Cited as *IR*.

Lily B. Campbell. *Shakespeare's Tragic Heroes: Slaves of Passion* (1930). In later editions, appendices on Bradley.

Lionel C. Knights. *How Many Children Had Lady Macbeth? An Essay in the Theory and Practice of Shakespeare Criticism* (1933). The most influential attack.

J. W. Mackail. *Proceedings of the British Academy* 21 (1935): 385–92.

John Middleton Murry. *Katherine Mansfield and Other Literary Portraits* (1949).

Anne Paolucci. "Bradley and Hegel," *Comparative Literature* 12 (1964): 211–25.

Morris Weitz. *Hamlet and the Philosophy of Literary Criticism* (1964), 3–18.

George K. Hunter. "A. C. Bradley's 'Shakespearean Tragedy,' " in *Essays and Studies of the English Association,* ed. W. S. Roe and H. W. Simeon Potter (1968).

Katherine Cooke. *A. C. Bradley and His Influence on Twentieth Century Shakespeare Criticism* (1972). Gives ample references.

NOTES TO PAGES 28–41

1. "Andrew Bradley," in *Katherine Mansfield and Other Literary Portraits* (1949), 114.

2. "A Retrospect," in *Scrutiny* 20 (1963): 12.

3. M. Richter, *The Politics of Conscience: T. H. Green and His Age* (1964), 14.

4. See index to *ST*; for Rötscher, see *OL*, 252; Gervinus, *M*, 208, and *OL*, 271n.; Ten Brink, *OL*, 298.

5. *Correspondance générale* (1932) 3:31.

6. See Peter Szondi, *Versuch über das Tragische* (1961); cf. Josef Körner,

"Tragik und Tragödie," in *Preussische Jahrbücher* 225 (1931): 59–75, 157–86, 260–84.

7. *Shakespeare's Tragic Heroes: Slaves of Passion* (1930). See Appendices: "Bradley Revisited: Forty Years After," repr. from *SP* 44 (1947), and "Concerning Bradley's Shakespearean Tragedy," repr. from *HLQ* 7 (1949).

8. *ST,* 12f. The saying can be traced back to a fragment of Heraclitus, ἦθος ἀνθρώπῳ δαίμων. See G. Kirk and J. E. Raven, *The Presocratic Philosophers* (1957), 213.

9. Konstantin Stanislavsky, *Building a Character* (1949) and *An Actor Prepares* (1936).

10. See letter quoted by John Britton in "A. C. Bradley and Those Children of Lady Macbeth," in *SQ* 12 (1961): 349–51.

11. London Times, April 7, 1905, repr. in *Drama and Life* (1907), 137n.

12. Sir Ifor Evans in Helen Gardner, *King Lear* (1967), preface.

13. "Christopher North," in *Blackwood's Magazine* (November 1849, April and May 1850).

14. Terence B. Spencer, "The Tyranny of Shakespeare," *British Academy Annual Shakespeare Lecture, 1959,* 163.

15. *The Wheel of Fire* (1930), 7, 10.

16. Prefatory note to the 1949 edition of *The Wheel of Fire,* v.

17. *The Imperial Theme* (1931), prefatory note to the 1951 edition, v.

18. J. Kirkman in *The New Shakespeare Society Transactions* (1877).

19. *The Structure of Complex Words* (1951), 125, 229, 153, 231.

20. "Diabolic Intellect and the Noble Hero," in *The Common Pursuit* (1952), 146f.

21. *ST,* 71ff., and the paper "Shakespeare's Theatre and Audience," in *OL,* 361–93.

22. See Jan Kott, "King Lear or Endgame," in *Shakespeare Our Contemporary,* trans. Boleslaw Taborski (1964), 87–194. Octavio Paz, *The Bow and the Lyre,* trans. Ruth L. C. Simms (1974).

23. *The Uses of Poetry,* English Association Leaflet no. 20 (1912), 13.

24. *Wordsworth and Schelling: A Typological Study of Romanticism* (1960), see p. 5 on Bradley.

25. *The Wheel of Fire,* 39, 45.

26. *On Hamlet* (1948); cf. review by J. D. Wilson, repr. in *What Happens in Hamlet* (1935), 321–33.

27. *The Lion and the Fox* (1927).

28. Expounded seriously by Stanley Edgar Hyman in *Iago: Some Approaches to the Illusion of His Motivation* (1970), 101–21.

29. *Language as Symbolic Action* (1966), 92, 96; cf. my article, "Kenneth Burke and Literary Criticism," in *The Sewanne Review* 79 (1971), esp. 181.

30. Murry quotes both A. C. and F. H. Bradley on the first page.

31. See Richard Wollheim, "Eliot and F. H. Bradley," in *Eliot in Perspective,* ed. G. Martin (1970), repr. in *On Art and the Mind* (1973), 200–49; and Anne C. Bolgan, "The Philosophy of F. H. Bradley and the Mind and Art of T. S. Eliot," in *English Literature and British Philosophy,* ed. S. P. Rosenbaum (1971), 251–77; and the other items listed in these papers.

32. "John Middleton Murry," in *Neglected Powers: Essays on Nineteenth and Twentieth Century Literature* (1971), 352–67.

33. *To the Unknown God* (1930), 265.

ELTON, KER, GRIERSON AND GARROD

Oliver Elton. *The Augustan Ages* (1899). Cited as *AA.*
———. *Modern Studies* (1907). Cited as *MS.*
———. *Survey of English Literature. 1730–1780,* 2 vols. (1932); *1780–1830,* 2 vols. (1912); *1830–1880,* 2 vols. (1920).
———. *Essays and Addresses* (1939). Cited as *EA.*
L. S. Martin. Obituary of Elton in *Proceedings of the British Academy* 31 (1945): 317–34.

W. P. Ker. *Epic and Romance* (1896).
———. *The Dark Ages* (1904).
———. *English Literature: Medieval* (1912).
———. *The Art of Poetry* (1923).
———. *Collected Essays.* 2 vols. (1925). Cited as *CE.*

R. W. Chamber. On Ker in *Proceedings of the British Academy* 11 (1924/25): 413–26.
Arundell del Re. *William Paton Ker: An Appreciation* (n.d., 1929?). Good.
B. Ifor Evans. *W. P. Ker as Critic of Literature* (1955).

Sir Herbert Grierson. *The First Half of the Seventeenth Century* (1907).
———. *Metaphysical Lyrics and Poems of the Seventeenth Century* (1921). An Anthology.
———. *The Background of English Literature* (1925).
———. *Cross Currents in English Literature of the Seventeenth Century* (1929).
———. *Milton and Wordsworth: Poets and Prophets. A Study of Their Reactions to Political Events* (1937).
———. *Sir Walter Scott, Bart.* (1938).
———. *Essays and Addresses* (1941).

———, and J. C. Smith. *A Critical History of English Poetry* (1946). Cited as *CH*.

Sir Herbert Grierson. *Criticism and Creation* (1949).

René Wellek. "The Decline of Literary-History Writing," in *Western Review* 12 (1947): 52–54. Reviews Grierson's *A Critical History of English Poetry:* some passages are used verbatim in the chapter above.

David Daiches. On Grierson in *Proceedings of the British Academy* 46 (1960): 319–32. Reprinted in *More Literary Essays* (1968).

H. W. Garrod. *The Profession of Poetry and Other Lectures* (1929). Cited as *PP*.

———. "Jane Austen: A Depreciation," in *Essays by Divers Hands,* being the *Transactions of the Royal Society of Literature,* vol. 8, n.s. (1929), ed. L. Binyon, pp. 21–40.

———. *Poetry and the Criticism of Life* (1931). Cited as *PCL*.

SELECT BIBLIOGRAPHY: THE BLOOMSBURY GROUP

ROGER FRY AND CLIVE BELL

Clive Bell. *Art* (1913). Capricorn Books reprint (1958). Cited as *A*.

———. *Potboilers* (1918). An interesting foreword to a miscellany.

Roger Fry. *Vision and Design* (1920). Phoenix Library ed. (1928). Cited as *VD*.

———. *Transformations: Critical and Speculative Essays on Art* (1926). Cited as *T*.

Clive Bell. *Proust* (1928).

Virginia Woolf. *Roger Fry* (1940). A sympathetic biography.

J. K. Johnstone. *The Bloomsbury Group: A Study of E. M. Forster, Lytton Strachey, Virginia Woolf, and Their Circle* (1954). Contains chapters on "Bloomsbury Philosophy" and "Bloomsbury Aesthetics."

Clive Bell. *Old Friends: Personal Recollections* (1956). Contains an essay on Bloomsbury.

S. P. Rosenbaum, ed. *The Bloomsbury Group* (1975). A valuable "Collection of Memoirs, Commentary, and Criticism."

NOTES TO PAGES 56–59

1. *Principia Ethica* (1903; repr. 1928), 188.
2. *Two Memoirs,* introduction by David Garnett (1949), 83, 97–98.
3. Letter in Virginia Woolf, *Roger Fry,* 270.

4. Letter to Robert Bridges (1924), in Woolf, *Roger Fry*, 230.

5. Letter to G. L. Dickinson (1913), in Woolf, *Roger Fry*, 183.

6. Mauron published a pamphlet entitled *The Nature of Beauty in Art and Literature* (1928), printed by the Hogarth Press.

7. Rosenbaum, *The Bloomsbury Group*, 372, 373, 374, 375.

LYTTON STRACHEY

Landmarks in French Literature (1912). Cited as *LFL*.

Books and Characters, French and English (1922). Phoenix Library ed. (1928), cited as *BC*.

Portraits in Miniature and Other Essays (1931). Cited as *PM*.

Characters and Commentaries (1933). Cited as *CC*.

Spectatorial Essays (1964). Cited as *SE*.

Charles Richard Sanders. *Lytton Strachey: His Mind and Art* (1957). Contains chronological checklist of the writings.

Michael Holroyd. *Lytton Strachey and the Bloomsbury Group: His Work, Their Influence* (1971). Extracted from *Lytton Strachey: A Critical Biography*, 2 vols. (1967, 1968). A revised edition in one volume.

The discussion of the criticism in Sanders is superior to Holroyd's diffuse treatment, though Holroyd's biography has the great advantage of access to the intimate letters and diaries.

NOTES TO PAGES 59–65

1. In the *New Quarterly*, 1908; reprinted in *BC*.

2. Cf. *BC*, 74, with *Causeries du Lundi*, 1:414.

3. *BC*, 89; cf. *CC*, 107, with *Causeries du Lundi*, 1:431.

4. Review of George Paston's *Mr. Pope* (1909), reprinted in *SE*, 148–49.

5. *SE*, 149; *CC*, 268; Strachey alludes to Valéry's defense of arbitrary conventions.

VIRGINIA WOOLF

A Room with a View (1920).

The Common Reader (1925). Penguin ed. (1938), cited as *CR*.

A Room of One's Own (1929). Cited as *ROO*.

The Second Common Reader (1932). Harvest Book ed. (1956), cited as *SCR*.

The Death of the Moth (1942). Harvest Book ed. (1974), cited as *DM*.

The Moment and Other Essays (1948). Harvest Book ed. (1974), cited as *M*.

The Captain's Death Bed and Other Essays (1950). Harvest Book ed. (1950), cited as *CDB*.

A Writer's Diary, ed. Leonard Woolf (1954). Cited as *WD*.

Granite and Rainbow (1958). Harvest Book ed. (1975), cited as *GR*.

Contemporary Writers, preface by Jean Guiguet (1965). Cited as *CW*.

The Letters of Virginia Woolf, ed. Nigel Nicolson (1975–81). Vol. 1 (1888–1912) contains little of interest for the study of her criticism. Cited as *Letters*.

David Daiches. *Virginia Woolf* (1942).

B. J. Kirkpatrick. *Virginia Woolf: A Bibliography* (1957). Invaluable for locating the uncollected reviews. Of the 375 articles listed there, 208 have been reprinted in the collections listed above.

Dorothy Brewster. *Virginia Woolf* (1962).

Jean Guiguet. *Virginia Woolf et son oeuvre* (1962). Engl. trans. by Jean Stewart (1965).

Quentin Bell. *Virginia Woolf: A Bibliography*. 2 vols. (1972). Contains much new information.

NOTES TO PAGES 65–84

1. She plowed through *Principia Ethica* in August 1908. See the convincing essay by S. P. Rosenbaum, "The Philosophical Realism of Virginia Woolf," in *English Literature and British Philosophy*, ed. S. P. Rosenbaum (1971), 316–56.

2. See this *History*, 4:186.

3. In *The Nation*, December 15, 1923 (the original version of the essay), 433; this phrase was deleted in the reprinting.

4. In *Guardian*, February 22, 1905 (badly cut); see *Letters*, 1:178.

5. Cf. Samuel Hynes, "The Whole Contention of Mr. Bennett and Mrs. Woolf," in *Edwardian Occasions* (1972), 24–38.

6. In *Cassell's Weekly* 2 (March 28, 1923): 47; reprinted in *Things That Interested Me: Third Series* (1926), 160–63.

7. Bell, *Virginia Woolf*, 2:54.

8. *WD*, 22; Bell, *Virginia Woolf*, 2:54.

9. Letter, November 1930, in Bell, *Virginia Woolf*, 2:162.

10. *WD*, 220–21, referring to *Men Without Art*, October 1934; Bell, *Virginia Woolf*, 2:168, apparently referring to Muriel C. Bradbrook's comments on *The Waves* in *Scrutiny* 1 (1932): 36: "No solid characters, no clearly defined situations and no structure of feelings; merely sensation in the void."

E. M. FORSTER

Aspects of the Novel (1927). Reprint ed. (1953), cited as *AN*.
Abinger Harvest (1936). Penguin ed. (1967), cited as *AH*.
Two Cheers for Democracy (1951). Penguin ed. (1965), cited as *TC*.

Lionel Trilling. *E. M. Forster* (1943).
Frederick Crew. *E. M. Forster: The Perils of Humanism* (1962). Good re-
    marks on the checks-and-balances notion of the writer's mind (see esp.
    93–94).
Frederick P. W. McDowell. "E. M. Forster's Theory of Literature," in
    Criticism 8 (1966): 19–43.
Wilfred Stone. *The Cave and the Mountain: A Study of E. M. Forster* (1966).
    Two relevant chapters, "Forster's Esthetics" and "Criticism: The Near
    and Far."

NOTES TO PAGES 84–89

1. *AN*, 25; cf. Eliot, *Sacred Wood* (1920), xiv.
2. *On the Margin* (1923), quoted in M. Philipson, ed., *On Art and Artists*
(1960), 144

DESMOND MACCARTHY

Remnants (1918).
Portraits (1931).
Criticism (1932). Cited as *C*.
Leslie Stephen (1937). The Leslie Stephen Lectures for 1937 (Cambridge).
Drama (1940).
Humanities (1953). Preface by Lord David Cecil. Cited as *H*.
Theater (1954).

SELECT BIBLIOGRAPHY: THE NEW ROMANTICS

JOHN MIDDLETON MURRY

Fyodor Dostoevsky: A Critical Study (1916).
Aspects of Literature (1920). Cited as *AL*.
The Evolution of an Intellectual (1920). Cited as *EI*.
Countries of the Mind (1922). Cited as *CM*.
The Problem of Style (1922). Cited as *PS*.
Pencillings (1923). Cited as *P.*
Discoveries (1924). Cited as *D*.

To the Unknown God (1924). Cited as *TUG*.

Keats and Shakespeare (1925).

Things to Come (1928).

Studies in Keats (1930).

Countries of the Mind: Second Series (1931). Cited as *CM2*.

Son of Woman: The Story of D. H. Lawrence (1931).

Reminiscences of D. H. Lawrence (1933). Cited as *R*.

William Blake (1933). Reprint ed. (1964), cited as *Blake*.

Between Two Worlds (1935).

Shakespeare (1936).

Heaven—and Earth (1938). Published in America as *Heroes of Thought* (1938).

Studies in Keats: New and Old (1939).

Katherine Mansfield and Other Literary Portraits (1949).

The Mystery of Keats (1949).

John Clare and Other Studies (1950).

Jonathan Swift (1954).

Keats, 4th ed., revised and enlarged (1955).

Unprofessional Essays (1956). Cited as *UE*.

Love, Freedom and Society (1957).

Katherine Mansfield and Other Literary Studies, foreword by T. S. Eliot (1959).

Selected Criticism, 1916–1957, chosen and introduced by Richard Rees (1960). An anthology.

Poets, Critics, Mystics: A Selection of Criticism Written between 1919 and 1955, ed. Richard Rees (1970). Cited as *PCM*.

William W. Heath. "The Literary Criticism of John Middleton Murry," *PMLA* 70 (1958): 41–57.

Derek Stanford. "Middleton Murry as Literary Critic," *Essays in Criticism* 8 (1958): 60–67.

F. A. Lea, *The Life of John Middleton Murry* (1959). A good "official" but not uncritical biography.

J. B. Beer, "John Middleton Murry," in *Critical Quarterly* 3 (1961): 59–66.

G. Wilson Knight, "J. Middleton Murry," in *Of Books and Humankind*, ed. John Butt (1964). Reprinted in G. Wilson Knight, *Neglected Powers* (1971), 352–67.

Ernest G. Griffin, *John Middleton Murry* (1969). A helpful, sympathetic monograph.

The John Middleton Murry issue of *The D. H. Lawrence Review,* vol. 2, no. 1 (Spring 1969), contains several useful articles.

NOTES TO PAGES 92–116

1. Eliot, *Selected Essays, 1917–1932* (1932; rpt. 1950), 136.
2. Eliot, *The Sacred Wood* (1920), 48.
3. Mary M. Murry, *To Keep the Faith* (1958), 158.
4. Eliot, *Selected Essays,* 28.
5. See T. S. Eliot, "Mr. Middleton Murry's Synthesis," *Monthly Criterion* 6 (1927): 340–47; Rev. M. C. D'Arcy, S.J., "The Thomistic Synthesis and Intelligence," ibid., 210–28; T. Sturge Moore, "Towards Simplicity," ibid., 409–17; Charles Mauron, "Concerning 'Intuition,' " ibid., 525–33; a letter to the editor by Charles Mauron, ibid., 7 (1928): 263–65. There is an extended account of the controversy in John D. Margolis, *T. S. Eliot's Intellectual Development, 1922–1939* (1972), 53–67.
6. Mirsky, preface to E. H. Carr, *Dostoevsky* (1931).
7. Hough, *The Dark Sun* (1956), 13.
8. C. W. Houtchens and L. H. Houtchens, *The English Romantic Poets and Essayists* (1957), 16.

D. H. LAWRENCE

The Letters, ed. Aldous Huxley (1932). Cited as *L.*
Studies in Classic American Literature (1923). Reprint ed. (1953), cited as *S.*
Selected Literary Criticism, ed. Anthony Beal (1955). Cited as *SLC.* Very useful.
The Collected Letters, ed. Harry T. Moore. 2 vols. (1962). Cited as *CL.*
The Complete Poems, ed. Vivian de Sola Pinto and Warren Roberts. 2 vols. (1964). Cited as *CP.*
The Symbolic Meaning: The Uncollected Versions of Studies in Classic American Literature (1918–21), ed. Armin Arnold (1964). Cited as *SM.*
Phoenix II: Uncollected, Unpublished and Other Prose Works, ed. Warren Roberts and Harry T. Moore (1970). Cited as *P2.*
Phoenix: The Posthumous Papers, ed. Edward D. McDonald (1972). Cited as *P.*

Most of the literature on Lawrence is biographical or concerns the novels, tales, and poems.

F. R. Leavis. Review of *Phoenix* in *Scrutiny* 6 (1937): 352–54.

William Y. Tindall. *D. H. Lawrence and Susan His Cow* (1939). Flippant in tone but instructive.

G. D. Klingopulos. "Lawrence's Criticism," *Essays in Criticism* 7 (1957): 294–303.

F. R. Leavis. "Genius as Critic," *Spectator,* March 24, 1961.

Richard Foster. "Criticism as Rage: D. H. Lawrence," in *D. H. Lawrence: A Collection of Critical Essays,* ed. Mark Spilka (1963), pp. 151–61.

Martin Green. "Studies in Classic American Literature," in *Re-Appraisals: Some Commonsense Readings in American Literature* (1965), pp. 231–47.

David J. Gordon. *D. H. Lawrence as a Literary Critic* (1966). A good though uncritical thesis.

George J. Zytaruk. *D. H. Lawrence's Response to Russian Literature* (1971). Collects all pronouncements and presses their importance.

Emile Delavenay. *D. H. Lawrence: The Man and His Work. The Formative Years: 1885–1919* (1972). Excellent, though prolix.

Richard Swigg. *Lawrence, Hardy, and American Literature* (1972). Makes much of the interrelationship of the criticism with the novels.

Philip Rahv. "On F. R. Leavis and D. H. Lawrence," in *Essays in Literature and Politics, 1932–1972* (1978), pp. 263–77.

G. WILSON KNIGHT

Myth and Miracle: An Essay on the Mystic Symbolism of Shakespeare (1929). Reprinted in *The Crown of Life.*

The Wheel of Fire: Essays in Interpretation of Shakespeare's Sombre Tragedies, introduction by T. S. Eliot (1930). Cited as *WF.*

The Imperial Theme: Further Interpretations of Shakespeare's Tragedies, including the Roman Plays (1931). Cited as *IT.*

The Shakespearian Tempest (1932). Cited as *ST.*

The Christian Renaissance with Interpretations of Dante, Shakespeare and Goethe (1933). Cited as *CR.*

Principles of Shakespearian Production with Special Reference to the Tragedies (1936).

The Burning Oracle: Studies in the Poetry of Action (1939).

The Starlit Dome: Studies in the Poetry of Vision (1941). Cited as *SD.*

The Olive and the Sword (1944).

The Crown of Life: Essays in Interpretation of Shakespeare's Final Plays (1947). Cited as *CL.*

Christ and Nietzsche: An Essay in Poetic Wisdom (1948).

Lord Byron: The Christian Virtues (1952).

Laureate of Peace: On the Genius of Alexander Pope (1948). Reprint ed., *The Poetry of Pope* (1965), cited as *PP.*

The Mutual Flame: On Shakespeare's Sonnets and "The Phoenix and the Turtle" (1955).

Lord Byron's Marriage: The Evidence of the Asterisks (1957).

The Sovereign Flower: On Shakespeare as the Poet of Royalism (1958). Cited as *SF.*

Ibsen (1962).

The Golden Labyrinth: A Study of British Drama (1962).

The Saturnian Quest: A Chart of the Prose of John Cowper Powys (1964).

Byron and Shakespeare (1966). Cited as *BS.*

Poets of Action (1967). Cited as *PA.*

Shakespeare and Religion: Essays of Forty Years (1967).

Neglected Powers: Essays on Nineteenth and Twentieth Century Literature (1971). Cited as *NP.*

Shakespeare's Dramatic Challenge (1977).

Symbol of Man: On Body-Soul for Stage and Studio (1979).

Shakespearian Dimensions (1984).

D. W. Jefferson, ed. *The Morality of Art: Essays Presented to G. Wilson Knight by His Colleagues and Friends* (1969). Contains bibliography and Francis Berry's essays, "G. Wilson Knight: Stage and Study."

A biography by John E. Van Domelen is announced as forthcoming.

NOTES TO PAGES 128–138

1. Herbert Read, *The Cult of Sincerity* (1968), 112.
2. See the review by Mario Praz in *English Studies* (1936), 177–81.
3. Frye, *Shakespeare and Christian Doctrine* (1963), 35.

HERBERT READ

Reason and Romanticism (1926). Cited as *RR.*

English Prose Style (1928).

Phases of English Poetry (1928).

The Sense of Glory (1929).

Julien Benda and the New Humanism (1930).

Wordsworth (1930).

Form in Modern Poetry (1932). Cited as *FMP.*

In Defense of Shelley and Other Essays (1936). Cited as *IDS.*

Collected Essays in Literary Criticism (1938). Cited as *CELC.*

A Coat of Many Colours (1945). Cited as *CMC.*

The True Voice of Feeling (1953). Cited as *TVF.*
The Tenth Muse (1957). Cited as *TM.*
Poetry and Experience (1967).
The Cult of Sincerity (1968).

Hans Walter Hausermann. *Studien zur englischen Literaturkritik 1910–1930* (1938). Has a substantial chapter on Read, pp. 164–200.
Henry Treece, ed. *Herbert Read: An Introduction to His Work by Various Hands* (1944). Contains translation of Hausermann's chapter.
Robin Skelton, ed. *Herbert Read: A Memorial Symposium* (1970). Contains Kathleen Raine's "Herbert Read as Literary Critic," pp. 135–57. Excellent. Full bibliography.
Worth Travis Harder. *A Certain Order: The Development of Herbert Read's Theory of Poetry* (1971).
George Woodcock. *Herbert Read: The Stream and the Source* (1972).

CHRISTOPHER CAUDWELL

Illusion and Reality: A Study of the Sources of Poetry. 1937. 1950 reprint used. Quoted as *IR.*
Studies in a Dying Culture, with an introduction by John Strachey (1938).
Further Studies in a Dying Culture, ed. and with a preface by Edgell Rickword (1949).
Romance and Realism: A Study in English Bourgeois Literature, ed. by Samuel Hynes (1970).

Stanley Hyman. *The Armed Vision* (1948), pp. 168–208.
David N. Margolies. *The Function of Literature: A Study of Christopher Caudwell's Aesthetics* (1969). Marxist.
Georg Lukács. *Probleme der Aesthetik* (vol. 10 of *Werke,* (1969), pp. 768–69 and in *Aesthetik,* vol. 1 of *Werke,* vol. 11 (1963), pp. 267–68. Lukács comments on Caudwell briefly.

SELECT BIBLIOGRAPHY: THE INNOVATORS

T. E. HULME

T. E. Hulme. *Speculations,* ed. Herbert Read (1924). Cited as *S.*
———. *Further Speculations,* ed. Sam Hynes (1955). Cited as *FS.*

Michael Roberts. *T. E. Hulme* (1938).
Murray Krieger. "The Ambiguous Anti-Romanticism of T. E. Hulme," *ELH* 20 (1953): 300–14.

Murray Krieger. *The New Apologists for Poetry* (1956), pp. 31–45.

Alun Richard Jones. *T. E. Hulme* (1960).

Jan J. Kamerbeek. "T. E. Hulme and German Philosophy: Dilthey and Scheler," *Contemporary Literature* 31 (1969): 193–212.

Cyrena Pondrom. "Hulme's 'A Lecture on Modern Poetry' and the Birth of Imagism," *Papers on Language and Literature* 5 (1969): 465–70.

Ronald Schuchard. "Eliot and Hulme in 1916," *PMLA* 88 (1978): 1083–94.

Miriam Hansen and Helmut Vierbrock. "Thomas Ernest Hulme's 'Speculations': Kunstphilosophie and Dichtungstheorie im Dienst von Weltanschauung," in *Englische und Amerikanische Literaturtheorie* (1979), ed. Rüdiger Ahrens and Erwin Wolff, 2:281–311.

EZRA POUND

The Spirit of Romance (1910). New Directions ed. (1953), with corrections and an inserted chapter, cited as *SR*.

Instigations (1920).

How to Read (1931).

ABC of Reading (1934). New Directions ed. (1960), cited as *ABC*.

Polite Essays (1937). Cited as *PE*.

Guide to Kulcher (1938). New Directions ed. (1952), with addenda, cited as *GK*.

The Letters of Ezra Pound (1907–41), ed. D. D. Paige (1950). Cited as *L*.

Literary Essays of Ezra Pound, ed. with an introduction by T. S. Eliot (1954). Reprint ed. (1968), cited as *LE*.

Pound/Joyce: The Letters of Ezra Pound to James Joyce, ed. Forrest Read (1967). Reprint ed. (1970), cited as *P/J*.

Selected Prose, 1909–1965, ed. William Cookson (1973).

There is a huge literature on Pound, biographical, exegetical, apologetical, but little is focused on the literary criticism.

Herbert Bergman. "Ezra Pound and Walt Whitman," *American Literature* 27 (1955): 56–61.

Peter Demetz. "Ezra Pound's German Studies," *Germanic Review* 31 (1956): 279ff.

Gian N. Orsini. "Ezra Pound: Critico letterario," *Letterature moderne* 7 (1957): 34–51. A devastating attack.

George Kennedy. "Fenollosa, Pound and the Chinese Character," *Yale Literary Magazine* 126 (1958): 24–36.

Donald A. Gallup. *A Bibliography of Ezra Pound* (1963). Indispensable.

N. Christoph de Nagy. *Ezra Pound's Poetics and Literary Tradition: The Critical Decade* (1966).
Richard Ellmann. "Ez and Old Billyum," in *New Approaches to Ezra Pound,* ed. Eva Hesse (1969), pp. 55–85.
Max Nänni. *Ezra Pound: Poetics for an Electric Age* (1973).
Miriam Hansen. *Ezra Pounds frühe Poetik und Kulturkritik zwischen Aufklärung und Avantgarde* (1979).
Ian F. A. Bell. *Critic as Scientist: The Modernist Poetics of Ezra Pound* (1981).

NOTES TO PAGES 152–169

1. See Ulrich Weisstein, *Yearbook of Comparative and General Literature* 13 (1964): 28–40; reprinted in *Expressionism as an International Literary Phenomenon* (1973), 167–80.
2. Fischer, *Ezra Pound: 22 Versuche,* ed. Eva Hesse (1966), 167–81.
3. Fleming, "Ezra Pound and the French Language," in *Ezra Pound: Perspectives,* ed. Noel Stock (1965), 129–50.
4. Brooke-Rose, *ZBC of Ezra Pound* (1971), 123f.
5. Kenner, *The Theory of Ezra Pound* (1951), 98.
6. Praz, "T. S. Eliot and Dante," in *T. S. Eliot: A Selected Critique,* ed. L. Unger (1948), 298f.
7. See "Vorticism," in *Fortnightly review,* n.s. 96 (1914): 461–71; and in *Gaudier-Brzeska: A Memoir* (1960), 84.
8. Ellmann, "Ez," 55–85.
9. See Thomas Parkinson, "Yeats and Pound," *Comparative Literature* 6 (1954): 256–64.
10. See *LE,* 288; "A Study of French Poets," in *Instigations*; "Approach to Paris" (1913), in *Selected Prose.*

WYNDHAM LEWIS

The Lion and the Fox (1927). Cited as *LF.*
Time and Western Man (1927). Cited as *TWM.*
Paleface (1929). Cited as *P.*
Men Without Art (1934). Cited as *MA.*
Rude Assignment (1950).
Letters, ed. W. K. Rose (1963).
Wyndham Lewis on Art: Collected Writings, 1913–1956, ed. Walther Michel and C. J. Fox (1969). Cited as *OA.*
Enemy Salvoes: Selected Literary Criticism, ed. C. J. Fox, introduction by C. H. Sisson (1975). Cited as *ES.* Excellent.

Hugh Kenner. *Wyndham Lewis* (1954).

Geoffrey Wagner. *Wyndham Lewis: Portrait of the Artist as the Enemy* (1957).
William H. Pritchard. *Wyndham Lewis* (1968). Has a good chapter on criticism.
————. "Wyndham Lewis," in *Profiles in Literature* (1972). Short extracts with commentary.
Fredric Jameson. *Fables of Aggression: Wyndham Lewis, the Modernist as Fascist* (1979).
Jeffrey Meyers. *The Enemy: A Biography of Wyndham Lewis* (1980).

SELECT BIBLIOGRAPHY: T. S. ELIOT

The Sacred Wood: Essays on Poetry and Criticism (1920). Cited as *SW*.
"A Brief Treatise on the Criticism of Poetry," *Chapbook* 2 (1920): 1–10. Cited as *BTCP*.
For Lancelot Andrewes (1928). Cited as *FLA*.
Preface to Ezra Pound, *Selected Poems* (1928). Cited as *SPEP*.
A Garland for John Donne, ed. Theodore Spencer (1930). Cited as *GJD*.
Introduction to G. Wilson Knight, *The Wheel of Fire* (1930). Cited as *WF*.
Selected Essays 1917–1932 (1932). Cited as *SE*.
John Dryden the Poet, the Dramatist, the Critic (1932). Cited as *JD*.
The Use of Poetry and the Use of Criticism (1933). Cited as *UP*.
After Strange Gods: A Primer of Modern Heresy (1934). Cited as *ASG*.
Preface to Marianne Moore, *Selected Poems by Marianne Moore* (1935). Cited as *SPMM*.
Essays Ancient and Modern (1936). Cited as *EAM*.
Points of View (1941). Cited as *PV*.
"The Social Function of Poetry," in *Critiques and Essays in Criticism,* ed. R. W. Stallman (1949), pp. 105–16.
"Poetry and Propaganda," in *Literary Opinion in America,* ed. Morton Dauwen Zabel (1951), pp. 97–107. Rev. ed., cited as *Z*.
On Poetry and Poets (1957). Cited as *OPP*.
Introduction to Paul Valéry, *Art of Poetry* (1958). Cited as *AP*.
Knowledge and Experience in the Philosophy of F. H. Bradley (1963). Cited as *KE*.
To Criticize the Critic and other Writings (1965). Cited as *CC*.

There is a huge literature on Eliot as a person, his poems and plays, his social, political, and religious views. I list items only directly concerned with literary criticism, though general books contain incidental discussions of the criticism, too.

Ans Oras. *The Critical Ideas of T. S. Eliot* (1932). The first monograph.

J. C. Ransom. "T. S. Eliot: The Historical Critic," in *The New Criticism* (1941).

Yvor Winters. "T. S. Eliot, or the Illusion of Reaction," in *The Anatomy of Nonsense* (1943).

Muriel C. Bradbook. "Eliot's Critical Method," in *T. S. Eliot: A Study of His Writings by Several Hands,* ed. B. Rayam. Reprint ed. (1966).

Leonard Unger, ed. *T. S. Eliot: A Selected Critique* (1948).

Victor Brombert. *The Criticism of T. S. Eliot: Problems of an "Impersonal Theory" of Poetry* (1949).

Kristian Smid. *Poetry and Belief in the Work of T. S. Eliot* (1949). London ed. (1961).

Edward J. Greene. *T. S. Eliot et la France* (1951).

Eliseo Vivas. "The Objective Correlative of T. S. Eliot," in *Creation and Discovery* (1955), pp. 175–90.

Vincent Buckley. *Poetry and Morality: Studies on the Criticism of Matthew Arnold, T. S. Eliot and F. R. Leavis* (1959).

Séan Lucy. *T. S. Eliot and the Idea of Tradition* (1960).

Lewis Freed. *T. S. Eliot: Aesthetics and History* (1962).

Herbert Howarth. *Notes on Some Figures behind T. S. Eliot* (1964).

Christian Karlson Stead. *The New Poetics* (1964).

Fei-pei Lu. *T. S. Eliot: The Dialectic Structure of His Theory of Poetry* (1966).

Allen Tate, ed. *T. S. Eliot: The Man and His Work. A Critical Evaluation by 26 Distinguished Writers* (1966).

F. R. Leavis. "T. S. Eliot as Critic," in *Anna Karenina and Other Essays* (1967), pp. 177–96.

Donald C. Gallup. *T. S. Eliot: A Bibliography* (1969). Indispensable.

Austin Warren. "Continuity and Coherence in the Criticism of T. S. Eliot," in *Connections* (1970), pp. 152–84.

Richard Wollheim. "Eliot and F. H. Bradley," in *Eliot in Perspective,* ed. G. Martin (1970). Reprinted in *On Art and the Mind* (1973), pp. 200–49.

John D. Margolis. *T. S. Eliot's Intellectual Development* (1972).

Mildred Martin. *A Half Century of Eliot Criticism: An Annotated Bibliography of Books and Articles in English, 1916–1965* (1972).

Armin Paul Frank. *Die Sehnsucht nach dem unteilbaren Sein. Motiv und Motivation in der Literaturkritik T. S. Eliots* (1973). Excellent.

Ronald Schuchard. "Eliot and Hulme in 1916: Towards a Revaluation of Eliot's Critical and Spiritual Development," *PMLA* 88 (1973): 1083–94.

Mowbray Allan. *T. S. Eliot's Impersonal Theory of Poetry* (1974).

Ronald Schuchard. "T. S. Eliot as an Extension Lecturer, 1916–1919," *Review of English Studies* (May, August 1974): 163–73; 292–304.

Allen Austin. *T. S. Eliot: The Literary and Social Criticism* (1974).

Harry Levin. *Ezra Pound, T. S. Eliot and the European Horizon: A Lecture* (1975).

Lyndall Gordon. *Eliot's Early Years* (1977).

David Newton-de Molina, ed. *The Literary Criticism of T. S. Eliot: New Essays* (1977).

Mechtild and Armin Paul Frank and K. P. S. Jochum, comp. *T. S. Eliot Criticism in English, 1916–65: A Supplementary Bibliography* (1978).

Lewis Freed. *T. S. Eliot: The Critic as Philosopher* (1979). On the influence of F. H. Bradley.

Brian Lee. *Theory and Personality: The Significance of T. S. Eliot's Criticism* (1979).

Edward Lobb. *T. S. Eliot and the Romantic Critical Tradition* (1981).

Michael Grant, ed. *T. S. Eliot: The Critical Heritage,* 2 vols. (1982). Confined to reviews of Eliot's poems and plays.

Piers Gray. *T. S. Eliot's Intellectual and Poetic Development, 1909–1922* (1982).

Ronald Bush. *T. S. Eliot: A Study in Character and Style* (1983). Quotes unpublished Clark lectures.

Gregory S. Jay. *T. S. Eliot and the Poetics of Literary History* (1983).

Michele Hannoosh. "Metaphysicality and Belief: Eliot on Laforgue," *Comparative Literature* 1985, forthcoming. Quotes unpublished lectures.

NOTES TO PAGES 176–220

1. Richard March and Tambimuttu, *T. S. Eliot: A Symposium* (1949), 86.

2. Bush, *T. S. Eliot,* 83.

3. See Frank, *Die Sehnsucht nach dem unteilbaren Sein,* 206ff.

4. See René Wellek, "Hofmannsthal als Literaturkritiker," *Arcadia,* 20 (June 1985), pp. 61–71.

5. *Interpretations of Poetry and Religion* (1900), 277.

6. *Essays on Truth and Reality* (1914), 190.

7. Vivas, *Creation and Discovery,* 189.

8. See "Shakespears Verskunst," in *Essays* (1949), ed. Helmut Viebrock, 103.

9. Introduction to Charlotte Eliot, *Savonarola* (1926), xi.

10. St. John Perse, *Anabasis* (1930), preface, 9.

11. Introduction to Johnson's *London* and *The Vanity of Human Wishes* (1930).

12. Preface to Harry Crosby, *Transit of Venus* (1931), ix.

13. *GJD*, 10.

14. "Cyril Tourneur," in *SE*, 190; cf. *EAM*, 152.

15. Johnson's *London* (1930) and *OPP*, 162ff.

16. In Lecture III of the unpublished Clark lectures, quoted in Bush, *T. S. Eliot.*

17. See his review of *Secentismo e marinismo in Inghilterra* in *TLS*, December 11, 1925, 878.

18. *Chroniques* 3 (1927): 162.

19. Hannoosh, quoting Lecture VIII, 170.

20. Hannoosh, quoting Lecture III, 5 and 8.

21. *Le Serpent* (1924), 8.

22. *Revelation* (1937), 28ff.

23. *D. H. Lawrence and Human Existence* (1951), viii.

SELECT BIBLIOGRAPHY: I. A. RICHARDS

The Meaning of Meaning, with C. K. Ogden (1923). Cited as *MM.*
Principles of Literary Criticism (1924). Cited as *PLC.*
Science and Poetry (1926). Cited as *SP.*
Practical Criticism (1929). Cited as *PC.*
Coleridge on Imagination (1934). Cited as *CI.*
The Philosophy of Rhetoric (1936). Cited as *PR.*
Speculative Instruments (1955). Cited as *SI.*
The Screens and Other Poems (1960). Cited as *Screens.*
Style in Language, ed. Thomas E. Sebeok (1960). Cited as *Style.*

J. C. Ransom. *World's Body* (1938).
———. *The New Criticism* (1941).
Stanley E. Hyman. *The Armed Vision* (1948).
R. S. Crane. *Critics and Criticism* (1952).
E. Vivas. *Creation and Discovery* (1955).
Murray Krieger. *The New Apologists for Poetry* (1956).
R. J. Foster. *The New Romantics* (1962).
W. H. N. Hotopf. *Language, Thought, and Comprehension: A Case Study in the Writings of I. A. Richards* (1965).
Jerome P. Schiller. *I. A. Richards's Theory of Literature* (1969).
John Paul Russo. "Richards and the Search for Critical Instruments," in *Twentieth Century Literature in Retrospect* (1971), ed. Reuben Brower.

Helen Vendler, Reuben Brower, and John Hollander, eds. *I. A. Richards: Essays in His Honor* (1973). Bibliography by John Paul Russo.
Murray Krieger. *Poetic Presence and Illusion* (1979).
John Needham. *The Completest Mode: I. A. Richards and the Continuity of English Literary Tradition* (1982).

NOTES TO PAGES 221–238

1. *Slovo a slovesnost* (Word and Literature) 3 (1937): 108–21.
2. Published in *Yale Review* 39 (1949): 108–18.
3. *Philosophical Review* 57 (1949): 145–57; reprinted in *SI*, 39–56.
4. *How To Read a Page* (1942), 15.
5. "The God of Dostoevsky," *Forum* 78 (1927): 97.
6. *The Use of Poetry and the Use of Criticism* (1933), 135.
7. *Sense of Beauty* (1896), 235.
8. *Forster: A Collection of Critical Essays*, ed. M. Bradbury (1966), 19–20.

SELECT BIBLIOGRAPHY: F. R. LEAVIS

How to Teach Reading: A Primer for Ezra Pound (1932) (repr. in *Education and the University*, 1943).
New Bearings in English Poetry (1932). Cited as *NB*.
Culture and Environment, with Denys Thompson (1933). Cited as *CE*.
For Continuity (1933).
Towards Standards of Criticism: Selections from the Calendar of Modern Letters, 1925–27 (1933).
Determinations: Critical Essays (1934).
Revaluation: Tradition and Development in English Poetry (1936). Cited as *R*.
Education and the University (1943). 2nd ed. (1948), cited as *EU*.
The Great Tradition: George Eliot, Henry James, Joseph Conrad (1948). Cited as *GT*.
The Importance of Scrutiny, ed. Eric Bentley (1948). Cited as *IS*.
The Common Pursuit (1952). Cited as *CP*.
D. H. Lawrence: Novelist (1955). Cited as *DHL*.
Scrutiny: A Retrospect (1963).
Two Cultures? The Significance of C. P. Snow's Richmond Lecture (1963).
Anna Karenina and Other Essays (1967). Cited as *AK*.
A Selection from Scrutiny, ed. F. R. Leavis (1968).
English Literature in Our Time and the University (1969). Cited as *EL*.
Lectures in America, with Q. D. Leavis (1969). Cited as *LA*.

Dickens: The Novelist, with Q. D. Leavis (1970). Cited as *D*.

"Wordsworth: The Creative Conditions," in *Twentieth-Century Literature in Retrospect*, ed. Reuben A. Brower (1971).

Nor Shall My Sword: Discourses on Pluralism, Compassion and Social Hope (1972). Cited as *NS*.

"Justifying One's Evaluation of Blake," in *William Blake: Essays in Honour of Sir Geoffrey Keynes*, ed. Morton Paley and Michael Phillips (1973).

Letters in Criticism, ed. John Tasker (1974). A collection of Leavis's letters to the press, containing items of interest. Cited as *LC*.

The Living Principle: "English" as a Discipline of Thought (1975). Cited as *LP*.

Thought, Words and Creativity: Art and Thought in Lawrence (1976). Cited as *TWC*.

Reading Poetry and Eugenio Montale: A Tribute (1979).

The Critic as Anti-Philosopher, ed. E. Singh (1982). See my review in *Modern Language Review* 79 (1984): 174–76.

René Wellek. "Literary Criticism and Philosophy," *Scrutiny* 5 (1937): 375–83 (repr. in *IS*, 23–30).

———. "Correspondence: Literary Criticism and Philosophy," *Scrutiny* 6 (1937): 195–96.

H. A. Mason. "F. R. Leavis and *Scrutiny*," *Critic* 1 (1947): 21–34.

Martin Jarett-Kerr. "The Literary Criticism of F. R. Leavis," *Essays in Criticism* 2 (1952): 351–68.

Bernard C. Heyl. "The Absolutism of F. R. Leavis," *Journal of Aesthetics and Art Criticism* 13 (1954): 249–55.

L. D. Lerner. "The Life and Death of *Scrutiny*," *London Magazine* 2 (1955): 68–77.

Lionel Trilling. "Leavis and the Moral Tradition," in *A Gathering of Fugitives* (1956).

Eliseo Vivas. "Mr. Leavis on D. H. Lawrence," *Sewanee Review* 65 (1957): 123–36.

Vincent Buckley. *Poetry and Morality: Studies in Criticism of Arnold, Eliot, and Leavis* (1959), pp. 158–213.

James Holloway. "The 'New Establishment' in Criticism," in *The Charted Mirror* (1960), pp. 204–26.

Andor Gomme. "Criticism and the Reading Public," in *The Modern Age*, vol. 7 of *The Pelican Guide to English Literature*, ed. Boris Ford (1961), pp. 350–76.

George Steiner. "F. R. Leavis," *Encounter* 18 (May 1962): 37–45 (repr. in *Language and Silence*, 1967, pp. 221–38).

Lionel Trilling. "Science, Literature and Culture: The Leavis-Snow Controversy," *Commentary* 33 (1962): 461–77 (repr. in *Beyond Culture*, 1965, pp. 145–77).

George Watson. *The Literary Critics* (1962), pp. 208–15.

E. Singh. "Better History and Better Criticism: The Significance of F. R. Leavis," *English Miscellany* 16 (1965): 215–79.

Andor Gomme. *Attitudes to Criticism* (1966).

Ronald Hayman. *Leavis* (1966).

D. F. McKenzie and M. P. Allum. *F. R. Leavis: A Checklist, 1924–64* (1966). Contains an out-of-date bibliography.

F. W. Bateson. "The *Scrutiny* Phenomenon," *Sewanee Review* 85 (1977): 144–52.

Robert Boyer. *F. R. Leavis: Judgment and the Discipline of Thought* (1978).

R. P. Bilan. *The Literary Criticism of F. R. Leavis* (1979).

Francis Mulhern. *The Moment of 'Scrutiny'* (1979). See my review of the previous three books in *Modern Language Review* 76 (1981): 175–80.

William Walsh. *F. R. Leavis* (1980). Also contains a chapter on Q. D. Leavis. See my review in *Modern Language Review* 77 (1982): 710–12.

P. J. M. Robertson. *The Leavises on Fiction: A Historic Partnership* (1981).

Denys Thompson, ed. *The Leavises: Recollections and Impressions* (1984).

Q. D. LEAVIS

Fiction and the Reading Public (1932).

Bibliography in *Scrutiny* 20 (1963).

Collected Essays, vol. 1 of *The Englishness of the English Novel*, ed. G. Singh (1983). Two more vols. to follow.

NOTES TO PAGES 239–264

1. *New York Times*, March 10, 1962. Leavis's lecture was printed as "The Significance of C. P. Snow," *Spectator* (1962): 297–303. Snow's pamphlet was his Rede Lecture, Cambridge, 1959.

2. Leavis, in "A New Preface for the American Reader'" to *Two Cultures? The Significance of C. P. Snow*, chides Trilling as "guilty of *la trahison des clercs*" (16), surprisingly and perversely.

3. *An Approach to Shakespeare* (1938; rpt. 1956) and *Shakespeare: The Last Phase* (1955).

4. *NB*, ix; *CP*, 280; and, more grudgingly, "T. S. Eliot's Stature as Critic," *Commentary* 26 (1958): 399.

5. *GT*, 2–3: "Life isn't long enough to permit one's giving much time to Fielding." "Sterne's irresponsible (and nasty) trifling."

6. Q. D. Leavis, "A Critical Theory of Jane Austen's Writings," *Scrutiny* 10 (1941): 61–87, 114–42, 272–94; and 12 (1944): 104–19, on the letters.

7. Leavis withdrew the suggestion that the novel could or should be divided into two (see introduction to G. Eliot, *Daniel Deronda* [1876; rpt. 1961], xiv; see *Commentary* 30 [1960]: 318).

8. "The Americanness of American Literature: A British Demurrer to Van Wyck Brooks," *Commentary* 14 (1952): 466–74.

9. *Sewanee Review* 70 (1962): 177–201; see also the essay on Conrad's *Shadow Line* in *Sewanee Review* 66 (1958): 179–200.

10. Originally in *Scrutiny* 6 (1937): 59–70; reprinted with my original letter in *IS*, 30–40, and without my piece in *CP*, 211–22.

11. "The New Antiquarianism," *Scrutiny* 16 (1949): 260–64.

12. "The Responsible Critic," *Scrutiny* 19 (1953): 182.

13. "Correspondence," *London Magazine* 2, no. 3 (1955): 77–83; a reply to L. D. Lerner's "The Life and Death of *Scrutiny*," ibid., no. 1, 68–77.

14. Review of M. M. Mahood's *Poetry and Humanism*, in *Scrutiny* 17 (1951): 278. The context shows that Walton is thinking of religion. Leavis was unable to locate the passage.

15. "The Responsible Critic," 174.

16. "Thought and Emotional Quality," *Scrutiny* 13 (1945): 60.

17. George Watson (*The Literary Critics* [1962], 209) goes too far when he denies that Leavis is "a verbal analyst." He knows only one analysis, that of Arnold's sonnet on Shakespeare (in *EU*). But there are two substantial articles, "Thought and Emotional Quality: Notes on the Analysis of Poetry" (*Scrutiny* 13 [1945]: 53–76) and "Imagery and Movement: Notes on the Analysis of Poetry (*Scrutiny* 16 [1948]: 119–34), which discuss words ("diurnal"), kinetic imagery, metrical effects, and so on. See also "*Antony and Cleopatra* and *All for Love*," *Scrutiny* 5 (1936): 158–69, for a comparison commenting on verbal and metrical effects.

18. *R*, 161, 164; on reverence see *DHL*, 75, 127–28, 235.

19. Reply to Robert D. Wagner, "Correspondence: Lawrence and Eliot," *Scrutiny* 18 (1951): 142; see also *DHL*, 25–26, 308.

20. *GT*, 60; see also *DHL*, 25–26, 75, 86.

21. On Flaubert, see preceding note. On Tolstoy, see "Note on Being an Artist," in *DHL*, 297–302, commenting on the episode in *Anna Karenina*, in Venice, with the painter Mikhaylov. See also "T. S. Eliot's Stature as Critic," *Commentary* 26 (1958): 401.

22. *DHL*, 122; "Imagery and Movement," *Scrutiny* 13 (1945): 124; *CP*, 102.

23. "Mr. Pryce-Jones, the British Council and British Culture," *Scrutiny* 18 (1951): 227.

24. "Criticism and Literary History," *Scrutiny* 4 (1935–36): 96.

25. *Reading Poetry and Eugenio Montale* (1979). See also my review in *Modern Language Review* 77 (1982): 710–12.

SELECT BIBLIOGRAPHY: F. W. BATESON

English Poetry and the English Language (1934). 3rd ed. (1972).
English Poetry: A Critical Introduction (1950).
"Linguistics and Literary Criticism," in *The Disciplines of Criticism* (1968),
    ed. Peter Demetz. Thomas M. Greene, and Lowry Nelson, Jr. Cited as
    DC.
Essays in Critical Dissent (1972). Cited as *ECD*.
The Scholar-Critic (1972). Cited as *SC*.

NOTES TO PAGES 265–274

1. See my "Fall of Literary History," in *Geschichte: Ereignis und Erzählung*, ed. R. Kosseleck and W. Stempel (1973); also in *Proceedings of the Eighth Congress of the International Comparative Literature Association, Bordeaux, 1970* (1975).

2. Edited by Peter Demetz, Thomas M. Greene, and Lowry Nelson, Jr. (1968).

3. J. S. Mill, *Dissertations and Discussions,* 2nd ed. (1867), 1:71–72.

4. *Scrutiny* 4:96–100, reprinted in *The Importance of Scrutiny,* ed. Eric Bentley (1948).

5. F. R. Leavis, *Lectures in America* (1969), 23.

6. See Bateson's review of E. D. Hirsch's *Validity in Interpretation,* in *Essays in Criticism* 18: 337–42.

7. Saussure, *Cours de linguistique générale,* 5th ed. (1955), 28.

8. Reprinted in Roger Fowler, ed., *The Languages of Literature* (1971).

9. For example, in "Stylistics, Poetics, and Criticism," in *Discriminations* (1970).

10. 1948; but the chapter dates back to an older paper, "The Theory of Literary History," in *Travaux du Cercle Linguistique de Prague* 6 (1936).

11. See "Organic Form: Some Questions about a Metaphor," in *Organic Form: The Life of an Idea,* ed. George Rousseau (1972), reprinted in *Day of the Leopards* (1976).

12. In *The Literary Criticism of T. S. Eliot,* ed. D. Newton-De Molina (1977).

SELECT BIBLIOGRAPHY: WILLIAM EMPSON

Seven Types of Ambiguity (1930). Cited as *STA.*
Some Versions of Pastoral (1935). Cited as *SVP.*
The Structure of Complex Words (1951). Cited as *SCW.*
Milton's God (1961). Cited as *MG.*
Using Biography (1984).

John Crowe Ransom. "Mr. Empson's Muddles," *Southern Review* 4 (1938/
39): 322–39.
I. A. Richards. "William Empson," *Furioso* 1 (1940): 44f. (Supplement).
Cleanth Brooks. "Empson's Criticism," *Accent* 4 (1944): 208–16.
———. "Hits and Misses," *Kenyon Review* 14 (1952): 669–78. Review of
SCW.
Elder Olson. "Wiliam Empson, Contemporary Criticism and Poetic Dic-
tion," in *Critics and Criticism: Ancient and Modern,* ed. R. S. Crane (1952),
pp. 45–82.
Hugh Kenner. "Alice in Empsonland," in *Gnomon: Essays on Contemporary
Literature* (1958), pp. 249–62.
Claude J. Rawson. "Professor Empson's Tom Jones," *Notes and Queries*
n.s.6 (1959): 400–04.
Robert Martin Adams. "Empson and Bentley: Scherzo," in *Milton and
the Modern Critics* (1966), pp. 112–27.
James Jensen. "The Construction of *Seven Types of Ambiguity*," *Modern
Language Quarterly* 27 (1966): 243–59.
———. "Some Ambiguous Preliminaries: Empson in *The Granta*," *Crit-
icism* 8 (1966): 349–61.
W. W. Robson. "Mr. Empson on *Paradise Lost*," in *Critical Essays* (1966),
pp. 87–98.
Roger Sale. "The Achievement of William Empson," *Hudson Review* 19
(1966): 369–90; repr. in *Modern Heroism: Essays on D. H. Lawrence, Wil-
liam Empson, and J. R. Tolkien* (1973).
J. H. Willis, Jr. *William Empson* (1969). In the Columbia Essays on Modern
Writers series.
Roma Gill, ed. *William Empson: The Man and His Work* (1974). Contains
a bibliography by Moira Megaw and essays by M. C. Bradbrook,
G. Fraser, and I. A. Richards on the criticism.
Horst Meller. *Das Gedicht als Einübung. Zum Dichtungsverständnis William
Empsons* (1974).
Christopher C. Norris. *William Empson and the Philosophy of Literary Crit-
icism,* with a postcript by William Empson (1978). Excellent. See my
review in *Modern Language Review* 75 (1980): 182–85.

NOTES TO PAGES 275–292

1. In *T. S. Eliot: A Symposium* (1949), ed. Richard Marsh and Tambimuttu, p. 35.

2. Rosalie Colie, *The Echoing Song* (1970), 161.

3. *British Journal of Aesthetics* 2 (1962): 36–54.

4. First published in *Kenyon Review* 20 (Spring 1958): 217–49; a revised version, cited here, appears in R. Paulson, ed., *Fielding: A Collection of Critical Essays* (1962), 123–45.

5. In "William Empson," 55.

6. Rawson, "Professor Empson's Tom Jones."

7. Ibid., 402–03.

CHRONOLOGICAL TABLE
OF BOOKS

1900	A. Symons:	*The Symbolist Movement*
1903	W. B. Yeats:	*Ideas of Good and Evil*
	W. Raleigh:	*Wordsworth*
1904	W. P. Ker:	*The Dark Ages*
1905	A. C. Bradley:	*Shakespearean Tragedy*
1907	W. Raleigh:	*Shakespeare*
	O. Elton:	*Modern Studies*
	H. Grierson:	*The First Half of the Seventeenth Century*
1909	A. Symons:	*The Romantic Movement*
	A. C. Bradley:	*Oxford Lectures on Poetry*
1910	E. Pound:	*The Spirit of Romance*
1912	O. Elton:	*A Survey of English Literature, 1780– 1830*
	W. P. Ker:	*English Literature: Medieval*
	L. Strachey:	*Landmarks of French Literature*
	H. Grierson:	*Edition of John Donne*
1913	C. Bell:	*Art*
1914	G. Murray:	*Hamlet and Orestes*
1916	A. Quiller-Couch:	*On the Art of Writing*
	J. M. Murry:	*Fyodor Dostoevsky*
1919	G. Moore:	*Avowals*
1920	O. Elton:	*A Survey of English Literature, 1830–80*
	R. Fry:	*Vision and Design*
	J. M. Murry:	*Aspects of Literature*
	T. S. Eliot:	*The Sacred Wood*
1921	H. Grierson:	*Metaphysical Lyrics*
1922	J. M. Murry:	*The Problem of Style*
		Countries of the Mind
	L. Strachey:	*Books and Characters*

1923	D. H. Lawrence:	*Studies in Classic American Literature*
	I. A. Richards and C. K. Ogden:	*The Meaning of Meaning*
1924	J. M. Murry:	*Discoveries*
	I. A. Richards:	*Principles of Literary Criticism*
	G. Moore:	*An Anthology of Pure Poetry*
		Conversations in Ebury Street
	T. E. Hulme:	*Speculations*
1925	J. M. Murry:	*Keats and Shakespeare*
	V. Woolf:	*The Common Reader*
1926	I. A. Richards:	*Science and Poetry*
	H. Read:	*Reason and Romanticism*
	H. W. Garrod:	*Keats*
1927	W. Lewis:	*The Lion and the Fox*
	E. M. Forster:	*Aspects of the Novel*
	R. Graves and L. Riding:	*A Survey of Modernist Poetry*
	T. S. Eliot:	*Shakespeare and the Stoicism of Seneca*
1928	W. B. Yeats:	*A Vision*
	W. Lewis:	*Time and Western Man*
	T. S. Eliot:	*For Lancelot Andrewes*
1929	H. Grierson:	*Cross Currents in English Literature of the Seventeenth Century*
	G. W. Knight:	*Myth and Miracle*
	I. A. Richards:	*Practical Criticism*
1929	T. S. Eliot:	*Dante*
1930	G. W. Knight:	*The Wheel of Fire*
	H. Read:	*Wordsworth*
	W. Empson:	*Seven Types of Ambiguity*
	D. H. Lawrence:	Preface to Dostoevsky's *The Grand Inquisitor*
1931	W. B. Yeats:	*Oxford Anthology of English Poetry*
	J. M. Murry:	*Countries of the Mind*, second series
	L. Strachey:	*Portraits in Miniature*
	H. W. Garrod:	*Poetry and the Criticism of Life*
	G. W. Knight:	*The Imperial Theme*
	J. M. Murry:	*Son of Woman, The Story of D. H. Lawrence*
1932	O. Elton:	*A Survey of English Literature, 1730–80*
	V. Woolf:	*A Second Common Reader*
	D. MacCarthy:	*Criticism*

	G. W. Knight:	*The Shakespearian Tempest*
	F. R. Leavis:	*New Bearings in English Poetry*
	Q. D. Leavis:	*Fiction and the Reading Public*
	T. S. Eliot:	*Selected Essays*
1933	O. Elton:	*The English Muse*
	J. M. Murry:	*William Blake*
	L. Strachey:	*Characters and Commentaries*
	L. C. Knights:	*How Many Children Had Lady Macbeth?*
	G. W. Knight:	*The Christian Renaissance*
	T. S. Eliot:	*The Use of Poetry and the Use of Criticism*
1934	E. Pound:	*ABC of Reading*
	I. A. Richards:	*Coleridge on Imagination*
	W. Lewis:	*Men Without Art*
	F. W. Bateson:	*English Poetry and the English Language*
	A. Quiller-Couch:	*The Poet as Citizen*
	T. S. Eliot:	*After Strange Gods*
		Elizabethan Essays
1935	W. Empson:	*Some Versions of Pastoral*
	C. Spurgeon:	*Shakespeare's Imagery and What It Tells Us*
1936	J. M. Murry:	*Shakespeare*
	E. M. Forster:	*Abinger Harvest*
	H. Read:	*In Defense of Shelley*
	F. R. Leavis:	*Revaluation*
	I. A. Richards:	*The Philosophy of Rhetoric*
1937	H. Grierson:	*Milton and Wordsworth*
	E. Pound:	*Polite Essays*
	L. C. Knights:	*Drama and Society in the Age of Jonson*
	C. Caudwell:	*Illusion and Reality*
1938	H. Read:	*Essays in Literary Criticism*
	E. Pound:	*Guide to Kulchur*
1939	O. Elton:	*Essays and Addresses*
	G. W. Knight:	*The Burning Oracle*
1941	G. W. Knight:	*The Starlit Dome*
1942	T. S. Eliot:	*The Classics and the Man of Letters*
		The Music of Poetry
1944	G. W. Knight:	*The Olive and the Sword*
1945	H. Read:	*A Coat of Many Colours*
	T. S. Eliot:	*What is a Classic?*
1946	H. Grierson:	*A Critical History of English Poetry*
1947	G. W. Knight:	*The Crown of Life*
	L. C. Knights:	*Explorations*

	T. S. Eliot:	*Milton*
1948	F. R. Leavis:	*The Great Tradition*
	T. S. Eliot:	*Notes towards a Definition of Culture*
		From Poe to Valéry
1950	F. W. Bateson:	*English Poetry: A Critical Introduction*
1951	E. M. Forster:	*Two Cheers for Democracy*
	W. Empson:	*The Structure of Complex Words*
	T. S. Eliot:	*Poetry and Drama*
1952	G. W. Knight:	*Lord Byron: The Christian Virtues*
	F. R. Leavis:	*The Common Pursuit*
1953	D. MacCarthy:	*Humanities*
	H. Read:	*The True Voice of Feeling*
	T. S. Eliot:	*American Literature and the American Language*
		The Three Voices of Poetry
1954	E. Pound:	*Literary Essays*
	F. W. Bateson:	*Wordsworth*
	G. W. Knight:	*The Laureate of Peace*
1955	I. A. Richards:	*Speculative Instruments*
	G. W. Knight:	*The Mutual Flame*
	F. R. Leavis:	*D. H. Lawrence: Novelist*
1956	T. S. Eliot:	*The Frontiers of Criticism*
1957	H. Read:	*The Tenth Muse*
	T. S. Eliot:	*Of Poetry and Poets*
1961	W. Empson:	*Milton's God*
1962	T. S. Eliot:	*George Herbert*
1963	F. R. Leavis:	*Two Cultures? The Significance of C. P. Snow*
1964	T. S. Eliot:	*Knowledge and Experience in the Philosophy of F. H. Bradley*
1965	T. S. Eliot:	*To Criticize the Critic and Other Writings*
1967	F. R. Leavis:	*Anna Karenina and Other Essays*
	H. Read:	*Poetry and Experience*
1968	H. Read:	*The Cult of Sincerity*
1969	F. R. and Q. D. Leavis:	*Lectures in America*
	F. R. Leavis:	*English Literature in Our Time*
1970	F. R. and Q. D. Leavis:	*Dickens: The Novelist*
1972	F. R. Leavis:	*Nor Shall My Sword: Discourses on Pluralism, Compassion and Social Hope*

INDEX OF NAMES

INDEX OF TOPICS AND TERMS